Region

REGION

Planning the Future of the Twin Cities

MYRON ORFIELD AND THOMAS F. LUCE JR.

*with Geneva Finn, Baris Gumus-Dawes, Jill Mazullo,
Eric Myott, Sharon Pfeifer, and Nick Wallace*

Published in cooperation with the
Institute on Race and Poverty
at the University of Minnesota

UNIVERSITY OF MINNESOTA PRESS
MINNEAPOLIS • LONDON

Portions of chapter 4 are from or are based on Thomas Luce, Myron Orfield, and Jill Mazullo, "Access to Growing Job Centers in the Twin Cities Metropolitan Area," *CURA Reporter* 36, no. 1 (Spring 2006). Portions of chapter 5 were previously published as "Growth Pressures on Sensitive Natural Areas in DNR's Central Region," Ameregis and the Minnesota Department of Natural Resources, 2006.

Unless otherwise credited, all maps copyright 2009 by the Institute on Race and Poverty, University of Minnesota, http://www.irpumn.org.

The maps were created by William Lanoux, Eric Myott, and Aaron Timbo.

Design and composition by Yvonne Tsang at Wilsted & Taylor Publishing Services

Published by the University of Minnesota Press
111 Third Avenue South, Suite 290
Minneapolis, MN 55401-2520
http://www.upress.umn.edu

Library of Congress Cataloging-in-Publication Data

Orfield, Myron.
  Region : planning the future of the Twin Cities / Myron Orfield and Thomas F. Luce Jr. ; with Geneva Finn . . . [et al.].
      p.   cm.
  "Published in cooperation with Institute on Race and Poverty."
  Includes bibliographical references and index.
  ISBN 978-0-8166-6556-3 (hc : alk. paper)
  ISBN 978-0-8166-6557-0 (pb : alk. paper)
   1. Regional planning—Minnesota—Minneapolis Metropolitan Area. 2. Regional planning—Minnesota—Saint Paul Metropolitan Area. I. Luce, Thomas F. II. University of Minnesota. Institute on Race and Poverty. III. Title.
  HT394.M6O75 2009
   307.1'209776579-dc22   2009009248

Printed in Canada on acid-free paper

The University of Minnesota is an equal-opportunity educator and employer.

16 15 14 13 12 11 10   10 9 8 7 6 5 4 3 2 1

CONTENTS

ILLUSTRATIONS

Figures

Maps

Tables

INTRODUCTION

Myron Orfield and Thomas F. Luce Jr.

People and jobs are steadily decentralizing into the suburbs of the Twin Cities and most other U.S. metropolitan areas. This trend threatens to undermine a host of regional policy objectives, including controlling sprawl; increasing opportunities for disadvantaged populations; implementing transit; decreasing racial, ethnic, and economic segregation; and conserving natural assets and open space. These trends are especially detrimental to low-income households and people of color, who are often concentrated in lower-opportunity inner-city neighborhoods and inner-ring suburbs. Because these policy problems transcend municipal boundaries, regional approaches are required to ensure a more equitable and sustainable arrangement of opportunities in metropolitan areas.

The Twin Cities metropolitan area provides an excellent case study of these issues. The region's highly fragmented system of local governance helps explain several undesirable recent trends in the region, including increasingly scattered development patterns, increasing segregation, growing fiscal inequality, and threats to the area's natural assets. At the same time, comparisons to other metropolitan areas suggest that the region's relatively strong regional planning system helps mitigate these patterns.

Region: Planning the Future of the Twin Cities is an effort to bring much better regional data to bear to illuminate how the region operates, to refine the goals of regional policy, and to reinvigorate interest in reshaping regional policy. It is about using more in-depth data and analysis to think more clearly about the socioeconomic polarization that is occurring in the region and to become more explicit about what to do—and what not to do—about it.

The analysis presented here adds a perspective not often used in the Twin Cities, namely, race. Historically one of the least racially diverse areas in the country, the region is rapidly becoming more diverse. Not only has race become a central factor in the evolution of the region's development, it must also now be added to governance, taxes, land use, the economy, and partisan politics as an essential consideration when evaluating potential solutions for regional problems. Race is not included because it is easier to do so or because current thinking demands it. Quite the opposite: adding race to the equation invariably complicates issues, and Americans are more and more prone to dismiss it as a central question in policy debates.

Race is a focus because policy solutions that do not address race are not likely to make much difference to the deepest problems of inequality and segregation.

The focus of this book is the Twin Cities metropolitan area, but it is intended to inform policy discussions and analysis in other regions as well. The problems and policies it deals with are universal to U.S. metropolitan areas, and wherever possible the Twin Cities experience is compared to other areas through the use of a large comparative data set for other large metropolitan areas or by more in-depth direct comparison with a few other metropolitan areas.

The book begins by documenting how the Twin Cities region is governed, how it has grown, and the great diversity of its local areas. As in most metropolitan areas, the region's public sector is highly fragmented. Area municipalities, school districts, special districts, and counties overlap, resulting in more than 1,700 unique combinations of tax rates and public services. Perhaps more important, the region has nearly three hundred cities and townships, each pursuing its own land use agenda. Reflecting this, undeveloped land (and farmland) has been converted to urban uses at significantly greater rates than population has grown. Population growth has followed the classic pattern of American metropolitan areas with much more rapid growth in second- and third-ring suburbs than in the core. Current projections predict more of the same in coming decades.

Unbalanced growth is reflected in fiscal inequality. Tax bases are growing most slowly in the core, and tax rates are highest and increasing most rapidly there. But stress is not limited to the central cities. Analysis of suburban diversity using tax base, socioeconomic, and job data shows several distinct types of suburbs in the region. Nearly a third of suburban households live in cities or townships experiencing the kinds of stress formerly associated solely with central cities. These "stressed suburbs" show low and slow-growing tax bases combined with high and fast-growing social costs. Another 45 percent live in rapidly growing areas with only modest fiscal resources. These "developing job centers" and "bedroom developing" suburbs are middle-class areas facing increasing school costs and congestion. Only a quarter of suburban households live in areas with strong tax bases and few social costs—"developed job centers" and "affluent residential suburbs." However, even these areas must deal with the costs of growth—especially the congestion associated with rapid growth in the large, relatively low-density job centers and scattered job sites that dominate growth patterns in modern America.

Chapter 2 describes the history and powers of the institution with the greatest capacity to alter these patterns—the Twin Cities Metropolitan Council. The council is empowered to coordinate planning and development in the region and has undoubtedly mitigated many of the disparities documented in chapter 1. For instance, although the region shows many of the same difficulties seen in metropolitan areas across the country, it also shows lower fiscal inequality and less sprawl than would be expected given the extreme fragmentation in its local governance structure.

Since the Met Council's inception in the early 1970s, the legislature has periodically increased its powers, especially during the 1990s. It is now the most powerful regional government in the country. However, in recent years the council has retreated from policy leadership in many areas. It has reduced the impact of the metropolitan urban service area (MUSA)—the boundaries within which the council supports growth with regional services such as wastewater collection and treatment. In 1986, for instance, 78 percent of urbanized land in the council's seven-county area was inside the MUSA. But only 52 percent of land that urbanized in the next sixteen years was inside the MUSA.

The Met Council has also retreated from many of the more proactive development objectives of its "youth," such as a long-standing emphasis on promoting growth in job clusters large enough and dense enough to support transit. Although the region is now pursuing a (very) long-term strategy to develop alternatives to the automobile—light-rail transit and commuter rail—the Twin Cities still has one of the least developed transit systems in the country among large metropolitan areas, more than thirty years after the formation of the Met Council.

Finally, numerous attempts to make the council more responsive by converting it from an appointed to an elected body have failed. As a result, the council is still at risk of switching from 100 percent one party to 100 percent the other every time a new governor is elected. This means not only that the council is almost never truly representative of a region that is fairly evenly split between the parties and between fully developed core areas and growing suburbs, but also that it tends to lurch from one philosophy of regional growth to another, reducing its long-run impact.

Chapter 3 documents the region's rapidly growing racial diversity and the increasing degree to which the races are separated into segregated neighborhoods and schools. Historically one of the least diverse regions in the country, the Twin Cities have seen very rapid growth in African American, Asian, and Latino populations, including many recent immigrants from East Africa, Laos, and Central America. Recent estimates put the number of languages spoken at home by students in the Minneapolis public school district at more than eighty. As nonwhite populations grew, many of the region's core neighborhoods and schools initially became integrated. However, most neighborhoods and schools that were integrated at a point in time were actually in transition, and very high shares of the region's African American, Asian, and Latino populations now attend schools or live in neighborhoods that are predominantly nonwhite. Segregation is increasing for most residents of color, even as it is declining for whites.

Racial segregation is not just about race. It is about access to opportunity. Where you live affects your access to jobs, good schools, and basic economic prospects in life. If racial segregation limits people's residential choices, then it undermines equality of opportunity. Segregation especially hurts residents of color by limiting their residential choices to lower-opportunity parts of the region. Racial steering in housing markets, for instance, often pushes residents of color toward less affluent neighborhoods with struggling schools and high crime rates.

Racial segregation is not simply the result of the housing market's neutrally sorting people according to their preferences and economic status. Discriminatory behavior by a number of public and private actors has shaped housing markets. Actions by private actors (e.g., steering by real estate agents and discriminatory business practices of financial institutions, mortgage brokers, and insurance agents) perpetuate segregation. Public actors also contribute to the problem. Housing policies of the federal government, decisions by school districts, and land use policies in municipalities all contribute to racial segregation. Segregation is not written in stone; it can be reversed by eliminating the policies and practices that generate it.

Court action toward schools has not produced long-term integration because federal courts have been unwilling to enforce remedies across district or municipal boundaries. State court solutions, like the Choice Is Yours interdistrict transfer program, have been promising but are small scale, and many of the inner suburbs participating in the program are now going through racial transitions themselves.

Chapter 4 looks at the spatial organization of the labor markets using a relatively new tool—the commuter shed. Data on where people live and work are used to illustrate a variety of features of the regional labor market. Jobs tend to cluster into job centers, and not surprisingly, middle and outer suburban job centers are growing much more rapidly than those in inner suburbs or the central cities. At the same time, the tendency for jobs to cluster at all is weakening. The region's jobs are both decentralizing into middle and outer suburbs and deconcentrating into scattered-site developments. The result is that the automobile has become even more of a necessity and transit has become less viable. Three important results of this shift are decreasing access to growing parts of the region for lower-income workers, increasing average vehicle miles traveled across the region, and continuing residential sprawl into the periphery—a distressing set of inequitable and environmentally unfriendly outcomes.

These patterns at least partly reflect policy. Early in the Met Council's history, its planning objectives clearly encouraged clustering. This emphasis has nearly disappeared from more recent plans.

Unbalanced growth, decentralization, and deconcentration have also led to increasing congestion, especially in the suburbs. Commuter sheds—the area within which workers can commute to a particular job center in a reasonable time—are shrinking everywhere, but most rapidly in the suburbs. Commuter sheds for the fastest-growing areas in middle and outer suburbs also include little of the region's affordable housing and few of its people of color. This kind of unbalanced access to opportunity is an important contributor to inequality across incomes and races.

The decentralization of population and jobs documented in chapters 1 and 4 frames the analysis of environmental issues in chapter 5. The Twin Cities have a diverse ecology and there are nearly 500,000 acres of unprotected sensitive natural areas left in the region, including 120,000 acres classified as high-quality wetland and terrestrial habitats. More and more of the region's lakes and streams are now classified as "impaired," including 27 percent of stream miles and 37 percent of lake area. In addition, Lake Pepin, which is just beyond the region's official boundaries along the Mississippi River, was recently reclassified as impaired. EPA restrictions resulting from this directly affect the entire metropolitan area because virtually all of the region's lakes and streams feed eventually into Lake Pepin.

The spatial analysis of sensitive natural areas in the region shows clearly that they tend to cluster in local areas with lower than average tax capacities—areas with the fewest resources to protect them and the most incentives to develop them. In addition, sensitive lands cluster in the area just beyond the region's fully developed suburbs, putting them directly in the path of projected future growth. Municipality-by-municipality simulations of projected growth show that unless future growth occurs at much higher densities than in the recent past, either much of the region's sensitive natural areas will be developed or growth will be pushed farther and farther to the periphery. One group of fast-growing suburbs with modest fiscal resources (developing job centers in the community classification presented in chapter 1) in particular is expected to receive more growth than those suburbs will be able to accommodate.

Chapter 6 summarizes the regional policies proposed in each of the earlier chapters in five policy areas: land use planning, housing and schools, economic development and transportation, the environment, and governance. In land use planning, the focus is on more aggressive administration of the MUSA, stricter review of local plans by the Met Council, and the need for a reinvigorated state planning system. Housing and school policy suggestions focus on equalizing access to opportunity across races and income groups with more aggressive pro-integrative policies in housing markets and the school system. Improved transit, more efficient use of the existing highway system, and increased emphasis on redevelopment activities in fully developed areas are underscored in the economic development and transportation policy discussion. The importance of integrating environmental concerns into local and regional planning processes is stressed in the growth and environment discussion. Finally, the governance section emphasizes the need to create or strengthen institutions with the geographic scope appropriate for each policy area. For most of the highlighted policy areas, the appropriate scale is clearly regional. The regional scale of housing and labor markets means that local planning, housing, school, transportation, economic development, and environmental policies inevitably have an impact on neighboring communities and, often, the region as a whole. If these costs and benefits are ignored when policies are designed and implemented, then the region as a whole will clearly be shortchanged by the results.

The overriding theme of the analyses and the policy discussions is that metropolitan systems—transportation networks, infrastructure, labor and housing markets, natural systems, schools—must be viewed as an interconnected whole. Policy decisions in one policy area affect goals in other areas, and actions in one part of the region affect residents in other parts. Effective policy making in this kind of environment requires regionwide analysis, policy design, and implementation.

Chapter 7 analyzes the political geography of the region, highlighting potential coalitions for the policy agenda outlined in chapter 6. Since the early 1990s, the region grew more polarized, both across party lines and geographically. Places experiencing social and economic stress in the developed core of the region, including the central cities and inner suburbs, became more Democratic, while fast-growing places in the outer suburbs became more Republican. Voters across the region also became less "volatile"—less likely to split their ticket and vote for candidates of different parties in different races. In recent elections, the region's most volatile voters have been in middle suburbs, especially in developing and developed job centers. The region's political battleground thus coincides with the "bow wave" of development. More and more, to win elections in Minnesota, parties and candidates must appeal to voters in the local areas most directly affected by the way the region is growing. In recent elections, voters in these areas have shown themselves willing to vote for either party, meaning that it is candidates and issues that decide elections in these parts of the region.

The brand of regionalism espoused in this book can potentially appeal to politicians and voters of both parties in these areas. For instance, regional policies to focus growth in already developed parts of the region or in an orderly fashion in areas directly adjacent to the fully developed core should appeal to urban and suburban Democrats with historical ties to the core and strong concerns for the environment as well as to suburban Republicans with ties to the periphery and a desire to maintain the status quo in those areas. The political calculus is not simple, of course, but a "regional agenda" should not be viewed as the sole property of either party. The history of regionalism across the country makes this clear. Many of the most important regional policy initiatives in the Twin Cities in the early 1970s—for instance, the Fiscal Disparities Act of 1971, a tax-base sharing program—were championed by moderate Republicans from the (then) developing fringe and now have broad bipartisan support across the region. Similarly, Republicans initiated regional consolidation in Indianapolis and played a significant role in the bipartisan movement that resulted in the formation of Portland Metro in Oregon. The key is to accentuate the benefits to voters across the political spectrum when building coalitions for change.

Region

Local Governance, Finance, and Growth Trends

Myron Orfield, Thomas F. Luce Jr., and Eric Myott

Americans are governed by a wide array of local governments, especially those who live in metropolitan areas. Political power and service responsibilities are divided among tens of thousands of local governments, from general-purpose governments like cities and counties to special governments, such as school and water districts. Each type of government is financed by its own mix of local, state, and federal funds. Given this complexity, it is not surprising that almost no one is aware of all the governments that serve them or of how their services are financed.[1]

This fragmented mosaic is largely the result of the legal and cultural priority given to local government—cities, towns, and townships—over other levels, particularly in making land use decisions. Although cities and townships derive their power from the state, they generally can and do make policy without considering the repercussions on the region as a whole. Whether they realize it or not, city officials compete with each other, seeking tax wealth and social status in the form of businesses and high-income housing. While some economists and legal scholars view some aspects of this competition in a positive light, most view the overall ramifications as negative. Interlocal competition hurts all types of communities, city and suburban, rich and poor, integrated and segregated. It also affects the strength of regional economies and the quality of the environment in many ways.

Recently a small group of scholars—the "new regionalists"—have focused on the implications of interlocal competition, particularly between cities and suburbs.[2] They advocate measures to reduce growing inequality, discourage competition for tax base, and remove barriers to cooperative land use planning. Given the pervasiveness of localism, however, most scholars and activists who believe in regional reform are pessimistic about the prospects for reform.

The Twin Cities metropolitan area is an excellent case study of these issues. The Minnesota portion of the region is home to more than 60 percent of Minnesota's total population, 3.1 million people in 2005, and the region's role is increasing. The metropolitan economy is the state's major growth engine—84 percent of statewide population growth between 2000 and 2005 occurred there, and the region is expected to expand by another million people by 2030.

Effectively governing this dynamic economy is often problematic, however. The Twin Cities has one of the most fragmented local government systems in the United States—it ranks as the fifth most fragmented system among the 50 largest U.S. metropolitan areas.[3] The region includes 172 cities, 97 townships, 76 school districts, more than 100 special districts, and 11 counties. This makes it difficult to coordinate actions in the many policy areas like planning and economic development that are handled primarily by local governments and special districts. The existence of the Metropolitan Council, which covers seven of the eleven counties, helps but, as will be described in chapter 2, the council has limited powers in some policy areas and limited ambition in others.

The region's growth patterns reflect the fragmented public system. Like most metropolitan areas in the United States, the Twin Cities area has seen significant decentralization of population and jobs in recent decades. While this pattern is not as pronounced as in some other large metropolitan areas, the way the region is growing threatens many of the open spaces and sensitive natural areas that make the area so attractive to prospective residents and businesses. The "bow wave" of new growth continues to move outward. In the 1980s and 1990s, it went through a ring of middle suburbs like Blaine and Coon Rapids in the north; Plymouth, Minnetonka, and Eden Prairie in the west; Burnsville and Apple Valley in the south; and Woodbury in the east. By the early 2000s, however, most of the developable land in these areas was gone and the wave had moved still farther outward into places like Lakeville, Shakopee, Chanhassen, Maple Grove, Andover, Ham Lake, Lake Elmo, Cottage Grove, and Rosemount. At the same time, many parts of the core experienced shrinking population and school closings.

Continuing decentralization also has created rapidly increasing traffic congestion on suburban roads that were not designed to serve as major commuting routes and reduced the opportunities available to populations "left behind" in the core. All too often, the "left behind" are new immigrants and racial minorities isolated in neighborhoods of concentrated poverty in the core cities and a few inner suburbs. The extra costs associated with high poverty and large numbers of non-English speakers place extra burdens on the municipalities and school districts least able to afford them. Fragmentation contributes to this process as well, by creating and nurturing incentives for developing areas to restrict growth only to the types of development that "pay their way."

Fragmentation and decentralization also contribute to fiscal disparities and segregation by race and income. And this is not just a city versus suburb issue.

Increasingly, growing disparities among suburban areas reflect growing concentrations of economic, social, and fiscal problems historically associated with central cities. Metropolitan areas, including the Twin Cities, can no longer be viewed as struggling central cities surrounded by prospering suburbs. Suburban areas now present a widely varying assortment of places, including areas with fiscal stress, racial segregation, and poverty concentrations like those in central cities. Public policies must reflect this fact.

This chapter lays the groundwork for the rest of the book by providing an overview of local governance, growth patterns, and fiscal disparities in the region. A set of local characteristics is then used to classify the region's 270 municipalities and townships, documenting the diversity of places in the region and providing a framework for the analysis in subsequent chapters.

LOCAL GOVERNANCE IN THE TWIN CITIES

The Twin Cities provide a classic example of fragmentation of local governance. The region's local public sector consists of several layers that make and enforce laws, set public policy, collect revenues, and spend those revenues for services and infrastructure. The resulting geography of powers is amazingly complex. For instance, none of the various layers are perfectly contiguous with the other layers: some municipalities or townships cross county lines; most school districts include all or parts of more than one municipality; many municipalities are in more than one school district; and special districts often cut across several municipalities, school districts, or counties as they follow watersheds or other naturally determined service areas.

There is, of course, some method to the madness. In principle, multiple layers and types of governance are meant to balance a number of factors that determine the ideal scale for providing local public goods and services. Three factors, in particular, come into play most often when deciding on the appropriate scale for providing a particular service.

First, the desire to maximize accountability to voters means that services should be provided on the smallest possible scale. It is often argued that smaller governments are "closer" and more responsive to voters and that as many services as possible should therefore be provided at the local level. A corollary is that local provision of services provides as much choice as possible among different mixes of public services. When deciding where to live, consumers can "vote with their feet" by finding the local area that provides a mix of public services best suited to them.

Second, economies of scale mean that some services can be provided more efficiently at large scales. For example, large treatment plants can process wastewater for return to the environment at a lower cost per gallon than small treatment plants. This implies that the "best" scale would not be at the local level because this would require the use of many small treatment plants—a method that would be much more expensive than the use of a small number of large treatment plants. The consolidation movement in primary and secondary education is another example of the impact of economies of scale. Changes in transportation technology and infrastructure made school districts with larger areas possible at the same time that many school districts, especially in rural areas, were losing population. The result was that in many areas, the trade-off between transportation costs (including time) and the advantages of efficiently sized schools changed, making consolidation a much more desirable alternative.

Finally, when determining how much of a good or service should be provided, all the potential costs and benefits should be taken into consideration. This means that service areas should be large enough to encompass all the costs and benefits of providing the service. For instance, many of the benefits of a freeway through one town are enjoyed by residents of other towns. If freeways were a purely local responsibility, then individual towns would provide too few freeway lanes because they would face all the costs of the road within their boundaries but many of the benefits would accrue to nonresidents who pay no taxes in that particular town. Local officials would have no incentive to account for those benefits when deciding how much road to build.

Each of the three factors creates the potential for controversy, but the third—scaling services based on the scope of costs and benefits—creates the greatest challenges in a growing metropolitan area. The costs and benefits of many public policies are spread across a region by a variety of markets, for example, housing, labor, and consumer goods markets. In a modern economy, few people live, work, and shop in the same town. As a result, people do not decide where to live based solely on the characteristics of one town. The characteristics of nearby places matter as well. And once the home location decision is made, people consume public services such as transportation and public safety in other towns (where they do not pay taxes) as they work, shop, and play.

Similarly, the scope of many public services traditionally regarded as "local goods" in many places—goods or services with only local consequences—spreads to include neighboring areas as metropolitan economies grow in scale and complexity. For instance, as metropolitan areas extend into undeveloped exurban areas, planning decisions that previously affected only local residents (e.g., lot size rules or the sewer vs. septic decision) begin to have consequences on a larger scale, influencing neighboring communities and the larger metropolitan areas in various ways. Current lot size decisions determine whether densities can be increased in the future through infill, which, in turn, affects development pressures in neighboring communities. The same lot size decisions also have consequences for transportation and environmental services funded at larger scales. The potential for controversy is great in these situations because the benefits of overruling local decisions are spread over large areas, across large numbers of people, while the costs are focused locally.

The "correspondence principle" is a standard developed to accommodate these factors.[4] In essence, it maintains that local public services should be provided at the lowest level of government consistent with economies of scale and the scope of costs and benefits. The first half of the principle pushes service provision toward the local end of the spectrum (as "close to voters" as possible), while the second pushes it toward higher levels of government. Balancing the two parts can be difficult, involving as it often does deciding between the advantages of diversity in the mixes of public goods available (greater choice and responsiveness to voters) and the disadvantages (higher costs, service inequality, tax base disparities, and service levels that are "wrong" because they don't account for all costs and benefits).

The result of this balancing act in the Twin Cities is a complex mosaic of municipalities, townships, school districts, special districts, counties, and the Metropolitan Council. The following sections describe the situation as it stands now. The questions to keep in mind are the following: Does the current state of affairs meet the requirements of the correspondence principle? And how can we accommodate the changing realities on the ground (resulting from growth and change in the regional economy) by modifying public entities that are inherently resistant to change?

Size and Scope of Local Governments

As in most states, the scope and powers of local governments in Minnesota are determined by the state legislature. There are two types of local multipurpose government in the state: cities and townships. Historically, both types followed boundaries based on congressional townships (generally thirty-six square miles) laid down when the state was still a territory. As townships transformed to cities with more powers to tax and spend, boundaries sometimes changed to follow development patterns. In other cases, townships maintained their boundaries when they became cities.[5]

There are 172 cities in the eleven-county area of the Twin Cities. Most are in the core of the region where populations are great enough to justify the additional powers associated with cities (Figure 1.1). For the most part cities are much more significant actors in the local economy than townships. In 2004 current expenditures by cities in the region totaled $2.6 billion, or $617 per capita, compared to just $63 million, or $145 per capita, for townships. This reflects a greater range of responsibilities taken on by city governments. Two service categories—public safety and transportation—dominate township current expenditures; cities devote more than

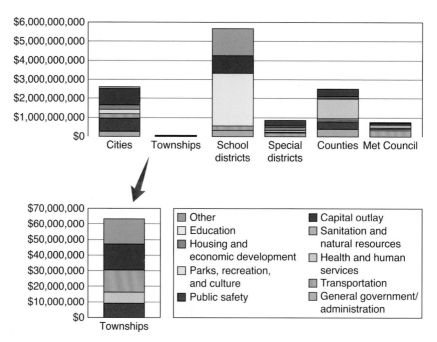

FIGURE 1.1. Expenditures by Twin Cities local governments, 2004. *Source:* Minnesota State Auditor.

10 percent of current spending to each of these categories plus two others—parks and recreation, and housing and economic development.

The property tax (including special assessments) is the primary revenue instrument for both cities and townships, representing 40 percent of current revenues in cities and 52 percent in townships. The difference is due to much greater reliance on intergovernmental revenues (or aid) by cities: 19 percent for cities versus 7 percent for townships (Figure 1.2).

School districts are a form of special district responsible for overseeing schools and support services, such as transportation and school bus yards. In Minnesota, school district boards are elected and governed by six or seven members who serve four-year terms. There are seventy-six school districts in the eleven-county area. School district boundaries rarely conform to other government boundaries in the area and often overlap several municipalities.

School districts spend more money than any other layer of local government—$5.6 billion in 2004. However, school districts rely much more heavily on funding from higher levels of government (primarily the state). State and federal sources represented more than 60 percent of school district revenues in the region in 2004—55 percent from the state and 5 percent from the federal government. As a result, their property tax revenues were similar to those for counties, cities, and townships:

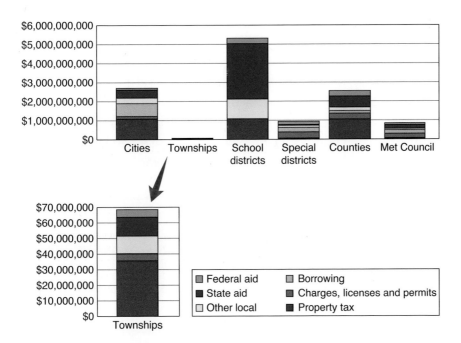

FIGURE 1.2. Revenue sources by Twin Cities local governments, 2004. *Source:* Minnesota State Auditor.

$990 million for schools, $983 million for counties, and $890 million for cities and townships.

Special taxing districts are governmental units set up to serve a single purpose, such as watershed management, airports, sports facilities, or housing redevelopment. They may be governed by either elected or appointed officials, and their boundaries rarely coincide with other governmental units such as cities or townships. Special districts also include special service districts completely within another governmental unit that are financed from service charges assessed only within its neighborhood.

Since they are so diverse, special districts are very hard to categorize. The most common form in the Twin Cities region is the watershed district. Watershed districts were created to address water management issues such as drainage management, flood control, and water quality within the region's watersheds. Since their boundaries are determined solely by natural systems, their boundaries usually cut across cities, townships, and counties, but every point in the region is contained within at least one district.

In addition to watershed districts, there are three special districts that contain the region's seven core counties—Anoka, Carver, Dakota, Hennepin, Ramsey, Scott, and Washington. The Metropolitan Airports Commission, the Metropolitan

Sports Facilities Commission, and the Metropolitan Mosquito Control Commission were created to complement the activities of the Metropolitan Council. Their combined budgets are roughly $230 million.

Because they are single-function organizations, special districts often rely on revenues other than property taxes, most commonly service charges or contributions from the state or cities and townships within their boundaries. Combined special district budgets in the region are similar to that of the Metropolitan Council: their revenues totaled $943 million in 2004 and they spent $864 million.

Counties are the primary subdivision of U.S. states. In Minnesota, counties have different options in how they can structure their government. Each county must include an elected or appointed treasurer, sheriff, auditor, attorney, recorder, and coroner.[6] To make offices appointed, a county must undergo a referendum. Some offices may also be combined, such as an auditor-treasurer.[7]

In the Twin Cities, counties took in $2.5 billion in revenues in 2004. The most common revenue for counties was from property taxes (40 percent), followed by state aid (23 percent) and charges (12 percent), and federal aid (11 percent).

The Metropolitan Council is a multipurpose regional government that provides direct services to voters and municipalities (such as transit and wastewater collection and treatment); engages in regional planning for transportation, housing, and drinking water; and oversees local planning by cities, townships, and counties.

The Federal-Aid Highway Act of 1962 required that urbanized areas of more than fifty thousand residents regionally coordinate highway expenditures in order to receive federal assistance.[8] Metropolitan Planning Organizations (MPOs) were born out of this requirement.[9] The Metropolitan Council, along with the Minnesota legislature–created Transportation Advisory Board (TAB),[10] serves as the designated MPO for the Twin Cities metropolitan area, comprising the seven counties of Anoka, Carver, Dakota, Hennepin, Ramsey, Scott, and Washington.[11]

One of the Metropolitan Council's primary planning tools is the metropolitan urban service area (MUSA). The MUSA designates the area within which the council provides wastewater collection and treatment infrastructure and services. The council also takes a more active role in planning within the MUSA, but its planning powers are not limited to that area.

The Metropolitan Council's annual budget is roughly $850 million, significantly less than counties, school districts, or cities. However, because of its role in providing regional infrastructure, the council is very active in bond markets. In 2005, its bonded debt exceeded $1 billion, more than that of its seven component counties combined. The council's primary source of revenue is charges to consumers (for transit services, for instance) and municipalities (for wastewater collection and treatment), representing 27 percent of current revenue in 2005. However, it also receives significant amounts of money from the state and federal governments

(24 and 11 percent, respectively), borrowing (22 percent), and taxes (8 percent). It assesses property taxes and receives a share of the state-administered motor vehicle excise tax.

All Levels Combined

Taken together, the different types of local governments in the Twin Cities region present a strikingly complex picture (Figure 1.3). Assembling all the boundaries in a single map illustrates this point very well (Figure 1.4). Every resident in the seven core counties area is served by at least eight local governments—a city or township, a school district, a watershed district, a county, the Metropolitan Council, and three seven-county special districts for airports, sports facilities, and mosquito control. And this number is a lower bound because the map does not include all special districts.

Another way to illustrate the complexity of the system is the total number of unique combinations of local governments that can be found in the region. Because school districts and watershed districts are, for the most part, not contiguous with cities and townships or with each other, this number is enormous. It can be represented visually by the number of polygons in Figure 1.4: 1,714. This represents the upper bound on the number of different public service mixes in the region. The average number of people in areas with each of the possible combinations is just 1,730.

One manifestation of this complexity is that there are many more "taxing districts" in the region than municipalities. A "taxing district" in this context is a coterminous area with its own unique total tax rate. Map 1.1 shows how this plays out with property taxes in the eleven-county metropolitan area. The map shows total property tax rates—city or township plus school district plus special districts (if they use a property tax) plus county plus Metropolitan Council—across the region.[12] The total number of "taxing districts" on the map is 526. In other words, since very few special districts use the property tax, a total of 350 governmental units (cities plus townships plus school districts plus counties plus the Metropolitan Council) combine in such a way as to create 526 different property tax rates. The degree of fragmentation in the region is even greater than typical measures, such as the number of governments per ten thousand residents, imply.

This complexity makes it very difficult for residents and potential residents in a place to evaluate the mix of total public services they receive and the total tax rate they pay. These differences can segment the housing market in a single town. When, for instance, a city is split between two school districts (as is true for Golden Valley, Medina, and Eagan) with significantly different characteristics, the housing market reacts and the differences are reflected in housing values. This means that two

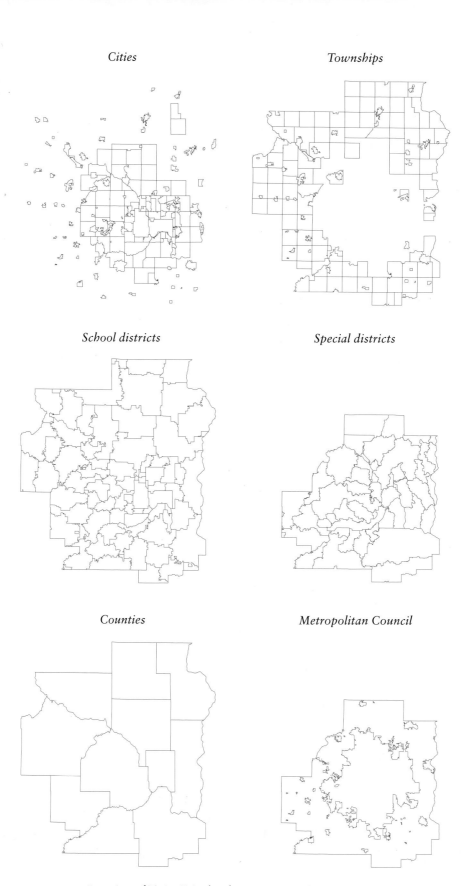

FIGURE 1.3. Location of Twin Cities local governments. *Source:* U.S. Census Bureau.

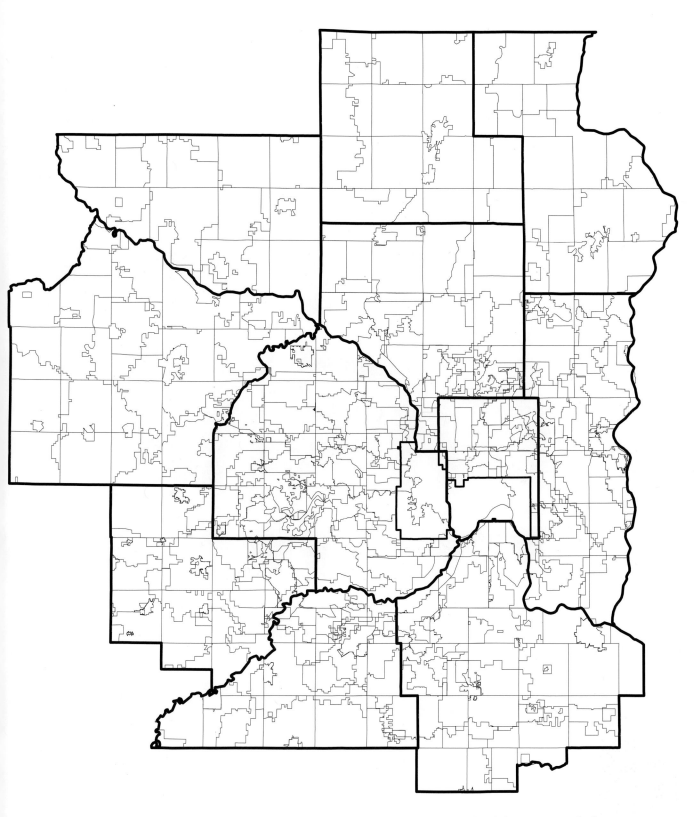

FIGURE I.4. Twin Cities area local government boundaries: cities, townships, school districts, watershed districts, counties, and the metropolitan urban service area. *Source:* U.S. Census Bureau.

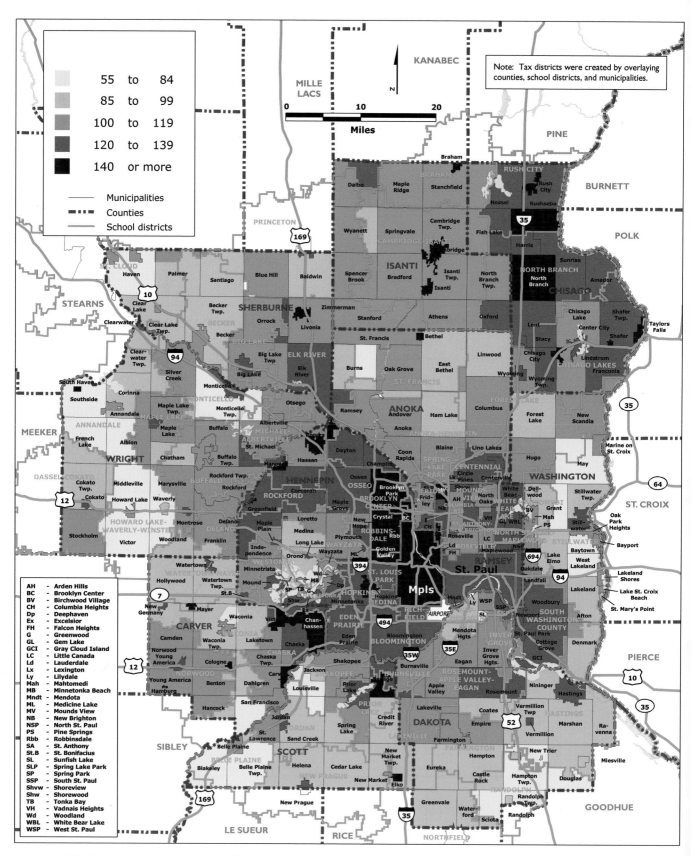

MAP 1.1. Total tax rates (total property-tax levies as a percentage of net tax capacity) by tax district, 2004. *Source:* House Research, Minnesota House of Representatives

identical households living in identical houses in different parts of town will pay different amounts of property tax to the city (because their home values vary), despite the fact that they receive identical municipal services from the city government.

Who Pays Local Taxes?

An important characteristic of a tax system is how tax collections affect taxpayers with different incomes. In a regressive tax system, lower-income taxpayers pay a higher percentage of their income in taxes than do higher-income taxpayers; in a progressive system, higher-income taxpayers pay the higher share; in a proportional system, all pay the same share of income. Most local tax systems in the United States rely on one or more of three taxes—property, sales, and income taxes. Most often, property and sales taxes are regressive while income taxes are usually proportional or progressive. As Figure 1.2 shows, the property tax is the primary tax for local governments in Minnesota. Minnesota's property tax has some features that reduce the regressivity of the tax. For instance, the first $72,000 of the value of a home is taxed at a lower rate than the value above $72,000. When all is said and done, however, property taxes in Minnesota are regressive. In 2004 residential property taxes hit lower-income taxpayers significantly harder (measured as a percentage of income) than higher-income taxpayers. For instance, taxpayers between the tenth and twentieth income percentiles paid 3.6 percent of their income on average in property taxes while those between the eightieth and ninetieth percentile paid 2.2 percent.[13]

Of course, Minnesota taxpayers also pay state taxes, and state taxes support significant parts of local expenditures. The state government's primary taxes are sales and income taxes. The Minnesota sales tax is a regressive tax: taxpayers in the tenth to twentieth percentile range paid 5.0 percent of income to the sales tax compared to just 2.8 percent in the eightieth to ninetieth percentile range. The income tax, on the other hand, is progressive: 0.6 percent at the tenth to twentieth percentile range and 4.6 percent at the eightieth to ninetieth percentile range.[14] How the big three taxes—property, sales, and income—are combined determines the overall regressivity or progressivity of the total tax system.

In 2004 the way the three taxes were combined resulted in a mildly regressive state–local tax system. However, the combination has changed over time. Figure 1.5 shows how changes have affected the system. It shows the Suits index, a commonly used measure of regressivity/progressivity from 1994 to 2004 along with the expected change in the index by 2009 from changes already written into the tax code. The index is negative throughout the period, implying that state and local taxes in Minnesota were regressive over the entire period. However, the system became significantly more regressive between 1994 and 1998, less regressive from 1998 to 2002, and more regressive since then.[15]

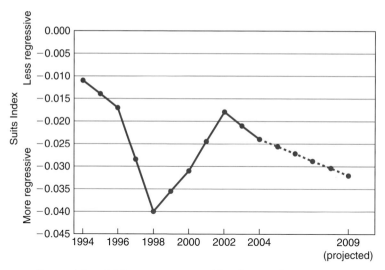

FIGURE 1.5. Regressivity of Minnesota state and local taxes. *Source: 2007 Minnesota Tax Incidence Study: An Analysis of Minnesota's Household and Business Taxes*, Minnesota Department of Revenue, Tax Research Division, March 2007.

GROWTH PATTERNS

The eleven-county study area is home to 3.1 million people, more than 60 percent of the state's population, and contains Minnesota's primary growth engine: the Twin Cities metropolitan area economy. The eleven-county metropolitan area is projected to grow significantly by 2030, with the seven core metropolitan counties continuing to receive the majority of the state's new residents and jobs.

Like most metropolitan areas in the United States, the Twin Cities metro has seen significant decentralization of population and jobs during recent decades. This pattern has not been as pronounced as in many large metropolitan areas, owing, at least in part, to the existence of relatively strong (compared to other metropolitan areas) regional institutions like the Metropolitan Council and the Twin Cities Fiscal Disparities tax base sharing program.[16]

Population Growth

Recent population growth patterns in the Twin Cities are common to most American metropolitan areas in the United States, namely, decline or lower than average growth in core areas surrounded by much greater growth rates in a wide band of suburbs (Map 1.2). Although both of the core cities of Minneapolis and St. Paul gained population overall between 1990 and 2004, the two cities grew at a substantially slower rate than the region as a whole: 1.3 percent for Minneapolis and 3.0 percent for St. Paul, compared with a regional rate of 22.5 percent.

Many inner-ring suburbs, on the other hand, actually lost population during

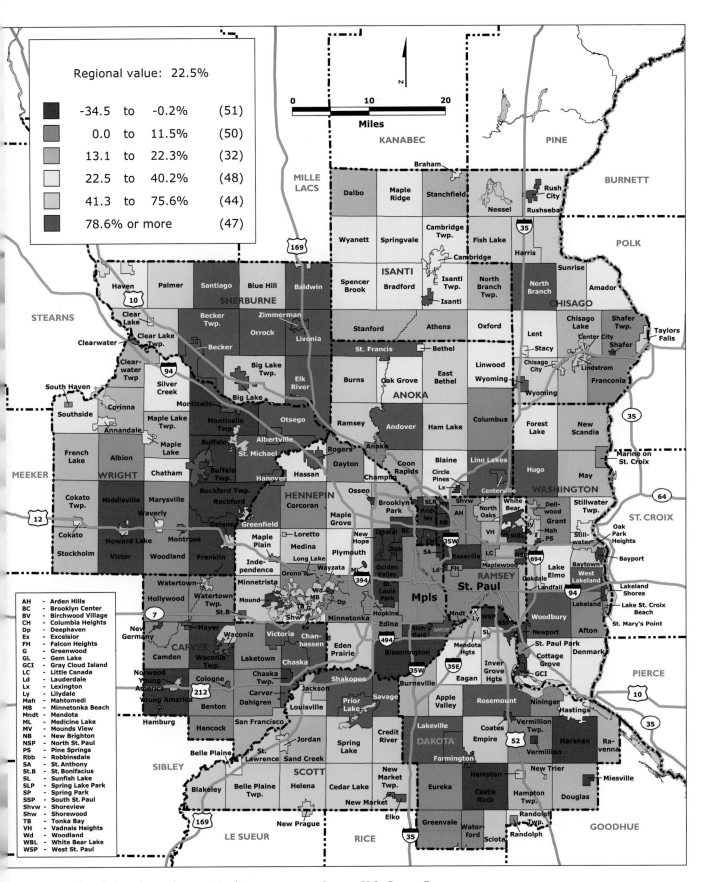

Regional value: 22.5%

	−34.5	to	−0.2%	(51)
	0.0	to	11.5%	(50)
	13.1	to	22.3%	(32)
	22.5	to	40.2%	(48)
	41.3	to	75.6%	(44)
	78.6% or more			(47)

0   10   20
Miles

AH   - Arden Hills
BC   - Brooklyn Center
BV   - Birchwood Village
CH   - Columbia Heights
Dp   - Deephaven
Ex   - Excelsior
FH   - Falcon Heights
G   - Greenwood
GL   - Gem Lake
GCI - Gray Cloud Island
LC   - Little Canada
Ld   - Lauderdale
Lx   - Lexington
Ly   - Lilydale
Mah - Mahtomedi
MB   - Minnetonka Beach
Mndt - Mendota
ML   - Medicine Lake
MV   - Mounds View
NB   - New Brighton
NSP - North St. Paul
PS   - Pine Springs
Rbb - Robbinsdale
SA   - St. Anthony
St.B - St. Bonifacius
SL   - Sunfish Lake
SLP - Spring Lake Park
SP   - Spring Park
SSP - South St. Paul
Shvw - Shoreview
Shw - Shorewood
TB   - Tonka Bay
VH   - Vadnais Heights
WBL - White Bear Lake
WSP - West St. Paul

MAP 1.2. Population change by municipality, 1990–2004. *Source:* U.S. Census Bureau.

this period. In fact, the majority of suburbs that bordered one of the core cities showed declines. The greatest growth rates occurred in second- and third-ring suburbs and even farther out along the major freeway corridors—along Highway 169 and I-35 in the north, I-94 in the east, and I-35 in the south.

The places that grew by 10,000 people or more were virtually all second- and third-ring suburbs, forming a nearly complete ring around the region: Woodbury (29,340), Lakeville (22,951), Eden Prairie (20,159), Maple Grove (18,436), Plymouth (18,375), Eagan (16,597), Savage (15,296), Shakopee (14,942), Apple Valley (14,340), Andover (13,722), Blaine (11,450), Brooklyn Park (11,400), Chanhassen (10,392), St. Michael (10,344), and Farmington (10,120).

Urbanization

While the spatial pattern of population growth is an important way to track growth, it does not capture everything that is important in growth patterns. The direct effect of growth and development on the landscape—the development of previously undeveloped land—is also of great importance. Data on new subdivision development and remote sensing from satellite imagery and aerial photography provide two ways of visualizing these changes.

The locations of new subdivisions, shown in Maps 1.3 and 1.4, highlight that much of the growth in the region is consuming previously undeveloped land. The greatest numbers of new subdivisions occurred in virtually the same list of places showing the greatest numbers of new residents: Woodbury, Cottage Grove, Lakeville, Shakopee, Eden Prairie, Plymouth, Maple Grove, Brooklyn Park, Andover, and Blaine.

Urbanization rates in the seven-county core region over the period 1986–2002 reflect this pattern as well.[17] Maps 1.5 and 1.6 show urbanized land in 1986 and 2002. (Urban land is defined as land used for residential, commercial, industrial, transportation, or communications.) Map 1.7 shows just the land that became urbanized during the period. Based on satellite imagery analyzed by the University of Minnesota's Department of Forest Resources, the maps show how growth in population and employment consumed previously undeveloped land during the sixteen-year period.[18]

Two patterns are clear. First, rapid urbanization occurred in areas immediately adjacent to previously urbanized areas (in inner and middle suburbs), as well as in locations along major roads and highways. Places like Woodbury, Savage, and Brooklyn Park made rapid transitions from largely undeveloped in 1986 to nearly fully developed just sixteen years later.

Second, the 2002 distribution of urbanized land is much more "scattershot" in outer parts of the region. In 1986, urbanized land was largely confined to contiguous areas in the core, but in 2002, there are many smaller tracts of urban land scattered across the outer parts of the region.

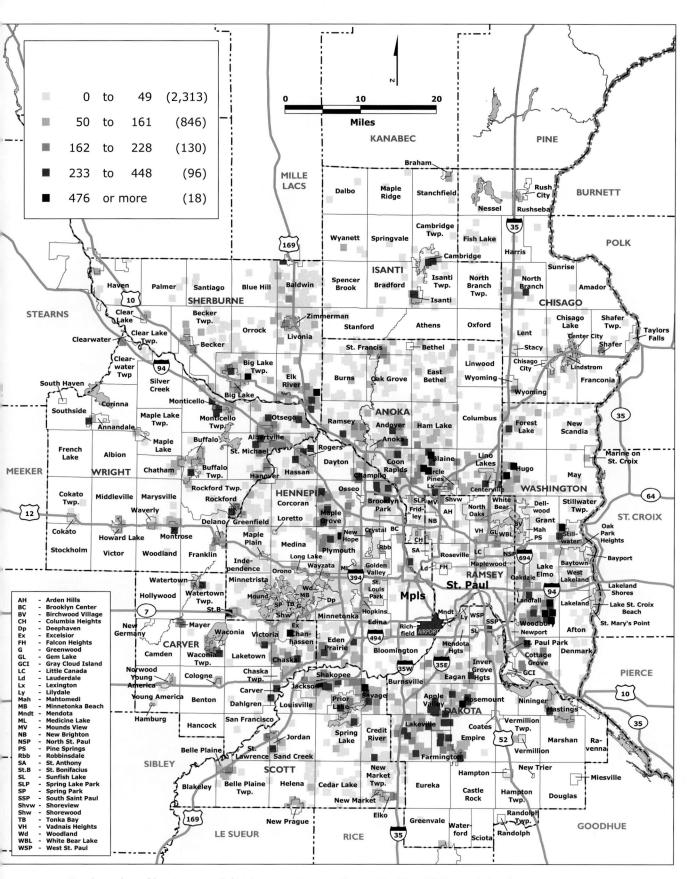

MAP 1.3. Total number of lots in new subdivisions, 1998–2005. *Source:* Residential Research Services.

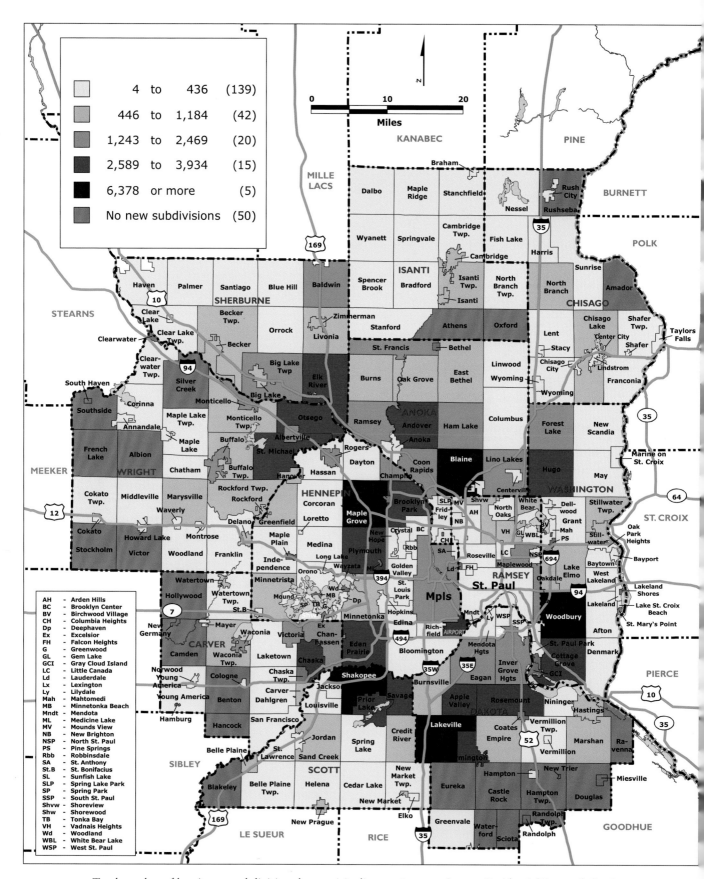

MAP 1.4. Total number of lots in new subdivisions by municipality, 1998–2005. *Source:* Residential Research Services.

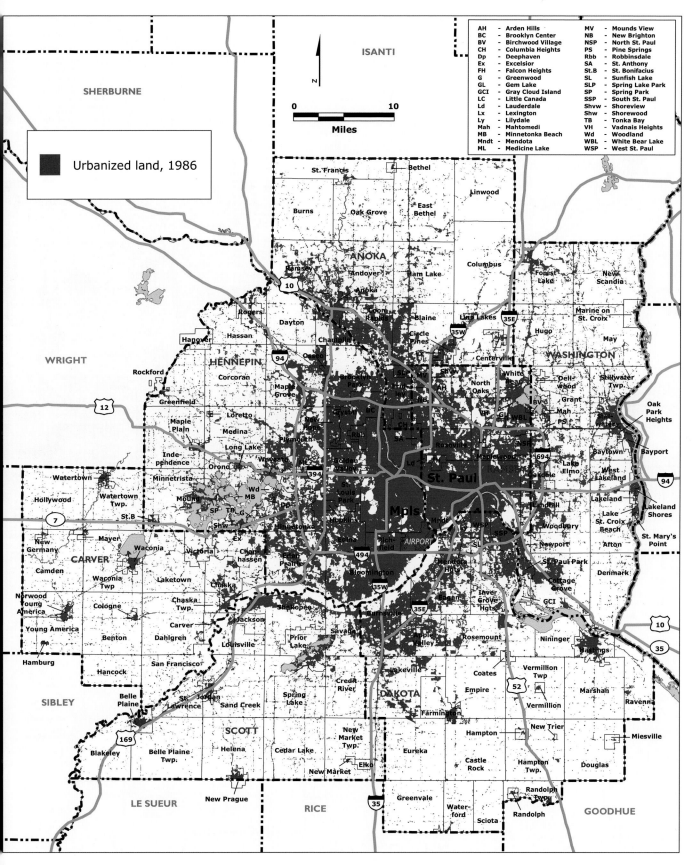

MAP 1.5. Urbanized land, 1986. *Source:* Remote Sensing and Geospatial Analysis Laboratory, University of Minnesota.

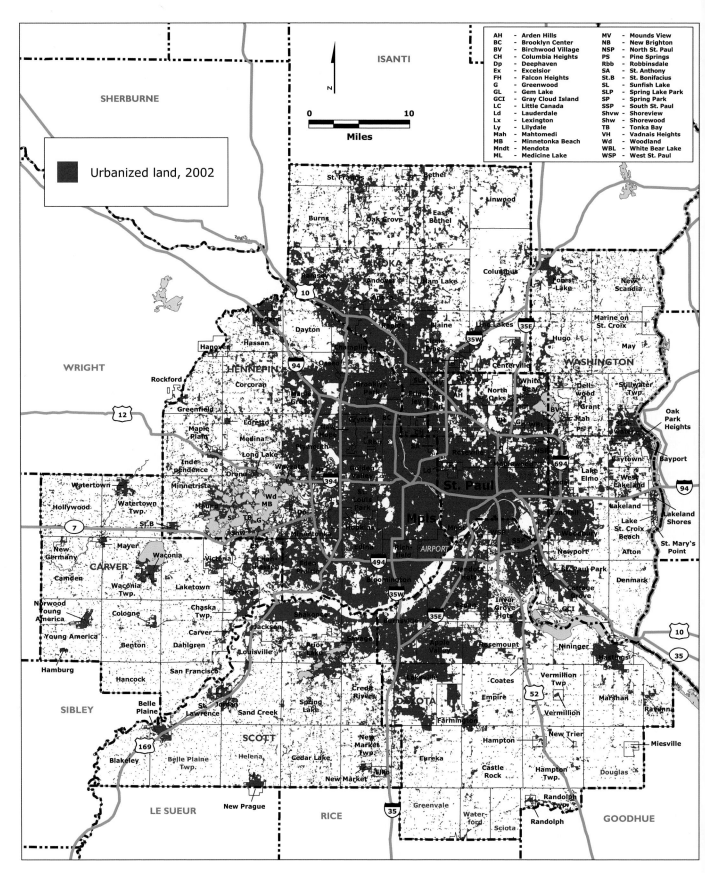

MAP 1.6. Urbanized land, 2002. *Source:* Remote Sensing and Geospatial Analysis Laboratory, University of Minnesota.

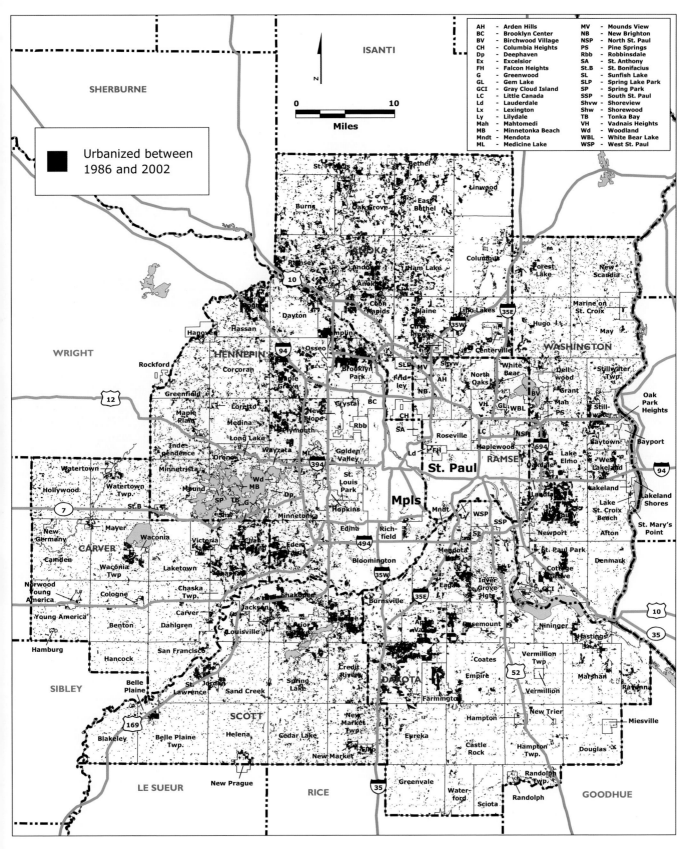

MAP 1.7. Land that became urbanized between 1986 and 2002. *Source:* Remote Sensing and Geospatial Analysis Laboratory, University of Minnesota.

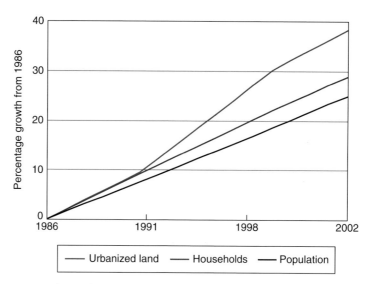

FIGURE 1.6. Growth in urbanized land, population, and households, Twin Cities seven-county metropolitan area, 1986–2002. *Sources:* Remote Sensing and Geospatial Analysis Laboratory, University of Minnesota; U.S. Census Bureau.

Overall, the data show a pattern seen in most American metropolitan areas: as the region has grown, it has become less dense, consuming (or urbanizing) land at a rate greater than population has grown. This is true even in the most densely settled parts of the region. Between 1986 and 2002, the amount of urbanized land in the seven-county metropolitan core grew from 450,000 to 625,000 acres, or by 38 percent. During the same period, population grew by just 25 percent—the growth rate in urbanized land was 53 percent greater than the population growth rate (Figure 1.6).

Current population projections show the seven-county region growing by 33 percent between 2003 and 2030. If this growth urbanizes land at the same rate as in the recent past, then the amount of urbanized land in the seven-county region will grow by another 50 percent during that period, consuming hundreds of thousands of acres of previously undeveloped land.

An important factor contributing to this pattern of growth is the region's highly fragmented system of local governance. Data for the fifty largest U.S. metropolitan areas for the period from 1970 to 2000 show a clear relationship between the degree of fragmentation (the number of municipal governments per ten thousand residents) and sprawl rates (the ratio of population growth to urban land growth). Higher levels of fragmentation are clearly correlated with greater sprawl rates.[19] Figure 1.7 shows the relationship.

The number of municipal governments per ten thousand residents varies from

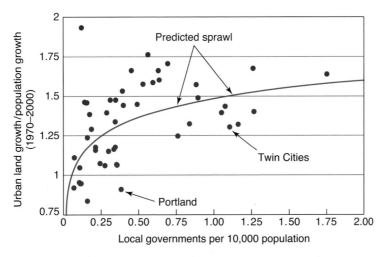

FIGURE 1.7. Fragmentation and sprawl in the fifty largest U.S. metropolitan areas. *Source:* U.S. Census Bureau.

.07 to 1.75 across the fifty metropolitan areas. The value for the Twin Cities is the fifth highest at 1.10. The sprawl measure varies from .74 to 1.93. (A value less than 1 implies that population grew more quickly than urbanized land; a value greater than 1 implies that urbanized land grew more quickly.) The Twin Cities fall in the middle of this range (twenty-second out of fifty) at 1.31. The curved line ("Predicted sprawl") in Figure 1.7 shows the curvilinear relationship between the two measures.[20] The line shows the predicted sprawl for every possible value of the fragmentation measure. If the actual value for a metropolitan area falls below the predicted value, this means that its sprawl measure is lower than would be predicted by its fragmentation measure. The predicted sprawl measure for a metropolitan area with 1.10 governments per ten thousand residents (the Twin Cities value) is 1.50. The actual value for the Twin Cities was 1.31, which implies that the Twin Cities did better in controlling sprawl than expected, given the area's high degree of fragmentation. The most likely explanation of this is the existence of the Metropolitan Council. Only two of the fifty metropolitan areas—Portland and the Twin Cities—have regionwide (or nearly so) metropolitan governments with a mandate to oversee local planning decisions. Not surprisingly, both of these metros do better than expected.

The Twin Cities clearly could do better, however. The area's actual sprawl measure is 13 percent lower than predicted (1.31 compared to 1.50) while Portland's is 31 percent lower (.91 versus 1.32). The implication is that Portland's regional government does a better job of counteracting the incentives for sprawl implied by the region's degree of fragmentation.

Jobs

Historically, jobs have tended to follow people to the suburbs. As areas became suburbanized, firms followed to be nearer their workforces and customers. In addition, many of the same factors that draw households to the suburbs directly affect businesses as well, such as cheaper land and improving access as a result of substantial transportation investments like the interstate highway system.

However, not only do jobs follow people, but people follow jobs. The spread of significant numbers of jobs to middle and outer suburbs enables many workers to live farther and farther from the core of the region while remaining within reasonable commutes from their jobs. In addition, for a select group of workers, technological advances in communications—the Internet and wireless communications—have made telecommuting possible.

All these factors have made living at the edges of the metropolitan area much more practical. In many cases, these are areas with little (or none) of the physical infrastructure (such as sewers and wastewater treatment facilities) needed to support low-impact development. They are also often the parts of the region that retain natural habitats with significant ecological value.

A trend toward decentralization is clearly evident in the job and job change data for the region. Like population, jobs still tend to cluster in the core of the metropolitan area. However, job growth has been significantly greater in middle and outer suburbs (Map 1.8). Growth was negative or below the regional average in the core of the metropolitan area, including both central cities of Minneapolis and St. Paul and most of the older, inner-ring suburbs. High percentage gains in jobs between 1993 and 2003 were concentrated in growing suburban communities just inside or at the boundaries of the seven-county core area where much of the urbanization in recent years occurred.

Beyond the seven-county metropolitan area, job concentrations tend to be much lower. Many of these rural or exurban areas show significant job growth, but it is from such small numbers that the increases represent relatively few jobs in absolute numbers.

As with sprawl, the data for large metropolitan areas show a clear relationship between political fragmentation and job growth rates. Figure 1.8 shows the relationship. The Twin Cities and Portland again stand out with growth rates significantly above what would be expected given their political fragmentation. The Twin Cities growth rate was nearly double the expected—29 percent versus 16 percent—and Portland's was about two-thirds higher than expected—39 percent compared to 24 percent.[21]

The preceding sections show very clearly that the dominant trends in the metropolitan economy involve the decentralization of jobs and people and that the influence of the core metropolitan area is spreading farther out into the region. The places where this can be seen most clearly are the four collar counties—Chisago,

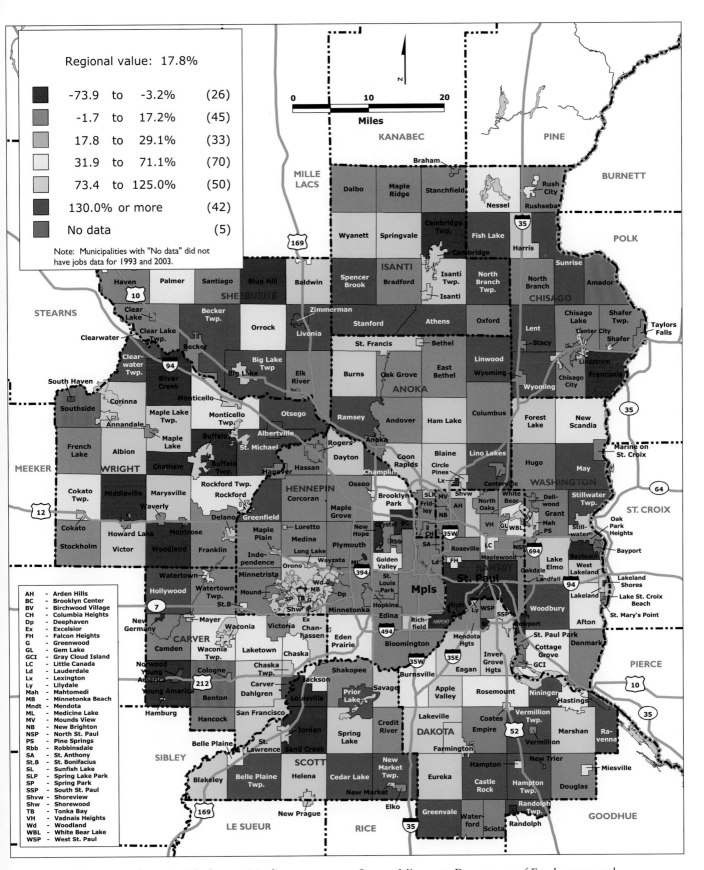

MAP 1.8. Percentage change in jobs by municipality, 1993–2003. *Source:* Minnesota Department of Employment and Economic Development.

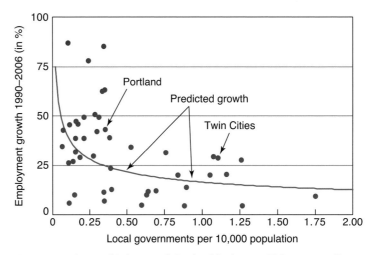

FIGURE 1.8. Fragmentation and job growth in the fifty largest U.S. metropolitan areas. *Sources:* Bureau of Labor Statistics; various state and local sources.

Isanti, Sherburne, and Wright. These counties, which were not added to the census-designated "metropolitan area" until the 1970s or 1980s, are rapidly making the transition from rural to suburban—a transition clearly being driven by the metropolitan economy.

Table 1.1 shows one measure of how much more connected to the core of the metropolitan area the collar counties have become: increases in the number of workers commuting from residences in the collar counties to jobs in the seven-county core. The total number of workers residing in these four counties almost quadrupled between 1970 and 2000, from about 31,500 to 118,225. During the same time period, however, the number of workers living in the collar counties and working in the core seven counties increased by *more than six times,* from just 8,900 to more than 56,000. By 2000, 48 percent of the workers living in these counties commuted to jobs in the seven-county core, compared to just 28 percent in 1970.

How can this kind of change occur? Transportation improvements made a significant contribution, but another important factor was the growth of jobs in the middle and outer sections of the core seven counties—growth that is evident in Map 1.8. The rapid growth in jobs at the fringes of the seven-county core area opens up opportunities for individuals to live in parts of the region well beyond the current urbanized area. While it may not be practical for someone living in western Wright County to commute to the Minneapolis central business district, it might very well be practical for that same person to commute to Maple Grove. Growth of job centers at the fringes of the core region allows individuals previously residing within the urbanized area to take advantage of cheaper land and housing outside the metropolitan core without giving up employment opportunities.

Commuting data for 1990 and 2000 show how accessible residences on the

TABLE 1.1   Integration of the collar counties into the
Twin Cities metropolitan area, 1970–2000

County	Total resident workers			Workers commuting to the core 7 counties		
	1970	2000	Change (%)	1970	2000	Change (%)
Chisago	5,935	20,772	250	1,732	11,754	579
Isanti	5,597	16,085	187	1,611	7,319	354
Sherburne	6,037	34,084	465	1,643	14,265	768
Wright	13,921	47,284	240	3,945	22,960	482
Total	31,490	118,225	275	8,931	56,298	530

County	Percentage of resident workers commuting to the core 7 counties		Percentage of residents working in county of residence	
	1970	2000	1970	2000
Chisago	29	57	42	34
Isanti	29	46	56	40
Sherburne	27	42	38	32
Wright	28	49	63	43
Total	28	48	53	38

Source: U.S. Census Bureau.

fringes of the region have become. Maps 1.9 and 1.10 show commuting patterns into a representative cluster of jobs in the inner suburbs—in the Fridley–Coon Rapids area—and various commute times to that job center in 1990 and 2000 (i.e., within zero to twenty minutes, twenty to thirty minutes, and thirty to forty minutes). These commuter sheds were derived using data about where commuters to the job center live and how long their commutes took.[22] The Fridley–Coon Rapids job center had 14,500 jobs in 1990 and grew by 45 percent, to 21,000 jobs in 2000. (Chapter 4 is devoted to a much more extensive analysis of data for forty job centers across the region.)

Map 1.9 shows that, in 1990, workers in this job center could live relatively far out on the fringes of the metropolitan area and still have reasonable commuting times to their jobs. At that time, much of Isanti and Sherburne counties, and significant parts of Chisago and Wright counties, were within a forty-minute commute of the job center.

However, rapid population and job growth in this part of the region during the

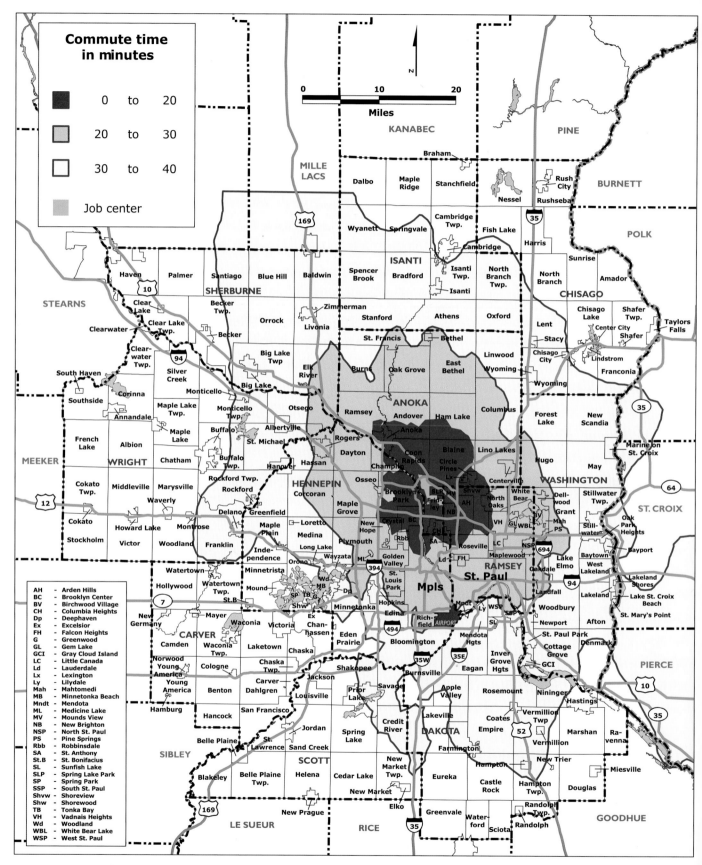

MAP 1.9. Commuter shed for Fridley–Coon Rapids job cluster, 1990. *Source:* U.S. Census Transportation Planning Package.

1990s led to increasing traffic congestion, making these commutes more and more difficult. By 2000, although the commuter shed still reached into Chisago, Isanti, and Sherburne counties, the area within a forty-minute drive of the job center had shrunk considerably (Map 1.10).

Increasing congestion on the fringes of the region could have different effects. On the one hand, slower commutes make the farthest fringes less desirable to potential residents–commuters. On the other hand, firms locating or relocating to this part of the region have incentives to move even farther away from the core to remain within a "reasonable" commute of the area's growing workforce.

Overall, it is clear that the collar counties are rapidly transforming from largely self-contained rural environments to more suburban communities with strong links to the metropolitan economy. As long as that economy continues to grow, this part of the region can expect to see growing demand drive development of currently undeveloped land.

Projected Future Growth

Past population and job growth trends can help us understand the forces at work in defining the demographic and economic face of a region. Past patterns do not, however, always foretell the future, so it is worthwhile to examine projections that account for a variety of factors. Population projections of this nature are available for the entire region. Such projections are subject to error, of course, but they provide the best available basis for evaluating future growth pressures.

Map 1.11 shows projected population growth from 2000 to 2030 as estimated by the Office of the Minnesota State Demographer and the Twin Cities Metropolitan Council in the early 2000s.[23] The vast majority of growth in the region was projected to fall in the seven-county core area: roughly 970,000 new residents were expected within the seven-county metropolitan core and an additional 140,000 in the four collar counties.

The greatest projected growth rates in the seven-county metro area were in the second- and third-ring suburbs. These high growth areas lie almost uniformly adjacent to land that made up the urbanized core of the region in 2002, implying that a large share of future growth will most likely consume currently undeveloped land.

Overall, growth within the seven-county metropolitan area is expected to be strongest in the western half, with nearly all remaining nonurbanized areas of Hennepin, Carver, and Scott counties seeing high percentage population growth rates. Many of the municipalities in the four collar counties show similarly high projected growth rates. The highest rates fall in western Chisago County, all but the westernmost tip of Sherburne County, and extreme northeastern Wright County. Notably, the growth in the collar counties falls almost exclusively in areas directly adjacent to or one municipality removed from major transportation corridors: U.S. Highway 10

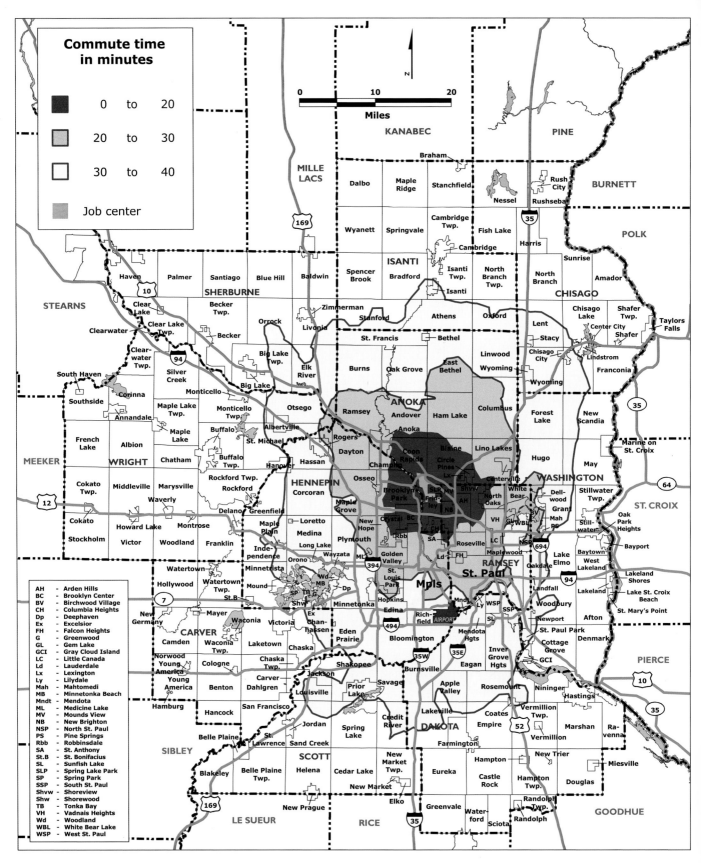

**Commute time
in minutes**

■	0	to	20
▨	20	to	30
□	30	to	40

■ Job center

N

0   10   20
Miles

AH - Arden Hills
BC - Brooklyn Center
BV - Birchwood Village
CH - Columbia Heights
Dp - Deephaven
Ex - Excelsior
FH - Falcon Heights
G - Greenwood
GL - Gem Lake
GCI - Gray Cloud Island
LC - Little Canada
Ld - Lauderdale
Lx - Lexington
Ly - Lilydale
Mah - Mahtomedi
MB - Minnetonka Beach
Mndt - Mendota
ML - Medicine Lake
MV - Mounds View
NB - New Brighton
NSP - North St. Paul
PS - Pine Springs
Rbb - Robbinsdale
SA - St. Anthony
St.B - St. Bonifacius
SL - Sunfish Lake
SLP - Spring Lake Park
SP - Spring Park
SSP - South St. Paul
Shvw - Shoreview
Shw - Shorewood
TB - Tonka Bay
VH - Vadnais Heights
Wd - Woodland
WBL - White Bear Lake
WSP - West St. Paul

MAP 1.10. Commuter shed for Fridley–Coon Rapids job cluster, 2000. *Source:* U.S. Census Transportation Planning Package.

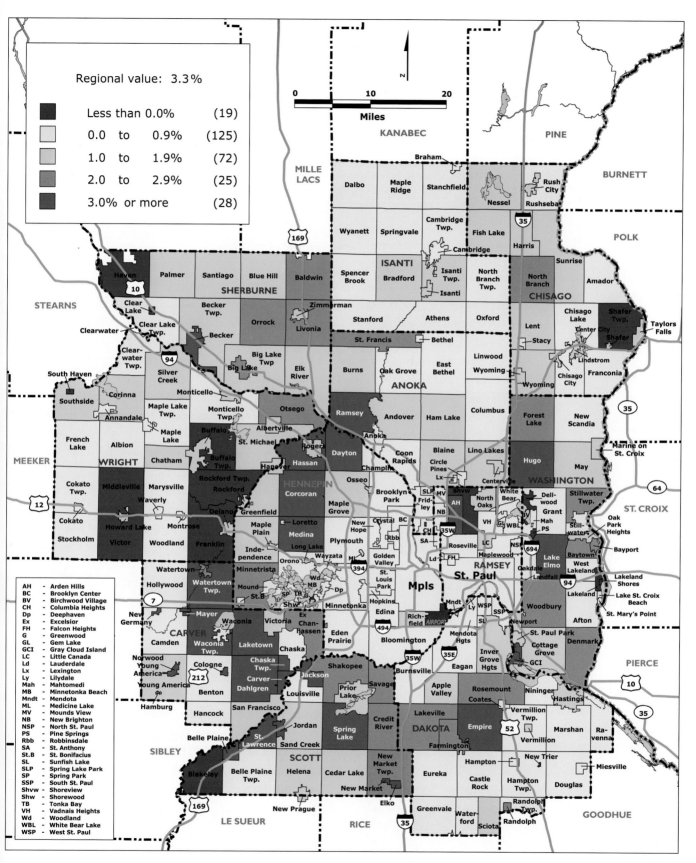

MAP I.II. Percentage change per year in projected population by municipality, 2000–2030. *Source:* State of Minnesota Department of Administration, State Demographic Center.

and I-94 through Sherburne and northeastern Wright counties, U.S. Highway 169 through eastern Sherburne County, and I-35 through western Chisago County.

Although this growth is from relatively small numbers compared to the high-growth areas of the seven-county core metro, the 140,000 people expected to settle in these areas represent significant growth: 65 percent for the four counties as a whole. Further, since much of the land in these counties is currently nonurban, this growth is also likely to represent significant consumption of currently undeveloped land.

Projected Growth Patterns versus Actual Growth, 1975–2000 and 2000–2005

Predicting the future is an inexact science. Growth projections like those represented in Map 1.11 must always be used with caution. In addition, these projections were not developed as pure forecasts. Indeed, for the seven core counties they were developed by an agency, the Metropolitan Council, with the power to directly affect the pattern of future growth. As a result, the projections represent goals to some extent, instead of pure forecasts.

It is therefore worthwhile to examine how well growth projections have matched actual patterns and how well the forecast in Map 1.11 has tracked actual growth since 2000. Maps 1.12 and 1.13 do this.

Map 1.12 shows the difference between actual population growth between 1975 and 2000 and the growth projections developed by the Metropolitan Council in the early 1970s for the seven-county core area. In red areas population grew more slowly than projected, while in blue areas it grew more quickly than projected. There is a clear pattern. Overall, inner parts of the region grew more slowly than expected, while outer parts, especially in the north and south, outperformed the projections.

Map 1.13 shows the same measure for the period from 2000–2005. Although the color scheme varies a bit in the suburbs compared to Map 1.12, the overall pattern is the same: slower than predicted growth in the core and greater than predicted growth on the fringes of the region.

The similarity between the two maps clearly suggests that the Metropolitan Council's growth projections tend to reflect two of the agency's most important overall mandates—to guide growth as much as possible to core areas and to limit growth on the periphery as much as possible to areas immediately contiguous with already urbanized areas. Both sets of projections (1975 and 2000) were ambitious, in the sense that they projected strong growth in the core. Unfortunately, actual growth in these areas did not fulfill the expectations. The clear implication is that future growth is likely to consume even more currently undeveloped land than the projections in Map 1.11 imply.

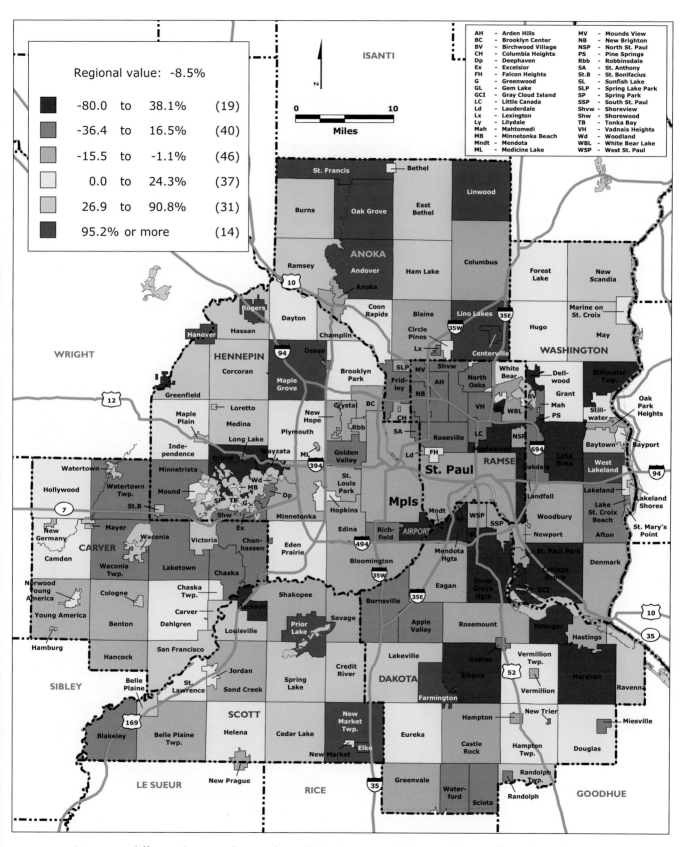

Regional value: -8.5%

■	-80.0 to 38.1%	(19)
■	-36.4 to 16.5%	(40)
■	-15.5 to -1.1%	(46)
□	0.0 to 24.3%	(37)
■	26.9 to 90.8%	(31)
■	95.2% or more	(14)

AH	– Arden Hills	MV	– Mounds View
BC	– Brooklyn Center	NB	– New Brighton
BV	– Birchwood Village	NSP	– North St. Paul
CH	– Columbia Heights	PS	– Pine Springs
Dp	– Deephaven	Rbb	– Robbinsdale
Ex	– Excelsior	SA	– St. Anthony
FH	– Falcon Heights	St.B	– St. Bonifacius
G	– Greenwood	SL	– Sunfish Lake
GL	– Gem Lake	SLP	– Spring Lake Park
GCI	– Gray Cloud Island	SP	– Spring Park
LC	– Little Canada	SSP	– South St. Paul
Ld	– Lauderdale	Shvw	– Shoreview
Lx	– Lexington	Shw	– Shorewood
Ly	– Lilydale	TB	– Tonka Bay
Mah	– Mahtomedi	VH	– Vadnais Heights
MB	– Minnetonka Beach	Wd	– Woodland
Mndt	– Mendota	WBL	– White Bear Lake
ML	– Medicine Lake	WSP	– West St. Paul

MAP 1.12. Percentage difference between the actual population in 2000 and the 2000 forecasted population from 1975. *Source:* Metropolitan Council.

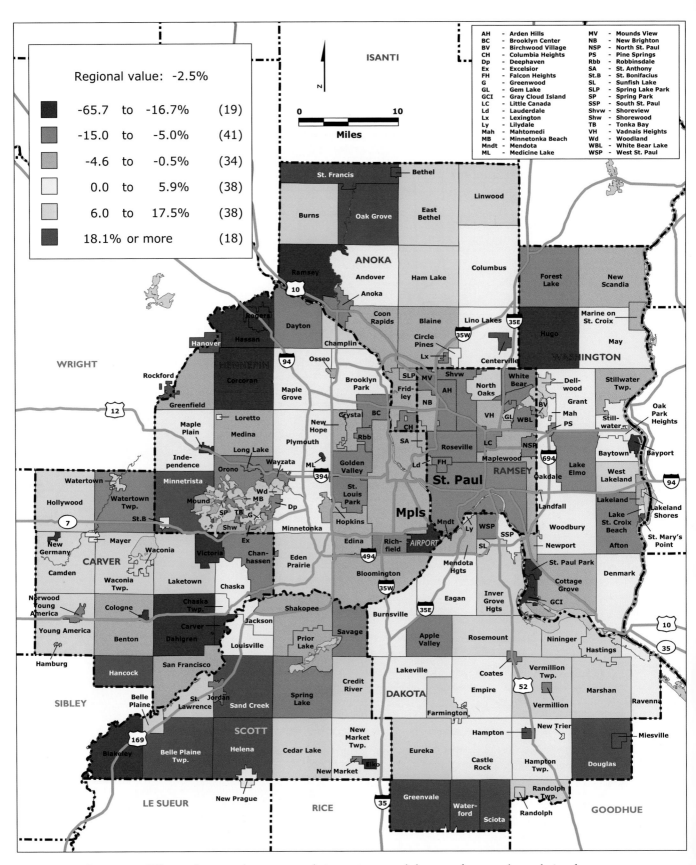

MAP 1.13. Percentage difference between the 2005 population estimate and the 2005 forecasted population from 2000.
Source: Metropolitan Council.

LOCAL FISCAL CAPACITY

Several layers of government are involved in determining how metropolitan areas grow. However, local governments, with their powers to regulate land use, are the most important actors. Municipal governments often have the first and last word on whether specific parcels of land can or will be developed.

While it is true that local governments are best positioned to handle the nuts and bolts of growth, they are not particularly well suited to regulate many aspects of development. For instance, they are not well positioned to evaluate the environmental effects of development decisions. The full benefits of conserving natural resources are rarely concentrated in a single community. But, at the same time, the costs of protecting may be highly localized. In this situation, local governments do not face the proper incentives. If the benefits of protection are undervalued (because many of the benefits accrue to other areas), while the costs are not (because they are fully borne locally), then local governments can be expected to do too little to protect sensitive natural areas.

This happens not because residents or public officials value the resources any less than others or behave irrationally. Environmental assets clearly have value to local actors—recent initiatives in Woodbury and Eden Prairie to raise local taxes to preserve open space illustrate this principle.[24] However, local residents often receive only a portion (often small) of the benefits of protection, biasing decisions made solely at the local level away from conservation.

Similar incentives also push local areas to favor some types of development over others. Local tax policy and land use regulations are closely related. Local taxes must finance municipal services like police and fire protection and public schools. The amount of revenue a local government can generate on its own depends largely on the value and types of land within its boundaries. If the property tax is the primary local tax, as it is in Minnesota, then local governments have a direct incentive to develop a land use plan that maximizes the value of property.

Different types of development often imply different obligations on the expenditure side of local budgets as well. Commercial–industrial development may enhance the tax base without increasing the demand for school services, for instance. In the end, it is the balance of costs (expenditure needs caused by the development) and benefits (the revenues generated) about which local officials care.

The net effect of the revenue and expenditure side factors is that local governments have incentives to favor high-value residential, commercial, and industrial development that generates little demand for public services over other uses such as apartment buildings or moderate-value homes. For residential development, this often means favoring lower-density development over higher densities. The cumulative effect of this over an entire metropolitan area is a tendency to consume land (especially on the fringes) at greater rates than necessary.

The ability of local governments to raise revenues is clearly an important component of local development decisions. Tax base–rich areas face less incentive to develop currently undeveloped land. In Minnesota, the primary local tax instrument is the property tax. State law sets the rate structure for different types of property; for instance, the rate per dollar of assessed value is greater for commercial–industrial property than for owner-occupied residential property. A particular locality's mix of property types then determines how productive its tax base is (in terms of revenue generated per dollar of property values). This is the locality's "tax capacity." Local governments then determine their overall tax rate by varying the percentage of tax capacity that they tap.

Tax capacity—the revenue the property tax would generate if the locality taxed its capacity at 100 percent—per household is therefore the proper measure of local ability to raise tax revenue. Maps 1.14 and 1.15 show this measure in 2004 and the percentage change during the prior ten years for each municipality in the Twin Cities region.

The maps show great diversity in the capacity of local governments to absorb the potential costs of natural resource conservation. Tax capacities per household in 2004 varied from as low as $794 per household in the city of Landfall in Washington County to as high as $12,866 in the city of Becker in Sherburne County. The distribution is relatively even between these extremes, and 80 percent of municipalities fall in the range between $1,505 and $3,909 per household (Figure 1.9).

However, there are significant variations across the region in tax capacities. Municipalities in the core and at the northern fringe of the metropolitan area share lower-than-average capacities for the most part, while second- and third-ring suburbs, especially in the eastern, southern, and western parts of the region, are largely

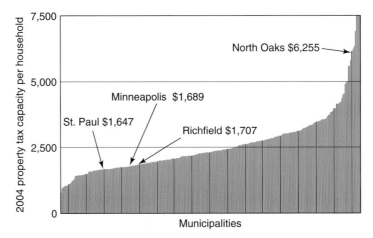

FIGURE 1.9. Property tax capacity per household by municipality, 2004. *Source:* Minnesota State Auditor.

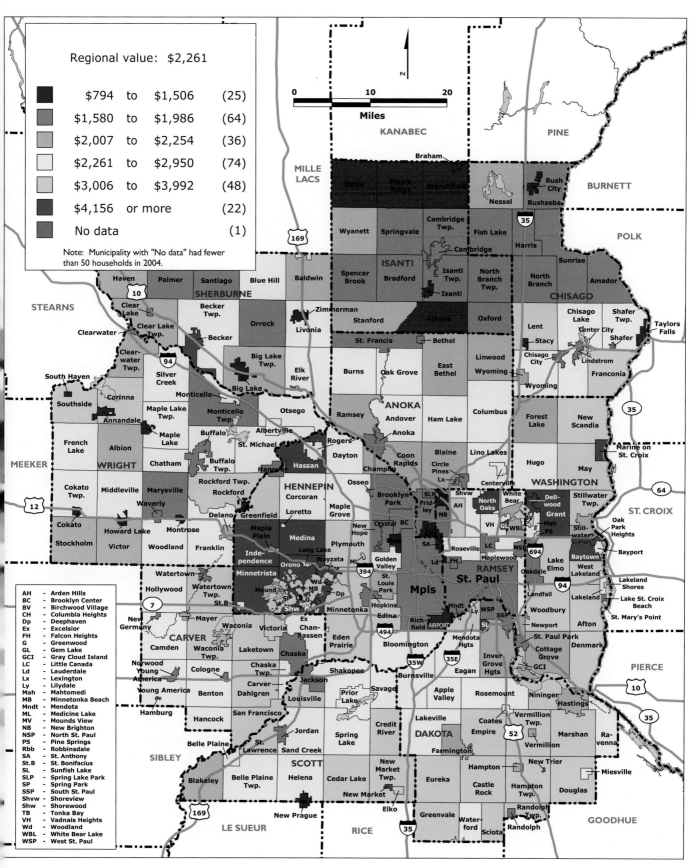

MAP 1.14. Tax capacity per household by municipality, 2004. *Source:* Minnesota State Auditor.

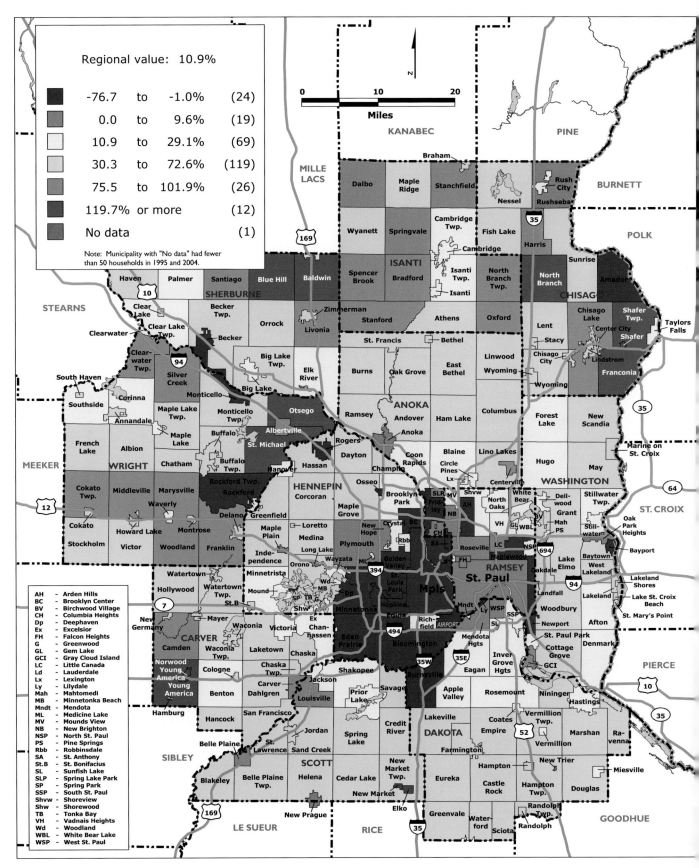

MAP 1.15. Percentage change in tax capacity per household by municipality, 1995–2004. *Source:* Minnesota State Auditor.

above average. The highest capacities are in the southwest and western suburbs and along the St. Croix River valley.

The pattern of changes in tax rates is even clearer. The developed core of the region, including several second- and third-ring suburbs, lost tax base or grew more slowly than average between 1995 and 2004, while the rest of the region gained base. Part of the explanation for this dichotomy is the changes in state law that occurred during this period. The changes decreased tax rates on commercial–industrial property compared to residential property, leading to decreasing values of tax bases in places rich in commercial–industrial property (e.g., the core of the metro area) compared to places with less commercial–industrial property (e.g., largely residential suburbs).

Although fiscal disparities in the Twin Cities are significant, the region actually compares relatively well to other large metropolitan areas. Table 1.2 shows a commonly used measure of inequality—the Gini coefficient—for each of the twenty-five largest U.S. metropolitan areas in 1993 and 2001. The region ranks sixth best among the twenty-five, and inequality declined during the period. This is a surprising result given the degree of fragmentation in the Twin Cities. Figure 1.10 shows that there is a relatively strong relationship between fragmentation rates and fiscal inequality: greater fragmentation is associated with higher rates of inequality.

The number of municipal governments per ten thousand residents varies from .07 to 1.75 across the fifty metropolitan areas. The value for the Twin Cities is the fifth highest at 1.10. The Gini coefficients vary from .11 to 45. (The larger the Gini coefficient, the greater the fiscal inequality.) The curved line ("Predicted inequality") in Figure 1.10 shows the curvilinear relationship between the two measures.[25] The line shows the predicted inequality for every possible value of the fragmentation measure. If the actual value for a metropolitan area falls below the predicted value, this means that its inequality is lower than would be predicted by its fragmentation measure. The predicted sprawl measure for a metropolitan area with 1.10 governments per ten thousand residents (the Twin Cities' value) is .26. The actual value for the Twin Cities was .17, which implies that the Twin Cities did better in controlling inequality than expected, given the area's high degree of fragmentation.

However, just as it could do better with sprawl, the Twin Cities could clearly do better with tax base equality. Although its actual Gini coefficient is 35 percent lower than predicted (.17 compared to .26), other metropolitan areas do even better than this. Portland's actual inequality is 50 percent lower than predicted, for instance (.11 vs. .22). Again, the implication is that Portland's regional development planning does a better job of distributing tax base evenly across the region.

The most likely explanation for the Twin Cities' relatively strong showing in the fiscal inequality comparison is the existence of the Fiscal Disparities Program. The Fiscal Disparities Program, the only regionwide tax base sharing program in

TABLE 1.2   Fiscal equity: Gini coefficients for tax capacity
per household, 1993, 2001

Metropolitan area	1993	2001	Change (%)
Atlanta	0.13	0.14	0.01
Boston	0.22	0.25	0.03
Chicago	0.30	0.30	0.00
Cincinnati	0.44	0.45	0.00
Cleveland	0.34	0.31	-0.03
Dallas–Fort Worth	0.22	0.26	0.03
Denver	0.20	0.36	0.16
Detroit	0.32	0.30	-0.02
Houston	0.14	0.15	0.01
Kansas City	0.19	0.21	0.02
Los Angeles	0.20	0.23	0.03
Miami	0.19	0.21	0.02
Milwaukee	0.25	0.29	0.04
Minneapolis–St. Paul	0.19	0.17	-0.02
New York	0.27	0.34	0.06
Philadelphia	0.30	0.28	-0.03
Phoenix	0.13	0.20	0.07
Pittsburgh	0.26	0.26	0.00
Portland	0.12	0.11	-0.01
San Diego	0.10	0.11	0.01
San Francisco	0.18	0.19	0.02
Seattle	0.32	0.22	-0.10
St. Louis	0.36	0.39	0.03
Tampa	0.17	0.15	-0.02
Washington, D.C.	0.29	0.37	0.08
Average	0.23	0.25	0.02

Source: Various state and local government agencies.

the country, is designed to reduce fiscal inequality, as well as incentives for inefficient competition for tax base among cities and towns. The program covers the seven core counties of the Twin Cities metropolitan area. There are 192 municipalities, 50 school districts and more than 100 special districts covered by the program. In existence since 1971, it pools 40 percent of the growth in commercial–industrial

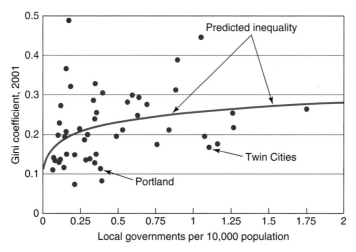

FIGURE 1.10. Fragmentation and fiscal inequality in the fifty largest U.S. metropolitan areas. *Sources:* U.S. Census Bureau; various state and local sources.

tax base since that time and redistributes it based on population of total local property tax base per capita.

As of 2004, 32 percent of the region's commercial–industrial tax base was in the pool and 64 percent of the region's population lived in municipalities that were net beneficiaries of the program. The program reduces tax base inequality in the region by about 20 percent, as measured by the Gini coefficient. The effects are even more pronounced at the extremes of the distribution. The program reduces the ratio of the highest to lowest tax base per household from twenty-five to eight, and of the second highest to second lowest from ten to four. The region's two central cities are affected in significantly different ways. St. Paul, with much of its prime real estate devoted to state office buildings and other nonprofit purposes, is a major beneficiary of the program. Its average tax on a homesteaded residence is about 9 percent lower than it would be in the absence of the program. Minneapolis, on the other hand, has had periods when it contributed more to the pool than it received from it and other times when it has been a net receiver.

Map 1.16 shows how the program's fiscal benefits are distributed. Net payers into the pool are clustered along the I-494 corridor south and west of the central cities, where much of the growth in the region's commercial–industrial tax base is occurring. Net receivers from the pool are scattered across the region, but especially in the core, where tax base growth has lagged in recent years and in the outermost parts of the region, where most tax base growth is in residential, rather than commercial–industrial, base.

The Fiscal Disparities model is very flexible. For instance, the redistribution formula can take a variety of forms. It can be aggressively redistributive and use local tax base or poverty rates as a primary component. Or it can be relatively neutral

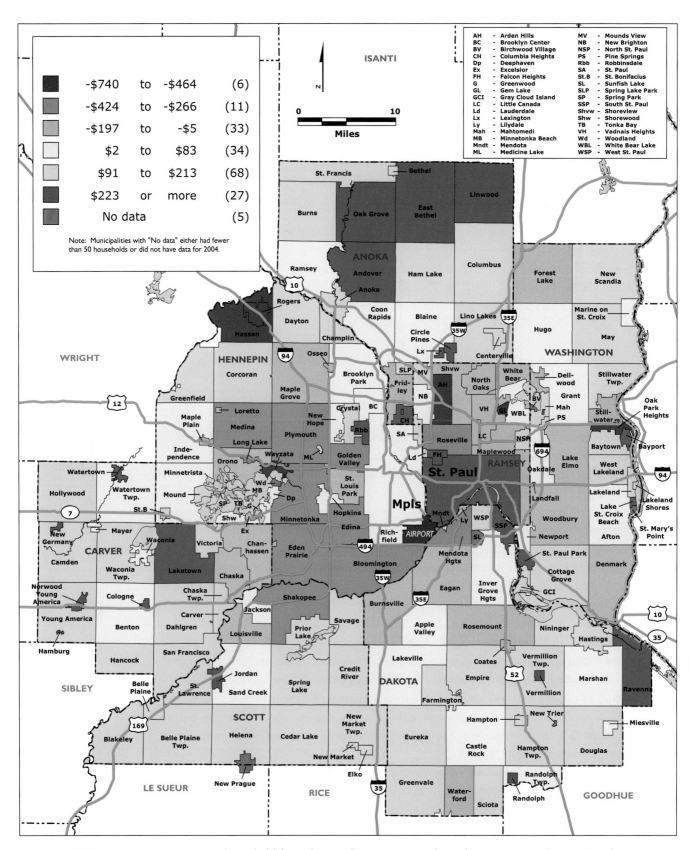

MAP 1.16. Net gain in tax capacity per household from the Fiscal Disparities tax-base-sharing program by municipality, Minneapolis–St. Paul region, 2004. *Source:* House Research, Minnesota House of Representatives.

and use local population or household counts. It can also be designed to compensate local areas for extra costs of public services. The age of the housing stock—a good proxy for the age of infrastructure—could be used in this way. In any of these cases, because contributions to the pool are based on local tax bases, the net effect of the system will be to reduce fiscal disparities across the region.

If the contribution formula is designed properly, tax base sharing can also improve the efficiency of the local tax system. In the model used in the Fiscal Disparities Program, communities contribute 40 percent of the increase in commercial–industrial property tax base to the pool, which is then redistributed with a formula based on population and local tax base. On the one hand, the design reduces the incentives for communities to compete for tax base, because they do not keep all the resulting revenues. On the other hand, because localities retain enough of the tax base to cover the costs of growth, the incentive is not so strong that local areas will be unwilling to allow new development.[26]

For all these reasons, the Fiscal Disparities Program is an excellent model for other metropolitan areas.

COMMUNITY CLASSIFICATION

Local government revenues are not the only important dimension to consider when evaluating the capacity of local governments to provide public services. Local fiscal stress or health also depends on factors affecting the demand side of local budgets. (See the sidebar on cluster analysis for more on this topic.)

Metropolitan areas are often viewed as if they are composed of troubled central cities and prosperous suburbs. However, recent work in metropolitan areas across the country has documented the wide diversity of communities within metropolitan areas, especially suburban areas.[27] In most metropolitan areas, many fully developed, relatively densely settled suburban areas show signs of stress much like those seen in central cities. In addition, another group of suburbs usually exhibits modest, roughly average tax bases and high rates of population or job growth—a combination that can also produce stress because of the costs associated with growth.

No single dimension, such as tax base, income, or poverty, is adequate to describe the diversity of communities in the metropolitan landscape. For this work, cluster analysis was used to group municipalities based on similarities and differences across several dimensions, including both sides of local budgets, that is, the capacity to raise revenues and the need for or costs of providing services.

Table 1.3 and Map 1.17 show the results of the analysis for the municipalities in the eleven-county metropolitan area. The analysis divided the 270 municipalities in the eleven-county region into six groups: central cities, stressed suburbs, developing job centers, bedroom developing communities, developed job centers, and affluent residential areas. Table 1.3 shows how the groups vary across the characteristics

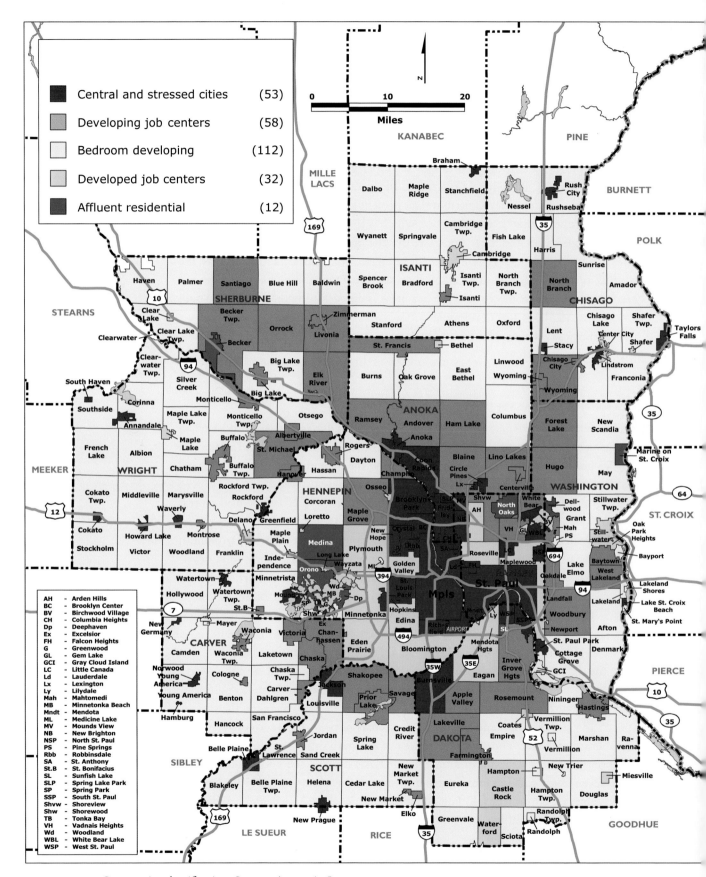

Legend:

- Central and stressed cities (53)
- Developing job centers (58)
- Bedroom developing (112)
- Developed job centers (32)
- Affluent residential (12)

MAP 1.17. Community classification. *Source:* Ameregis, Inc.

TABLE 1.3   Characteristics of community types, Twin Cities metropolitan area

						Variables included in the cluster analysis		
Community type	Number	Percentage of regional households	Tax capacity per household 2003	Jobs per household 2003	Poverty rate 2000	Percentage growth in households 1993–2003	Households per square mile 2003	Median housing age 2000
Central cities	2	24	1,821	1.7	16	1	2,972	58
Stressed suburbs	53	23	1,943	1.2	6	7	1,371	32
Developing job centers	58	25	2,503	1.0	3	56	364	14
Bedroom developing	112	8	2,639	0.3	3	24	36	29
Developed job centers	32	19	3,375	2.3	3	15	793	30
Affluent residential	12	1	7,047	0.9	2	19	173	34
Region	269	100	2,429	1.4	7	18	287	27

Source: U.S. Census Bureau; various state and local government agencies; Ameregis, Inc.

used in the clustering: tax capacity per household, jobs per household, poverty rate, percentage growth in households from 1993 to 2003, household density (households per square mile), and median housing age.

Two groups—two central cities and fifty-three stressed municipalities—are home to 47 percent of metropolitan households. These two community types, found largely in the core of the region, show a combination of capacities and costs that imply significant fiscal stress. In these places, lower than average tax capacities are combined with higher than average cost factors. Notable cost factors include significant job concentrations that increase demand for services by nonresidents; higher poverty rates that increase needs; much greater than average household densities that can create congestion costs; and greater than average housing ages, which generally indicate older infrastructure that is more expensive to maintain or upgrade.

Another group of fifty-eight developing job centers, representing 25 percent of the metropolitan area's households, shows roughly average tax capacity but some higher than average cost characteristics. In particular, these places are likely to be stressed by growth: they show the highest growth rates for both households and jobs among the six clusters. Developing job centers lie in two arcs of second-ring suburbs in the southern and northern parts of the metro and along the I-94 corridor to the northwest.

The bedroom developing group consists of 112 municipalities at the perimeter of the metropolitan area and represents 8 percent of households. It is similar to the developing job centers except that these places do not show job concentrations like those in the job centers. They also show roughly average tax resources coupled with rapid population growth.

The final two community types—thirty-two developed job centers and twelve affluent residential areas—are largely second-ring suburbs across the south and west of the region and in the area around Lake Minnetonka to the west. They show few signs of stress. Representing just 20 percent of regional households, these places enjoy relatively rich tax bases with few cost factors.

In sum, like most metropolitan areas, the Twin Cities region shows a great deal of diversity in community types, especially in the suburbs. Just under half of the region's households live in places showing clear signs of stress and another third live in communities that must plan carefully to manage the costs of growth with only average local resources.

The community typology, based as it is on local characteristics affecting both sides of the fiscal ledger, provides a better system for comparing suburban areas than simple geography (such as "inner suburbs" and "outer suburbs"). For instance, it provides a way to evaluate projected growth patterns to see whether growth is expected to occur in high-, moderate- or low-stress places. High- and moderate-stress places are the areas where the need to ensure that new growth "pays its way" is greatest—where, for instance, pressure to ensure that residential development is limited to high-end, large-lot development is the greatest.

Table 1.4 shows the distribution of population across the community types in 2003 and the distribution of projected growth from 2003 to 2030. The lion's share of growth is projected to occur in developing job centers and bedroom developing

TABLE 1.4   Distribution of projected population growth by community type

Community type	Population 2003	Share	Projected growth 2003–30	Share	Projected growth rate
Central cities	653,592	22	112,408	11	17
Stressed suburbs	645,427	22	114,438	11	18
Developing job centers	828,609	28	468,038	47	56
Bedroom developing	275,432	9	223,531	22	81
Developed job centers	536,051	18	69,467	7	13
Affluent residential	28,896	1	14,808	1	51
Total	2,968,007	100	1,002,690	100	34

Source: U.S. Census Bureau; Minnesota Department of Administration, State Demographic Center.

communities. These places are currently home to 37 percent of the region's population but are projected to receive 69 percent of growth after 2003. Developing job centers, in particular, can expect to face significant growth pressures during the next two decades. The other community types also show modest growth. In particular, central cities and stressed suburbs—fully developed places that for the most part have not grown much in the recent past—show modest growth rates. This indicates, as noted earlier in the discussion of growth projections, that the Metropolitan Council's projections for infill development are ambitious.

Are bedroom developing communities and developing job centers well positioned to face the growth pressures forecast for them? The answer is mixed. On the one hand, they are not as highly stressed as the central cities or stressed suburbs. Their poverty rates are relatively low, and the developing job centers provide reasonable employment opportunities. However, both types of communities have just average fiscal resources, implying that they will feel pressure to limit growth in ways that could limit opportunities for lower-income residents of the region. These places will not have the luxury of ignoring (or at least compromising on) the pressures to make growth "pay its way" as developed job centers or affluent residential areas could.

History also suggests that the Metropolitan Council's ambitions for growth in the central cities and stressed suburbs are unlikely to be realized. In fact, during the first six years of the projection period (2000–2006), the central cities and stressed suburbs actually lost population, meaning that there was greater growth pressure on other parts of the region than expected. All this "extra" growth (and more) went to the developing job centers. Figure 1.11 shows that, during this period,

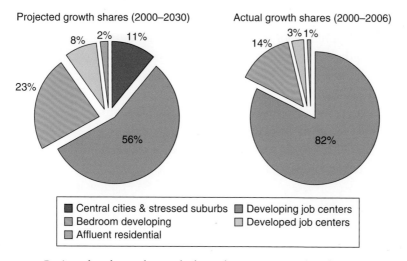

FIGURE 1.11. Projected and actual growth shares by community classification in the Twin Cities metropolitan area. *Sources:* Metropolitan Council; U.S. Census Bureau; Ameregis, Inc.

CLUSTER ANALYSIS: HOW IT WORKS

Because there are more than 260 jurisdictions included in the study area, it is impossible to individually measure each one against the others. Instead this assessment relies on a statistical procedure called cluster analysis to assign municipalities to groups that are as internally homogeneous and as distinct from one another as possible, based on specified social, fiscal, and physical characteristics. Grouping was accomplished using the *k-means* clustering procedure in SPSS. For more on cluster analysis in general, and *k*-means clustering in particular, see *StatSoft, Inc. Electronic Statistics Textbook* (Tulsa, OK: StatSoft, 2002; www.statsoft.com/textbook/stathome.html).

The characteristics used to group the municipalities were property tax base per household (2003), poverty rate (2000), household growth (1993–2003) and household density (2003), jobs per household (2003), and median age of the housing stock (2000). (All variables were standardized—expressed as the number of standard deviations from the mean—to minimize scale effects.)

These demographic and fiscal variables provide a snapshot of a community in two dimensions—its ability to raise revenues from its local tax base and the costs associated with its social and physical needs. Fiscal capabilities are measured by tax base and jobs per household.

Need measures capture a range of local characteristics that affect the cost of providing public services. High poverty is a well-documented contributor to public service costs. It both generates greater needs for services and increases the cost of reaching a given level of service. Both population declines and large increases tend to increase the per-person costs of long-lived assets such as sewers, streets, or buildings. When population declines, the costs of these assets must be spread across fewer taxpayers. When population is growing rapidly, the costs for new infrastructure tend to fall disproportionately on current residents (compared to future residents) because of the difficulty of spreading the costs over the full lifetime of the assets. Density is another important predictor of cost. Very low densities can increase per-person costs for public services involving transportation (e.g., schools, police, and fire protection) and for infrastructure (roads and sewers). Moderate to high densities, on the other hand, can help limit per-person costs. Housing age is used as a proxy for the age of the community's infrastructure—older infrastructure is more expensive to maintain.

These variables also capture a cross section of the socioeconomic characteristics that define a community's character. Demographics, population growth, and density are among the factors people examine when deciding whether a community is "their kind of place."

Because of their unique history and characteristics, the Twin Cities central cities—Minneapolis and St. Paul—were placed in their own group before clustering.

developing job centers absorbed a much greater share of regional growth than planned: 82 percent compared to 56 percent. The implication is that these places will "fill up" even more quickly than expected. The result could either be to push growth still farther out into the bedroom developing areas or inward to the core. History implies that, unless regional growth planning is much more aggressive about promoting growth in the core than it has been, growth is likely to be pushed farther and farther outward.

CONCLUSIONS

The Twin Cities region has one of the most fragmented local government systems in the country, and it sits in an area very like the proverbial "featureless plain." With so many localities competing for economic activity and so few physical barriers to development, one would expect it to sprawl across the landscape and bifurcate into extremes of rich and poor places. This has not happened. Based on most measures, the region is, as Garrison Keillor claims, above average.

Its sprawl rate is typical of large American metropolitan areas and better than similarly situated areas. Fiscal inequality in the region is considerably lower than average, even compared to places with less political fragmentation. The region's economy has also outperformed most others, especially other Frost Belt metropolitan areas.

The region's relative strength has many sources. An important one is that the region has the largest, and arguably the most sophisticated, multipurpose regional government in the country—the Metropolitan Council. It also home to one of the most innovative regional fiscal institutions in the country—the Fiscal Disparities tax base sharing program. The council and the Fiscal Disparities Program serve as counterbalances, moderating the potential effects of the area's highly fragmented local planning system.

However, the situation is not ideal by any means. To say that the region is typical of large American metropolitan areas is to say that its:

- Population and economy are decentralizing and deconcentrating—moving outward into the periphery and scattering across the landscape;
- Older core areas, including older suburbs, house disproportionate shares of the region's low-income and minority populations and are growing very slowly or not at all;
- Local governments have widely varying capacities to finance public services; and
- Future is forecast to provide more of the same.

The clear implication is that there is more to be done. The following chapters present more detailed information on important aspects of the region's development with policy proposals.

2

Governing the Twin Cities

Myron Orfield, Nick Wallace, Eric Myott, and Geneva Finn

SPRAWL, FRAGMENTATION, AND REGIONAL GOVERNMENT

Fragmented metropolitan areas in the United States are sprawling, and this sprawl is damaging the social, economic, and environmental quality and potential of American society. Urban land development that outpaces population growth exacerbates social separation and traffic congestion. The rapid outward growth of metropolitan areas strains the financing of existing urban infrastructure and puts pressure on sensitive environmental areas. Because metropolitan urban growth is often regional in nature and can have adverse social, economic, and environmental consequences, regional planning and governing structures are necessary to minimize the negative impacts of growth.

The fragmented structure of government in U.S. metropolitan areas makes regional planning difficult. Metropolitan areas have multiple localized jurisdictions with a variety of missions, goals, and incentives that plan and govern at cross-purposes. Regional planning and governing institutions can guide regional growth, coordinate with local jurisdictions, and equitably set policy for issues that are regional in scale.

In the Twin Cities, there is a unique system of regional government and planning: the Metropolitan Council (Met Council). The Met Council has the power to ensure orderly planning for growth, efficient regional services, and infrastructure, and to provide resources equitably to benefit all people in the region. The Met Council has unprecedented legal powers and policy tools, but has not fulfilled its regional goals, has been cautious and deferential in exerting its authority, and remains an unelected, often unmotivated governing body.

Portland, Oregon, has a similar regional governing structure that has more effectively limited sprawl even though it has fewer legal and policy powers over urban services and infrastructure than the Met Council. The relative success of Portland's elected regional government shows that the Twin Cities' Met Council has the ability to make a greater difference in addressing urban growth. Stronger regional governance in the Twin Cities will help the region's economy, help counter resegregation, and improve the environment in a way that will benefit all people in the region.

This chapter first describes the development of the Met Council. Second, it details how the Met Council has used and not used its extensive powers. Third, it compares the effectiveness of the Met Council to Portland's regional government. Finally, it suggests policy reforms that will lead to a more efficient and effective regional government in the Twin Cities region. The story that underlies both this chapter and the development and continued operation of the Met Council is the role of party politics at the state level and local government opposition to losing power to the regional government. This chapter highlights the problematic role of politics and local governmental opposition in effective regional governance and suggests how the Met Council can overcome these challenges.

THE CREATION OF REGIONAL GOVERNANCE IN THE TWIN CITIES: THE METROPOLITAN COUNCIL

The Minnesota legislature formed the Met Council in 1967 to fulfill federal requirements and to address growing issues of state land use planning, wastewater coordination, and transit funding after decades of ad hoc cooperation between local governments in the Twin Cities region.[1] Federal laws requiring intergovernmental coordination of planning spurred the Met Council's development. For example, the Demonstration Cities and Metropolitan Development Act of 1966 required that all federal grant or loan applications for the planning or construction of public facilities be submitted to an area planning agency for review or comment.[2] Similarly, the Intergovernmental Cooperation Act of 1968 required that state enabling legislation establish area-wide planning agencies.[3]

Planning struggles were evident from the start of the Met Council, and the tug-of-war between local governments attempting to preserve their own power and the growing need for comprehensive regional planning is the enduring political legacy of the Met Council. Two competing bills that authorized the Met Council's formation envisioned two very different Met Councils. One bill would have created a powerful elected council; the other, an appointed advisory body. The Rosenmeier-Albertson bill (1967) called for establishment of a coordinating body, appointed by the governor, without authority to provide services or set policy. The alternative, the Ogdahl-Frenzel bill (also 1967), provided for an elected, policy-setting body with power to veto local plans not consistent with metropolitan plans developed by the new agency.[4] A slightly strengthened version of the Rosenmeier-Albertson bill prevailed. The new Met Council had both coordinating authority and the ability to set policies and veto plans of other metropolitan commissions. The conservative approach of the bill reflected the reluctance of county officials, who were experiencing increased revenue and power from suburban population growth, to cede power to a regional authority.

Although a provision to elect the Met Council failed in a tie vote, the desire to strengthen the political power of the Met Council by creating an elected body has remained alive. This issue was raised thirty years later; although a bill for an elected Met Council passed the legislature, Governor Arne Carlson vetoed it. In 2007, an elected Met Council bill was defeated again in the Senate by a margin of 36 to 26. Recent arguments for an elected Met Council centered on the accountability of council members and the appointed council's power to tax. In presenting the recent bill, author Senator Charles Wiger echoed the colonial-era demand for "no taxation without representation."[5] Senators opposed to the bill argue that the Met Council's powers, including its powers to tax, were merely administrative tools granted by the legislature. Opponents also argued that accountability for the Met Council rests with members of the legislature, who grant the Met Council its powers.

Arguments that an elected council would be partisan and/or parochial eliminated the opposition. Wealthier southern suburbanites believe the system that makes up the council is unconstitutional, while many in the central cities find that the council's transportation policy saps away funds to the core for major highway projects in the outer suburbs. Working-class northern suburbs are also concerned about their ability to compete against wealthier sections of the region. These political conflicts operate in a system where the council is appointed and less accountable to the common good for the region.

Developers also have had a dominant voice in the council and have often eschewed nonregulatory solutions to affordable housing and environmental concerns. In 1996 six of the seventeen appointed council members were either developers or actively involved in the development industry. A lawyer for the Minnesota Orchestra sat on the council at the same time the orchestra was seeking council approval on a major amphitheater that could be used to stage shows.[6] Another was accused of financial conflict of interest by promoting the expansion of a sewer interceptor and highway near undeveloped land he owned.[7] This power struggle has played out over time through long-running arguments over the function of the Met Council: is it a policy-making body or a local governmental body? In reality, the Met Council is both, guiding regional policy and planning and providing governmental services.

The Expansion of the Met Council's Power

While the legislature did not originally intend the Met Council to operate government services, it gradually expanded the council's duties—creating a regional government with significant financial resources and operational duties. By the late

1990s, the council administered the metro's transit systems, managed water and sewer systems, set the regional planning and development agenda, and distributed affordable housing around the region. In 2009 the Met Council has the financial resources to match its power. The Met Council receives its funding from several sources: In 2006, the Met Council received approximately 35 percent of its $646 million in revenues from state and federal funds. About 29 percent of the Met Council's revenues came from user fees derived from such sources as transit fares and wastewater treatment. The remaining 36 percent of the Met Council's revenue is derived from debt service, pass-through funds, and a seven-county property tax. The Met Council's revenues are primarily spent on wastewater collection and treatment, transit, and grants to local governments for community development.[8] The Met Council's activity can be divided into two rough spheres, namely, the coordination of regional government operations and regional planning. Today, the coordination of regional services is less controversial than the council's original planning and policy-setting function.

Coordinating Services: The Metropolitan Reorganization Acts of 1974 and 1994

Shortly after the legislature created the Met Council, it created several new special-purpose commissions, including the Metropolitan Transit Commission and Metropolitan Sewer Board. These new agencies and the Met Council were often in conflict over who had superior regional planning authority.[9] These conflicts led to the passage of the Metropolitan Reorganization Act of 1974, which gave the Met Council the authority to approve the Metropolitan Transit Commission's and the Metropolitan Waste Control Commission's budgets and long-range plans as well as the power to appoint the members of both commissions.[10] Twenty years later, the Met Council absorbed the functions of the Metropolitan Transit Commission, Regional Transit Board, and the Metropolitan Waste Control Commission. The passage of the Metropolitan Reorganization Act of 1994 further aligned the regional policy-making and operational functions of the Met Council.[11] There are a few services that should be regionally supplied that the Met Council does not provide or directly administer. Prime examples are water supplies and watershed protection. However, the Met Council still has power over these policy areas through its planning authority.

The Metropolitan Council's Planning Authority

In 1976, the Minnesota legislature passed the Metropolitan Land Planning Act (MLPA), which recognized the interdependency of local government units and the need for comprehensive planning to deal with air and water pollution, the development of regional infrastructure, and orderly economic development.[12] The MLPA requires all local governments in the seven-county metropolitan area to adopt comprehensive plans that are consistent with the regional systems identified by the Met Council that include (1) transportation, (2) wastewater, (3) airports, and (4) parks. These systems have a heightened legal significance in terms of the MLPA, for if local comprehensive plans are inconsistent with these systems, they can be invalid. There are other substantial policy areas that the council operates, such as housing, that are not "systems." The MLPA gives the Met Council final authority over local planning; it has the authority to require local governments to modify their plans if they have a potential substantial impact on or substantial departure from metropolitan system plans. This chapter will talk about two important systems related to regional equitable development: transportation and wastewater. It will omit discussion of airports and parks, although they are important, and argue for two addition systems—housing and water—that should be more important.

Tax Base Sharing

Although the Fiscal Disparities Act of 1971 is not under the legal or political control of the council, regional tax base sharing (discussed at greater length in chapter 1) is a critical part of the land use planning system. Tax base sharing is the political glue that allowed the MPLA to pass initially and that has sustained it over the years politically. There was powerful opposition to the MPLA, particularly from the low fiscal capacity suburbs and more affluent bedroom places like Lake Elmo that wanted to develop on two-acre lots. These places politically accepted the MPLA only when it became clear that they were recipients of tax base sharing. Sadly, many of the places that benefited from tax base sharing continue to flout the Met Council and have ignored prior council guidelines on rural residential densities.

MET COUNCIL AS METROPOLITAN PLANNING ORGANIZATION

Metropolitan Planning Organizations (MPOs) are regional planning entities that solicit and evaluate applications for federal transportation funding. Since the early 1970s, the federal government has mandated that any urbanized area with more than fifty thousand residents have an MPO that is composed of members of an elected body and that they generate regional plans based on a continuing, cooperative, and comprehensive ("3 C") planning process. The Intermodal Surface Transportation Efficiency Act of 1991 (ISTEA) gave MPOs great power over a portion of transportation funds and the flexibility and authority over the suballocation of transportation funds within a region.[13]

The flexibility given by the federal government in structuring MPOs has resulted in a variety of governing systems and funding priorities. For instance, Portland, Oregon, has a centralized, directly elected governing body, which serves jointly with a

TAB-like board of local elected officials, that has given priority to supporting transit. Although it is not the MPO, it has had a major influence on the MPO. The MPO in Atlanta, Georgia, operates as a regional council of governments represented by officials of various city, county, and other governments within the metropolitan area, which has historically emphasized building roads in growing outer suburban areas. The process of apportioning MPO members also varies among MPOs. Members do not necessarily have equal voting powers or represent residents in equal proportions, which opens up the possibility of bias in favor of one set of a region's constituents over another. For instance, 78 percent of Detroit's MPO board members are white, while 52 percent of its represented residents are people of color. In terms of apportionment, the city itself is significantly underrepresented in voting strength on the MPO.[14]

As mentioned earlier, federal law requires that MPOs must be composed of elected public officials. The Metropolitan Council had a history of regional planning in the Twin Cities that made it a great candidate to become the MPO for the region. However, the Met Council is a body appointed by the governor. Therefore, to conform to federal law, the legislature created the Transportation Advisory Board (TAB), a more traditional MPO board that serves jointly with the Met Council as an MPO for the Twin Cities Metropolitan Area. The TAB has an advisory role to the council but takes the first and often determinative cut on highway allocation.[15]

The fact that both the Met Council and the TAB fulfill the role of the MPO has created confusion about the role and responsibility of each organization. As a practical matter, the Met Council often rubber-stamps transportation funding allocations made by the TAB, although the TAB also pays attention to council allocations. One such conflict arose when the Met Council successfully pressed for funding a light-rail system, against the wishes of the TAB, which advocated for greater highway funding. Ultimately it appears that the Met Council has final authority, but there have been growing disagreements.

Regional Planning Frameworks

In 1975 the council released the *Metropolitan Development Guide (MDG)* to document the council's policy vision for the region. Subsequent planning frameworks (also called blueprints) replaced the *MDG* with amendments and additions of Met Council policies.[16] While each policy document is different and reflects the aspirations of the governor and appointed council, there have been emerging policy trends from the 1970s to the present that have affected the way the region has developed. Early Met Councils attempted to guide urban growth within a well-defined urban boundary, often with the concern about the public costs associated with extending urban services. While the early councils did not greatly contain growth from the rural portions of the region, the council's rural policies enacted in the 1990s became even vaguer, and rural guidelines were established that encouraged urban sprawl in the Twin Cities. By 2002, the council's long-standing concern about containing growth within its designated urban areas became greatly diminished, putting even greater development pressure on rural areas.

The most recent regional planning guide is *Framework 2030,* a plan adopted in 2004. *Framework 2030* represents a major planning policy change: *Framework 2030* reoriented regional growth strategy toward the arrangement and pattern of land uses rather than attempting to limit sprawl at the fringe of the metro area.[17] The consequences of the effective abandonment of the metropolitan urban service boundary (MUSA) and the adoption of a "hub-and-spoke" planning around transit centers are described later in this chapter.

Local Comprehensive Planning

Local government units, including school districts' capital improvement programs, must review and update their local comprehensive plans within three years from when the Met Council establishes its planning guide. The Met Council reviews local planning documents to ensure that they are consistent with and comparable with the adopted policies, forecasts, and systems plans of the Met Council.[18] If local plans are inconsistent with the Met Council's plans, the council can require the locality to modify its local plan. The local governments then negotiate with the Met Council and with neighboring localities, which also review local plans. Once the local plan is accepted, local governments may not adopt fiscal devices, zoning ordinances, or other official controls that would conflict with the established local comprehensive plan.[19]

In practice the council has narrowly reviewed local plans for systems compliance. Professor Brian Ohm argues that the Met Council has great flexibility in interpreting when a local plan constitutes a "substantial impact" or "substantial departure" from regional systems plans under the MPLA and that the council should exercise more scrutiny when reviewing local plans.[20]

Regional Affordable Housing: The Livable Communities Act

Affordable housing organizations pushed for the passage of the Metropolitan Livable Communities Act (MLCA) after a series of publicized cases in which suburbs refused to allow the construction of low-income housing.[21] This bill enticed suburbs to create and maintain low-income housing by offering incentives and withheld state money from suburbs that refused to build their share of affordable housing.[22] The final version of the MLCA allows the Met Council to negotiate goals and withhold regional services from cities that do not voluntarily participate.[23] The MLCA allows for participating communities in the seven-county metropolitan area to receive grants for livable community projects, including pollution cleanup for land redevelopment, new jobs and affordable housing, new development or redevelopment that demonstrates efficient land use, and the creation of additional affordable housing opportunities.

It is important to note that the MLCA was weakened by legislative amendments. Major concessions were made to appease conservative legislators in the wealthier suburbs and avoid a veto by Governor Arne Carlson. Because of these concessions, the MLCA does not explicitly state that communities must make progress on the act's goals. Even if the Met Council set solid benchmarks for affordable housing, local governments are not required to meet these benchmarks and could avoid their affordable housing responsibilities by effectively not participating in the program. The program also suffers because its benchmarks are based on the existing levels of affordable housing in subsections of the region, rather than on the actual affordable housing need of households in the region. Finally, the development of affordable housing through the Metropolitan Livable Communities Act is underfunded.[24]

Legal Challenges to the Met Council's Planning Authority: Lake Elmo

The Minnesota legislature granted the Met Council expansive powers, powers that constrained the powers of municipalities. Unsurprisingly, the bodies that lost power to the Met Council fought back. While the Minnesota Supreme Court has recognized the right of cities to limit property development through zoning, it was not clear until the court's *Lake Elmo* decision that the Met Council had the ability or will to restrict cities' zoning and planning.[25]

In *City of Lake Elmo v. Metropolitan Council,* Lake Elmo challenged the Met Council's decision to require that the city's comprehensive plan conform to the Met Council's water resources management and transportation policy plans by exhausting the city's land supply by 2020.[26] The Minnesota Supreme Court found that the MLPA empowers the Met Council to require, by resolution, a municipality to modify its comprehensive plan if it "may have a substantial impact on or contain a substantial departure from metropolitan system plans."[27] The court determined that Lake Elmo's comprehensive plan was a substantial departure from the Met Council's systems plans and that the cost to the Met Council for the implementation would have a substantial impact on the systems plans. The *Lake Elmo* holding gives the Met Council great flexibility in interpreting what constitutes "substantial impact" or "substantial departure" under the MPLA. The affirmation of the court provides an additional source of power to the Met Council to ensure that municipalities conform to regional planning objectives.

While the Minnesota courts upheld legal challenges to the Met Council's exercise of power, a political turnover in the governor's office in 1991 created an appointed Met Council that was even less willing to exercise its power to encourage orderly and economic development than previous councils had been. As the law becomes stronger and clearer, the council became less and less willing to encourage orderly planning.

The Met Council uses considerable restraint in flexing its regulatory muscle under the Metropolitan Land Planning Act. Individuals are often frustrated when the council fails to exercise its power, while municipalities are frustrated when the Met Council enforces its regional comprehensive plans. Individuals, however, cannot make the Met Council enforce its plans; an intermediate appellate court has found that there is no private cause of action under the MLPA, whereas municipalities can challenge the Met Council's plans and decisions in state courts. [28] Court review of the Met Council's actions, however, has only strengthened the hand of the Met Council under the MLPA.

REGIONAL PLANNING POLICIES IN THE TWIN CITIES

The Met Council is responsible for regional planning in the Twin Cities, and it has multiple tools and powers to guide urban growth in the region. But the council often has failed to act to prevent regional development problems, especially urban sprawl. The Met Council has had some notable successes, and its regional governance has made the Twin Cities a leader in regional planning. The Met Council, however, has not fulfilled its potential. For example, the council has consistently prioritized maintaining existing highway infrastructure, a position that counteracts urban sprawl, yet the council has failed to give policy priority to job centers that could integrate and strengthen regional transportation, land use, economic development, and housing goals. This section looks at the Met Council's six largest planning areas, the MUSA, rural and urban geographic policy areas, job centers, wastewater, transit, and housing, and discusses the Met Council's successes and failures as a regional government and planner.

Population Growth and the Metropolitan Urban Service Area

The metropolitan urban service area (MUSA) is the area in which the Met Council provides urban regional facilities and services within seven core counties of the Twin Cities metropolitan area. The MUSA was the Met Council's response to its growing regulatory and planning powers and responsibilities, balancing the demand for land development and the public costs associated with urban service extensions.

In a sense, the MUSA is the conglomerate urban development boundary reflecting all local comprehensive plans for the region, which represents where urban development and services exist or are planned for the future. Through MUSAs, the council can coordinate and direct municipalities' development plans to be in accordance with the council's broader vision for the planned development of the Twin Cities area.

The size of the MUSA is officially determined by Met Council projections of municipal growth over a thirty- to forty-year period. The Met Council makes assumptions about future developed land for municipalities that either fully developed to their borders or that are still developing within the MUSA boundary. The council's projections underpin the amount of land development that cities and townships can undertake in the Twin Cities.

The council's attitudes toward growth at the fringe of the MUSA shape the council's projections and the MUSA. In the 1970s, the Met Council's scenario allowed the MUSA to increase by 244 square miles between 1973 and 1990.[29] Similarly, in 1988 the council assumed that the existing MUSA would effectively capture growth through 2000, setting strict requirements for granting MUSA extension requests. Yet by the 1990s council blueprints contained substantially less language about the costs of MUSA extensions and instead focused more on planning approaches that are more consensus based with localities.[30]

In *Blueprint 2030* the Met Council no longer requires a contiguous MUSA boundary, specifying only that jurisdictions develop no more than the amount of urban land allotted by the Met Council.[31] This more flexible type of MUSA allows local government to experiment more with various types of development, but with Met Council emphasis on more intensive land uses near major highway nodes. The lack of a contiguous MUSA has the potential to encourage major land acquisitions at the expense of a more compact form of urban development in the region.[32] Over time the MUSA has continued to expand, and its definition has been blurred by noncontiguous changes in its boundary and by increased spillover of urbanlike densities in the rural areas surrounding the MUSA.

The MUSA and Growth in the Twin Cities

Over the past thirty years, the Twin Cities population has outpaced the size of the MUSA. While the Met Council has consistently expanded the size of the MUSA, the population living outside the MUSA has exploded.

Figure 2.1 shows past and future projected growth of the MUSA and the population of the seven-county metropolitan area between 1970 and 2030. Population expanded much faster than the MUSA, especially beginning in 1990. Between 1990 and 2000, MUSA growth was more gradual compared to population growth, which continued to increase rapidly. This lengthening gap between fast-growing population and the slower-growing MUSA corresponds to the 1988 Met Council's reluctance to expand the MUSA. The council forecast similar MUSA growth and population growth rates between 2000 and 2010. Post-2010 projections show MUSA growth slowing compared to population growth.

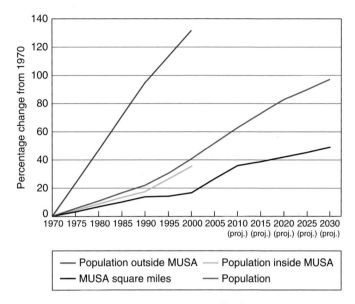

FIGURE 2.1. Twin Cities seven-county population and urban service area, 1970–2030. MUSA square miles and population were interpolated for 1975, 1980, 1985, and 1995. *Source:* Metropolitan Council.

Growth outside the MUSA has far outpaced growth within the MUSA. Between 1970 and 2000, population outside the MUSA increased more than 130 percent, while population inside the MUSA increased less than 40 percent. In 2002, the population living outside the MUSA made up about 10 percent of the region's total population, while 30 percent of the region's urbanized land was outside the MUSA.[33]

The future trajectory of urban growth in the Twin Cities illustrated in Map 2.1 shows the planned urban growth and services in the Twin Cities region. The 2010–40 MUSAs contain more islands of urbanization outside the core, reflecting the recent council's noncontiguous MUSA boundary. The noncontiguous urban growth is likely to spur sprawl because the Met Council has not aggressively regulated densities in the surrounding rural service area.

Growth Projections in Rural and Urban Geographic Policy Areas

The Metropolitan Council directs growth by developing separate guidelines for urban and rural areas. This designation of an area as urban or rural limits the localities' land use planning and development in those areas. Within the urban service area, the current Met Council distinguishes between fully developed and developing communities:

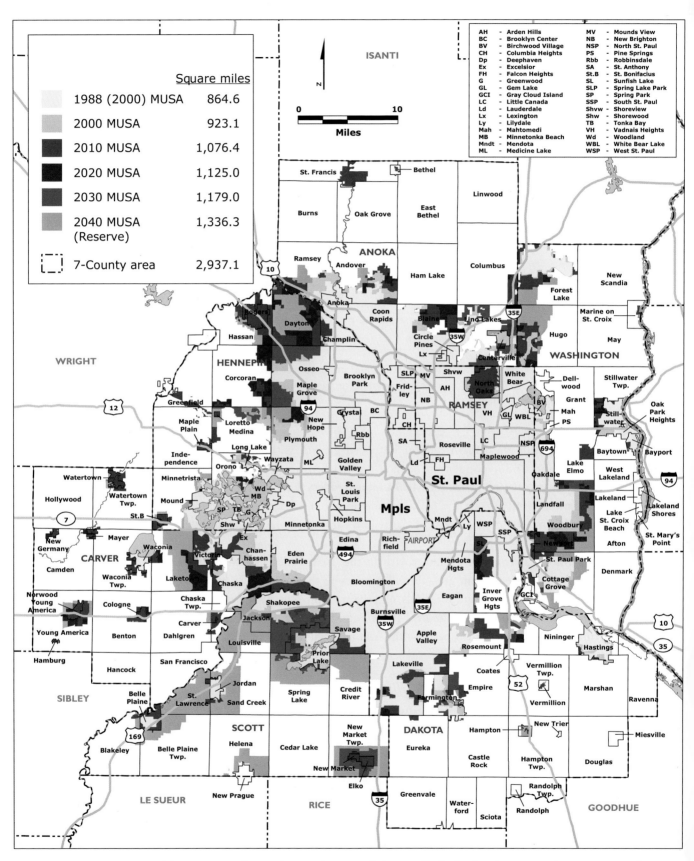

MAP 2.1. Past, current, and future metropolitan urban service areas, Minneapolis–St. Paul region, 2006. *Source:* Metropolitan Council (November 13, 2006).

Developed communities are jurisdictions where more than 85 percent of the land within the urban service area is fully developed. The Met Council's goals in these areas include maintaining and improving infrastructure and supporting integrative land uses. In *Framework 2030*, housing density goals are about 15 units per residential acre for central cities and 6 units per acre for fully developed suburban communities.[34]

Developing communities are jurisdictions where more than 15 percent of the land within the urban service area is vacant and developable. Developing communities are expected to receive the most residential growth in the region. The Met Council's goals in these areas include supporting planned development and accommodating places that are in the process of urban growth in the periphery of the MUSA. In *Framework 2030*, housing density goals are about 3.5 units per residential acre for developing communities.[35]

Rural portions of the seven-county Twin Cities area outside of the MUSA are a growing service area of the Met Council. In the rural service area, the Met Council plans for future urban use, or agricultural or natural preservation, distinguishing between rural centers, rural growth centers, rural residential areas, diversified rural communities, and agriculture areas:

Rural centers are small towns located in the rural service area where future growth is not foreseen.[36]

Rural growth centers are rural centers that are interested in and show a potential for growth. In *Framework 2030*, housing density goals are set at 3.7 units per residential acre for rural growth centers.[37]

Rural residential areas are areas where there are no plans to provide urban infrastructure such as wastewater systems. The Met Council currently designates these areas with no more than at one unit per 2 acres residential densities, an increase from one unit per 10 acres in the 2002 guidelines. Environmentalists have argued that this increase in rural density reflects recent Council concessions with rural jurisdictions that have developed near urban densities; densities that contradicted earlier Council guidelines on rural areas.[38]

Diversified rural communities are the sparsely developed areas that host a wide variety of farm and non-farm land uses. They include a small mix of large-lot residential areas and clustered development. The Met Council limits growth into these areas at no more than 1 unit to 10 acres, preserving them for post-2030 urban development.[39]

Agriculture areas are large contiguous land areas zoned and planned to maintain agriculture as the primary land use, due to their favorable soils for current and future agricultural uses. Agricultural areas have residential density limits of 1 unit to 40 acres.[40]

The Met Council forecasts that between 2000 and 2030, there will be an additional 485,000 housing units, 60 percent built in the developing area, 27 percent in developed areas, 5 percent in rural growth centers, and 8 percent in rural areas.[41] The council calculates the additional acreage needed for development by prescribing densities for developed areas, developing areas, and rural growth centers and the type of housing in demand, including single family, multifamily, rural residential, and mixed use.[42]

It is important to note that the Met Council has consistently underestimated the growth in the periphery of the region and overestimated growth in the core of the region. Chapter 1 showed that inner-ring cities like Bloomington and Richfield did not grow as fast in the 1970s as predicted, nor are they on pace to grow as fast as predicted for 2010. At the same time, jurisdictions, particularly in rural and rural residential areas, have continuously grown faster than expected. Although the council has set goals to guide growth toward the core of the region, it has failed to meet these expectations.

The Urbanization of Rural Areas

The Met Council has failed to prevent suburban-like development in rural service areas, which has led to the inevitable loss of prime agricultural land. A major recent change for rural policy areas has been changes in rural density guidelines. Permanent rural areas had density requirement changes from 1 unit to 40 acres in 1988 to as high as 1 unit to 10 acres in 2002.[43] Likewise, rural residential areas saw a density requirement change from one unit to ten acres in 1988 to one unit to two acres in 2002.[44] Maps 2.2 and 2.3 illustrate the changes in the Met Council's geographic planning areas between 1988 and 2006, showing projected future growth for the region. While the Met Council has attempted to prevent development of rural agricultural land, many agricultural areas will convert into suburban development over the next thirty years. Already, places like Cottage Grove and Denmark Township, southeast of St. Paul, had much agricultural area destroyed by exurban growth generated by upwardly mobile households that drove up surrounding land prices.[45] In Scott County, another area with significant farmland, both resident and farming advocates are concerned about the future of development and oppose mass suburbanization into the area. They aim to preserve prime agricultural land in the

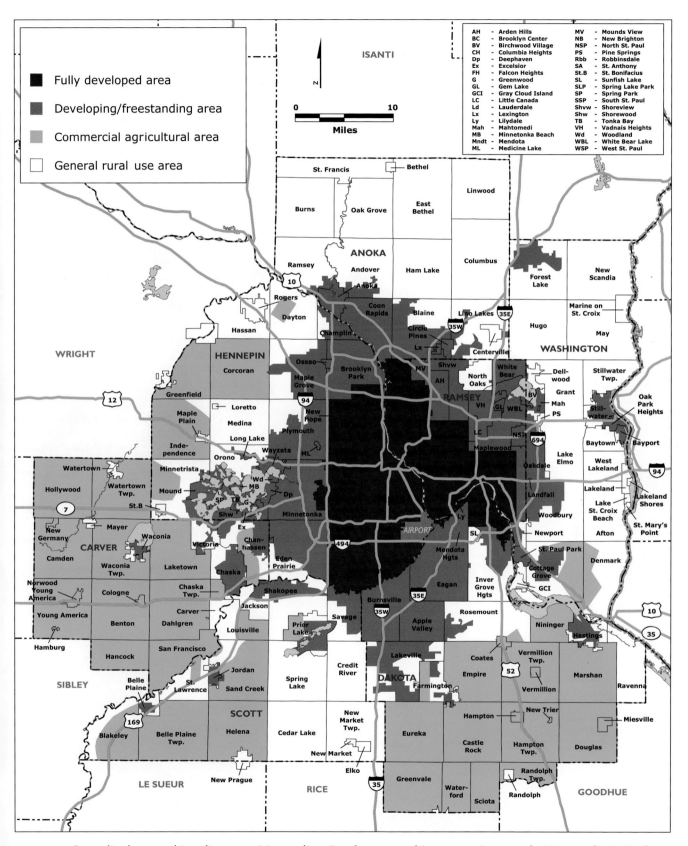

MAP 2.2. Generalized geographic policy areas, Metropolitan Development and Investment Framework, Minneapolis–St. Paul region, 1988. *Source:* Metropolitan Council, Metropolitan Development and Investment Framework, 1998. The map's spatial boundaries were digitized by the Institute on Race and Poverty, University of Minnesota.

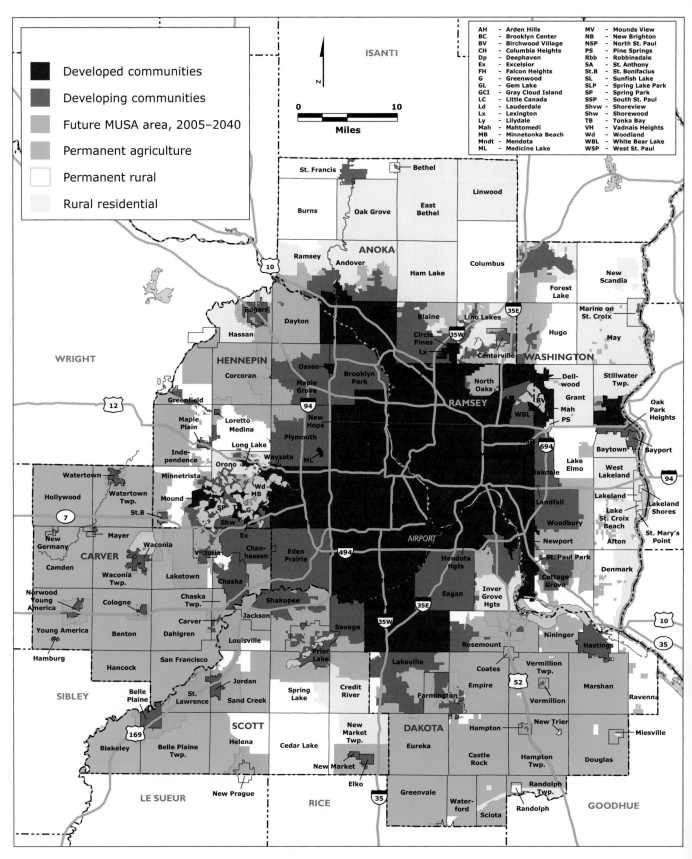

MAP 2.3. Geographic planning areas, comprehensive planning composite, Minneapolis–St. Paul region, 2006.
Source: Metropolitan Council (September 6, 2006).

county permanently, some advocating for greater densities in surrounding cities like Shakopee.[46]

The Met Council has, nevertheless, increasingly allowed flexibility in its rural service area policy, viewing its rural policy as nonintegral to its system plans used to establish the MUSA and assess the conformity of local planning. Under this view the council cannot enforce the planned densities of rural jurisdictions. While the Met Council did successfully challenge development plans within the MUSA in *Lake Elmo,* it has never challenged a predominately rural jurisdiction that creates land use plans with near suburban housing densities, and instead has simply changed its guidelines to reflect increasing rural densities outside the MUSA.[47]

Another recent policy that could greatly impact agricultural areas is the Met Council's reclassification of rural centers as "developing communities." The Met Council has allowed changing the designation of rural centers in a Council attempt to manage and operate wastewater systems in those areas. The main requirement for a rural center to become a developing community is that the locality include in its comprehensive plan a contiguous urban growth boundary.[48] Such a requirement for rural centers, given the council's recent view that the MUSA can be noncontiguous, makes growth more diffuse.

The extension of metro wastewater systems into rural centers will create strong market incentives for development of rural and agricultural areas that surround rural centers. For instance, there has been strong developmental pressure on suburban Ham Lake after its neighbor East Bethel reached an agreement with the Met Council to develop a wastewater treatment center in the municipality. Because Ham Lake is between East Bethel and the MUSA, there are both concerns about losing the rural character of the area and the potential of economic development opportunities leapfrogging north into growing East Bethel.[49]

Growth in the Collar Counties of the Region

Development pressures in the seven-county metropolitan region have also spilled over into counties just outside the region. The fastest population and job growth rates are now outside the seven counties. Collar county officials find it difficult to coordinate and guide such growth in a free-for-all system, but have few incentives to cooperate with one another or the region as a whole. Public resources in the collar counties are used inefficiently because municipal planning is highly localized, often working at cross-purposes with neighboring jurisdictions. Unfortunately, local officials in collar counties report that they are given little guidance from state agencies.[50]

Legislative efforts to include collar counties in the Met Council's planning process have also failed. One effort would have required that the Met Council include officials from Minnesota and Wisconsin counties adjacent to the seven counties to serve as nonvoting affiliate members of the council. Such an effort would familiar-ize these officials with the planning process at the council and help them coordinate planning with the council concerning issues that affect their collar counties.[51] With the seven-county area quickly developing its remaining land, it is imperative for col-lar counties to be involved with the Met Council.

Job Centers

The Met Council has had an interest in the concentration of jobs in the downtown areas and the surrounding suburban beltway since the 1970s because strong job centers in the region's core act as a magnet for development and job creation, help-ing to prevent excessive infrastructure maintenance costs and urban sprawl. These areas contain higher job densities and an intensity of urban services, such as water and utility lines, roads, and transit. If jobs cluster in spatial concentrations, trans-portation can operate more efficiently, as more passengers will travel to specific rather than spread-out destinations.

The Met Council has had an uneven interest in job centers. In 1988, the council gave job centers the highest priority for council investments, as a way of maintain-ing existing infrastructure and restraining public costs associated with excessive sprawl.[52] By the 1990s, however, job centers no longer had policy preference at all.[53] In 2002, the issue of traffic congestion in the region rekindled Met Council inter-est in integrated land use and transportation planning. *Blueprint 2030* promoted transit to address growing concerns about traffic congestion.[54] The Met Council provided detailed descriptions about land uses it envisioned for transportation cor-ridors and activity centers that had concentrations of jobs, housing, and a greater potential for transit usage. Under *Blueprint 2030* guidelines, the council recom-mends housing densities between eight and thirty housing units per acre within transportation corridors and nearby job centers.[55]

The Dispersion of Jobs

Clustered employment was the strongest policy priority of the Met Council in the 1970s and 1980s, but was not a priority geographic policy area in the 1990s and has since become a very inconsistent policy. While the 2002 Council began to reestab-lish regional planning for job-clustered areas and describe ideal land use patterns for them, two years later the council dropped the detailed land use descriptions as-sociated with transportation corridors and job centers in its *Framework 2030*.[56]

During the 1990s, the Twin Cities saw a steady trend toward decentralization of jobs. In 1990, 55 percent of all jobs were densely clustered, often located near the core of the region. By 2000, only 52 percent of the regional jobs remained clustered (see chapter 4). If this trend continues, most regional jobs in the Twin Cities today may be sprawled across the region. A sprawled job market contributes to more housing in the periphery of the region, magnifies the spatial mismatch between housing and jobs, and makes mass transit less viable in the region. These trends exacerbate the inequality of opportunity for low-income workers and contribute to congestion in the region.

Framework 2030 does recommend making investments along major transportation corridors, where many jobs cluster, but does not discuss how integrated land uses and transportation goals will curtail traffic congestion, urban sprawl, and the viability of the region's transit system. Unfortunately, *Framework 2030* relies more on traffic management and transportation engineering strategies to address the region's growing traffic problems at the expense of seriously incorporating transportation land use planning goals.[57]

Wastewater and Regional Water Planning

The Met Council develops the region's water policy plans, including a wastewater systems plan, which guides local comprehensive plans. The water policy plans aim to protect the region's water supply and manage the wastewater service through the Metropolitan Council's Environmental Services (MCES) Division. The council currently is involved in three major water-planning functions: wastewater services, water supply planning, and surface water management.[58]

While water supply planning and surface water management are important mechanisms for environmental protection, the Met Council's wastewater services are the most relevant to local and regional planning. The extension of wastewater systems is a tool for development that makes land more valuable for urban development. Wastewater extensions may also conflict with budgetary constraints of extending other public projects and services, such as roads and schools. To prevent excessive urban growth, regional governments can ensure that local development plans remain consistent with regional wastewater plans.

Today, MCES provides wastewater collection and treatment for approximately 2.5 million people and 103 communities in the Twin Cities region. Up to 300 million gallons of wastewater are processed a day through six hundred miles of regional interceptors and eight wastewater plants.

Map 2.4 shows the eight wastewater treatment plants that include the metro system, one of the nation's largest, which processes about three-fourths of the region's wastewater and covers the cities of Minneapolis and St. Paul, suburban Ramsey County, and large portions of Hennepin, Anoka, and Washington counties.[59] Medium-sized systems in the Twin Cities include the extensive Blue Lake system in the fast-growing southwest metro; the Seneca system in Bloomington, Burnsville, and Eagan; and the newly constructed Eagles Point interceptor system that covers Woodbury and Cottage Grove in the east metro.

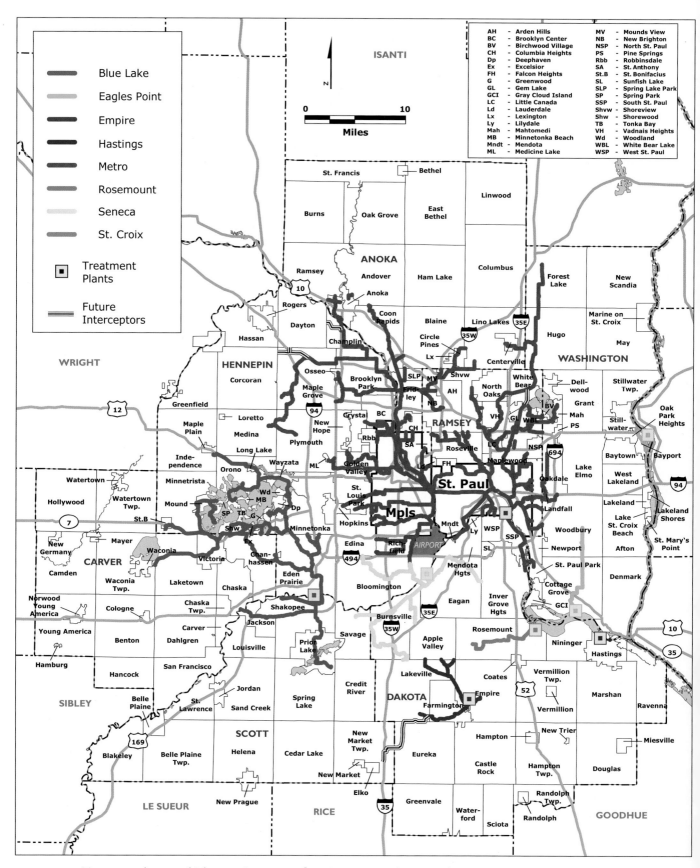

MAP 2.4. Treatment plant to which sewer interceptor flows in Minneapolis–St. Paul region. *Source:* Metropolitan Council.

Regional Wastewater Quality/Equity

Rapid Twin Cities urban development has resulted in inequity in regional payments for wastewater. MCES charges jurisdictions largely on a uniform basis. MCES also collects revenues through its Service Availability Charges (SACs) for the increased volume or connections to the wastewater system. The SACs are an attempt to account for new users and differing usage rates between the various wastewater systems; however, SACs make up a small proportion of MCES's overall revenues: about 19 percent compared to the 74 percent collected from the uniform rate charges.[60]

The current Met Council projects that over the next twenty-five years it will need to invest $3.7 billion for building, replacing, and maintaining the region's wastewater treatment facilities, including treatment plants and interceptors.[61] Map 2.5 shows large extensions of the wastewater system into low-density suburban areas. An entirely new treatment plant and interceptor system, called Eagle's Point, has been established for Woodbury and Cottage Grove.[62] The Met Council is also considering constructing new plants in Carver and Scott counties.[63]

The urban core is paying more than its share for the urban expansion of the Twin Cities wastewater system. Past research in the Twin Cities has shown that sewage treatment service charges have not covered the full costs of developing and maintaining the system, because of subsidies in the Twin Cities wastewater rate system. Luce, Lukermann, and Mohring found that if Twin Cities consumers had paid the actual costs of using the wastewater system, rather than paying uniform rates, they would have paid about 20 to 36 percent more than they did. The researchers also found that users of the Metro system, which services the core of the region, were subsidizing users of other plants that service much lower-density suburban areas. On average, other plant users would be paying 70 percent more for wastewater services if the charges reflected the costs of operating their systems compared to the Metro system.[64]

Regional Water Planning

The region's urbanized land growth has put enormous pressures on the region's natural environment. Water quality is often substandard in the region: in 2004, the Minnesota Pollution Control Agency found that fifteen of the region's twenty-five streams were impaired, having one or more pollution violations.[65] Thirty to forty percent of lakes received a poor quality rating due to their poor water clarity.[66] Furthermore, the rapid development occurring outside the seven-county metro area is depleting water aquifers, which are shallow and susceptible to pollution.

The regional water supply plan is developed by the Met Council, reviewed by the Minnesota Department of Natural Resources, and is reported to the Minnesota legislature.[67] The council does not centrally manage or operate a drinking water system, but is involved in the approval process for local drinking water providers.

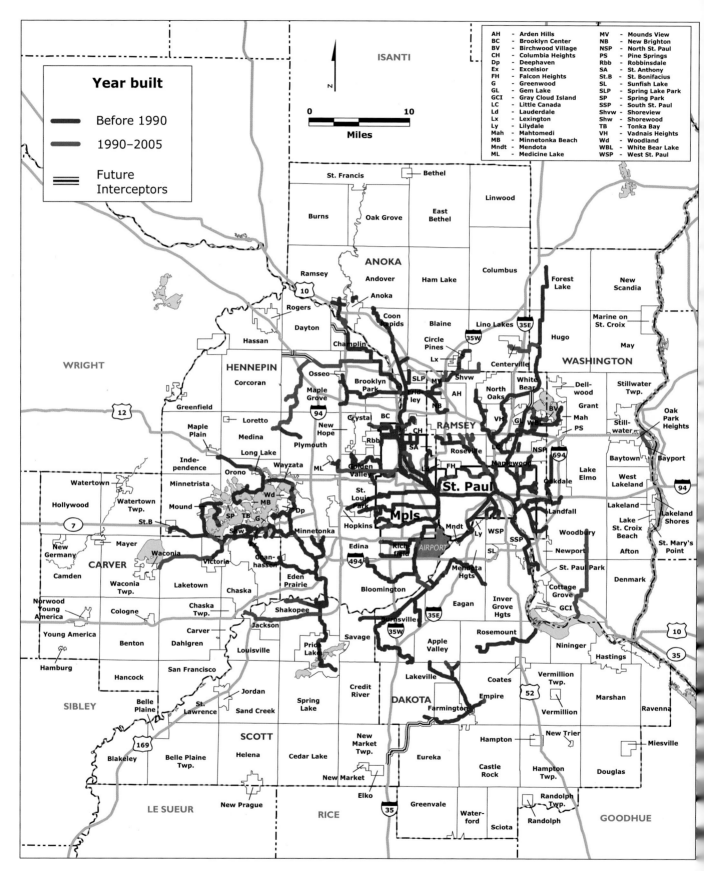

MAP 2.5. Year sewer interceptor system built, Minneapolis–St. Paul region. *Source:* Metropolitan Council.

In the Twin Cities there are 108 separate local public entities that supply drinking water and that must establish local water supply plans subjected to approval from the Met Council, Minnesota Department of Natural Resources, and Department of Health.[68] The council has similar involvement with watershed planning in the region.[69] The Met Council has proposed to the Minnesota legislature that its water supply plan have the same powers of other systems plans. If the Met Council proposal comes to fruition, local water supply plans would need to demonstrate consistency with the regional water supply plan.[70]

Regional Transportation: Transit, Highway Expansion, and Repairs

The Met Council is responsible for creating a regional plan for transportation in the Twin Cities, including both highways and mass transit. The Met Council has obtained leverage with state and federal agencies over highway funding, which allows it to be an effective regional transportation planner.[71] The Met Council's current transportation systems plan includes a twenty-year long-range regional transportation policy plan (TPP) every four years and a three-year preparation of transportation improvement program (TIP), which includes all federally funded transportation projects.[72] TIP is developed in close cooperation with the Minnesota Department of Transportation. The most recent TPP goals focus on improving alternative means of transportation in the region to slow traffic congestion, improving accessibility to jobs, and protecting the natural environment.[73] Like prior transportation systems plans, the current TPP also establishes that maintaining the existing highway system is the council's first priority.[74]

Transportation, Mass Transit, and Land Use

Since 1967 the Met Council has consistently supported the maintenance over the expansion of the highway system. A large share of regional highway financing has been directed toward the core of the region's transportation system (see chapter 5).[75] The council has attempted to counter a "roads only" approach by advocating for transit funding. The council strongly argued for and leveraged transportation funds to establish the Hiawatha light-rail line and expanded plans for 2020 to include five additional railways and three busways with dedicated lanes.[76] The mass transit plans fit within the council's goal to slow traffic congestion in the area by increasing travel choices in the Twin Cities region.

Metropolitan sprawl gets in the way of effective mass transit. The lack of clear and articulated goals for an integrated land use–transportation plan has been the greatest problem with the Met Council's planning for mass transit. Housing density is necessary for effective mass transit, and the fastest-growing suburbs are not dense enough for a serviceable and effective mass transit system.[77] The Twin Cities currently has more than eight thousand miles of transit routes; however, only about

2 percent of those miles are routes that provide service frequently, and these routes barely make their way into suburban areas.[78]

Moreover, the Met Council policies to integrate transportation–land use programs are poorly conceived. The establishment of the U.S. Transportation Equity Act for the 21st Century (TEA-21) helped the Met Council establish benchmarks for housing performance. TEA-21 authorized funding for transportation and helped to better define prior transportation policy and law. It also emphasized the flexible use of highway funds to promote transit and protect the environment. Because counties were usually the recipients of TEA-21, local benchmarks were often unreported, even though the funding often benefited localities. Additionally, there has been little funding of the Met Council's Affordable Housing Enhancement Demonstration (AHED) that allows localities to take advantage of federal highway dollars to make transportation enhancements in conjunction to affordable housing development.[79]

Counties Asserting Power over New Transit Money

In 2008, the legislature allowed metropolitan counties to increase the sale tax and created another form of metro governance. It created the Country Transit Improvement Board (CTIB) in March 2008 and empowered it to increase the state sales tax by a quarter point in counties that agreed to the increase and to use the funds for transit. The CTIB collects the extra sales tax in the counties that opt to collect the tax, and grants the funds to capital projects in the Twin Cities area. It has bonding authority secured by the tax revenues. The board's membership includes ninety-five representatives from the five counties that have thus far passed the tax and five members representing the Met Council. It will control an estimated $100 million annually for transit. Many argued that power over the new funds should have gone to the Met Council, but others argued that the unelected council should not be granted more authority than it already has. In the end the naysayers won, and the governance arrangement effectively bypasses the Met Council.

Subsidized and Affordable Housing

Although housing is not officially a "system," metropolitan housing policy plays an important role with the Met Council. The council establishes housing densities in geographic policy areas inside and outside the MUSA as a way to forecast the amount of future developable land in the region. Under the Metropolitan Land Planning Act and the Livable Communities Act, the council also reviews, comments on, and negotiates local affordable housing goals within local comprehensive planning documents. The Metropolitan Land Planning Act further empowered the Met Council to serve as a housing authority, and to operate federally assisted housing programs in any suburban community requesting assistance.[80]

The Met Council experienced one of its greatest successes in the 1970s with the development of thousands of affordable low-income housing units. A number of factors, including the availability of federal money for subsidized housing construction and conversion,[81] contributed to the dramatic increase in the number and proportion of subsidized housing units in Twin Cities suburbs during the 1970s. The proactive housing policies adopted by the Met Council in 1971 made it possible for the Twin Cities region to effectively leverage federal funds when they became available beginning in 1974. The Met Council's policies, which were part of an effort to expand the stock of subsidized housing in the suburbs, contributed to a substantial increase in the number and share of units available in the suburbs between 1971 and 1974 (Figure 2.2).[82]

The Twin Cities metropolitan region experienced a net gain of 12,255 subsidized housing units between 1974 and 1979.[83] Fifty-four percent were newly constructed project-based Section 8 units, and 46 percent were existing units subsidized through Section 8 certificates and vouchers.[84] From 1974 to 1979, the Twin Cities metropolitan area gained 7,300 Section 8 new construction units and 6,334 Section 8 existing units, for a total of 13,634 new Section 8 units.[85]

Under the Livable Communities Act, the Met Council negotiates with local governments to create affordable housing based on how well local governments compare to neighboring communities. The council then reports local progress on affordable housing goals to the legislature.[86] In 2001, the council began giving localities a housing performance score based on how well local jurisdictions provide affordable and life cycle housing in the region. The council uses the ranked performance scores to evaluate funding requests from localities, particularly for TEA-21 funds.[87]

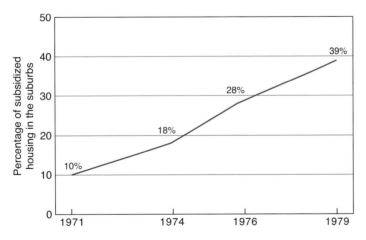

FIGURE 2.2. Twin Cities subsidized housing in the suburbs, 1971–79. *Source:* Metropolitan Council.

The Met Council, through the Metropolitan Council and Redevelopment Agency (Metro HRA), administers Section 8 vouchers and other subsidized housing, but it does not allocate low-income housing tax credits (LIHTC). The Minnesota legislature has given the state's Minnesota Housing Finance Agency (MHFA) the responsibility to allocate LIHTC. MFHA in turn grants funds to multiple suballocators, including the planning and development agency in Minneapolis, St. Paul's Housing and Redevelopment Agency, and suburban Dakota County and Washington County housing and development agencies.[88]

Subsidized and Affordable Housing Successes and Failures

Since the 1970s, the Twin Cities has proactively placed subsidized family housing in the suburbs. Currently, 46 percent of family project–based Section 8 units, 54 percent of Section 8 vouchers, and 62 percent of family LIHTC units are located in Twin Cities suburban areas (Table 2.1). Around 40–50 percent of the suburban subsidized unit households are racial minorities, smaller proportions than in the central city, but not monolithically white either.[89]

The Minnesota Housing Finance Agency is more successfully allocating LIHTC units into the suburbs, in greater proportions than the current project-based Section 8 and Section 8 voucher programs. In fact, all housing programs in the Twin Cities have done a better job placing subsidized units in the suburbs than have most other metropolitan areas. The prominence of Minneapolis and St. Paul in the suballocation of LIHTC funding, however, has resulted in more subsidized units in the central cities, making the program less integrative than it could be.[90]

While the placement of subsidized housing in the suburbs has been successful in the Twin Cities, the overall development and distribution of affordable housing in the Twin Cities has been less than stunning. Two major laws promote the development of affordable housing throughout the Twin Cities region's municipalities: the Metropolitan Land Use Planning Act (MLPA) and the Livable Communities Act

TABLE 2.1 **Suburban subsidized housing in the Twin Cities, 2004**

	Number of units	Percentage of regional total	Percentage minority in suburban housing
Section 8 project (family)	3,405	45.5	47.1
Section 8 vouchers	9,198	53.8	43.1
LIHTC (family—2002)	3,340	62.2	44.2

Source: Minnesota Housing Finance Agency.

Note: Includes only core seven counties. Estimate based on 53% survey sample of Low Income Housing Tax Credit units in Twin Cities in 2002. Only units with children were included in the data.

(LCA). A major drawback of the policy structure of both laws is that their formula calculation relies on future housing production and population increases, not current affordable housing needs. Both MLPA and LCA have excluded approximately 170,000 low-income residents in need of affordable housing in 2000.[91] Even excluding current affordable housing needs, there will be an estimated shortfall of 33,000 affordable units by 2010.[92]

There is a strong concentration of market rate affordable housing in the central cities of the Twin Cities. In 2000, the central cities of Minneapolis and St. Paul capture 51 percent of the region's housing units that are affordable to households making 50 percent or less of regional income (or $26,652).[93] The Twin Cities have successfully integrated subsidized housing in the suburbs, but the private market has not located affordable housing in many suburban jurisdictions, often because of suburban resistance to affordable housing and suburban zoning regulations that prohibit it.

Recently, the Met Council has established new criteria for MLPA affordable housing goals for the increase in households between 2011 and 2020 that may help increase affordable housing in the suburbs. The new MLPA goals call for fewer affordable units than the LCA goals, but also have lowered income eligibility criteria, with MLPA guidelines established for households with 60 percent of the region's median income, compared to 80 percent of regional income for low-income households in LCA. The MLPA affordable housing goals attempt to place units near entry-level jobs and in suburbs that lack affordable housing.[94]

TWIN CITIES–PORTLAND REGIONAL PLANNING COMPARISON

The fragmentation of local government in both the Twin Cities and Portland contributes to sprawl.[95] When multiple local governments exist in a metropolitan area, there is a propensity for local planning goals to conflict with regional planning goals, which creates sprawl. The curvilinear relationship between the sprawl and fragmentation ("Predicted sprawl") is shown in Figure 2.3.[96]

Both Portland and the Twin Cities experienced considerably less sprawl than expected, given their respective fragmentation of local governments.[97] The better than predicted growth patterns correspond to the strength of the regions' regional governments.

Regional policies matter when it comes to urban growth. While the Twin Cities regional governing body, the Metropolitan Council, has been given a greater range of budgetary[98] and policy responsibilities,[99] it has accomplished less than Portland's elected regional governing body, Metro, which has fewer regional governance responsibilities.[100] Much of Portland's success is due to the impact of Oregon's state

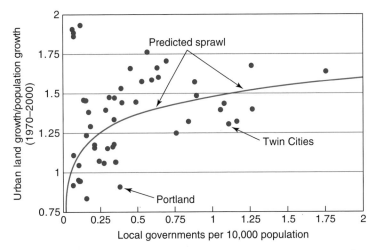

FIGURE 2.3. Fragmentation and urban sprawl in the fifty largest U.S. metropolitan areas. *Source:* U.S. Census Bureau.

land use laws on guiding development within urbanized areas, Portland's stronger development guidelines within urbanized areas, and Metro's stronger planning linkage of transportation to a compact urban form.

LAND USE PLANNING LAWS AND POLICIES

The laws that support geographic planning areas are one of the greatest differences between sprawl in the Twin Cities and Portland. While urban land use policy in the Twin Cities applies only to the Met Council's core seven-county metropolitan area, throughout the state of Oregon there is a strict limitation on new housing development outside an established urban growth boundary (UBG).[101] Oregon's Comprehensive Land Use Planning Coordination Act of 1973 authorizes the state's Land Conservation and Development Commission (LCDC) to establish state planning goals and other regulations, including the UGBs.[102]

In Portland there is an elected regional government called Metro, approved by voters in Multnomah, Washington, and Clackamas counties in 1978. Metro is chartered to create a regional framework plan and adopts an urban growth boundary; both are subject to review by the LCDC. What makes the UGB of Portland (and other Oregon cities) unique and effective is its mandate by comprehensive statewide policy and law.

Every city and county in Oregon localities must devise a comprehensive plan that is consistent with the LCDC's statewide planning goals.[103] In contrast, the Met Council approves local comprehensive plans only within its core seven-county area. Because there is no statewide plan that addresses urban growth, there are often concerns that Met Council policies that guide growth in the MUSA might generate rapid development outside the seven-county area. Even within the Met Council's seven-county area, there are near-suburban densities emerging in rural areas outside the MUSA, whereas in Portland there is a strict limitation on new housing development outside the UGBs established by Oregon state law.[104]

A critical difference between regional governance in the Twin Cities and Portland is that council members of Metro are elected, while in the Twin Cities the governor appoints council members. In Portland, there is greater public knowledge of growth management issues because of the publicizing of Metro council elections. Elected public officials help the public understand how regional issues affect the day-to-day lives of ordinary people. An elected government structure is also more accountable to the public than an appointed one. If elected officials attempt to seize too much power over regional affairs, other elected officials and the public can challenge their authority within a checks-and-balances system.

A regional government that is elected by the public will more likely challenge competing agencies and interests whose actions contradict the welfare of the region. An appointed body, however, has a duty to the appointing authority and is less likely to exercise discretion in decision making. Appointed bodies also have no incentive to publicize the decision-making process. In the Twin Cities, the public is often scarcely aware of the decision-making process of the Met Council and has little recourse to challenge the council's actions.

Another positive feature of governance in Portland that is absent in the Twin Cities is a statewide court system that helps streamline land use disputes that the public has with Oregon's regional governments. Oregon also has a specialized court system to handle land use appeals and a private right of action to enforce regional planning laws in Portland called the Land Use Board of Appeals (LUBA), replacing the LCDC and circuit courts appeal jurisdiction over land use disputes. LUBA is a court system not found elsewhere in the United States that helps simplify the appeals process and makes timely resolutions in land use disputes with legal consistency. Anyone who participated in the proceedings of the local government, state agency, or special district may file a notice of intent to appeal petition to LUBA for review of a land use decision. In addition, Oregon's Land Conservation and Development Act allows individuals to request adoption of an enforcement order if they believe a local government's comprehensive plan, limited land use decision, land use regulation, or other land use decision does not comply with the LCDC's goals.

Development Guidelines of Geographic Areas

In the Twin Cities and in Portland, regional planning emphasized forecasting the supply and demand of land, but these governments use different development densities in their urban land development calculations.[105] Portland's Metro establishes much higher suburban housing densities within the UGB than the Met Council does within its MUSA: Oregon's 1981 LCDC rule established minimum housing densities of 6 dwelling units (DUs) per acre for several small cities, 8 DUs per acre in Clackamas and Washington counties and midsized cities, and 10 DUs per acre in Multnomah County and large cities.[106] In contrast, the Met Council planning density recommendations are 6 units per acre for fully developed suburbs and 3.6 units per acre in developing suburban areas.[107] The lower development densities in the Twin Cities, pound for pound, make the MUSA larger than Portland's UGB, because the Council assumes more land consumption per household than does Portland's Metro.

Transportation Planning and Land Use Planning for Transit

The Twin Cities' and Portland's transportation plans both target investments into regional corridors and job centers, but Portland's plans emphasize land use that is favorable to transit services, while the Met Council's regional plans often focus on day-to-day operations. Portland's 1982 and 1989 Regional Transportation Plans (RTPs) used freeway and transit investments, as well as travel demand management, to guide growth in a cost-effective manner. To guide growth in transportation planning infrastructure, investments are targeted toward improving regional corridors.[108] The 2000 regional transportation plan explicitly links urban form to transportation, especially transit. The RTP directs infrastructure investments toward downtown Portland, regional centers, industrial areas, and intermodal facilities. The 2000 system also develops infrastructure for modes of transportation alternative to the automobile.[109] In contrast, the Met Council's *Framework 2030* goals focus on traffic engineering strategies to slow traffic congestion, rather than advocating for a compact urban form more suitable for transit operations.[110]

Regional policies matter when it comes to urban growth, and the Met Council has the power to serve as a stronger regional government and better contain sprawl. The passage of Measure 37 has challenged Portland's regional governance regime; however, legal challenges such as *Lake Elmo* have strengthened the powers of the Metropolitan Council.[111] Portland's greater success in containing sprawl shows that the Met Council can and should use its greater powers to guide the Twin Cities region to a more efficient and equitable future.

POLICY RECOMMENDATIONS

The Metropolitan Council is a leading regional government. The council has accumulated strong regional planning powers, but has failed to achieve goals set forth in regional planning documents and, instead, has often minimized or dropped such goals altogether when they are not achieved. Creating an elected Met Council, establishing statewide land use laws, protecting rural areas, and establishing equitable policies that make the core of the Twin Cities region vital will make the council more accountable and improve the likelihood that the council will reach its regional planning goals.

Elected Metropolitan Council

An elected Metropolitan Council would help the council reach its regional goals. With an elected body, there would be no confusion over whether the council or the Transportation Advisory Board holds ultimate power over regional planning. The Met Council could be the sole Metropolitan Planning Organization in the region, responsible for developing regional planning documents and soliciting and evaluating applications for federal transportation funding. An elected Metropolitan Council would also better represent and be accountable to the general public. For instance, it would have been tougher for an elected Met Council to delay the implementation of transit rail corridors until 2030 when the public has clearly demonstrated wide public support for rail transit in the region.

Statewide Land Use Planning Policies

The state of Minnesota should establish urban and rural land use policies that apply to the entire state of Minnesota and that are supportive of metropolitan regional plans throughout the state. In Minnesota, unlike Oregon, there are no statewide land use goals, and this lack of statewide planning makes regional planning less effective, contributing to concerns that more stringent development requirements would lead to suburban-like development outside the core metropolitan seven counties.

Strengthening Council Geographic Policies

Without stronger planning and regulation in the urban and rural service area, regional development will reproduce development inefficiencies and inequities, and endanger the natural environment. The council should reestablish a contiguous MUSA and insist that rural jurisdictions maintain low housing densities. The council's de-emphasis of the MUSA is a major detriment to its other regional goals. The lack of a meaningful MUSA makes transit less viable, makes the maintenance of transportation and wastewater infrastructure difficult and costly, and can minimize the public's access to work, parks, and other urban amenities. Without the council's guidance of growth into a more compact urban area, future regional problems may become insurmountable.

Land Use: Transportation Policies and Job Centers

In Portland, successful transportation planning primarily focuses on devising land uses that are favorable for public transportation. Likewise, the Met Council should create programs with strong funding leverage for development near job centers, including transit and housing. Without meaningful funding support for intensive development near corridors and job centers, the council will have difficulty establishing development conditions more conducive to transit and affordable housing. To illustrate, programs that could be beneficial to job centers, such as AHED, only support a small fraction of funding needed to integrate and align regional housing and transportation investments.[112] With funding leverage in place, the council should give much greater policy preference to intensive forms of development in and nearby job centers.

Water Policy

The Twin Cities wastewater system uniform rate system promotes an inequitable payment structure whereby residents in high-density communities pay to service residents in low-density communities. This funding structure both supports the outward growth of low-density development and detracts from the council's goal to maintain the existing system. The council should explore the full costs of building and operating wastewater systems and devise a funding structure that does not punish users in the core of the region by making them pay more for services that are provided at a cheaper cost. The council should also have more power over the conservation and protection of the region's water supply.

Housing Policy

The Met Council still possesses great power to guide the development of low-income housing in suburban areas, authority increased by the passage of the Livable Communities Act in 1995 and recent state court decisions. If the Met Council used its regulatory stance to promote better transportation–land use planning and if the LCA were strengthened and exercised in coordination with expanded school choice, the resulting increase in low-income housing would also strengthen regional integration efforts, by deconcentrating the poverty from units clustered in Minneapolis and St. Paul toward jurisdictions with better schools and stronger economic growth.

The council should generate more incentives for localities to zone and develop affordable housing. The Met Council has relatively little funding from the state legislature, with affordable housing the smallest funding stream within the Livable Communities Demonstration Account.[113] Affordable housing revenue streams should have much greater funding. Yet when affordable housing funding does exist, the council should punish localities that fail to adopt policies that aid the development of affordable housing (e.g., setting housing densities below minimum standards).

Regional Performance Plan

The council has often failed to reach its regional goals and when it has missed them, the council has often opted out of such goals rather than report them. It has become exceedingly difficult to assess within the blueprints whether much regional progress has occurred. Regional blueprints and frameworks should have a consistent performance plan section that contains measures of performance for regional goals reported in regional planning blueprints. In Portland, such performance plans exist and help demonstrate progress made in attaining regional goals and policies over a fifty-year period.[114]

3

Neighborhood and School Segregation

Myron Orfield, Baris Gumus-Dawes,
Thomas F. Luce Jr., and Geneva Finn

ollowing the release of the 2000 Census, scholars from all disciplines were eager to celebrate the decline of racial segregation in the nation. Study after study documented the decline in broad measures of racial segregation in many metropolitan areas during the 1990s.

While broad measures like metrowide dissimilarity indexes do a good job of showing overall segregation trends across metros, they fail to paint the full picture. In fact, a closer look at racial segregation in metropolitan areas reveals disturbing trends. In today's more racially diverse society, a new type of segregation is emerging for communities of color. This new type involves segregation of nonwhites from whites rather than of individual races from whites.

As racial diversity expands, different communities of color are mixing with each other in nonwhite segregated schools and neighborhoods but not with whites. While fewer whites are in predominantly white schools and neighborhoods, more people of color find themselves in nonwhite segregated schools and neighborhoods. As a result, segregation is increasing for most students and residents of color, even as it is declining for whites.

Racial segregation is a significant problem even in a predominantly white region like the Twin Cities. Elsewhere in the nation, in metros with more racially diverse populations, racial segregation is even more pronounced. Segregation is likely to be especially severe in regions with highly fragmented governance structures because smaller localities are more likely to be able to effectively engage in the kinds of exclusionary behavior that create or maintain racial segregation.

Racial segregation is not just about race. It is about access to opportunity. Where one lives affects one's access to jobs, good schools, and decent economic prospects in life. To the extent that racial segregation limits people's residential choices, it undermines equality of opportunity.

Residential segregation especially hurts residents of color by limiting their residential choices to low-opportunity neighborhoods of the region. As a result of racial steering, residents of color often find themselves in less affluent neighborhoods that offer poor-quality public services and schools. These neighborhoods also suffer from higher levels of crime and social disorganization.

Residential segregation also creates segregation in schools—one of the most important determinants of one's opportunities in life. Due to segregation, students of color are much more likely to attend racially segregated schools with high concentrations of poverty than white students. High-poverty schools are associated with a wide range of negative educational and life outcomes, which affect students of color much more disproportionately.

Racial segregation has an impact on various types of communities in the region. Many neighborhoods in the central cities have already been hard hit by the disinvestment caused by segregation. Once a problem confined to central cities, racial segregation is now a regional concern, threatening the vitality of suburban communities as well. In some suburban areas, schools—powerful indicators of a community's health—are already experiencing social and economic changes leading to growing segregation.

Segregation does not just affect the core of the region and inner suburbs—it undermines the economic vitality of the entire region. A region jeopardizes its competitive edge and long-term quality of life by allowing segregation to damage educational opportunity and neighborhood stability in its urban core and adjacent suburbs. The economies of a region's central cities and its suburbs are related. Vibrant central cities can be engines of growth for metropolitan areas.

Racial segregation is not simply the result of private residential preferences. It is not simply the "natural state" of the housing market neutrally sorting people according to their socioeconomic status. In fact, there is nothing neutral about the ways housing markets operate. The discriminatory policies and practices of a number of public and private actors shape the institutional structure of housing markets. Racial segregation in housing markets emerges as a result of these discriminatory policies and practices.

On the private side, steering by real estate agents as well as the discriminatory business practices of financial institutions, mortgage brokers, and insurance agents perpetuate segregation. On the public side, housing policies of the federal government, decisions of school districts, and land use policies of municipalities all contribute to racial segregation. This means that segregation is not written in stone; it can be reversed by eliminating the policies and practices that generate it.

Growing racial diversity in metropolitan areas does not have to lead to increasing racial segregation. Regional policies can interrupt harmful racial transition trends and eventually reverse segregation in neighborhoods and schools. The actions of individual school districts and municipalities matter, but local actors cannot erase the ugly imprint of segregation from their schools and neighborhoods by themselves. Addressing racial segregation effectively in a metro requires first and foremost collaboration among communities and a regional orientation toward solutions. Regional governance mechanisms that counteract the harmful effects of regional fragmentation are an important part of these solutions.

These solutions also require a significant change in the nature of advocacy. Advocacy by and for low-income residents of color is even more fragmented than local government structures, usually operating at neighborhood scale. These efforts are often portrayed as the less controversial alternative to comprehensive regional reforms that are necessary to reverse segregation. In many cases, these organizations try to preserve their fragile status in a fragmented, unequal region. This often means that their self-interest leads them to oppose the very reforms that the region must undertake to expand its vitality.

Regionally scaled advocacy groups can overcome this hyperfragmentation in advocacy by articulating the needs of individual communities and schools in the context of the regional trends that shape their well-being. Metropolitan areas need regional advocates to promote the regional reforms that will help *all* communities, rather than pitting community against community.

Neighborhood and school segregation shape each other. Segregated neighborhoods create segregated schools because schools draw students from nearby neighborhoods. Conversely, segregated schools lead to segregated neighborhoods. Real estate agents and families use the socioeconomic and racial composition of schools to evaluate the desirability of surrounding neighborhoods. Racial transition in schools usually becomes a trigger for racial transition in neighborhoods.

Because of this, regionwide measures that address school and neighborhood segregation can generate synergistic outcomes. For instance, most low-income students of color in school choice programs must travel great distances to attend higher-quality schools. If the families of these children were given the first choice to live in affordable housing near those higher-quality schools, the need for student transportation would be significantly reduced. Strategically linking housing choice with school choice can thus maximize the integrative impact of school desegregation programs. Simulations show that choice-driven housing programs currently in operation in the Twin Cities metropolitan area have the potential to cut school segregation in half with relatively gradual changes.

Similarly, integrating schools can also help integrate neighborhoods. When implemented on the metro scale, school desegregation can promote residential integration and enhance neighborhood stability. If parents know that their children will attend an effective, integrated school regardless of where they live, they will be less likely to flee racially mixed or changing neighborhoods.

This chapter starts with a discussion of why segregation is important, followed by findings from the Twin Cities region. After covering the factors that contribute to segregation, the chapter concludes with a discussion of regional policies that can help reverse segregation in the Twin Cities region.

WHY DOES RACIAL SEGREGATION MATTER?

Racial Segregation Undermines Equality of Opportunity

Racial segregation is not just about race. It is also about access to jobs, good schools, and decent economic prospects in life. Where one lives significantly determines the availability and quality of opportunities such as public education, employment, and wealth accumulation and thus dramatically influences one's life chances. To the extent that racial segregation limits people's residential choices, it undermines equality of opportunity.

Access to opportunities varies significantly by race and income in most metropolitan areas.[1] Metropolitan housing markets sort people by both race/ethnicity and income. However, race/ethnicity and income do not contribute equally to the process. Only a third of residential segregation in 2000 was due to income sorting, while the remaining two-third was due to race/ethnicity.[2]

As in many other metropolitan areas, opportunities are very unevenly distributed in the Twin Cities metropolitan area. The community classification discussed in detail in chapter 1 suggests how the opportunities offered by different types of communities vary systematically. Map 3.1 illustrates the geographical stratification of opportunity in the Twin Cities region by community types.

As places with low tax capacity and high service costs, central cities and stressed suburbs offer limited opportunities to their residents. In contrast, developed job centers and affluent residential areas can offer better opportunities to their residents thanks to their high tax capacities, low service costs, and access to growing job centers. Developing job centers and bedroom developing communities provide their residents with moderate opportunities.

Racial segregation restricts the residential choices of people of color. Map 3.2 demonstrates the concentration of residents of color in central cities and stressed suburbs in the core of the Twin Cities region. A comparison of Maps 3.1 and 3.2 illustrates how racial segregation exiles residents of color into neighborhoods with limited opportunities. Table 3.1 further illustrates this point.

More than three-quarters of the region's residents of color live in central cities and stressed suburbs—communities that offer very limited opportunities to their residents (Table 3.1). In contrast, only two-fifths of the region's white residents

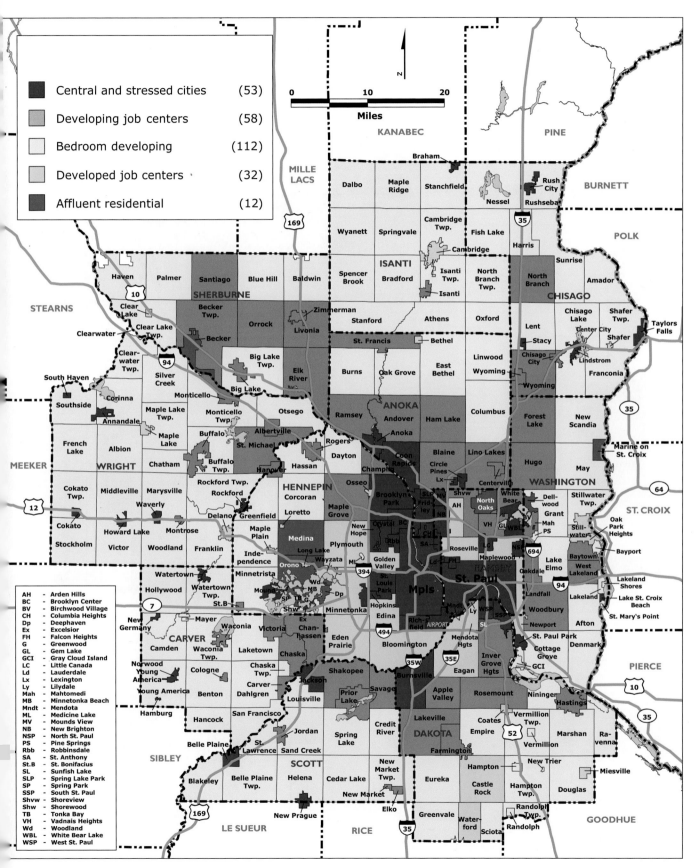

MAP 3.1. Community classification. *Source:* Ameregis, Inc.

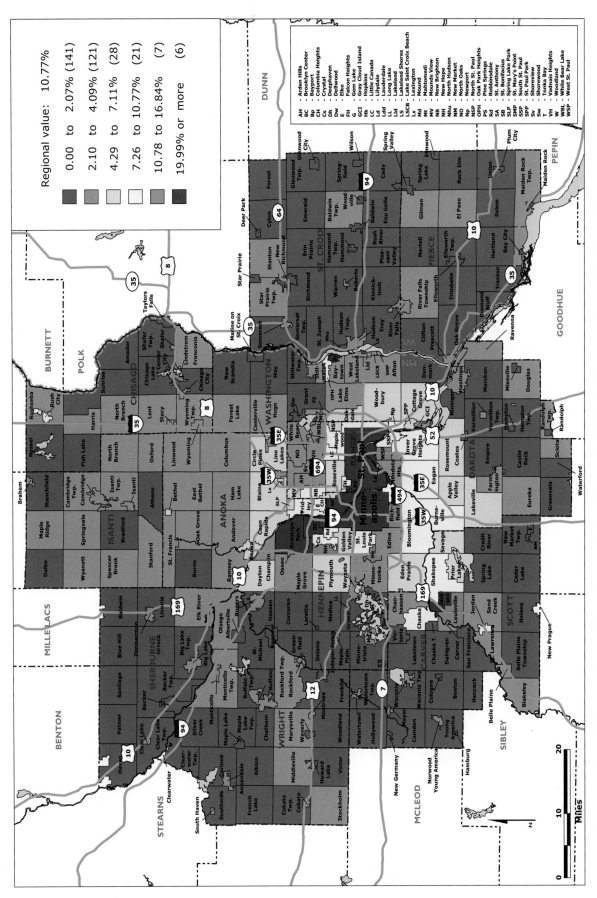

MAP 3.2. Percentage of non-Asian minority population by municipality, Minneapolis–St. Paul region, 2000. *Source:* U.S. Census Bureau.

Regional value: 10.77%

0.00 to 2.07%	(141)
2.10 to 4.09%	(121)
4.29 to 7.11%	(28)
7.26 to 10.77%	(21)
10.78 to 16.84%	(7)
19.99% or more	(6)

AH – Arden Hills
BC – Brooklyn Center
Bp – Bayport
CH – Columbia Heights
Cs – Crystal
Dh – Deephaven
Dw – Dellwood
E – Elko
FH – Falcon Heights
G – Gem Lake
GCI – Gray Cloud Island
Hk – Hopkins
LC – Little Canada
Ld – Lilydale
Ldd – Lauderdale
Ll – Long Lake
LL – Lake Lake
LS – Lakeland Shores
LSCB – Lake Saint Croix Beach
Lx – Lexington
Md – Mound
Mt – Mahtomedi
MV – Mounds View
NB – New Brighton
NH – New Hope
Nhu – North Hudson
NM – New Market
NO – North Oaks
Np – Newport
NSP – North St. Paul
OPH – Oak Park Heights
PS – Pine Springs
Rd – Robbinsdale
SA – St. Anthony
SB – St. Bonifacius
SLP – Spring Lake Park
SMP – St. Mary's Point
SSP – South St. Paul
SPP – St. Paul Park
Sv – Shoreview
Sw – Shorewood
T – Tonka Bay
VH – Vadnais Heights
W – Woodland
WBL – White Bear Lake
WSP – West St. Paul

TABLE 3.1   Distribution of racial groups across community
types in the Twin Cities region, 2000

	White	Black	Hispanic	Asian	Native American	Total nonwhite
Central cities	18	65	53	48	54	55
Stressed suburbs	23	20	20	21	19	21
Developing job centers	28	5	14	13	14	11
Bedroom developing communities	10	1	3	1	5	2
Developed job centers	20	8	10	17	7	11
Affluent residential	1	0	0	0	0	0

Sources: U.S. Census Bureau; Ameregis, Inc.

live in these low-opportunity communities. On the other side, only a quarter of the region's residents of color live in moderate- and high-opportunity communities compared to almost three-fifths of the region's white residents.

Racial segregation restricts residential choices of everyone but especially residents of color, forcing them to live in low-opportunity communities and neighborhoods of concentrated poverty. Poor white residents still have a higher likelihood of living outside neighborhoods with concentrated poverty compared to poor minority residents.[3] But it is not only poor residents of color who are trapped in poor neighborhoods. For instance, the average black family earning over $60,000 in the United States lives in a community with a higher poverty rate than the average white family earning less than $30,000.[4]

Racial segregation in neighborhoods is particularly harmful because it creates segregation in schools, which is closely associated with school failure. Attending a good school is one of the most important determinants of one's opportunities in life. In most places, residents send their kids to nearby schools. This generates a strong connection between residential segregation and segregation in schools, and influences one's likelihood of attending a good school.

Attending racially segregated schools hurts students of color because these schools have high concentrations of poverty.[5] In 2002, the average poverty rate in the nonwhite segregated schools of the twenty-five largest U.S. metros was six times the rate in predominantly white schools and more than two and a half times the rate in integrated schools (Figure 3.1).[6]

The difference was even greater in the Twin Cities. The poverty rate in nonwhite segregated schools was eight and a half times the poverty rate in predominantly white schools and two and a half times the poverty rate in integrated schools (Figure 3.2).

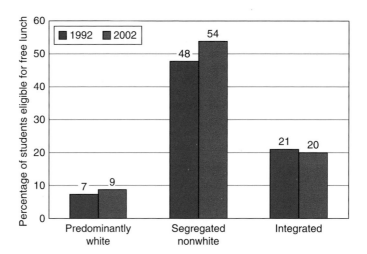

FIGURE 3.1. Percentage of elementary school students eligible for free lunch in the twenty-five largest U.S. metropolitan areas. *Source:* National Center for Education Statistics.

High-poverty schools have a number of characteristics that undermine quality education. These schools typically have less qualified and less experienced teachers due to high turnover among teachers.[7] They tend to offer limited curricula taught at less challenging levels, limiting the educational and occupational options of students.[8] High-poverty schools fail to provide positive peer competition and influence, and produce lower educational expectations.[9]

Attending a high-poverty school harms students because there is a well-documented relationship between poverty in schools and a wide range of negative educational and life outcomes. High-poverty schools produce lower test scores,[10]

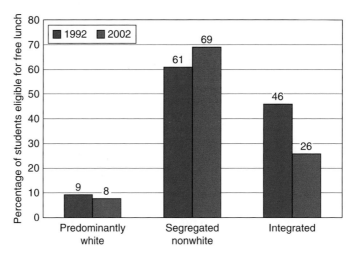

FIGURE 3.2. Percentage of elementary school students eligible for free lunch in the Twin Cities region. *Source:* National Center for Education Statistics.

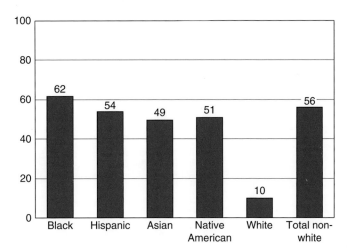

FIGURE 3.3. Percentage of students attending schools with high poverty rates (free and reduced lunch rates greater than 40 percent), 2006–7. *Source:* Minnesota Department of Education.

higher dropout rates,[11] lower college attendance rates,[12] lower earnings later in life,[13] higher imprisonment rates, and greater risk of being poor as adults.[14]

These negative effects are especially harmful to students of color, who are much more likely to attend high-poverty schools than white students. For instance, students of color in the Twin Cities metro are more than five times as likely to attend schools with high concentrations of poverty as white students (Figure 3.3). The numbers are even more striking for very-high-poverty schools. Students of color are almost thirty times as likely as white students to be in schools where more than 75 percent of students are poor (Figure 3.4).

Integrated Schools Help Students

Integrated schools boost academic achievement, attainment, and expectations; improve opportunities for students of color; and generate valuable social benefits. Integrated schools also enhance the cultural competence of white students and prepare them for a more diverse workplace and society.

Attending racially integrated schools and classrooms improves the academic achievement of minority students measured by test scores.[15] Minority students graduating from desegregated schools tend to complete more years of education, have higher college attendance rates, and tend to choose more lucrative occupations in which minorities are historically underrepresented.[16] Minority students who attended integrated schools have higher incomes than their peers in segregated schools.[17] Both white and nonwhite students tend to have higher educational aspirations if they have cross-race friendships.[18]

Students who experience interracial contact in integrated school settings are

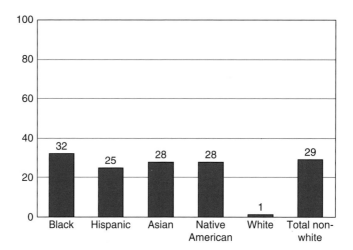

FIGURE 3.4. Percentage of students attending schools with very high poverty rates (free and reduced lunch rates greater than 75 percent), 2006–7. *Source:* Minnesota Department of Education.

more likely to live, work, and attend college in more integrated settings.[19] Integrated classrooms improve the stability of interracial friendships and increase the likelihood of interracial friendships as adults.[20] Interracial contact in desegregated settings decreases racial prejudice among students and facilitates more positive interracial relations.[21] Students who attend integrated schools report an increased sense of civic engagement compared to their segregated peers.[22]

Integrated schools make sense not only from a moral point of view but also from an economic point of view. Giving all children a fair start with the choice to attend opportunity-rich middle-class schools helps create the skilled workforce metropolitan regions need to replace impending baby boom retirements. During a period of skilled labor shortages nationwide, today's students are the next generation of workers who will replace these retirees.[23]

While the retirees of the Twin Cities region will be 90 percent white, the region's next generation of workers will be 75 percent white.[24] Segregated schools and a wide gap between white and nonwhite graduation rates will not yield the skilled workers needed for the region's economy.[25] Even if it is not morally moved by fairness to offer genuine educational opportunity to all children, the region cannot ignore the costs of failing to educate all of its children.

Integrated Schools Help Communities

If school integration involves all of a region's socioeconomic groups, its benefits can extend from students to neighborhoods. When implemented on a metrowide scale, school integration can promote residential integration and enhance neighborhood stability.[26] If parents know their children will attend an effective, integrated school regardless of where they live, they will be less likely to flee racially mixed or changing neighborhoods. This improves the odds that integrated neighborhoods will remain integrated, making it easier to prevent resegregation, neighborhood decline, and the costs associated with segregation.

Between 1970 and 1990, regions with metrowide school desegregation plans had residential segregation decreases twice the national average.[27] Research reported later in this chapter also demonstrates that large-scale school desegregation enhances neighborhood stability. The findings reveal that integrated neighborhoods become more likely to resegregate than to remain integrated once their share of nonwhite residents reaches a relatively modest level. In contrast, in metropolitan areas with large-scale school desegregation plans, integrated neighborhoods are more likely to stay integrated than to resegregate regardless of their initial racial composition.[28]

Metrowide plans prevent two problems that can make small-area plans counterproductive. First, metrowide plans reach beyond areas of residential segregation to include enough schools and students to ensure that all schools can be effective middle-class schools. Second, they prevent the destructive consequence of concentrating desegregation efforts in only a few less-affluent white neighborhoods that often already are struggling to maintain racial balance and stable integration. By asking every school to educate a small share of low-income children, a region prevents further concentration of poor children and eliminates the need for families to flee schools with high poverty enrollments.

In contrast, desegregation plans affecting only a small portion of a metro region, usually a central city, trigger greater residential segregation and worsen school segregation. This is the case because a single-district desegregation effort typically isolates schools where the majority of students are low-income and nonwhite and encourages flight to nearby districts.[29] Desegregation plans covering small geographic areas enable racially identifiable schools to persist.[30] When school desegregation plans do not cover a sufficiently large scale, real estate practices and preferences remain school identified and race based.[31]

Integration Is Necessary for Regional Vitality

Racial and economic segregation destabilizes communities and undermines their economic vitality by triggering a process of disinvestment in these communities. This process of disinvestment reduces housing values and drives out the businesses generating jobs and tax base. In addition, racial segregation and concentration of poverty impose a number of social costs on communities, inflating the expenditure side of their fiscal ledgers. Communities are put in a double bind, as racial segregation and concentration of poverty sap their fiscal capacities while their financial obligations accelerate as a result of growing social costs. As a result, they become less competitive in the marketplace.

Racial and economic segregation affects communities across the entire region, not only the parts of the central cities already hit hard by the disinvestment caused by segregation. Racial and economic segregation is now a regional concern that threatens the strength of many suburban communities. Schools, important indicators of a community's health, are already experiencing social and economic changes that signal growing segregation in many stressed suburbs.

However, stressed suburbs are not alone in experiencing these disturbing segregation patterns. Such patterns are emerging even in some higher-income, suburban job centers that are in close proximity to the stressed suburbs of the region. These suburban communities face the risk of decline unless they can preempt spreading racial and economic segregation before it undermines the vitality of their communities.

A metropolitan area jeopardizes its competitive edge and long-term quality of life by permitting segregation to damage educational opportunity and neighborhood stability in its central cities and adjacent suburbs. The success of a region's central cities and suburbs tends to move together.[32] Vibrant central cities can be engines of growth for metropolitan areas.[33] Population growth and economic growth correlate for both cities and regions.[34] In addition, economic growth in a large central city can have positive spillover effects of 1–2 percent on its suburbs for every 1 percent increase in the central city.[35]

HOUSING SEGREGATION TRENDS

Housing Segregation Continues to Impair Opportunities for People of Color

Scholars celebrating the decline of segregation in neighborhoods have been too hasty. While it is true that the share of segregated neighborhoods declined over time, this decline has been due to a sharp drop in the number of white segregated neighborhoods. This positive trend, however, is accompanied by a more disturbing one: the rapid proliferation of nonwhite segregated neighborhoods.[36] Nonwhite segregated neighborhoods have mushroomed in metropolitan areas as previously integrated neighborhoods became segregated. For residents of color, nonwhite segregated neighborhoods are the new face of segregation.

As a result of these changes in neighborhoods, segregation diminished primarily for white residents but not for people of color.[37] In 2000, two-thirds of blacks and Hispanics and nearly a third of Asians still lived in segregated neighborhood settings (Figure 3.5).[38] In contrast to whites, whose exposure to segregation dimin-

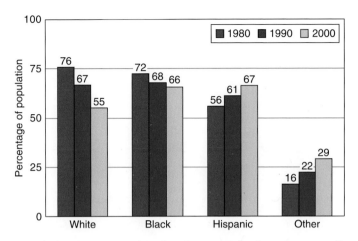

FIGURE 3.5. Population in segregated settings in twenty-five largest metropolitan areas. *Source:* U.S. Census Bureau.

ished, most people of color experienced growing segregation. A new type of residential segregation is emerging for communities of color. As racial diversity expands, different communities of color are mixing with each other in nonwhite segregated neighborhoods and not with whites.

The Twin Cities had smaller shares of people of color living in segregated neighborhood settings, due to its small population of people of color. Segregation trends in the region, however, were far more alarming, especially during the 1990s (Figure 3.6).[39] Segregation climbed much faster among people of color in the Twin Cities than it did in the twenty-five largest U.S. metropolitan areas.

This rapid increase in segregation was not merely the product of a very white

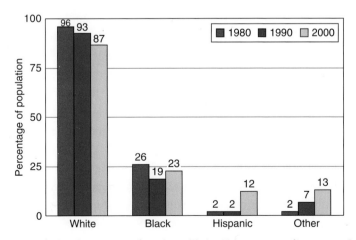

FIGURE 3.6. Population in segregated settings, Twin Cities metropolitan area. *Source:* U.S. Census Bureau.

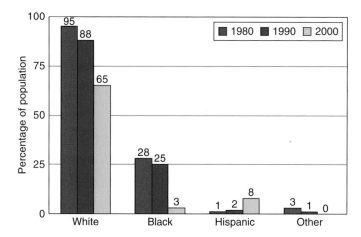

FIGURE 3.7. Population in segregated settings, Portland metropolitan area. *Source:* U.S. Census Bureau.

metro area becoming more racially diverse. Portland, a comparably white metro area, became as racially diverse without experiencing the rapid resegregation the Twin Cities experienced (Figure 3.7).[40] While black segregation climbed in the Twin Cities, black residents in Portland became far more integrated during the 1990s. Similarly, Asians became more segregated in the Twin Cities, while segregation was not an issue for Asians living in Portland. While Hispanic segregation increased in both metros, it did so much more rapidly in the Twin Cities than in Portland.

Neighborhood Integration: A Temporary Phenomenon

Many neighborhoods that are integrated at a given time are actually in transition. Segregated neighborhoods, in contrast, tend to remain segregated. The combination of these two trends limits the extent to which neighborhoods can remain stably integrated.

This is especially a problem in the Twin Cities metro, where neighborhoods are resegregating at a much faster rate than other metros. In the Twin Cities, 56 percent of the neighborhoods that were integrated in 1980 became segregated in 2000, compared to 43 percent in the twenty-five largest U.S. metropolitan areas and only 19 percent in Portland.[41]

At the same time, segregation was more intractable in the Twin Cities region than elsewhere. Of the neighborhoods that were segregated in 1980 in the region, 83 percent were still segregated two decades later, compared to 69 percent in the twenty-five largest U.S. metropolitan areas and 64 percent in Portland.[42]

Racial diversity in neighborhoods is frequently only a temporary stop along the way to persistent segregation. Resegregation rates show a common pattern: as

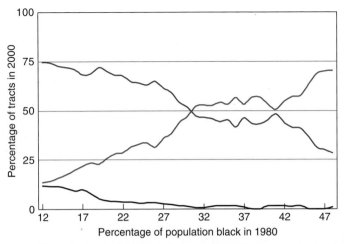

When the black population share was 30 percent or greater in 1980, the tract was more likely to resegregate during the next twenty years than it was to remain integrated.

FIGURE 3.8. Status in 2000 of 1,943 tracts that were white–black integrated in 1980 in the twenty-five largest U.S. metropolitan areas. *Source:* U.S. Census Bureau.

a neighborhood's nonwhite population share increases, it becomes more and more likely to segregate. The higher the share of nonwhite residents in a neighborhood, the greater is the likelihood that the neighborhood could eventually become segregated.

Figure 3.8 illustrates the relationship for neighborhoods that were black–white integrated in 1980. The figure includes three lines, each corresponding to a neighborhood transition status. The blue line shows the percentage of white–black neighborhoods that remained integrated from 1980 and 2000. The red line shows the percentage of white–black neighborhoods that became nonwhite segregated by 2000. Finally, the black line indicates the white–black neighborhoods that became predominantly white in 2000.

On the horizontal axis, the figure shows the black population shares in 1980, ranging from 10 percent to 50 percent because these percentages constitute the lower and upper limits for a neighborhood to be classified as white–black integrated. The solid line crosses 50 percent at 30 percent black. This means that a white–black integrated neighborhood that was 30 percent or more black in 1980 was more likely to make the transition to one of the segregated categories than it was to remain integrated during the next twenty years.

The analysis of racial change in neighborhoods revealed *turnover points* for each of the integrated neighborhood types. Turnover points are the minority share in a neighborhood at which it becomes more likely than not that the neighborhood will resegregate. The analysis shows turnover points are relatively modest—between 24 and 38 percent nonwhite, depending on the type of neighborhood. Neighborhoods that were white–Hispanic integrated in 1980 were more likely to resegregate by 2000 than to remain integrated if their Hispanic share exceeded 24 percent. The corresponding percentages for white–black or multiethnic integrated neighborhoods were 30 and 38 percent.[43]

The Geography of Racial Transition in Neighborhoods

Maps 3.3 through 3.5 document the geography of racial transition in the Twin Cities region from 1980 to 2000. These maps reveal the steady expansion of contiguous, segregated zones in the region's core within which different communities of color are mixing with each other and not with whites. They show the expansion of nonwhite segregated neighborhoods in the region as more and more integrated neighborhoods reach their turnover points over time.

The maps show two processes at work. As nonwhite residents attempt to flee segregated neighborhoods, the integrated rings around the segregated zones expand, especially along the I-94 and I-35 transportation corridors. Subsequently, however, resegregation erodes these integrated rings in areas adjacent to the segregated core, further expanding the size of the contiguous, segregated zones.

The 1980s: Integration of Neighborhoods
Surrounding the Segregated Cores

Despite its limited racial diversity, the Twin Cities already had three relatively small segregated areas in 1980. These segregated zones, near downtown St. Paul and Minneapolis, expanded significantly as the rapid influx of Asians into black neighborhoods created black–other segregated neighborhoods adjacent to the existing segregated black neighborhoods. At the same time, the ring of integrated neighborhoods around these segregated zones expanded.

Black residents left these segregated zones in large numbers to move to more integrated settings. This increased the number of white–black integrated neighborhoods surrounding the segregated zones. Asians also moved in large numbers to both existing segregated zones and to predominantly white and integrated neighborhoods in the urban core. This increased the number of white–other and multiethnic integrated neighborhoods in the region. Finally, Hispanic immigration into the region contributed to the rise in the number of multiethnic integrated neighborhoods around the segregated zones.

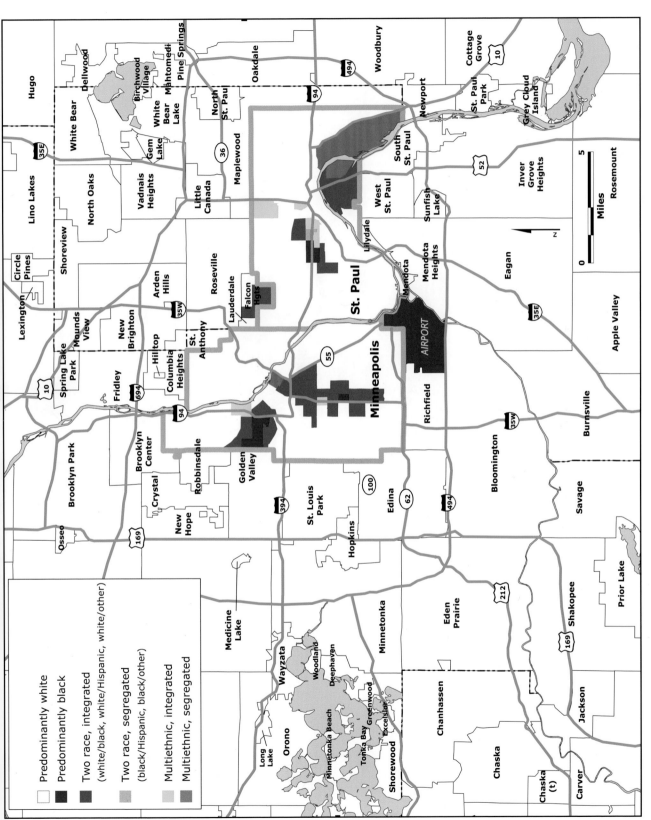

Legend:

- Predominantly white
- Predominantly black
- Two race, integrated (white/black, white/Hispanic, white/other)
- Two race, segregated (black/Hispanic, black/other)
- Multiethnic, integrated
- Multiethnic, segregated

MAP 3.3. Neighborhood classifications in Minneapolis–St. Paul area, 1980. *Source:* U.S. Census Bureau.

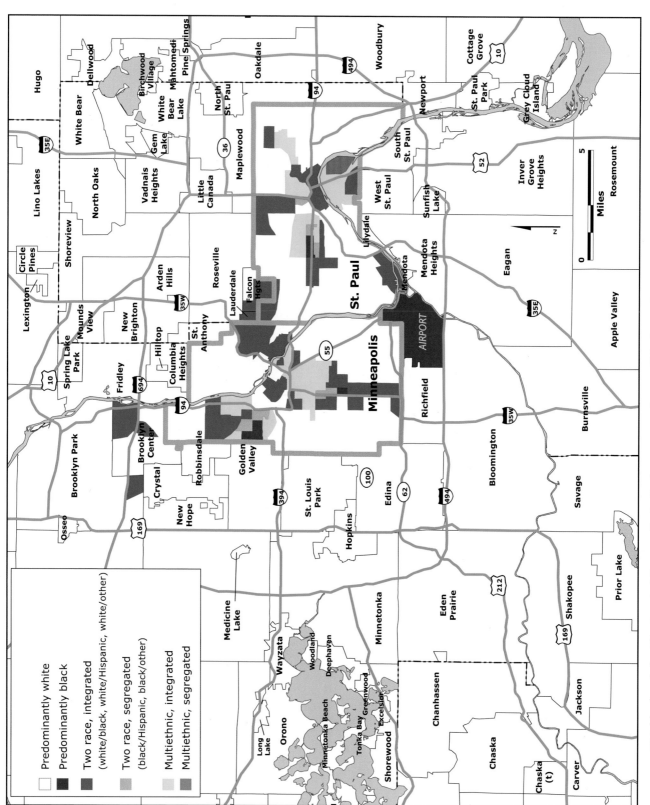

Legend:

- Predominantly white
- Predominantly black
- Two race, integrated (white/black, white/Hispanic, white/other)
- Two race, segregated (black/Hispanic, black/other)
- Multiethnic, integrated
- Multiethnic, segregated

MAP 3.4. Neighborhood classifications in Minneapolis–St. Paul area, 1990. *Source:* U.S. Census Bureau.

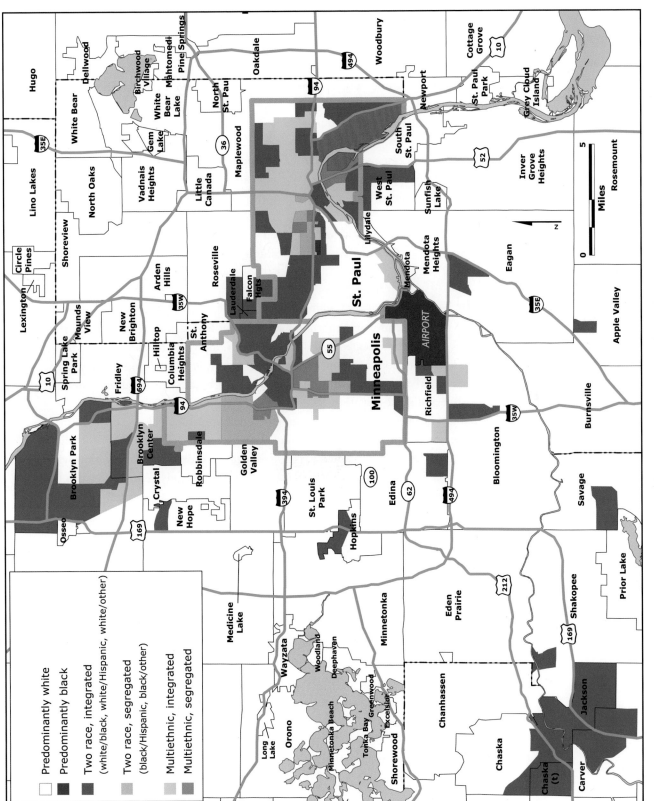

MAP 3.5. Neighborhood classifications in Minneapolis–St. Paul area, 2000. *Source:* U.S. Census Bureau.

The 1990s: Growing Racial Diversity, Resegregation, and the Expansion of the Segregated Cores

By 1990, the multiethnic neighborhoods were the most prominent component of this integrated ring around the segregated zones. These neighborhoods, which made up 43 percent of all the integrated neighborhoods in the region in 1990, were highly prone to resegregation. By the end of the 1990s, more than half of the multiethnic neighborhoods had resegregated, further expanding the segregated urban core.

The accelerated growth of Asian and Hispanic residents in the region's urban core further broadened and transformed the existing segregated zones in the 1990s. The number of Hispanics living in the Twin Cities region nearly tripled while the number of Asians almost doubled during the decade. This rapid immigration enlarged existing segregated zones and dramatically changed their racial composition.

2000: The New Face of Segregation—Multiethnic Segregated Neighborhoods

At the end of the decade, neighborhood segregation had a multiethnic face in the Twin Cities. Multiethnic segregated neighborhoods, along with black–other neighborhoods, were the most common forms of segregated neighborhoods. The size of the segregated urban core continued to expand both because of resegregation and because of persisting segregation.

While the racial composition of segregated neighborhoods changed over time, their segregated status remained constant. Over four-fifths of neighborhoods that were segregated in 1980 remained segregated after two decades. Segregation was even more persistent in nonwhite segregated neighborhoods. All of the neighborhoods that were nonwhite segregated in 1980 were still segregated in 2000. In contrast, more than half of the neighborhoods that were integrated became segregated.

SCHOOL SEGREGATION TRENDS

Intensifying School Segregation Erodes Opportunities for Students of Color

School segregation rates, measured very broadly, were largely unchanged in the twenty-five largest U.S. metropolitan areas. In both 1992 and 2002, nearly two-thirds of all schools in these metros were segregated (Table 3.2). However, this was the result of two trends: declining shares for white segregated schools but increasing shares for nonwhite segregated schools.

While the number of white segregated schools declined, the number of nonwhite segregated schools increased rapidly between 1992 and 2002. As a result, school

TABLE 3.2   Distribution of school types, 1992 and 2002

	% White segregated		% Nonwhite segregated		% Integrated	
	1992	2002	1992	2002	1992	2002
25 largest U.S. metros	39	28	27	37	35	35
Twin Cities	79	54	2	20	22	26

Source: National Center for Education Statistics.

segregation increased for all students of color while it decreased for white students. In 2002, three-quarters of all black and Hispanic students were segregated, in contrast to less than half of white students (Figure 3.9).[44]

Just as in neighborhoods, a new type of segregation is emerging in the schools of the twenty-five largest U.S. metros. Students of color are increasingly attending nonwhite segregated schools with other students of color and not with whites. As white students experience further integration, more and more students of color attend segregated schools.

The pattern in the Twin Cities was very similar. Although overall segregation declined a bit, school segregation for students of color got dramatically worse during the decade. The number of nonwhite segregated elementary schools in the Twin Cities jumped from 9 to 109 in just one decade, while the number of students of color attending these segregated schools skyrocketed from 2,832 in 1992 to 29,788 in 2002.

The share of black elementary school students in segregated school settings

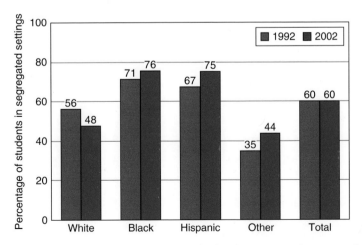

FIGURE 3.9. Percentage of students in segregated school settings in the twenty-five largest U.S. metropolitan areas. *Source:* National Center for Education Statistics.

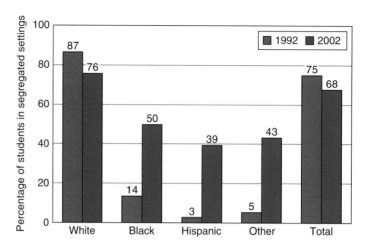

FIGURE 3.10. Percentage of students in segregated school settings in the Twin Cities metropolitan area. *Source:* National Center for Education Statistics.

more than tripled from 14 percent in 1992 to 50 percent in 2002. The share of Hispanic and other students attending segregated school settings jumped even more—increasing from 3 percent to 39 percent for Hispanics, and from 5 percent to 43 percent for other students of color (Figure 3.10).[45]

As a result of this growing segregation, the exposure of students of color to white students declined sharply during the 1990s. Table 3.3 breaks down the percentage of white students in the school attended by the average student of color for each racial/ethnic group. As the table shows, the exposure of all students of color to white students declined dramatically from 65 to 44 percent within just one decade.

Students of color in the Twin Cities region still attend segregated schools with

TABLE 3.3   **Exposure indexes for Twin Cities schools**

	1990	2000
Black Students with white students	59	38
Hispanic Students with white students	74	55
Asian Students with white students	70	48
All students of color with white students	65	44

Note: The exposure index shows the percentage of white students in the school attended by the average student of color.

Source: State University of New York at Albany, Lewis Mumford Center for Comparative Urban and Regional Research.

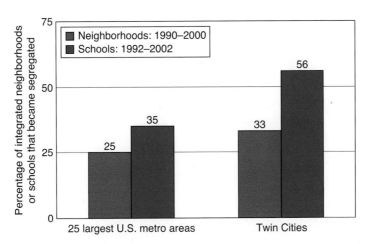

FIGURE 3.11. Average resegregation rates in neighborhoods (1990–2000) vs. schools (1992–2002). *Sources:* U.S. Census Bureau; National Center for Education Statistics.

high concentrations of poverty while a vast majority of white students attends schools with very low poverty rates. Rapid resegregation of integrated schools contributes to this unfortunate reality.

School Resegregation Is Severe

Resegregation is a clear threat to the stability of integrated schools in the twenty-five largest U.S. metros. As a result, students of color who leave segregated schools for integrated ones often find themselves eventually trapped once again in segregated schools. Meanwhile, once segregated, schools hardly ever reintegrate.

Integrated schools in the Twin Cities were exceptionally unstable when compared to integrated schools in other metro areas. Fifty-six percent of the region's integrated schools resegregated after a decade, compared to 35 percent in the twenty-five largest U.S. metros and 33 percent in the Portland metro.[46] Meanwhile, more than three-quarters of the Twin Cities schools that were segregated in 1992 remained segregated a decade later.[47]

Resegregation trends are more pronounced in schools than in neighborhoods. One in three integrated schools in the twenty-five largest U.S. metros resegregated after a decade, compared to only one in four neighborhoods (Figure 3.11). In the Twin Cities, this difference was even greater. While only a third of integrated neighborhoods resegregated from 1990 to 2000, 56 percent of the schools that were integrated in 1992 became segregated in 2002.

Schools, like neighborhoods, had turnover points—minority shares at which integrated schools become more likely than not to resegregate. These turnover points also varied according to the racial and ethnic makeup of the school. For all

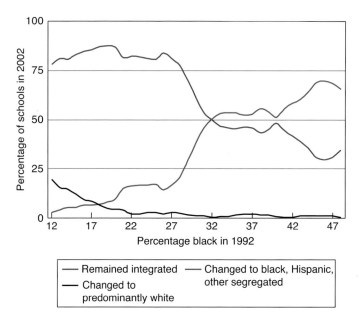

FIGURE 3.12. Status in 2002 of 1,669 schools that were black–white integrated or multiethnic integrated in 1992 in the twenty-five largest U.S. metropolitan areas. Schools that were more than 31 percent black in 1992 were more likely to resegregate than to remain integrated by 2002. *Source:* National Center for Education Statistics.

integrated schools, however, resegregation was likely to occur once the share of minority students exceeded relatively modest levels. Schools that were white–black integrated in 1992 were more likely to resegregate by 2002 than to remain integrated if their black student share exceeded 31 percent in 1992 (Figure 3.12). The corresponding percentages for white–Hispanic and multiethnic integrated schools were 36 and 48 percent.[48]

The Geography of Racial Transition in Schools

Maps 3.6 and 3.7 illustrate the spatial pattern of school segregation in the Twin Cities in 1992 and 2002. These maps show the rapid proliferation of nonwhite segregated schools in the region's core due to the resegregation of previously integrated schools. As the schools in the region's urban core rapidly segregated, students of color attempted to escape segregated urban schools. This created a new wave of school integration in suburbs farther away from the urban core.

Rapid Resegregation in the Urban Core

In 1992, there were only two small, but noticeable, clusters of segregated schools in the Twin Cities region, both in Minneapolis. There were only a few nonwhite

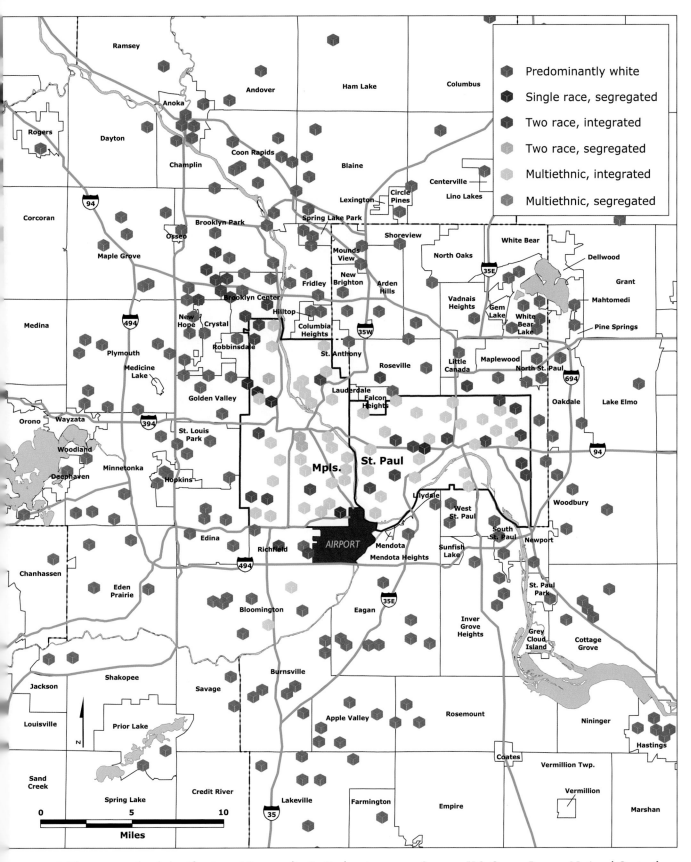

MAP 3.6. Elementary school classifications, Minneapolis–St. Paul region, 1992. *Sources:* U.S. Census Bureau; National Center for Education Statistics.

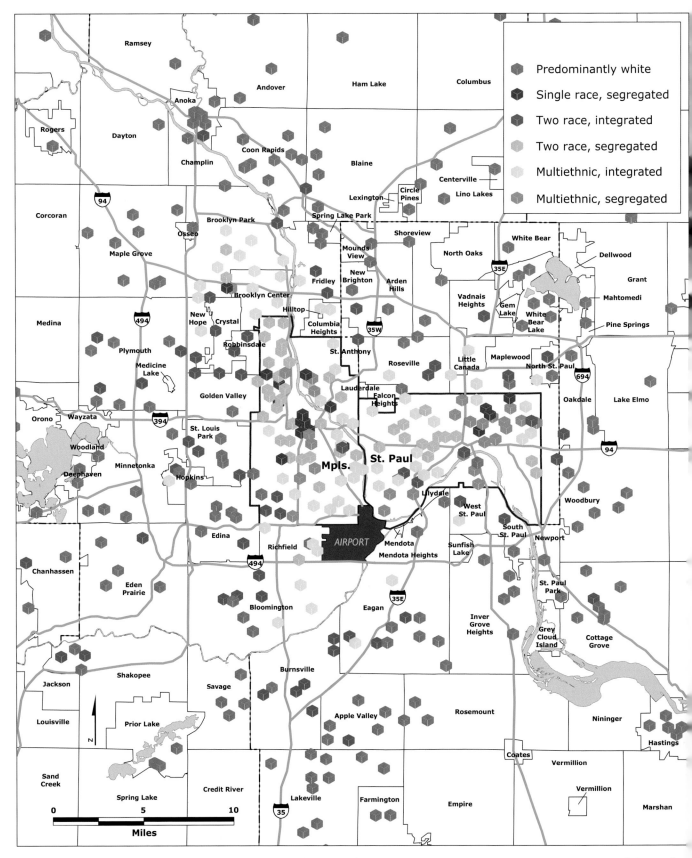

MAP 3.7. Elementary school classifications, Minneapolis–St. Paul region, 2002. *Sources:* U.S. Census Bureau; National Center for Education Statistics.

segregated schools in the region outside of these two clusters. The majority of the schools in the region's urban core were multiethnic integrated schools. Two-race integrated schools surrounded these multiethnic integrated schools at the fringes of the central cities and in the first-ring suburbs.

These integrated schools, however, were so unstable that by 2002 the urban core had large, contiguous clusters of nonwhite segregated schools. The multiethnic integrated schools in the urban core resegregated rapidly: within a decade, 57 percent became segregated. The two-race integrated schools surrounding the urban core also resegregated quickly. Nearly two-thirds of white–other integrated schools and half of white–black integrated schools resegregated during the 1990s. Almost all of the rest of these two-race integrated schools became multiethnic integrated— a school type that is itself highly prone to resegregation.

Resegregation of integrated schools triggered a rapid rise in the number of black–other and multiethnic segregated schools in the urban core. The number of black–other segregated schools jumped from three in 1992 to thirty-nine in 2002. More than one-quarter of integrated schools in the region became black–other segregated, and most were clustered around north Minneapolis and in and around downtown St. Paul.

There was a similar rise in the number of multiethnic segregated schools. While the region had no multiethnic segregated schools in 1992, it had thirty-one of them in 2002. More than one-fifth of integrated schools became multiethnic segregated, and most of these schools were in Minneapolis and east St. Paul.

Within just a decade, school segregation had spread out from two relatively small clusters of nonwhite segregated schools to cover almost the entire urban core of the region.

The Scope of Integration Moves from the Core to the Suburbs

As the schools in the region's urban core rapidly segregated, a new wave of school integration started in the suburbs. Resegregation in the core changed the geographic distribution of integrated schools, pushing them farther into first- and second-ring suburbs away from the urban core. In 1992, over four-fifths of the integrated schools were in the central cities. A decade later, less than two-fifths were in St. Paul or Minneapolis.

Two-race integrated schools led the expanding ring of school integration in the region. These schools rapidly proliferated in the first-ring suburbs and started appearing in second-ring suburbs. Closer to the core, in the first-ring suburbs a different type of racial transition took place. Many of the two-race integrated schools in these suburbs became multiethnic integrated by 2002. Noticeable multiethnic integrated school clusters emerged especially in the northern and southern first-ring suburbs of Minneapolis.

It is likely that these first-ring suburbs are going through the first stages of what has already happened in the central cities. In the central cities, most multiethnic integrated schools transitioned into multiethnic segregated schools during the 1990s. Given this instability, multiethnic integrated clusters in first-ring suburbs are likely to turn into clusters of multiethnic segregated schools unless regional measures are taken to keep the school system integrated. For example, signs of resegregation are already visible in a newly emerging cluster of segregated schools in Brooklyn Park.

THE DYNAMICS OF NEIGHBORHOOD AND SCHOOL SEGREGATION

Neighborhood and School Segregation Are Intertwined

The dynamics of neighborhood and school segregation reciprocally shape each other. It is well understood that segregated neighborhoods produce segregated schools because schools draw students from surrounding neighborhoods. The fact that resegregation trends in schools can intensify the instability of neighborhoods has not yet been as widely recognized. The Twin Cities case is illustrative.

Racial transition in schools outpaced racial transition in neighborhoods by a large margin in both the urban core and inner suburbs of the Twin Cities region (Maps 3.4–3.7). School resegregation clearly had detrimental consequences for neighborhoods. In fact, the racial dynamics of schools were largely driving the changing spatial pattern of residential segregation. A comparison of the 1992 school map (Map 3.6) with the 2000 neighborhood map (Map 3.5) shows strong geographic overlap between the racial makeup of schools in 1992 and the racial makeup of neighborhoods in 2000.

These maps demonstrate that the location of racially integrated schools in 1992 was a good predictor of the racially integrated neighborhoods in 2000. They also show that the location of racially segregated school clusters in 1992 was by and large a good predictor of the racially segregated cores in 2000. This strong geographic overlap between the racial makeup of schools in 1992 and the racial makeup of neighborhoods in 2000 testifies to the intertwined nature of segregation in schools and neighborhoods.

How Racial Segregation Happens— Unstable Integration Followed by Resegregation

Segregated schools and neighborhoods are tightly linked in a self-perpetuating neighborhood cycle. Segregated neighborhoods produce segregated schools and segregated schools create segregated neighborhoods. Real estate agents and families use the socioeconomic and racial composition of schools to evaluate the desirability of the surrounding neighborhoods. Perceptions regarding the quality of schools influence people's neighborhood choices. The process of segregation and resegregation usually works as follows.

Middle-class nonwhite families are usually the first minorities to move to slightly integrated suburbs. When middle-class residents of color reach a critical mass in a predominantly white neighborhood and its associated schools, the neighborhood starts to resegregate. Middle-class white families with school-age children are usually the first to leave the neighborhood because they perceive increasing percentages of students of color in area schools as a sign of school decline.

These perceptions are not formed in a vacuum. They are shaped by the steering practices of real estate agents. Real estate agents use schools as a proxy for signaling the quality of the neighborhoods to white residents to steer them away from integrated neighborhoods.[49] Rather than telling home purchasers to avoid certain neighborhoods because of their racial composition, many real estate agents tell them to avoid certain schools. This common practice of using schools as a proxy for neighborhood racial composition spreads misconceptions regarding school quality and racial composition and becomes the basis of geographic steering.

The families who leave integrated neighborhoods are not replaced by other white households. This happens because real estate agents steer potential white home purchasers away from integrated neighborhoods on the claim that "the schools are bad." Meanwhile, they recommend and market these very same schools as "integrated schools" to minority residents to steer them into these neighborhoods.[50] Through their steering practices, real estate agents start changing the racial composition of the neighborhood.[51]

Initially, the change in the racial composition of the neighborhood does not imply a change in its socioeconomic composition. But as steering practices further tilt the racial balance of these integrated neighborhoods, demand for housing declines along with home prices because middle-class families of color are not numerous enough to sustain the demand in the neighborhood. As home prices go down, low-income residents of color soon move into the housing left behind by white flight. As a result, the socioeconomic composition of the area and its schools gradually changes along with its racial composition.

Meanwhile, businesses and jobs soon follow the white middle-class, taking with them a portion of the tax base and further destabilizing these neighborhoods. As student poverty rates climb, the quality of the schools declines—making the presumed link between the racial composition of schools and their quality a self-fulfilling prophecy. Soon the middle-class minorities who initially moved into these neighborhoods find themselves in the same kind of neighborhoods they left behind.[52] The process of brief residential integration followed by gradual resegregation in neighborhoods and schools comes full circle.

WHY SEGREGATION PERSISTS

Racial segregation is not simply the result of private residential preferences. It is not simply the "natural state" of the housing market neutrally sorting people according to their socioeconomic status. In fact, there is nothing neutral about the ways housing markets operate. The discriminatory policies and practices of a number of public and private actors shape the institutional structure of housing markets. Racial segregation in housing markets emerges as a result of these discriminatory policies and practices.

On the private side, steering by real estate agents, as well as the discriminatory business practices of financial institutions, mortgage brokers, and insurance agents, perpetuates segregation. On the public side, housing policies of the federal government, boundary decisions of school districts, and land use policies of municipalities all contribute to racial segregation. This means that segregation is not written in stone; it can be reversed by eliminating the policies and practices that generate it.

Residential Preferences and Segregation

People's preferences regarding the race of their neighbors influence where they live.[53] As a result, people's residential preferences impact patterns of segregation. Racial segregation, however, is not caused by the desire of people of color to self-segregate and live with neighbors of the same racial and ethnic background.[54] Preference surveys show that most people of color prefer to live in integrated neighborhoods with a substantial group of same-race/co-ethnic neighbors.[55] These surveys also find whites to be less tolerant of integration than nonwhites.[56]

The preferences of whites play a more significant role than the preferences of nonwhites in shaping the actual racial composition of neighborhoods.[57] Analyses of actual mobility patterns confirm the findings of preference surveys and reveal the importance of white avoidance of integrated neighborhoods in creating residential segregation.[58] Recent research further demonstrates that altering the residential preferences of whites toward integration dramatically affects the actual racial composition of their neighborhoods.[59]

People's preferences toward integration impact the possibility and stability of neighborhood integration to a significant extent. But what shapes these preferences? Literature points to ethnocentrism and perceived class differences as the main factors that shape people's preferences for segregation.[60] Recent research, however, shows that racial stereotypes shape these preferences far more extensively than either ethnocentrism or perceived class differences.[61]

Negative stereotypes about other racial and ethnic groups influence the preferences of people from all races and ethnicities. In fact, studies find a racial rank order of "out-groups" as potential neighbors commonly held by people of all races and ethnic backgrounds.[62] In this racial hierarchy of desirable neighbors, whites followed by Asians are the most desirable and blacks the least, while Hispanics fall somewhere between Asians and blacks. These stereotypes play an important role in perpetuating residential segregation by reducing people's openness to integration.[63]

Socioeconomic Status and Segregation

Many studies demonstrate that racial and ethnic segregation results at least in part from socioeconomic differences across groups.[64] After all, race and income are still highly correlated in the United States. Since people sort themselves by income to some extent, differences in the socioeconomic status of different races result in some racial and ethnic segregation, even in the absence of prejudice and discrimination.

Studies also reveal, however, that the extent to which one's socioeconomic status has an impact on one's neighborhood depends on racial or ethnic status. Socioeconomic status plays a more important role in shaping the residential locations of Hispanics and Asians in comparison to African Americans.[65] For African Americans, race/ethnicity still plays a far more important role than socioeconomic status.

In metropolitan areas, race/ethnicity and income both shape the residential choices of people; but they do not do so equally. Racial/ethnic segregation accounted for two-thirds of residential segregation in 2000, while socioeconomic segregation accounted for only one-third. While the role of income in determining the residential choices of people increased from 1970 and 2000, race/ethnicity still remains the main determinant of where one lives.[66]

Steering Practices of Real Estate Agents and Segregation

While housing discrimination has been declining in recent years, people of color still face significant levels of discrimination in the housing market.[67] Potential homebuyers and renters from different races and ethnic backgrounds face distinct types of discrimination.[68] The types of discrimination faced by people of color have also been changing over time. While outright discrimination in the form of denying information on available units to people of color has declined, other forms of more subtle discrimination such as geographical steering have been on the rise.[69]

As metropolitan areas became more racially diverse, the number of racially mixed and minority suburban neighborhoods increased. Some researchers argued that the greater number of such neighborhoods contributed to the growing willingness of real estate agents to provide minority homeowners with information on additional units.[70] By the same token, however, the rapid growth in the number of racially mixed and minority suburban neighborhoods enhanced the ability of real estate agents to engage in racial steering.[71]

A 2002 U. S. Department of Housing and Urban Development (HUD) study documents significant levels of discrimination through three distinct forms of racial steering: information steering, where whites get information about a wider variety of neighborhoods; segregation steering, where whites get directed to more predominantly white neighborhoods; and class steering, where whites are directed to more affluent neighborhoods.[72] Similarly, in April 2006, the National Fair Housing Alliance (NFHA) completed a three-year, twelve-city housing discrimination study.[73] Using 145 sales tests in three geographic regions across the country, the NFHA found three patterns of discrimination: outright denial of service to blacks and Latinos; significant financial incentives offered to whites but not to blacks or Latinos; and steering of potential purchasers on the basis of race or national origin.

The NHFA tests revealed steering at a rate of 87 percent among testers who were given an opportunity to see homes.[74] Testers were generally steered to neighborhoods based on race or national origin, as well as religion and family status. The NHFA also reports that real estate agents use schools as proxy for racial or ethnic composition of neighborhoods and communities. Rather than telling white testers to avoid certain neighborhoods because of racial or ethnic composition, many real estate agents would tell the tester to avoid certain schools—schools that were racially identifiable.[75] Similar tests by Margery Austin Turner and Stephen Ross found statistically significant steering against blacks and Hispanics in rental markets and significant steering against blacks in housing markets.[76]

Discrimination in housing and financing markets costs blacks and Hispanics, on average, more than $3,000 per household whether or not they actually encounter discrimination.[77] These costs are reflected in the length and breadth of housing searches that blacks and Hispanics must endure because of discrimination in the market. Minorities encounter other, uncounted social costs because of discrimination—loss of proximity to opportunity, benefits of diverse neighborhoods, and costs of racial isolation. Furthermore, the neighborhoods where blacks buy homes "tend to be less affluent, have poorer quality public services and schools, and experience more crime and social disorganization compared to the suburbs that comparable whites reside in."[78]

New Forms of Discrimination in Mortgage Markets

Discrimination in mortgage markets continues to restrict the residential choices of minority residents.[79] While the share of home purchase loans going to minority and low-income households and communities went up noticeably since the 1990s, private lenders continue to deny mortgages to potential minority homebuyers at disproportionate rates.[80] Moreover, the recent growth in the amount of loans going to minority and low-income households accompanied the rise of a dual mortgage market, which introduced new and more subtle forms of racial discrimination into mortgage markets.[81]

The dual mortgage market is the result of growing segmentation in mortgage markets, where low-income and credit-impaired borrowers are served with a different mix of mortgage products and by different types of lenders than those in mainstream markets. Typically, products that serve these borrowers—such as subprime loans— have higher interest rates and less favorable terms than conventional prime loans that serve the mainstream market. These products are usually provided by mortgage brokers, who operate outside the existing federal regulatory framework.

While some low-income households benefited from these mortgage products, the targeted marketing of high-cost loans to minority communities resulted in a remarkable lack of prime loans even among the highest-income minority borrowers.[82] This discrepancy partly results from the fact that, on average, minorities have lower credit scores. However, borrower race and neighborhood racial composition still appear to be significantly linked to access to prime loans even after controlling for risk factors that legitimately affect access.[83]

Moreover, the disproportionate servicing of minority households by mortgage lenders that operate outside the regulatory framework of mortgage markets created new avenues for racial discrimination in mortgage lending. Differential estimates of home price and total loan amount based on race and ethnicity constitute the most serious recent form of discrimination in mortgage lending.[84]

Mortgage brokers operating in secondary markets face an incentive structure that rewards overextension of mortgage lending. A growing body of evidence suggests that the presence of such incentives and the absence of a federal regulatory framework encourage mortgage brokers to engage in predatory lending practices, which have a disproportionate impact on minority applicants and neighborhoods.[85] These practices result in the concentration of foreclosures among minority households and in minority neighborhoods, further contributing to racial disparities in wealth accumulation.[86]

Maps 3.8 and 3.9 show the remarkable overlap between the geographic distribution of home mortgagors of color and subprime mortgages in the Twin Cities region. While not all subprime loans are predatory loans, all predatory loans are subprime loans; and most predatory loans end up in foreclosures. Maps 3.8 and 3.10 demonstrate the overwhelming concentration of foreclosures in the minority neighborhoods of the Twin Cities.

New Forms of Discrimination in Insurance Markets

Discrimination in insurance markets is an often unrecognized barrier to home ownership among minority households. Access to homebuyers' insurance is essential for homeownership. Prospective buyers cannot have access to loans without proof of insurance, and without loans it is almost impossible to purchase a home. Racial discrimination is a continuing presence in the property insurance industry.[87]

While the days of overt discrimination in the form of neighborhood redlining are over, racial profiling in the property insurance industry effectively acts as a subtler form of redlining to make property insurance less accessible and less affordable to minority residents.[88] Linguistic profiling, the identification of a person's

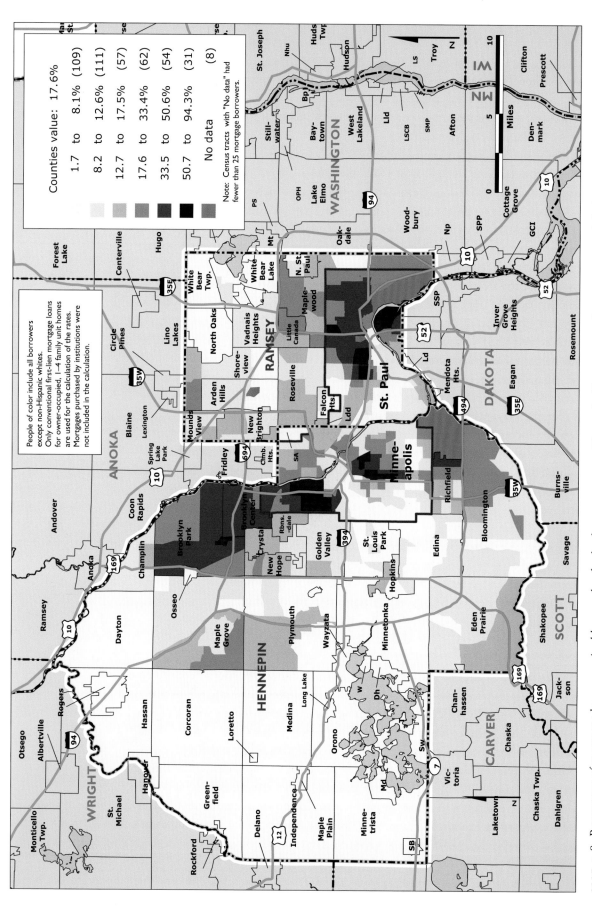

MAP 3.8. Percentage of mortgage loans acquired by people of color by census tracts, Hennepin–Ramsey counties, 2004–6. For full place-names, see Map 3.2. *Source:* Federal Financial Institutions Examination Council, Home Mortgage Disclosure Act data.

Counties value: 17.6%

1.7 to 8.1%	(109)
8.2 to 12.6%	(111)
12.7 to 17.5%	(57)
17.6 to 33.4%	(62)
33.5 to 50.6%	(54)
50.7 to 94.3%	(31)
No data	(8)

Note: Census tracts with "No data" had fewer than 25 mortgage borrowers.

People of color include all borrowers except non-Hispanic whites. Only conventional first-lien mortgage loans for owner-occupied, 1–4 family unit homes are used for the calculation of the rates. Mortgages purchased by institutions were not included in the calculation.

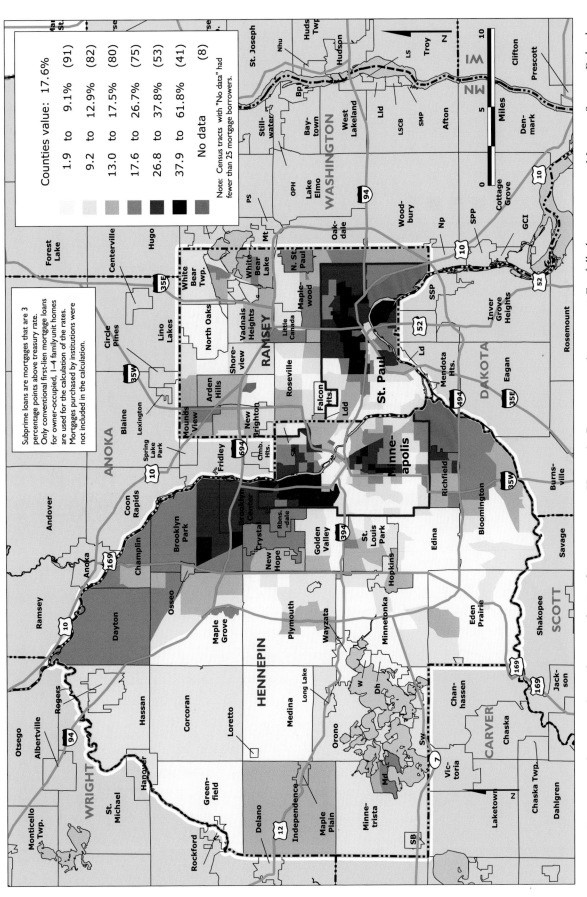

Counties value: 17.6%

1.9	to	9.1%	(91)
9.2	to	12.9%	(82)
13.0	to	17.5%	(80)
17.6	to	26.7%	(75)
26.8	to	37.8%	(53)
37.9	to	61.8%	(41)
		No data	(8)

Note: Census tracts with "No data" had fewer than 25 mortgage borrowers.

Subprime loans are mortgages that are 3 percentage points above treasury rate. Only conventional first-lien mortgage loans for owner-occupied, 1–4 family-unit homes are used for the calculation of the rates. Mortgages purchased by institutions were not included in the calculation.

MAP 3.9. Percentage of mortgage loans that are subprime by census tracts, Hennepin–Ramsey counties, 2004–6. For full place-names, see Map 3.2. *Source:* Federal Financial Institutions Examination Council, Home Mortgage Disclosure Act data.

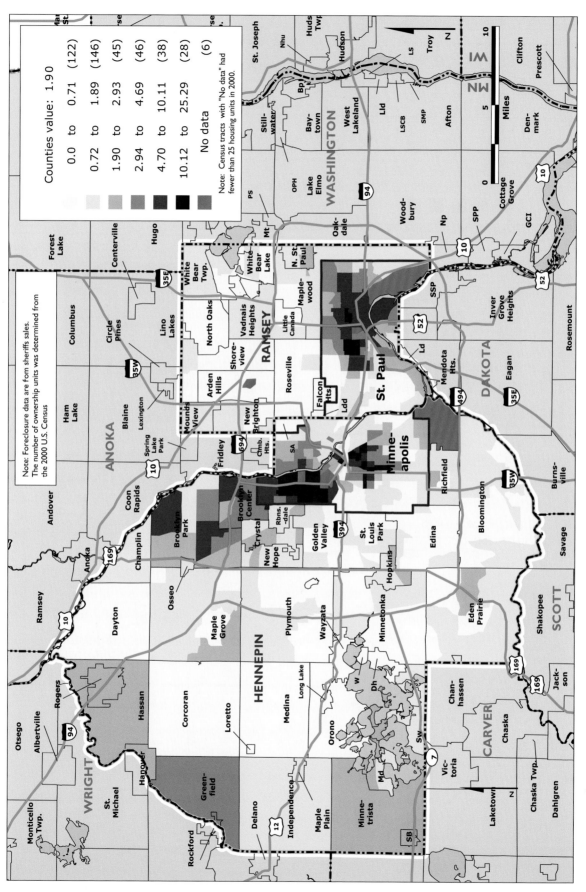

MAP 3.10. Foreclosures per one hundred owner housing units by census tracts, Hennepin–Ramsey counties, 2007. For full place-names, see Map 3.2. *Sources:* Hennepin and Ramsey County Sheriff Departments; University of Minnesota Center for Urban and Regional Affairs; U.S. Census Bureau.

Counties value: 1.90

	0.0	to	0.71 (122)
	0.72	to	1.89 (146)
	1.90	to	2.93 (45)
	2.94	to	4.69 (46)
	4.70	to	10.11 (38)
	10.12	to	25.29 (28)
	No data		(6)

Note: Census tracts with "No data" had fewer than 25 housing units in 2000.

Note: Foreclosure data are from sheriffs sales. The number of ownership units was determined from the 2000 U.S. Census

race from his or her speech patterns and the use of that information to discriminate on the basis of race, is also prevalent in the home insurance industry.[89] Moreover, underwriting guidelines used by many insurance companies have disparate adverse impacts on communities of color.[90]

Public Housing Programs and Segregation

The placement of affordable housing is a critical part of neighborhood segregation. Concentrating affordable housing in racially segregated or poor neighborhoods deepens segregation. By encouraging construction of affordable housing units in such neighborhoods, many government housing programs contribute to residential segregation.

In 1970 HUD created site and neighborhood standards to ensure that its housing programs complied with the requirements of the 1968 Fair Housing Act. These standards explicitly prohibit the construction of new affordable housing in racially segregated neighborhoods.

Since the early 1970s, however, HUD has weakened the enforcement of these antisegregation measures by establishing major exceptions to the standards.[91] These exceptions significantly eroded the integration potential of existing affordable housing programs such as public housing and Section 8.

Meanwhile, many new affordable housing programs that emerged in the past few decades do not have measures to prevent segregation in neighborhoods. In fact, programs such as the Low Income Housing Tax Credits (LIHTC) and the Community Reinvestment Act intensify segregation by providing incentives to construct low-income housing in poor neighborhoods, which tend to be racially segregated.[92]

HUD also carved out significant exceptions to the site and neighborhood standards in several of its important new programs, such as Hope VI and Housing Opportunities Made Equal (HOME). As a result, these programs tend to perpetuate residential segregation in metropolitan areas as well.[93]

The Low-Income Housing Tax Credit Program

The LIHTC program is the largest federal program that supports building low-income housing.[94] Created by the Tax Reform Act of 1986, the program provides more than $5 billion a year for the construction, acquisition, or rehabilitation of low-income housing.[95] The program allows investors in residential rental property to claim tax credits for the development or rehabilitation of property to be rented to low-income tenants.[96] While the Internal Revenue Service regulates the distribution of tax credits, state housing finance agencies make the decision to fund specific projects and administer the allocation of tax credits.

The program provides incentives to promote the construction of low-income housing in "qualified census tracts," which HUD defines as tracts "in which 50 percent or more of the households have an income which is less than 60 percent of the area median gross income for such year or which has a poverty rate of at least 25 percent."[97] As a result, many state agencies, including Minnesota's, have allocated significant numbers of credits to areas with high concentrations of minorities and people with low incomes.[98]

While the distribution of LIHTC units in the Twin Cities metro is less concentrated in the core than in most metropolitan areas, the location of these units appears to be pro-integrative in only a very few places (see Map 3.12 below).[99] Since the inception of the LIHTC program, approximately five thousand LIHTC units have been located in the Twin Cities suburbs and an equal number have been located in the central cities.[100] Although this fifty-fifty split seems "fair," it does not reflect the fact that Minneapolis and St. Paul represent just 23 percent of the region's total population.

Map 3.11 shows the location of LIHTC units in Minneapolis and the surrounding school districts. It is clear that these units are disproportionately located in Minneapolis neighborhoods, where the share of minority and low-income residents is already high. The map also highlights the concentration of LIHTC units in "qualified census tracts," demonstrating how the program's incentives to locate units in these tracts contribute to residential segregation in the Twin Cities metropolitan area.

The distribution of households of color who live in the LIHTC units further contributes to residential segregation in the metro. As Map 3.12 shows, this distribution is heavily skewed toward the central cities and stressed inner suburbs. Among the households living in LIHTC units, people of color have been much more likely to locate in the cities than in the suburbs. For instance, 65 percent of the black households in LIHTC units are in the central cities, compared to just 50 percent of the total LIHTC units in the cities.

The skewed distribution of households of color within LIHTC units worsens racial segregation, not only in neighborhoods, but also in schools. Map 3.13 shows the racial composition of the LIHTC unit occupants with children by unit site. The map demonstrates that the majority of the LIHTC households of color with children are located in racially segregated central cities as well as in stressed suburbs that are in racial transition.

Map 3.14 shows the highly segregated nature of the elementary school attendance zones in areas where the majority of the LIHTC households of color with children reside.

Overall, these patterns mean that affordable housing provided under the LIHTC program concentrates low-income households in racially segregated or transitioning neighborhoods and further intensifies school segregation by creating more racially identifiable schools with very high poverty enrollments.

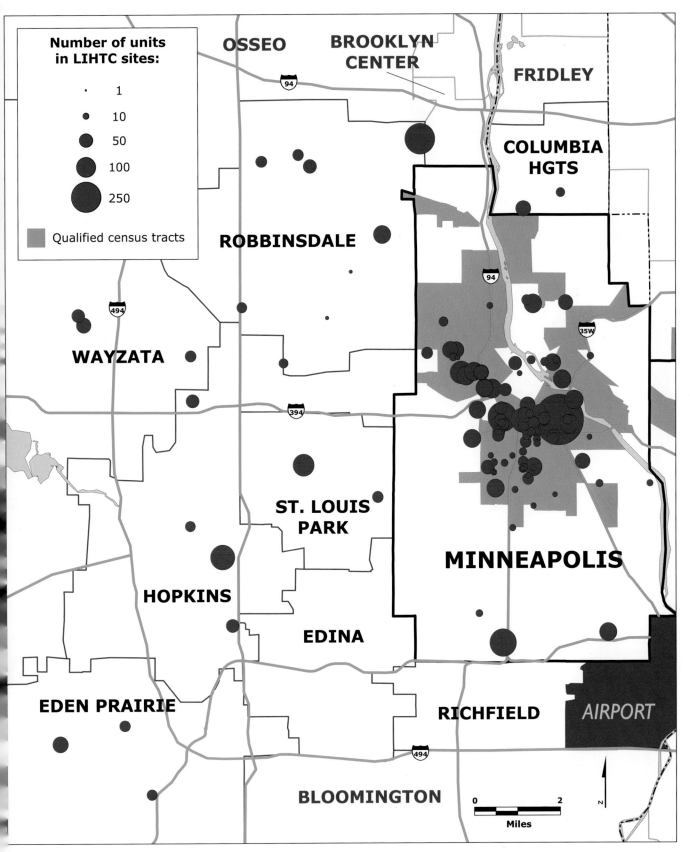

MAP 3.11. Low Income Housing Tax Credit (LIHTC) housing sites in Minneapolis and surrounding suburban school districts, 2005. *Source:* HousingLink Inventory of Assisted Rental Housing.

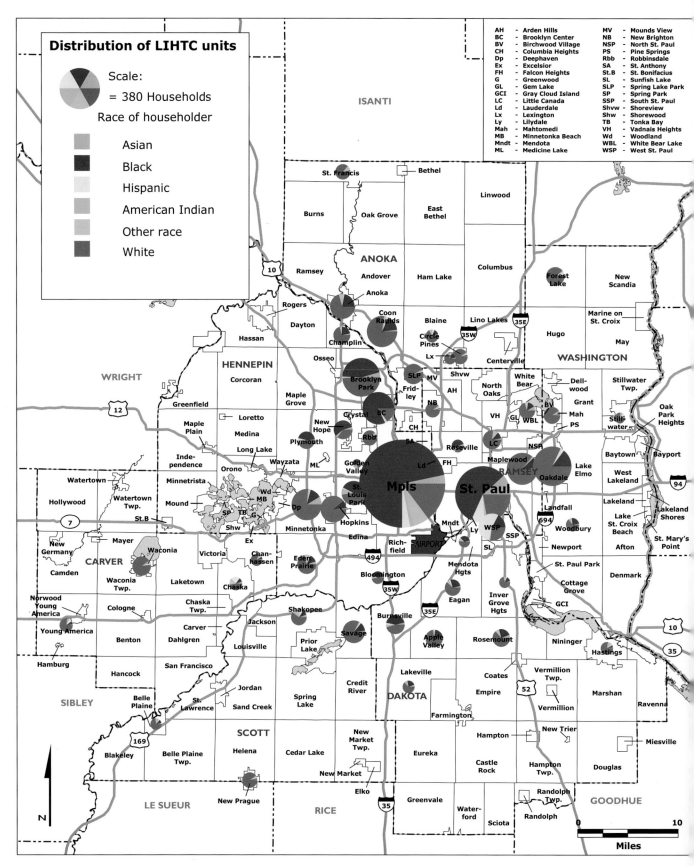

MAP 3.12. Racial composition of Low Income Housing Tax Credit survey units by county subdivision, Minneapolis–St. Paul region, 2002. *Source:* Minnesota Housing Finance Agency.

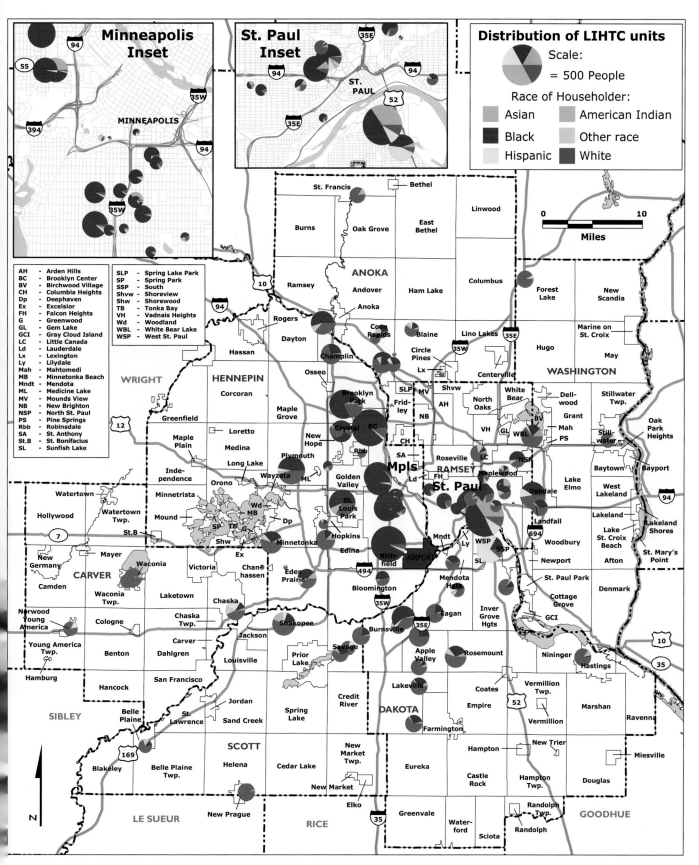

MAP 3.13. Racial composition of Low Income Housing Tax Credit households with children by survey site location, Minneapolis–St. Paul seven-county region, 2002. *Sources:* Minnesota Housing Finance Agency; Metropolitan Council; The Lawrence Group.

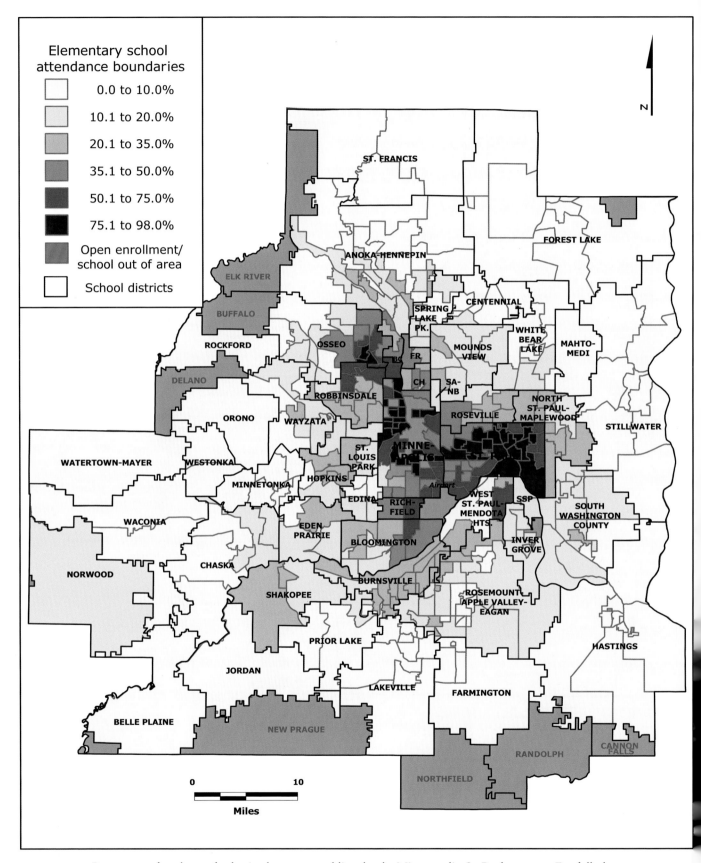

MAP 3.14. Percentage of students of color in elementary public schools, Minneapolis–St. Paul, 2002–3. For full place-names, see Map 3.2. *Sources:* Minnesota Department of Education; Minnesota Department of Land Management.

The Section 8 Program

The distribution of low-income housing under the Section 8 program also contributes to residential segregation in the Twin Cities region. Like the LIHTC units, low-income housing units and vouchers provided by the Section 8 program are located disproportionately in the central cities and stressed inner suburbs, where the shares of minority and low-income residents are already high. Similarly, the distribution of households of color who have access to housing through the Section 8 program is also heavily skewed toward the central cities and stressed inner suburbs.

The project-based Section 8 program was the primary federal low-income housing program from 1974 to 1983. Under this program, HUD provided assistance to public housing authorities and private owners for twenty to forty years after construction or substantial rehabilitation of low-income rental units.[101] During the nine years it was in effect, the project-based Section 8 program produced more than 750,000 new or substantially renovated subsidized housing units nationwide, an average of about 83,000 per year, many of which still function as low-income housing today.[102]

Map 3.15 shows the size, location, and racial composition of project-based Section 8 units in the Twin Cities region. Project-based Section 8 units are disproportionately in the central cities and inner-ring suburbs. In 2004, the central cities had 4,079—55 percent—of the region's 7,484 project-based Section 8 units. Map 3.15 also illustrates that the distribution of residents of color in these units was skewed toward the central cities and inner suburbs. For instance, while 55 percent of the project-based Section 8 units were in the central cities, 69 percent of project-based Section 8 households who were black were located in the central cities.

The other Section 8 program—the voucher program—was designed to promote housing choice and mobility for low-income residents. Despite this intention, it also contributes to segregation by concentrating low-income residents in racially segregated, high-poverty neighborhoods. Under the Section 8 voucher program, the administering public housing authority (PHA) pays a landlord the difference between 30 percent of household income and the PHA-determined payment standard—about 80 to 100 percent of the fair market rent. Section 8 vouchers are portable; a tenant who receives a voucher in one jurisdiction can take it to another for use.[103]

In 2004, there were 17,109 Section 8 vouchers used for housing in the Twin Cities. The vouchers contributed to residential segregation because, as Map 3.16 shows, they were used disproportionately in the central cities and stressed suburbs. While the central cities contained less than 23 percent of the population, they had 47 percent of the metro's Section 8 vouchers.

The program also further concentrated minorities in the central cities and stressed inner suburbs because households of color using the vouchers were more likely to locate in these areas (Map 3.17). Fifty-eight percent of black households

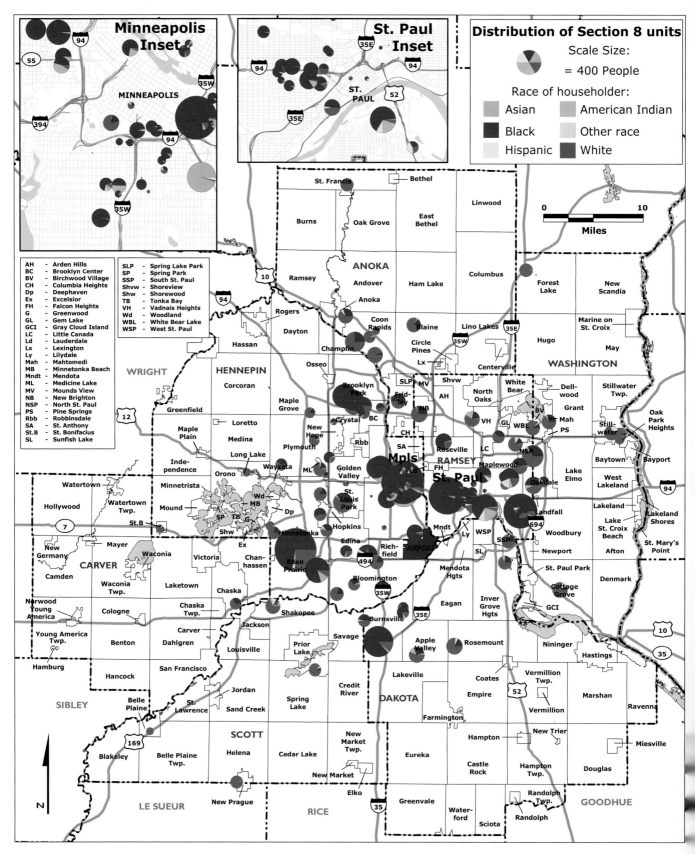

MAP 3.15. Racial composition of project-based Section 8 family households by site location, Minneapolis–St. Paul seven-county region, 2004. *Sources:* Minnesota Housing Finance Agency; Metropolitan Council; The Lawrence Group.

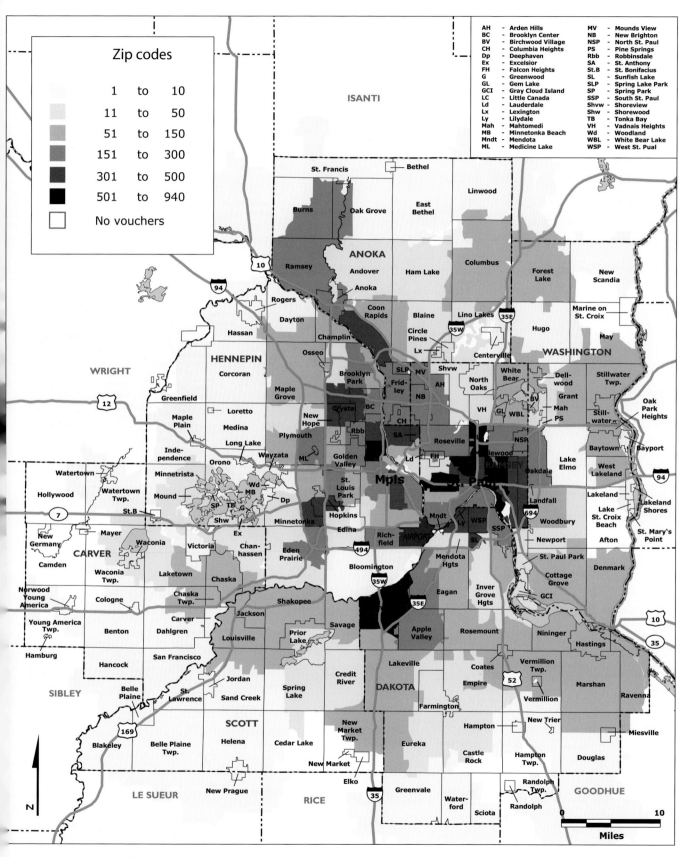

MAP 3.16. Number of Section 8 voucher householders by zip codes, Minneapolis–St. Paul seven-county region, 2004.
Sources: U.S. Department of Housing and Urban Development; Metropolitan Council; The Lawrence Group.

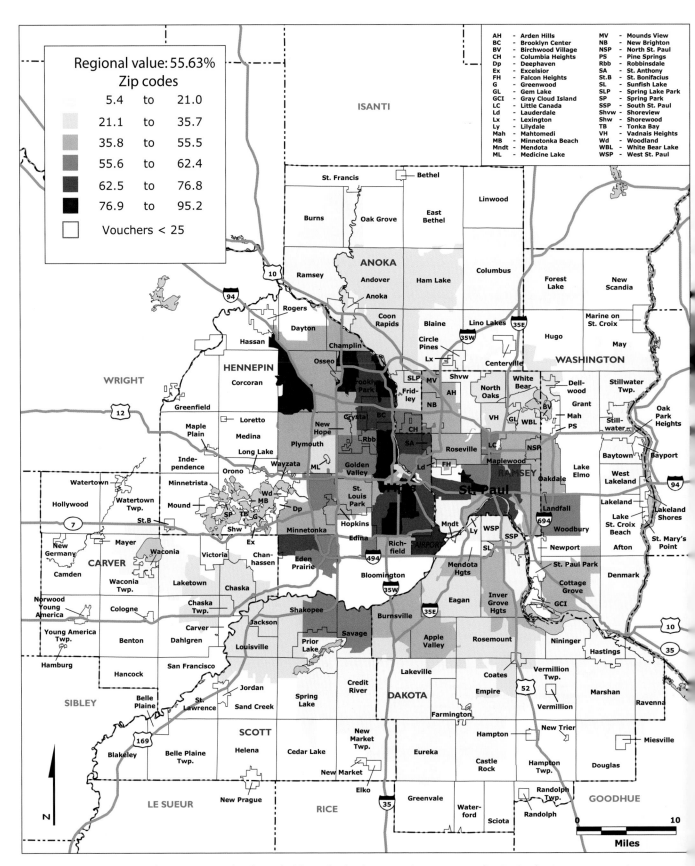

MAP 3.17. Percentage of Section 8 voucher householders of color by zip codes, Minneapolis–St. Paul seven-county region, 2004. *Sources:* U.S. Department of Housing and Urban Development; Metropolitan Council; The Lawrence Group.

used their vouchers in the central cities—in contrast to 46 percent of all the Section 8 voucher users who located in the central cities.

The skewed distribution of project-based Section 8 units and Section 8 vouchers not only leads to further concentrations of race and poverty in neighborhoods but also generates more racially identifiable schools with high poverty enrollments. By locating low-income residents of color and their children in highly segregated elementary school attendance zones, the Section 8 program intensifies school segregation in the region. A comparison of Maps 3.14, 3.15, and 3.16 establishes the geographic overlap between the distribution of Section 8 housing and the location of segregated school attendance zones.

As the federal housing programs and the state housing agencies that administer these programs concentrate affordable housing units in the central cities and stressed inner suburbs, they skew the regional distribution of affordable housing, intensify the spatial mismatch of jobs and housing in the region, and undermine the employment opportunities of people of color and low-income residents.[104] Map 3.18 illustrates the uneven geographic distribution of affordable housing units in the Twin Cities region, with the highest affordability rates concentrated in the core.

Figure 3.13 breaks down the availability of affordable housing by various community types in the region. While low-opportunity communities such as the central cities and the stressed suburbs had almost half of the region's total housing stock, they had nearly three-quarters of the region's housing units affordable to people

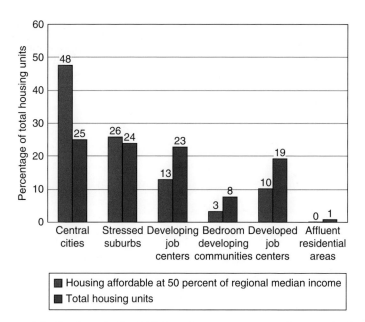

FIGURE 3.13. Distribution of affordable housing across community types in the Twin Cities, 2000. *Source:* U.S. Census Bureau.

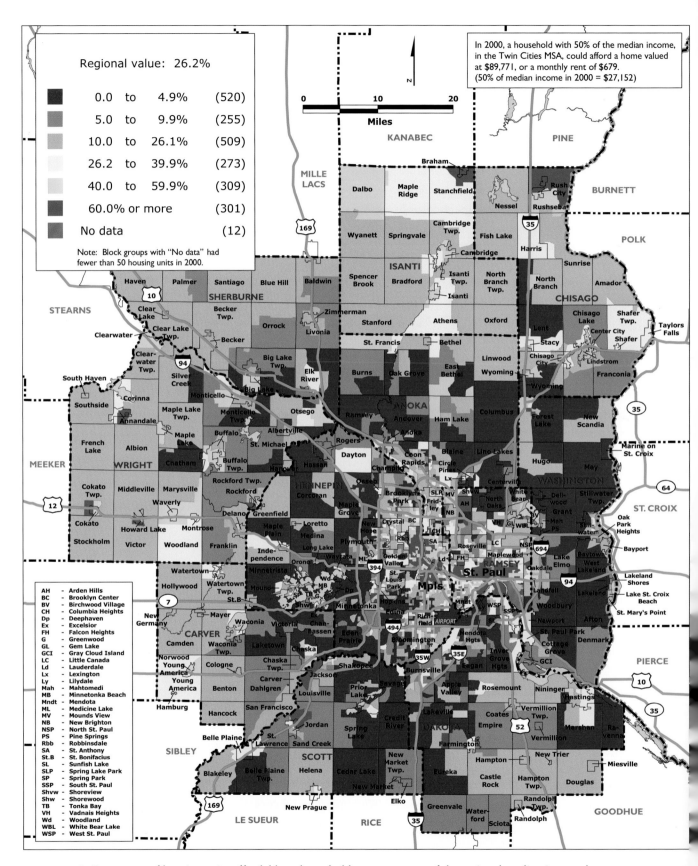

MAP 3.18. Percentage of housing units affordable to households at 50 percent of the regional median income by census block group, Minneapolis–St. Paul region, 2000. *Source:* U.S. Census Bureau.

with 50 percent of the regional median income. In contrast, the moderate- and high-opportunity communities had just a quarter of the region's affordable housing compared to half of the region's total housing units.

SCHOOL DISTRICT DECISIONS AND SEGREGATION

The decisions of school districts directly affect the racial distribution of schools and can often contribute to school segregation. School districts can intensify school segregation in a number of ways. They can manipulate their attendance zones in a racially segregative fashion. They can strategically select the sites of new schools in ways that foster racial segregation within districts. They can build racially identifiable schools. They can use mobile classrooms to segregate the student body. They can manipulate student transfer and transportation policies in ways that intensify districtwide racial segregation. They can use student, faculty, and staff assignment policies to racially segregate their students.

In Minnesota, although the state legislature has the overall power over Minnesota schools, in practice, local school boards shape the attendance boundaries of local schools. School districts redraw school attendance boundaries sporadically, when population or financial pressures demand opening a new school, closing an old school, or shifting students from one school to another. Few school districts in Minnesota have redrawn school attendance boundaries for the sole purpose of segregating students. However, when school districts shift boundaries, they often do so in ways that intensify preexisting racial isolation.

Discontinuous Attendance Zone Boundaries and Racial Segregation in the Rosemount–Apple Valley–Eagan School District

School districts can intensify racial segregation in their jurisdiction by gerrymandering attendance zone boundaries. Gerrymandering practices are often evident in discontinuous attendance zone boundaries, which either segregate whites from students of color or students of color from white students. Map 3.19 shows two attendance zones with discontinuous boundaries in the Rosemount–Apple Valley–Eagan School District: Cedar Park and Shannon Park.

Cedar Park Elementary School was racially isolated from the rest of the Rosemount–Apple Valley–Eagan School District from 2004 until 2007. Cedar Park's attendance zone was a discontinuous area consisting of a neighborhood with a high density of subsidized housing in the south and a manufactured home park in the north. These specific boundaries played an important role in making Cedar Park a racially isolated school.

The neighborhood surrounding Cedar Park is home to some of Apple Valley's public housing, which contains a disproportionate number of children of color. The

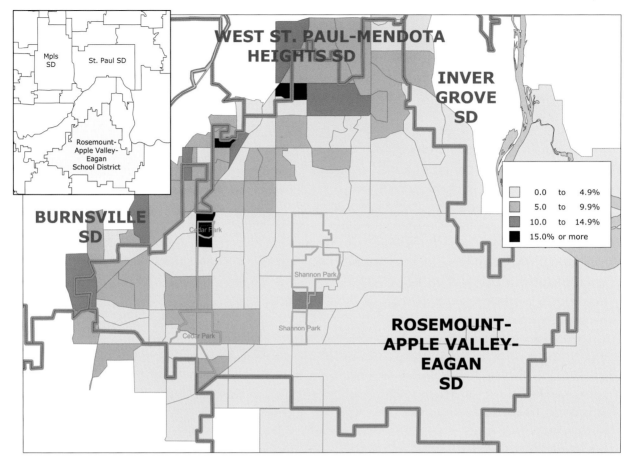

MAP 3.19. Selected elementary school attendance zones, 2004–7, and the percentage of non-Asian minority popula-tion for block group in the Rosemount–Apple Valley–Eagan School District, 2000. *Source:* U.S. Census Bureau and Rosemount–Apple Valley–Eagan School District.

manufactured home park in the northern part of the district is also home to many families of color. The inclusion of the manufactured home park and the public housing in the school attendance zone meant that a disproportionately high number of poor students and students of color attended Cedar Park.

The manufactured home park in the northern part of the district was closer to a number of other Apple Valley elementary schools. Yet, students living in this manufactured home park were bused across the district to Cedar Park. Simply al-lowing these students to attend an elementary school closer to their home would have decreased the racial isolation of the school. Moving the boundary would have been relatively easy, should have reduced transportation costs, and was the action requested by the Minnesota Department of Education.

The Minnesota Department of Education notified the district that the Cedar Park Elementary School was racially isolated in 2004. While the district continued to receive funding from the Integration Revenue Program, it did not take any action to integrate Cedar Park until 2006. In March of 2006, the attendance boundary committee suggested one attendance boundary change to facilitate school integration. Among the students who lived in the manufactured home park, newly entering kindergarten students who do not have an older sibling at Cedar Park would have a choice of three schools closer to their homes than Cedar Park. First graders without a sibling at Cedar Park could also choose to leave the school.[105]

The school district also created a magnet program at Cedar Park as part of its integration plan. However, the integrative potential of the Cedar Park science and math magnet program was diluted by the fact that the district created three magnet programs at the same time. In the fall of 2007, a small number of kindergarteners from the manufactured home park started school at other area schools. Nonetheless, Cedar Park has continued to become more racially isolated and most of the children from the manufactured home park continue to attend the school.

School districts are aware of intradistrict segregation—the Minnesota Department of Education makes districts aware of any school within district boundaries that has a student of color population 20 percent greater than other district schools.[106] School districts are also usually aware that school segregation often violates civil rights laws.[107] Even though districts get extra funding for segregated schools through integration revenue funding, many suburban districts do attempt to desegregate the district when the opportunity to adjust school attendance boundaries arises. These well-meaning attempts to create integrated schools often fail in the face of parental opposition. The process usually takes the following path. As more residents of color move to suburbs, some schools begin to have a sizable population of students of color. Eventually, the share of students of color in some of these schools exceeds the share of students of color in other schools in the district by 20 percent—the state's definition of a racially isolated school. When these districts need to change their school attendance boundaries—in response to changing student populations—the districts are aware that they should not make boundary decisions that increase the isolation of these schools. When the districts bring the possibility of integrative boundary decisions to the public, however, the white community comes out in force against "busing"—even though children had been previously bused across the district without public uproar.

White parents then put pressure on the school boards to adopt a "neighborhood schools" model, which supposedly would make sure that children attended the school closest to their residence. Frequently, these boundary decisions cement racial dividing lines within communities: while schools on one side of the line, the white side, prosper, schools on the other side do not. Some community members push for integrated schools, with the weak support of the department of school choice in the Minnesota Department of Education. These voices, however well they articulate the law and ethics of school desegregation, cannot overcome the demand for segregative school boundary decisions and the comfort of school boards with giving-in to the will of the community.

New School Site Decisions and Increasing Segregation in the Osseo School District

Recent experience in the Osseo School District provides an excellent example of the potential and the difficulties associated with boundary-based approaches to school desegregation by individual school districts. Osseo is one of the largest school districts in the state, and has a large achievement gap between white students and students of color. Osseo is also largely segregated, with seventeen of its twenty-six schools racially isolated. Today, many of Osseo's eastern schools are nearly all minority, while the schools in the western part of the district are nearly all white. Schools in the eastern part of the district are correspondingly high poverty and low performing, while schools in the west are low poverty and well known for their high test scores. Brooklyn Park (a stressed, first-ring suburb) is on the eastern end of the district, while Maple Grove (a developing job center) is on the western end of the district.

Demographic differences between these suburbs surely account for some of the racial division within the district. However, the school district's school construction practices and its school attendance zones also contributed to the segregation of schools in the district. Between 1990 and 1995, Osseo built four elementary schools on the western edge of the school district. As the Osseo School District constructed all-white schools on the western edge of the district, neighborhoods surrounding the then-integrated schools on the eastern end of the district began the process of becoming predominantly nonwhite, segregated neighborhoods.

Until 1995, children were bused across the district to balance enrollment and to prevent overcrowding. This meant that the district bused white children from the western part of the district to the eastern part of the district, creating schools that were more integrated than they would have been without the busing. Once schools were built on the western edge of the district, the school district redrew its attendance boundaries. Initially, the school board attempted to use the boundary changes to integrate schools. It ordered the newly formed Boundary Committee to "not consider any proposal that will increase the number of students of color in high concentration schools" and instructed the committee "to search for reasonable and workable boundary arrangements that have potential to reduce current concentrations of students of color."[108]

This charge proved highly contentious, and the Boundary Committee eventually recommended, and the school board adopted, a plan creating "neighborhood schools," which did nothing to integrate the district.[109] Students of color who wanted to attend the newly built, mostly white schools in the western part of the district had to "open enroll" into those schools.[110] After the move to neighborhood schools, school segregation rapidly increased.

In 1999, Osseo again redrew its school attendance boundaries and, again, some school board members sought to ensure that the new school boundaries would not worsen racial segregation.[111] The majority of the school board, however, refused to consider the racial impact of attendance boundary changes even though the school district knew its decisions likely violated state and federal desegregation laws.[112] While the school board eventually acknowledged that any boundary decision had to be in accordance with federal and state civil rights law, it nevertheless announced that the new attendance boundaries would place children in one of the buildings closest to their residences.[113] The resulting school attendance boundaries did nothing to integrate the district and maintained noncontiguous boundaries on both the east and the west sides of the district.[114] The final plan, however, did not bus students from east to west, fulfilling the prime demand of the Maple Grove parents who opposed school desegregation.[115]

The Minnesota Department of Education first notified Osseo that it had racially isolated schools in 1997. Osseo has received school integration revenue funding every year since. Osseo, unlike many Minnesota school districts, has used some of that money to transport students across the district in an attempt to integrate schools.[116] The Department of Education, although it was aware of the racially charged controversy surrounding Osseo's school attendance boundaries, did not request that Osseo integrate its schools through changes in attendance boundaries until 2006.[117]

In 2008 Osseo School District proposed to close two schools on the verge of becoming segregated and to turn an identifiably white elementary school on the western end of the district into a racially diverse magnet school. Maple Grove parents strongly oppose both of these proposals, which have the potential to address some of the racial segregation in the Osseo school district.[118] In the face of strong parental opposition, and without a state mandate to integrate, Osseo's plan may fail.

Even when school districts intend to integrate their schools, desegregating school districts one district at a time is very difficult. In fact, white parents often threaten to send their children to an adjacent school district through open enrollment when faced with school districts that pursue desegregation strategies in the Twin Cities. Hopkins School District provides the most recent example of the difficulty of desegregation under the threat of white flight.

In early 2006, Hopkins school district administrators discovered a $600,000 shortfall in the district's budget due to declining enrollments.[119] The district decided to close Katherine Curren Elementary School, the smallest and the most racially isolated school in the district.[120] The school board considered four options for redrawing school attendance boundaries in the wake of the elementary school closing.

The most integrative of the options would have dramatically increased the number of students of color at Glen Lake Elementary School in Minnetonka—the whitest school in the district.[121] White parents from Glen Lake threatened to open-enroll their kids out of Hopkins into the predominantly white Minnetonka School District unless the integrative option was taken off the table. Both Glen Lake parents, who opposed an influx of students of color into their school, and Katherine Curren parents, who hoped to save their school, opposed the most integrative option.[122] The school board consequently chose the school attendance boundary that produced the least integration.[123]

Open enrollment in Minnesota means that students who have the means to transport themselves across school district lines can leave integrating or resegregating schools. As white students leave school districts to avoid integrated schools, the districts themselves become segregated. This pattern of white flight is not unique to the Twin Cities. Crossing school boundaries by white students to avoid integrated schools has dramatically increased in the nation since the 1970s. As a result, between-district segregation replaced within-district segregation as the main source of school segregation in most metropolitan areas.[124] As Map 3.20 shows, today the greatest school segregation in the Twin Cities area is interdistrict, rather than intradistrict.

The implication is that school integration can only be stable when it is done at a regional scale. Attempts by individual school districts to desegregate their schools are unlikely to succeed when adjacent predominantly white school districts continue to present avenues for white flight. Only regionwide integration districts could effectively reduce the fuel for white flight. Moreover, within sufficiently large integration districts, incentives are needed to encourage all school districts in the region to work together to create strategic plans and share resources to effectively integrate the region's schools.

FRAGMENTATION, MUNICIPAL LAND USE POLICIES, AND SEGREGATION: EXCLUSIONARY ZONING

The fragmentation of local governments fosters racial and economic segregation in metropolitan areas.[125] Municipal fragmentation directly contributes to residential segregation by encouraging exclusionary zoning practices among municipalities.[126]

Through their land use and zoning decisions, municipalities exert a significant influence on a municipality's housing stock and in effect decide what types of people can reside within their boundaries. For instance, municipalities can effectively exclude low-income residents of all races from residing within their boundaries by severely limiting the land zoned for multifamily development or by requiring very large (and therefore more expensive) homes and lots.[127]

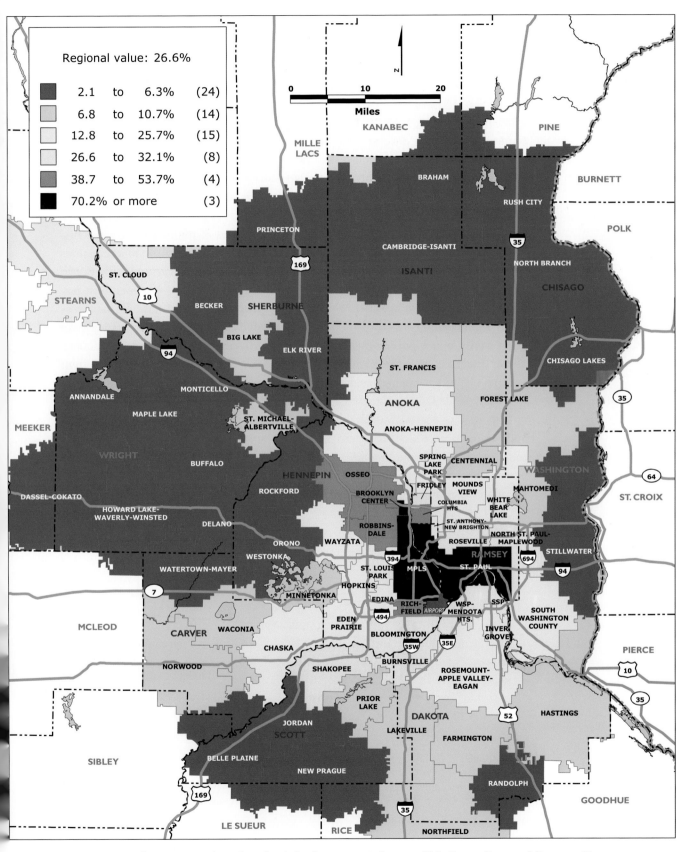

MAP 3.20. Percentage of minority students by school district, 2005–6. *Sources:* U.S. Census Bureau; Minnesota Department of Education.

Municipalities across the nation have fiscal incentives to exclude affordable housing from their jurisdiction through their zoning codes—a practice often called exclusionary zoning. In fact, most suburban municipalities frequently pursue such exclusionary zoning practices to expand their property tax bases. High-end residential and commercial developments augment a locality's tax base by more than the cost of local services they require. Large and expensive homes generate more property tax revenues per household for municipalities than multifamily units. Besides, residents of multifamily units, usually people with relatively modest incomes, tend to make demands for costly services while the residents of expensive homes rarely rely on public services and hardly add to the expenses of municipal governments.

When municipal fragmentation is high (i.e., when there are more municipalities competing for new development), competition for development is especially fierce. In the face of competition from other municipalities, local governments must pay extra attention to the net effect that any new development will have on local revenues and expenditures—on whether the proposed development "pays its way." In other words, municipal fragmentation creates additional incentives for exclusionary zoning practices by intensifying competition among municipalities. To the extent that municipalities pursue exclusionary zoning practices, they directly contribute to (economic and racial) residential segregation.[128]

Figure 3.14 demonstrates the relation between local government fragmentation and the extent to which white and black residents are segregated from each other in the fifty largest metropolitan areas. The figure confirms that metros with high levels of municipal fragmentation tend to experience higher levels of racial segregation. It is noteworthy that the two metropolitan areas with the most extensive regional

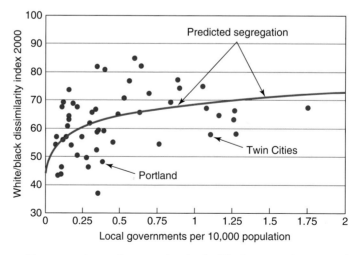

FIGURE 3.14. Fragmentation and segregation in the fifty largest U.S. metropolitan areas. *Sources:* U.S. Census Bureau; Mumford Center, State University of New York at Albany.

planning systems in the country—Twin Cities and Portland—exhibit less segregation than is predicted by their level of fragmentation.

Racial segregation continues to undermine equality of opportunity in most metropolitan areas. It undermines the life chances of people of color by forcing them
to live in low-opportunity neighborhoods and by exiling students of color to high-
poverty schools. Increasing racial diversity in metropolitan areas does not have to
result in growing racial and economic segregation and disinvestment in various
types of communities. The following section focuses on policies and remedies that
can reverse segregation in neighborhoods and schools.

LEGAL REMEDIES

More than fifty years ago, the U.S. Supreme Court in *Brown v. Board of Education*
struck the "evil of segregation down," and federal courts began remedial actions
"to eliminate from the public schools all vestiges of state-imposed segregation."[129]
Today, federal courts have sharply reduced the scope and extent of desegregation
remedies, and school segregation for minority students is quickly increasing. The
increasing number of nonwhite segregated schools is leading to an increase in residential segregation for families of color, cementing these families in high-poverty
neighborhoods and schools.

Students confined to these segregated, high-poverty schools have turned to state
courts. In state courts, students assert both their state equal protection rights and
their fundamental state rights to an education.[130] Further, in state courts, students
can use evidence of unequal opportunity in segregated schools to show violations
of these rights. School integration plans imposed by state courts—and, even more
promising, voluntarily adopted plans—are a way to avoid the limitations of federal
school desegregation remedies.

The Limited Scope of Federal Remedies under the Constitution

The Hope of *Brown v. Board of Education*

The Supreme Court declared segregation in education unconstitutional in 1954, but
held off on ordering desegregation until Brown II in 1955.[131] It was not until the
1960s that the Court began aggressively to define what it meant by "desegregation."
In *Green v. County School Board* in 1968, the Court held that a federal court order
for desegregation must take all steps necessary to desegregate schools by effectively
ordering the desegregation of student assignments, transportation, physical facilities, extracurricular activities, faculty assignments, and resource allocation.[132]

The Court expanded the scope of desegregation orders in 1971, when, in *Keyes
v. School District No. 1,* it held that Northern school district policies that created
segregated schools constituted unconstitutional segregation.[133] For the next twenty

years, federal courts ordered the desegregation of school districts across the country and monitored districts' compliance with the desegregation plans.

Two subsequent decisions, *Milliken v. Bradley* in 1974 and *School Board of Oklahoma City v. Dowell* in 1991, substantially limited the scope of desegregation orders and, eventually, brought the era of court-ordered and -monitored school desegregation to an effective end. As federal courts ended their oversight of segregation in U.S. schools, segregation rapidly increased.

Milliken: Restricting the Reach of Federal Court–Ordered Remedies

Federal desegregation law began breaking *Brown*'s promise just three years after *Keyes.* In its 1974 Detroit desegregation case, *Milliken v. Bradley,* the Supreme Court essentially limited federal remedies for school segregation to the area within the boundaries of a single school district.[134] After *Milliken,* to obtain an interdistrict remedy, plaintiffs have an enormous burden to show "a violation that caused segregation between adjoining districts," a nearly impossible burden to prove.[135] Because segregation dynamics operate at the scale of a metro area's housing market, the result of *Milliken* was to hobble the effectiveness of court-ordered desegregation orders unless the metropolitan area had a large, metrowide school district.[136]

The Supreme Court in the 1990s: Restricting the Extent of Court-Ordered Desegregation

In the 1990s the Supreme Court had lost its appetite for school desegregation cases and watered down the criteria for releasing school districts from the federal court's oversight. In 1991 the Supreme Court in *School Board of Oklahoma City v. Dowell* announced that school districts that were in general compliance with earlier plans should abandon their desegregation efforts, even if doing so would worsen racial segregation in their schools.[137] By 1995 the Court asserted that mostly all-black schools are "desegregated" as long as residential segregation is the current reason for the school segregation.[138]

Seattle Schools: *The Supreme Court Limits Secondary School Integration*

In 2007, the Supreme Court held that some race-based school integration plans are unconstitutional. While the Court's holding only extends to the use of an individual student's race in school admissions, the ruling may dissuade localities from attempting to remedy segregation through proactive measures and may give false assurance to segregated school districts that desegregation is no longer the law.[139] The Seattle decision, however, did not legalize segregation, nor did it prevent integration plans that do not assign individual students to area schools based on their race.[140]

State Court Remedies: The State Constitutional Right to Education

Minnesota, like all states, has a state constitutional duty to provide a public education. In Minnesota, public education is a fundamental right.[141] Minnesota's education clause, together with its equal protection clause, provides a powerful and promising tool for seeking redress for the inequities of severely segregated schools in the Twin Cities.

In *Skeen v. Minnesota,* a group of rural school districts challenged Minnesota's education funding scheme, asserting that the then-existing property tax system resulted in their districts receiving disparate per pupil funding.[142] The Minnesota Supreme Court in *Skeen* held that a constitutional violation exists when the state does not "establish a 'general and uniform system of public schools' which will secure a 'thorough and efficient system of public schools' . . . [that] meet[s] the basic educational needs of all districts."[143] The court did not resolve what constituted an inadequate education in Minnesota, leaving the door open to claims that a segregated education is inadequate and unconstitutional in Minnesota.[144]

Three years after *Skeen,* Minnesota's education and equal protection clauses were the basis for Minneapolis students' 1995 and 1998 desegregation lawsuits against the Minneapolis School District and various state defendants. Those cases led to a settlement that created the Choice Is Yours interdistrict remedy that is discussed later in this chapter. Those cases—and lawsuits that could be brought against the state in the future—flow from a state-court-based effort to rekindle *Brown*'s promise of equal educational opportunity. A Connecticut case successfully launched this new effort to make public educational opportunity meaningful for all children.

Sheff *and Other Desegregation Cases*

In *Sheff v. O'Neill,* minority plaintiffs claimed that de facto segregation in Connecticut schools deprived schoolchildren of a substantially similar educational opportunity under Connecticut's education and equal protection clauses.[145] The Connecticut courts ordered desegregation even though the court did not find intentional discrimination.

Sheff's success may be replicable in Minnesota. Connecticut's constitution, like Minnesota's, makes education a fundamental right.[146] The schools in the Hartford metro, like Twin Cities schools, were nonwhite segregated in the central city and white-segregated in the suburban districts. As in Minnesota, funding was substantially equalized. The court in *Sheff v. O'Neill* held, however, that adequate funding to segregated schools does not provide "a substantially equal educational opportunity" when schools are severely segregated.[147]

In Minnesota, the reasoning of *Sheff* and the promises of Minnesota's education and equal protection clauses were harnessed in the two 1990s cases out of which the Choice Is Yours Program was created. These cases are described later here in the discussion of school remedies for segregation.

HOUSING REMEDIES

Enforce Fair Housing Laws

Private markets provide most of the housing stock in the United States, and discrimination by private actors plays a significant role in segregating metropolitan areas. Reversing economic and racial segregation requires periodic monitoring of discriminatory practices and vigilant enforcement of fair housing laws. Monitoring and enforcement have been at best sporadic at the federal level.

In the absence of sustained federal commitment to fair housing, the Twin Cities region needs state-led efforts to enforce fair housing in the region. For instance, instituting a state-funded regional fair housing center that periodically conducts controlled tests to monitor discrimination by real estate agents, financial institutions, and mortgage and insurance brokers could be an effective way of enforcing fair housing in the region.

Implement Regionwide Fair Share Housing

The promotion of fair share housing is as essential as the enforcement of fair housing laws for reversing metropolitan segregation. Fair share housing requires that all communities in the region, not just central cities and stressed inner-ring suburbs, build their fair share of affordable housing within their jurisdictions.

In most metropolitan areas, "not in my backyard" attitudes and exclusionary zoning are the biggest impediments to fair share housing. Most suburban municipalities impede the construction of affordable housing by limiting the land zoned for multifamily housing and requiring excessively large lots.

This is especially a problem in hyperfragmented metros, where fragmentation creates additional incentives for exclusionary zoning practices by intensifying competition among municipalities. In the long run, this type of excessive, zero-sum local competition hurts metropolitan areas. For instance, it accentuates the regional mismatch between jobs and houses[148] and creates metrowide shortages of affordable housing. Only a regional governing body, armed with sufficient authority to implement a metrowide fair housing policy, could turn this harmful competition into healthy regional collaboration.

While the resistance of suburban governments to affordable housing looks insurmountable, this does not have to be the case. Regional fair share housing policies directed to increase the number and share of affordable housing in a region's suburbs can undermine such resistance and increase and widely distribute a region's affordable housing stock. The Twin Cities offer a very successful example of such fair housing policies. During the 1970s and early 1980s, the Metropolitan Council did a very good job of implementing regional fair share housing through its land use and housing policies.[149] A number of factors contributed to the success of the program.

The Metropolitan Council had not only the authority to implement a metro-wide fair housing policy but also the resources to make it happen. As an agency designated by the federal government, the council has the authority to review applications for federal grants for development infrastructure.[150] Through its Housing Policy 13 (later renumbered Policy 39), the council used this authority to encourage affordable housing development in the suburbs.[151] The council also gave infrastructure funding priority to suburbs that provided sufficient affordable housing in their jurisdictions.[152]

Starting with 1974, the council received a large influx of federal housing funds under the Section 8 New Construction Program.[153] The council's progressive housing policies were further supported by HUD's national fair housing initiative. In 1976, HUD initiated its Area-wide Housing Opportunity Program (AHOP) to encourage fair share housing across regions. The council was particularly well positioned to take advantage of this program, and immediately received additional funds from HUD to support its fair housing efforts.[154] As a result, the council's fair share housing program increased the suburban share of the region's affordable housing units from 18 percent in 1975 to 41 percent in 1983.[155]

Institute Region- or Statewide Inclusionary Housing Ordinances

An effective policy to resist exclusionary zoning has to happen at a regional level. However, federal tools are not the only tools to promote a more equitable distribution of affordable housing in a metropolitan region. When implemented on a region- or statewide scale, local tools such as inclusionary housing ordinances can also promote regional fair share housing. Inclusionary housing ordinances shift part of the burden of affordable housing provision onto private markets.

Inclusionary housing programs encourage the production of affordable housing by imposing affordability requirements on developers. In each proposed development, a certain percentage of the housing units is expected to be affordable to low- and moderate-income households. There are at least twelve jurisdictions in the nation with well-established inclusionary housing programs.[156]

Local governments are often the enforcers of inclusionary housing programs, which could either involve mandatory set-aside requirements or voluntary goals with built-in incentives to encourage developers to include affordable units within their developments. All inclusionary housing programs include some set-aside requirements, developer incentives, income targets for affordability, and a defined period of affordability, in addition to monitoring and enforcement rules.

Inclusionary housing is a popular strategy for achieving mixed-income housing in communities. Inclusionary housing programs enable low- and moderate-income people to live in opportunity-rich communities and make it easier for local businesses to hire and retain employees who live within reasonable commuting distance from their jobs. These programs serve two purposes at once: they increase the supply of affordable housing in individual communities and they disperse the supply of affordable housing across communities.[157]

Inclusionary housing programs, which usually apply to all new development in municipalities, make the production of affordable housing an integral part of the housing construction market. These programs can ease the shortage of affordable housing under different market conditions. When communities are gentrifying, inclusionary housing can prevent the displacement of low- and moderate-income people from their communities. In fast-growing suburbs, inclusionary housing can prevent the communities from being exclusive and generate affordable accommodation for low-income employees working for these communities.

Reduce Hyperfragmentation among Advocacy Organizations and Promote Advocacy at a Regional Scale

While many metropolitan areas show growing inequality that particularly hurts low-income residents of color, advocacy by and for low-income residents of color is even more fragmented than local government structures, usually operating at neighborhood scales. Hyperfragmented advocacy actually makes a region even more fragmented and dysfunctional.

Instead of helping create a regional identity and assisting residents in defining and advocating for regional reforms, these advocacy organizations do just the opposite. They urge residents to think in terms even smaller than their municipalities, encouraging them to change one neighborhood, one block, one school, and one wetland at a time.

Hyperfragmented advocacy efforts are often portrayed as the less controversial alternative to the comprehensive regional reforms that are necessary. In many cases, these organizations try to preserve their fragile status in a fragmented, unequal region. This often means that their self-interest leads them to oppose the very reforms that the region must undertake to expand its vitality.

Hyperfragmented advocacy hurts regional reform efforts by monopolizing the conversation regarding change, usurping philanthropic resources, and, in the end, failing to bring about substantial change for the communities they represent. It also undermines civic culture by exhausting idealistic activists with Sisyphean tasks that produce no results—ultimately reinforcing political cynicism rather than hope.

Regionally scaled advocacy groups can overcome this fragmentation in advocacy efforts by articulating the needs of individual communities and schools in the context of the regional trends that shape their well-being. Metropolitan areas need regional advocates to promote the regional reforms that will help all communities, rather than pitting community against community.

Community Development Corporations (CDCs) currently operate in a highly localized fashion to meet the affordable housing and economic development needs of individual communities. The strategies the CDCs use are often far narrower in scope than the regional strategies required to revitalize all impacted communities in a metropolitan area. These organizations compete for funds and often do not cooperate, since they are mostly focused on serving an individual neighborhood or town.

In 2006, there were thirty-seven CDCs operating in St. Paul and Minneapolis.[158] Collectively, these organizations raised and spent more than $83 million on economic development and affordable housing in 2006—more than the $77.5 million the Metropolitan Council spent for the same purpose in 2007. All of the CDCs operating in the region are located in the two central cities, and very few of these CDCs operate in the opportunity-rich suburbs of the region (Map 3.21).

CDCs struggle to bring economic development to their neighborhoods mostly because the neighborhoods they operate in do not compete on a level playing field. It is very difficult for neighborhoods with high levels of poverty to compete with developing suburbs. These suburbs attract businesses by offering them middle-class customers, cheap land, room for expansion and parking, low taxes, new highways, and relative freedom from crime and environmental problems.[159] Frequently, these CDCs lack the organizational capacity to make a significant impact on their neighborhoods, especially when regional forces that undermine the neighborhoods in the urban core work to negate their efforts.

In addition to their ineffectiveness in curbing regional inequalities, CDCs inadvertently contribute to these very same inequalities. Many CDCs work to bring affordable housing into their communities as part of their economic development efforts. By concentrating affordable housing in already poor neighborhoods, these CDCs end up locating low-income persons and people of color in places with relatively few opportunities.

This place-based strategy works against regional strategies, which aim to enhance opportunity for low-income persons and people of color by placing affordable housing in opportunity-rich suburbs. It also undermines regional strategies that aim to boost the stability of urban communities by creating mixed-income housing along transit nodes.

Foundations and philanthropic organizations could help by promoting and supporting regional CDCs that focus on regional issues. They can provide incentives to regional CDCs to advocate for pro-integrative distributions of affordable housing in the region. Regional CDCs could reduce harmful competition and foster

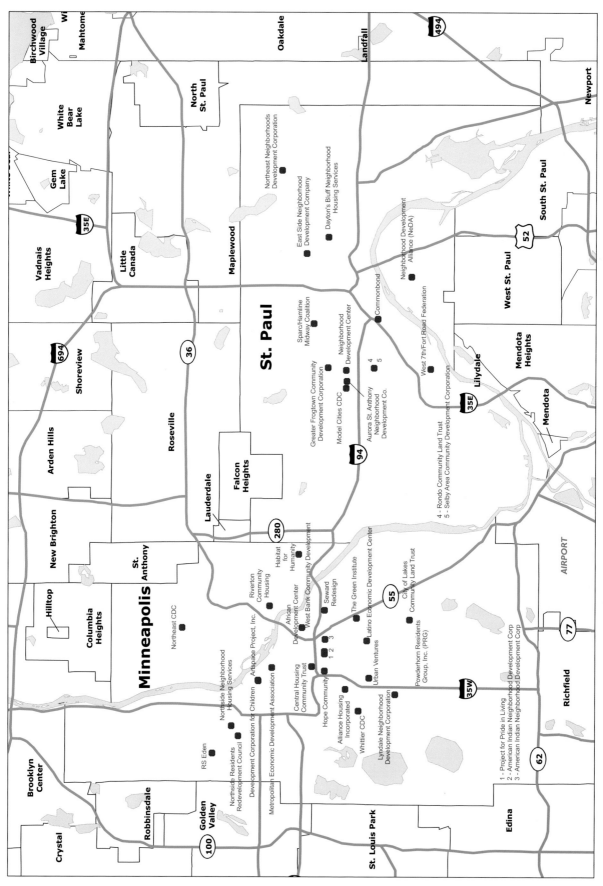

MAP 3.21. Locations of Community Development Corporations in the Twin Cities, 2006. *Source:* Metropolitan Consortium of Community Developers.

collaboration among CDCs to attain comprehensively defined regional goals. When CDCs work together to reach broader regional goals, local planning has greater chances of bringing growth and equity. Building the organizational capacity of regional CDCs would be an essential strategy to address regional inequality.

While most metropolitan areas lack the regional CDCs that could do the job, many have the prototypes of regional CDCs. Isles—a nonprofit community group from Trenton, New Jersey—is an example of a local CDC assuming the role of a regional CDC. While Isles is involved in "conventional" CDC activities, including promoting community gardens and providing low-interest loans and assistance to homeowners, it also focuses on the region and collaborates with other local and regional organizations.

In 2001, Isles cofounded the New Jersey Regional Coalition (NJRC) to promote socially equitable and environmentally responsible development in the state.[160] The NJRC includes planning, housing, civil rights, interfaith, labor, and community development organizations that are attempting to make systemic changes in regional development policy to counter urban sprawl, concentrated poverty, and environmental degradation.[161]

Hybrid organizations like Isles differ from many other local CDCs that promote affordable housing in already poor central city neighborhoods. Committed to a regionalist perspective, they resist the concentration of affordable housing in the region's urban core. For instance, in 2009, Isles, the NJRC, and other groups convinced the New Jersey legislature to abolish Regional Contribution Agreements (RCAs) that New Jersey suburbs used in the past to transfer their state affordable housing obligations to central cities.[162]

Regional CDCs such as Isles could effectively orchestrate and lead a coalition of local CDCs and bring much needed organizational capacity to community groups across the region. They can educate individual community groups on the benefits of regionalism and provide organizational resources for individual community groups that otherwise lack such resources.

In the Twin Cities, the Alliance for Metropolitan Stability is one organization that resembles a regional CDC. The alliance has a history of regional advocacy and understanding of the benefits of regionalism, and organizations like it could be good candidates for regional CDCs. The alliance could play an important role in enhancing equality of opportunity in the region by focusing on redirecting the development of affordable housing to opportunity-rich neighborhoods.

Organizations such as 1000 Friends of Minnesota and Transit for Livable Communities are also institutions with a regional focus. 1000 Friends of Minnesota has a history of addressing regional land use issues, and could be an important asset for a regionalist agenda. Similarly, with its current focus on enhancing the transit options of Twin Cities residents, Transit for Livable Communities could be instrumental in promoting a regionally beneficial transportation policy.

*Reform Existing Federal Public Housing Programs
to Promote Residential Integration*

While private markets provide most of the housing stock in the United States, public housing programs play a significant role in the provision of affordable housing. As a result, reforming existing federal public housing programs such as the LIHTC and Section 8 can go a long distance in reversing metropolitan segregation by redistributing affordable housing more fairly across regions.

Two changes could have pro-integrative effects on these programs, which contribute to segregation by placing disproportionate amounts of low-income housing in racially segregated, poor neighborhoods. First, efforts should be made to ensure that there is no correlation between an LIHTC or Section 8 household's race and its location. For instance, if 50 percent of LIHTC units are in the suburbs, then 50 percent of black households in LIHTC units would also be in the suburbs, rather than the actual share of 35 percent.

Second, subsidized low-income housing units should be evenly distributed across the region. If 77 percent of the region's total population is in the suburbs, then 77 percent of subsidized low-income housing development should be there as well, rather than the actual share of 45 to 50 percent (depending on the program). Many suburban housing and redevelopment authorities compete unsuccessfully with central city organizations for these tax credits. This imbalance needs to be rectified to reverse residential segregation in the Twin Cities region.

The LIHTC and Section 8 programs need to be restructured to redistribute the region's affordable housing stock into opportunity-rich areas. This would also involve connecting these opportunity-rich areas to transit opportunities for low-income residents of color to access these areas. Moreover, by restructuring its public housing programs, the region could desegregate its neighborhoods and schools simultaneously.

*Link Housing Choice to School Choice to Maximize the
Integrative Impact of School Desegregation Programs*

Regional fair housing policies could also reduce school segregation, enhancing educational opportunities for low-income persons and people of color. By promoting housing desegregation, such policies could bring about school desegregation and augment the integrative impact of existing school choice programs. A neighborhood that is racially integrated has a better chance of having schools that are also integrated. Most families of color who currently have their kids participating in school choice programs tend to have children traveling great distances to attend higher-quality schools. If these families were given the first choice to live in affordable housing near those higher-quality schools, the need for student transportation could be significantly reduced.

Linking housing and school choice could thus facilitate school integration and enhance the educational opportunities of low-income students and students of color. Examples from around the country illustrate that greater housing choice can be an effective strategy for improving opportunities for low-income persons and people of color when linked with school integration efforts. Louisville, Kentucky, and Yonkers, New York, for instance, have successfully fought school segregation by linking school choice with housing choice. In these places, the respective regional housing agencies made housing vouchers available on a priority basis to children involved in their desegregation programs.[163]

The Institute on Race and Poverty at the University of Minnesota conducted a simulation to demonstrate the potential integration impact of existing housing programs on schools in the Twin Cities metro area. This simulation attempted to quantify the impact of integrative changes to the LIHTC and Section 8 programs in the region. It also examined how a more integrative redistribution of low-income housing in the region would affect students who participate in an existing public school choice program, namely, the Choice Is Yours. The results of the simulation show that choice-driven housing programs currently in operation in the Twin Cities metropolitan area have the potential to cut school segregation in half with relatively gradual changes.

The Simulation Model

Before examining the potential effects on school integration of different types of remedies, it is necessary to estimate the scale of the changes needed to eliminate segregated schools in the region.[164] First, it is important to define *integrated*. Second, it is necessary to estimate the number of students who would have to change schools in order for all of the region's schools to be integrated.

For the purposes of these simulations, an *integrated* school is one with a black enrollment between 7 percent and 35 percent. Seven percent represents one-half the regional average share for black students, and 35 percent is roughly the turnover point for segregation in white–black integrated neighborhoods.

The starting point for the analysis is an estimate of the number of students who would have to change schools for all of the region's schools to be in the 7 percent to 35 percent range. In 2005, 375 of the roughly 1,000 schools in the seven-county region showed black shares in this range; 443 showed shares less than 7 percent and 184 schools had shares above 35 percent.

If integrating all schools were achieved simply by having students of appropriate races in the appropriate schools trade places, then roughly 9,900 black students in schools above the 35 percent ceiling would have to trade places with 9,900 white students in schools below the 7 percent floor. However, a choice program would be unlikely to result in one-for-one trades across schools.

If, instead, only 50 percent of the black students leaving predominantly black schools were replaced by white students, then about 12,500 black students would have to relocate to predominantly white and already-integrated schools in order for all schools to be below the 35 percent ceiling. If none of the black students leaving segregated schools were replaced by white students, then the number would increase to 15,250.

Thus, there is no single magic number of student moves that would result in integrated schools across the entire region. But 12,500 represents the middle of the range, and is used as the starting point for evaluating the potential impact of the Low Income Housing Tax Credit (LIHTC) and the project-based Section 8 programs.

Table 3.4 shows the potential impact of making two integrative changes in the LIHTC and Section 8 programs.[165] If LIHTC and project-based Section 8 units were assigned randomly by race, there would be an additional 1,527 black students in the suburbs—738 due to the LIHTC program and 789 due to Section 8. If, in addition, LIHTC and Section 8 units were located in proportion to population, there would be another 1,956 black students in the suburbs—655 due to the LIHTC program and 1,301 due to Section 8. These changes alone could bring the region nearly a third of the way to the goal of integrated schools: 3,483 (738 + 789 + 655 + 1,301) more black students would reside in the suburbs.

The location-specific race data needed to repeat the LIHTC and project-based

TABLE 3.4   **Metropolitan Integration Scenarios**

Number of black students who would have to change schools in order to achieve racial balance.	12,580
Number of additional black students who would already be in a racially integrated school if:	
• LIHTC units were assigned randomly by race.	738
• Section 8 project units were assigned randomly by race.	789
Number of additional black students who would already be in a racially integrated school if:	
• LIHTC units were distributed across the region in proportion to school enrollment.	655
• Section 8 project units were distributed across the region in proportion to school enrollment.	1,301
Additional Section 8 vouchers in the suburbs if they were distributed in same proportions as school enrollment.	4,750

Section 8 simulations for the Section 8 voucher program are not available.[166] However, at a very general level, if the distribution of vouchers were changed to reflect population shares, then there would be 4,750 more Section 8 vouchers used in the suburbs than is currently the case. At current average rates for the region as a whole, this would mean an additional 2,215 black households in the suburbs. These data suggest that there is probably as much potential for the Section 8 vouchers to affect school desegregation efforts as for each of the other two programs shown in Table 3.4. If this is the case, then adding Section 8 vouchers to the simulations would bring the totals in Table 3.4 up to roughly 50 percent of the number of students needed to achieve the goal of integrated schools across the entire seven-county region.

SCHOOL REMEDIES

In contrast to housing, which is primarily supplied by the private markets, education is mostly a publicly provided good. As a result, schools can be an effective venue for introducing public policy changes that can reverse metropolitan segregation. As discussed earlier, school segregation provides a powerful feedback to residential segregation, and integrating schools can help stabilize resegregating neighborhoods.

Moreover, integrating schools can be an effective way of changing racial attitudes in the society. School-age children are more amenable to change than adults, and introducing them to diverse experiences early in life in school can have long-lasting effects on their lives and future residential choices. School integration is thus pivotal to reversing metropolitan segregation trends.

Efforts to remedy school segregation and its harmful effects often involve piecemeal solutions, implemented on a much narrower scope than needed to ensure success. Such efforts frequently involve creating special programs for disadvantaged students of color or pushing school districts to desegregate schools within their boundaries. These piecemeal programs, however, cannot turn schools around in the context of white flight and local opposition to integration.

The severity of school resegregation trends outlined earlier in this chapter suggests that school integration can only be stable when it is implemented at a regional scale. School segregation is a regional problem that requires regional solutions. Regionwide school integration could only be achieved if all school districts in the metro work together to create strategic plans and share resources to effectively integrate the metro's schools.

The region has made many attempts to address racial inequalities in its public school system. Many of these attempts, however, failed to produce the results they were intended to produce. Others were more promising because they directly addressed school segregation as the root cause of these inequalities.

Reform the School District Integration Revenue Program

Regional school desegregation would require some changes to the School District Integration Revenue Program. The Minnesota legislature established this program in 1997 to provide funding to school districts for integration-related activities. The program distributed around $79 million in integration revenue to eighty school districts in 2005—70 percent of which came from state aid and the remaining 30 percent from matching local property tax levies by school districts.

Schools and school districts receive integration funds as part of the K–12 education formula, and their eligibility is based on their "protected student"—that is, nonwhite student—populations. School districts are eligible to receive integration funding if they fulfill one of four criteria: if they have at least one "racially identifiable school";[167] if they are a "racially isolated" district;[168] if they are adjacent to a racially isolated district; or if they work with a racially isolated district on a voluntary basis even if they are not an adjoining district.

The districts receive different per student funding rates depending on their specific eligibility criteria.[169] The total amount of integration revenue they receive depends on their total enrollment and the per student funding rate for which they are eligible. Racially isolated districts are required to establish a multidistrict collaboration council with adjoining districts to develop an "integration plan" to improve cross-district integration opportunities.

The program has a number of shortcomings, its most important limitation being the ambiguity of its main goal. The program's stated goal is to promote "interracial contacts." School districts have taken this term to mean a wide range of integration-related activities ranging from one-day multicultural activities to interdistrict magnet schools and cross-district transportation. The goal of the program needs to be clarified to unambiguously and directly encourage physical integration of school districts, schools, and classrooms.

Currently, the primary use of integration revenue in Minnesota appears to be to provide extra funding for poor and minority schools in the form of ESL teachers, support staff, and teacher training. While these are worthy purposes, integration revenue funding currently provides little or no incentive for school districts to desegregate their minority and low-income students. As a result, in practice, the program ends up providing an extra source of funding to cash-strapped districts that maintain segregation.[170]

The Office of the Legislative Auditor found that "the integration revenue funding formula has some unintended and potentially negative consequences."[171] Among other problems, the formula contains a financial disincentive to fully eradicate segregation in schools because school districts would no longer receive integration revenue once schools are fully integrated.[172]

The formula should be restructured to specifically reward affirmative efforts to integrate schools rather than simply distributing additional resources to segregated districts. In fact, school districts and schools that fail to take affirmative steps to actively integrate schools should lose integration revenue funding. Districts should be awarded the dollars on an as-needed basis to maintain programs, such as transportation programs, that make the districts and schools in the district more physically integrated than they would be in the absence of programs.

Enforce Integration Rules within Schools and School Districts

Another significant shortcoming of integration efforts is that they receive inadequate oversight from the Minnesota Department of Education. Although required by law, the department has failed to regularly review integration plans, to monitor the specific uses for which school districts used their integration revenues, and to give additional oversight to school districts that have had a racially identifiable school for three consecutive years.

The Minnesota Department of Education simply does not work very hard to enforce integration rules that are already on the books. It might be more effective to create an alternative institution outside the department that can exclusively focus on monitoring segregation within school districts. If given the authority to withhold integration revenue funding to school districts that do not actively desegregate or integrate their students, such an institution could more effectively secure school and school district compliance with program goals.

Funded at a more meaningful level with stronger rules, the School District Integration Revenue Program could be a model program that shows how states can incentivize integration that might otherwise be unappealing to school districts in the face of parental opposition. At a time when school districts across the country are scrambling for additional resources, states might play a key role in promoting school integration by providing a specialized funding stream that supports integration.

Spending Alone Cannot Replicate the Benefits of Integration in Segregated Schools

While specialized funding for integration makes sense, funding by itself cannot cure the problems associated with school segregation. Civil rights and public education advocates have fought to equalize education finance in many states, and they continue to do so.[173] While reducing funding inequalities is a necessary step in reducing educational inequalities, it is not sufficient to eliminate them. More spending alone, without racial and economic integration, cannot provide students with environments proven to support educational success.[174]

Historically, equalized funding has not succeeded in providing low-income students of color with an "equal education."[175] Minnesota was one of the states that increased resources going to racially and economically segregated schools. Minnesota's educational finance formula provides increased funding for each low-income child, as well as additional funds for schools with concentrated poverty. These funds are allocated directly to each school building.

As a result of this formula, average funding per student in schools and school districts with high concentrations of poverty vastly exceeds the state average. For instance, school districts and the state of Minnesota spent an average of $9,364 on each student in fiscal year 2007.[176] In contrast, Minneapolis Public Schools, a district with a high concentration of low-income students of color, averaged $11,988.[177] Some schools within the Minneapolis district spent significantly more than the district average, and invariably these were racially isolated schools of concentrated poverty.

Bethune Elementary was one of these racially and economically segregated schools. Students of color constituted 97 percent of its student body and 94 percent of its students were eligible for free or reduced-price lunch. Bethune Elementary received $18,073 per student in fiscal year 2007.[178] In contrast, Barton Open Elementary School, where only 21 percent of the student body was eligible for free or reduced-price lunches and where 65% of the students were white, received $9,016.[179]

Despite receiving almost twice as much as the state average in education funds, only 16 percent of the students who took the 5th Grade Math test in Bethune Elementary met or exceeded the standards in their MCASII scores in 2007.[180] In contrast, despite receiving per student funding below the state average, 74 percent of the students who took the same test in Barton Open Elementary School met or exceeded the standards in 2007.[181] The state's educational funding formula does very little to reduce student segregation in schools like Bethune Elementary. As a result, additional funding fails to overcome the poor performance results associated with high levels of segregation.

THE CHARTER SCHOOL OPTION

Minnesota pioneered the charter school concept in 1991.[182] Charter schools have been promoted to improve the performance of students who have no alternative to low-performing traditional public schools. Proponents claim that charter schools would extend school choice to low-income families and families of color, who do not have the choices that many families of means offer to their children. They suggest that by severing the link between neighborhoods and schools, charter schools would also allow students of color to escape the racially segregated schools they attend.

A 2008 analysis of all charter schools in the Twin Cities metro found that charter schools have failed to deliver on the promises made by charter school proponents.[183]

The study revealed that charter schools are far more segregated than traditional public schools in the metro, even in school districts where traditional public schools already have high levels of racial segregation. The analysis also showed that charter schools still perform worse than traditional public schools after nearly two decades of existence. The findings make it clear that charter schools offer a poor choice to low-income students and students of color—one between low-performing public schools and charter schools that do even worse. Compared to charter schools, other public school choice programs such as the Choice Is Yours offer much better choice schools to low-income students and students of color. Finally, the report found that charter schools hurt public education in the metro by encouraging racial segregation in the traditional public school system.

Charter Schools Are Severely Segregated

Charter school enrollments in Minnesota climbed rapidly from the early 1990s to around 24,000 students in the 2006–7 school year—about 3 percent of the K–12 student population.[184] Most of the increase in charter school enrollment has resulted from the rapid growth in enrollment of students of color (Figure 3.15). In 2007, more than half of charter school students were students of color, compared to about one-fifth of traditional public school students.[185]

Similarly, poverty concentrations are even higher in charter schools than in traditional public schools. In 2007, more than half of charter school students were eligible for free or reduced-price lunches, compared to 30 percent of traditional public school students.[186]

The uneven geographic distribution of charter schools contributes to the heavy concentration of low-income students and students of color in charter schools. Charter schools in the Twin Cities metro are mostly located in urban school dis-

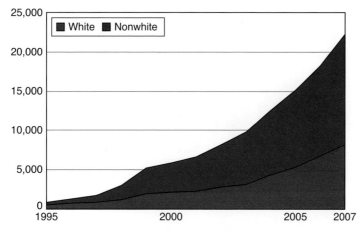

FIGURE 3.15. Growth of charter school enrollments in Minnesota, 1995–2007. *Source:* Minnesota Department of Education.

tricts or in inner suburban school districts, where the share of students of color and low-income students is much higher than the regional average. About a quarter of the state's charters are in Minneapolis, while St. Paul hosts about 20 percent.[187] The suburbs of the seven-county metro had more than a fifth of the state's charter schools, while a third were located outside the metro area.[188]

Charter schools are heavily segregated, not surprisingly, given their demographic makeup. By 2008, over half of charter schools were nonwhite segregated, compared to less than a fifth of the traditional public schools. Moreover, segregation among charter schools increased over time. In 1995, less than a third were nonwhite segregated. In 2008, this share was more than half. As a result, an overwhelming majority of students of color attending charter schools are in segregated settings. In fact, students of color who attended charter schools are more than twice as likely to be in a segregated school setting as their counterparts in the traditional public schools (Figure 3.16).

The claim that charter schools liberate students of color from racially segregated school districts by severing the link between the racial composition of schools and neighborhoods has no basis in the Twin Cities metro. On the contrary, the racial makeup of charter schools and the neighborhoods in which they are located strongly resemble each other (Map 3.22). Most nonwhite segregated charters are either in racially segregated urban school districts or in racially transitioning inner suburbs. White-segregated charters, in contrast, are mostly located in white suburban school districts, with a few in white urban neighborhoods with racially diverse district schools.

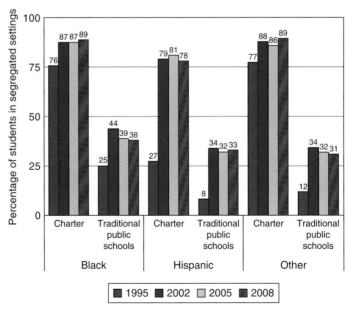

FIGURE 3.16. Students of color in segregated school settings by school type, Twin Cities, 1995–2008.

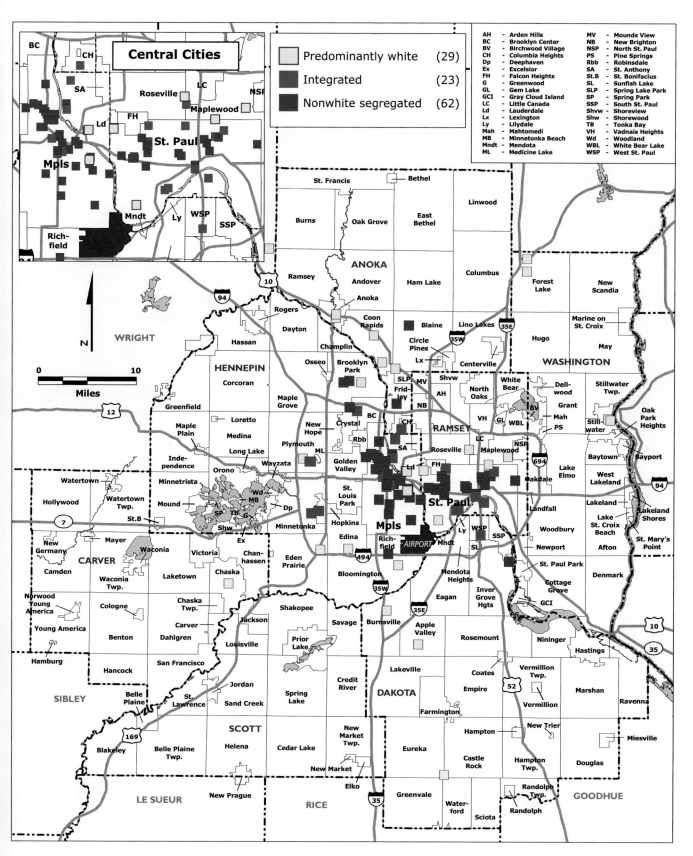

MAP 3.22. Charter school classifications, Minneapolis–St. Paul region, 2007–8. *Source:* Minnesota Department of Education.

Since the majority of charter schools are located in school districts that experience high levels of racial and economic segregation, comparing charter schools with traditional public schools at the metro level could make them look artificially more segregated. To correct for this problem, charter schools were compared to traditional public schools in the region's two urban school districts. The findings show that charter schools are still more segregated than the highly segregated traditional schools in St. Paul and Minneapolis.

In St. Paul, nearly 90 percent of all students of color who attended charter schools did so in segregated settings, compared to about three-quarters in traditional public schools.[189] Moreover, the presence of white-segregated charter schools in St. Paul means that charter schools are creating an avenue for white flight for the students who live in this racially diverse school district. In Minneapolis, segregation among charter school students was even more intense. More than 96 percent of the nonwhite students in Minneapolis charter schools attended school in segregated settings, compared to 80 percent of the nonwhite students in traditional public schools.[190]

Meanwhile, student poverty concentrations in Minneapolis charter schools grew rapidly. In 1995, student poverty rates in charters and traditional schools were similar—slightly over half of the students were eligible for free or reduced-price lunch. By 2008, 73 percent of the charter students qualified for free lunches, compared to 57 of traditional public school students.[191]

Student poverty trends in St. Paul were more complicated due to stark differences in the poverty patterns of white and nonwhite segregated charter schools. In 1995, average student poverty was higher in charter schools than in traditional district schools. By 2008, poverty rates among charter schools were lower than those in traditional district schools because of the growing number of white-segregated charter schools (up from only one in 1995 to seven in 2008) with low poverty rates.[192]

Less than 20 percent of the students who attended white-segregated charter schools in St. Paul were eligible for free lunches in 2008. In contrast, more than 84 percent of the students who attended nonwhite segregated charters and 71 percent of the traditional public school students qualified for free lunches in the district.[193] This pattern shows that segregation in charter schools hurts students of color much more than white students because students of color are much more likely to attend high-poverty charter schools, increasing the likelihood of negative educational and life outcomes.

Charter Schools Don't Perform as Well as Traditional Public Schools

Some charter school advocates argue that charter schools are worth investing in if they provide a better education for students than traditional public schools, even in segregated settings.[194] This argument, in the tradition of "separate but equal," posits that superior performance in charter schools balances the numerous harms that result from a segregated school system. A 2008 analysis of charter school performance in the Twin Cities metro found that charter schools are far from delivering the superior performance promised by charter school advocates.

Separate statistical models for reading and math proficiency showed that traditional schools outperformed charter schools after controlling for student poverty, race, special education needs, limited language abilities, student mobility rates, and school size.[195] Consistent with other research, student poverty was found to be the dominant factor in the performance of schools. Figures 3.17 and 3.18 demonstrate this relationship and how charter schools measure up. The predicted line in these figures corresponds to the performance level one would expect from schools given their student poverty rate. The figures break down the performance of charters, traditional public schools and a special subset of suburban schools that participate in

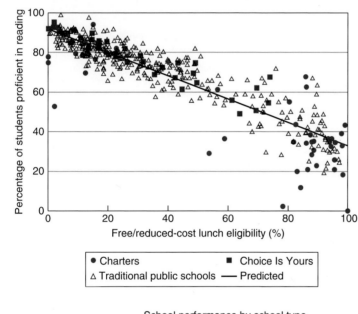

School performance by school type

	Percentage of schools performing better than expected given poverty rate	Percentage of schools performing worse than expected given poverty rate
Charter	24	76
Choice Is Yours	79	21
Traditional	54	46

FIGURE 3.17. Percentage of students proficient in reading and eligible for free or reduced-cost lunch in Twin Cities elementary schools (simple correlation = -.91). *Source:* Minnesota Department of Education.

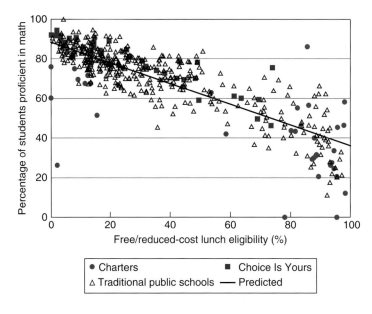

School performance by school type

	Percentage of schools performing better than expected given poverty rate	Percentage of schools performing worse than expected given poverty rate
Charter	21	79
Choice Is Yours	88	12
Traditional	53	47

FIGURE 3.18. Percentage of students proficient in math and eligible for free or reduced-cost lunch in Twin Cities elementary schools (simple correlation = -.84). *Source:* Minnesota Department of Education.

the Choice Is Yours Program—a public school choice program available to students in Minneapolis.

The figures show that charter schools are far from providing superior educational opportunities to students. In 2008, the reading performance of students in three-quarters of charter schools was lower than expected given the poverty levels of those schools. Similarly, almost four-fifths of charter schools performed worse than expected in math.

In striking contrast, four-fifths of the schools that participated in the Choice Is Yours Program performed better than expected in reading, and 88 percent performed better than expected in math. The Choice Is Yours clearly offers students a much better selection of schools than charter schools.

Charter schools were also clearly outperformed by traditional public schools. Only a quarter of charter schools performed better than expected in reading given their poverty levels, compared to more than half in traditional public schools. Charter schools lagged behind traditional schools in math proficiency as well: barely a fifth of charter schools performed better in math, compared to more than half in traditional public schools.

Charter School Competition Triggers Segregation in Traditional Public Schools

Charter schools in the Twin Cities metro are not only much more segregated than the traditional public schools but they also intensify segregation in the public education system by encouraging ethnic-based niche competition from the traditional school system. Charter school competition in ethnic niches particularly hurts students of color in the metro's traditional public school system because it deepens racial and economic segregation in traditional public schools. Traditional public schools in the Twin Cities metro have responded to charter competition in two ways that further intensify racial and economic segregation.

First, school districts in the Twin Cities metro sponsored charter schools of their own in an attempt to capture district students who left for charters. Like the vast majority of the charters in the Twin Cities metro, school district–sponsored charters were mostly nonwhite segregated schools with high concentrations of poverty.

In St. Paul, five of the eight charter schools sponsored by the district were nonwhite segregated schools with very high poverty rates; of the remaining three, one also had a very high poverty rate.[196] District-sponsored charters intensified racial and economic segregation in Minneapolis as well. Four of the five district-sponsored charters were nonwhite segregated schools with high poverty rates, while the other one was a predominantly white charter school with a low poverty rate.[197]

Second, school districts responded to ethnic niche–based competition from charter schools by initiating ethnocentric programs and magnet schools. In both Minneapolis and St. Paul, as the school districts lost students to Hmong-focused charter schools, they chose to compete with the charters by starting Hmong-focused programs or magnet schools.

In Minneapolis, the district responded to charter competition by initiating the Hmong International Academy—a Hmong-focused program within the Lucy Laney Elementary School. Located in north Minneapolis, this school had a relatively small group of Hmong students along with African American students who made up the majority of the student body. As participation in the program grew, the district moved the program to a separate building in north Minneapolis. Initially, the Hmong International Academy operated as a "school within a school" that separated Hmong students from the African American students. As the program moved to a different physical site, it resulted in the creation of two separate school facilities—each serving a specific racial/ethnic group.

In St. Paul, the district responded to charter competition by creating a Hmong-focused magnet school in Phalen Lake, a heavily Hmong-populated part of the district.[198] The district decided to convert the existing neighborhood school to a Hmong-focused magnet partially because as a magnet school, the school will be able to offer to Hmong students in other parts of the city the same transportation options offered by Hmong-focused charters.[199] The conversion decision will almost certainly increase the concentration of Hmong students at the school, where the share of Asian students is already 63 percent. Since these changes are very unlikely to reduce the school's extremely high student poverty rate—93 percent—the magnet conversion is unlikely to enhance the overall opportunities available to Hmong students.

To the extent that charter schools encourage ethnic-based competition, they deepen existing concentrations of poverty in traditional public schools and in the school system as a whole. This undermines the performance of students in both types of schools, especially students of color. The pattern harkens back to an earlier time when "separate but equal" was an accepted goal of the public education system—a goal discredited by research now just as much as in the time of *Brown v. Board of Education*.

THE CHOICE IS YOURS PROGRAM

The Choice Is Yours interdistrict transfer program was created in 2000 in response to a lawsuit filed by the NAACP and Xiong.[200] The plaintiffs who brought the lawsuit on behalf of the children enrolled in Minneapolis public schools argued that a segregated education violates the Minnesota State Constitution's education and equal protection clauses. They alleged that the state of Minnesota had not taken effective action to desegregate Minneapolis schools. The state came to a settlement agreement with the plaintiffs and created the Choice Is Yours Program as part of this agreement.

The settlement included an interdistrict student transfer component, which greatly expanded educational opportunities for low-income children in Minneapolis. Under the interdistrict transfer component of the Choice Is Yours, children of Minneapolis residents who qualify for free or reduced-cost lunch programs are eligible for priority placement in participating schools in eight suburban school districts, including Columbia Heights, Edina, Hopkins, Richfield, St. Louis Park, St. Anthony/New Brighton, Robbinsdale, and Wayzata.[201]

The program allocated a minimum of five hundred priority placement slots per year starting with the 2001–2 school year to eventually set aside an estimated two thousand slots over four years. While the legal settlement that resulted in the Choice Is Yours expired in June 2005, the interdistrict transfer component of the program continues to operate under the West Metro Education Program's comprehensive desegregation plan thanks to ongoing support.[202]

At the beginning of the 2005–6 school year, approximately 1,680 children were enrolled in the Choice Is Yours Program; 1,090 of these students were returning from the previous year. The majority of the Minneapolis public school students participating in the Choice Is Yours had previously attended overwhelmingly poor Minneapolis schools, like Jordan Park and Lincoln. In these schools, nearly all of the students were poor enough to qualify for free or reduced-cost lunch programs.[203]

The racial composition of the students enrolled in the Choice Is Yours was 63 percent black, 18 percent white, 10 percent Hispanic, 7 percent Asian or Pacific Islander, and 2 percent American Indian. In comparison, the racial composition of all the students enrolled in the Minneapolis district was 43 percent black, 27 percent white, 14 percent Hispanic, 12 percent Asian or Pacific Islander, and 4 percent American Indian.[204]

Map 3.23 shows the distribution of the Choice Is Yours students in the participating districts, as well as the number coming from each Minneapolis zip code. Table 3.5 demonstrates that although students from across Minneapolis participated, north Minneapolis neighborhoods were the largest contributors to the program—contributing 62.4 percent of the Choice Is Yours participants. During the 2005–6 school year, half of the Choice Is Yours participants came from the north Minneapolis neighborhoods shaded dark brown in Map 3.23.

Not surprisingly, the suburban district immediately adjacent to these neighborhoods—Robbinsdale—received more students under the program than any other district (Table 3.6). There were 583 program participants attending schools in the

TABLE 3.5 Choice Is Yours student residence locations in Minneapolis

	n	%
North	942	62.4
Northeast	118	7.8
Southwest	174	11.5
Southeast	275	18.2
Total	1,509	100.0

Note: Data do not include students attending the St. Anthony and Hopkins school districts.

Source: 2005 Wide Area Transportation.

TABLE 3.6 Choice Is Yours school district attendance

	n	%
Columbia Heights	196	10.5
Eden Prairie	6	0.3
Edina	170	9.1
Hopkins	230	12.4
Richfield	238	12.8
Robbinsdale	583	31.4
St. Anthony	99	5.3
St. Louis Park	177	9.5
Wayzata	159	8.6
Total	1,858	100.0

Note: Data do not include students attending the St. Anthony and Hopkins school districts.

Source: 2005 Wide Area Transportation.

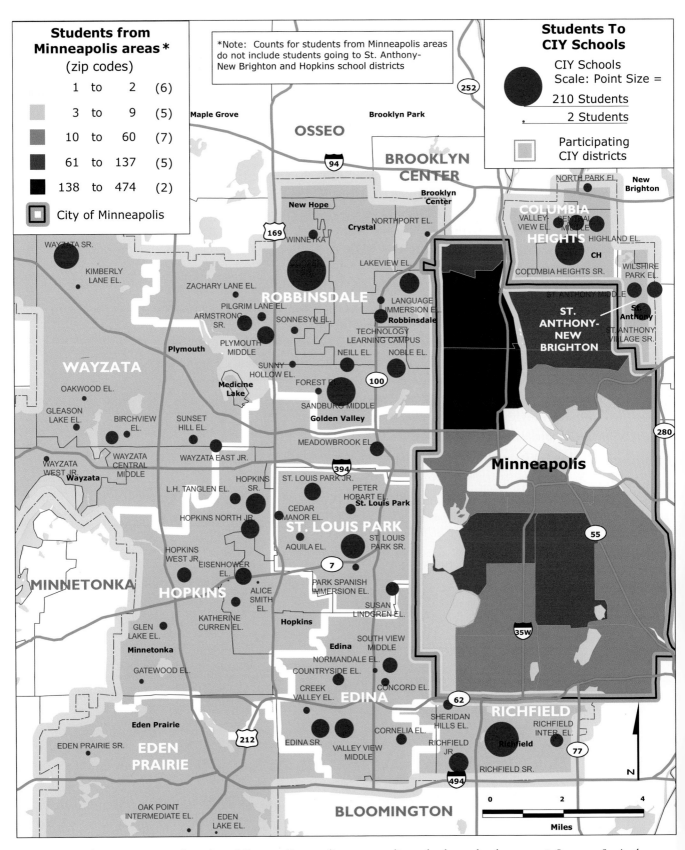

MAP 3.23. Choice Is Yours students from Minneapolis attending surrounding suburban schools, 2005–6. *Sources:* St. Anthony–New Brighton School District; West Area Transportation System; Hopkins School District.

Robbinsdale district compared to 238 in Richfield, the suburban district with the second most participants.

The Choice Is Yours Program Is a Promising School Choice Model for School Integration

According to a 2006 evaluation report prepared for the Minnesota Department of Education, students who participated in the Choice Is Yours Program benefited from significant achievement gains.[205] Averaged across all demographics, students from grades 3 through 7 made consistent and significant improvements in reading and mathematics. In comparison with the program-eligible but nonparticipating students, the Choice Is Yours suburban students made annual gains that were nearly a third higher.

Ideally, one needs to compare the test scores of the program participants with the scores of eligible students who were not accepted into the program to control for the self-selection bias of highly motivated students and parents who seek public choice programs. However, such a comparison is impossible since enrollment capacity limits for the Choice Is Yours Program have not yet been reached and no applicants have yet been rejected.

Instead, the Minnesota Department of Education attempted to correct for this self-selection bias by studying students who began in the program with a wide range of achievement levels. Students who scored below the fiftieth percentile initially made gains similar to other program participants. In both reading and mathematics, low-performing participants scored 19 percentile points higher in mathematics progress than nonparticipants and 13 to 22 percentile points higher in reading. These findings show that the Choice Is Yours holds promise for its academic quality.

The Choice Is Yours has been favorably regarded by parents, students, the Minnesota Office of the Legislative Auditor, and even the George W. Bush administration. As one of the nine choice programs nationwide to receive a federal grant while those monies were still available, the program was considered the best among these programs.[206] As a 2005 Minnesota Legislative Auditor report noted, unlike some of the activities for which state Integration Revenue funds were used, the Choice Is Yours Program was also "consistent with a traditional view of integration."[207]

A survey conducted to evaluate the first two years of the Choice Is Yours found that academic quality was the primary reason that parents enrolled their children in suburban school districts.[208] School safety was yet another reason parents chose to enroll their children in these suburban districts.[209] Interviews with parents of the students who participated in the program showed great satisfaction with the program. Parents rated the schools well on a variety of factors, including setting high standards for achievement, creating community, and making students feel welcome.[210]

Parent satisfaction with the interdistrict transfer component of the program was evident in the fact that 98 percent of all the parents whose children participated in the program claimed that they would recommend the program to others.[211] In fact, during the 2005–6 school year, 70 percent of the parents reported to have already recommended the program.[212] Indeed, word of mouth and direct contact through parents' social networks, rather than standard advertising techniques, continued to be the most common form of encouraging participation in the program.[213]

Parents seemed pleased with the suburban schools' approach to diversity. Nearly two-thirds of suburban participants reported that their schools could meet diverse needs, a proportion slightly less than the responses from nonparticipants remaining in city schools. Focus groups with participating children revealed that many felt suburban schools took learning more seriously, and that they did not have to be concerned with "bad" students interfering with their desire to learn. They did, however, feel they encountered some racism and hostility from teachers and students, and thought that the Choice Is Yours students received harsher discipline than did misbehaving suburban students.

Incoming students in city–suburban transfer programs around the country are reported to experience hostility in the suburbs.[214] In contrast, suburban school districts participating in the Choice Is Yours have been more receptive to incoming students partly because of their specific enrollment dynamics and partly due to the financial incentives built into the program. Many of the inner suburban districts receiving the Choice Is Yours students are facing declining or stagnating enrollments. In addition to facing such dire enrollment dynamics, these inner suburban school districts are also given financial incentives for receiving students.

Minnesota's school finance law rewards suburban districts for receiving students who participate in the Choice Is Yours Program because these students bring with them what is known as "compensatory revenue" in addition to the base amount of state aid allocated to all students. Compensatory revenue is awarded under a state formula based on the number of low-income children in each district. This means that suburban districts receive more state aid for the Choice Is Yours participants than they do for other students.

As a result, many of the inner suburban school districts have been more likely to see the Choice Is Yours participants as a boon than do the school districts in stable or growing outer suburbs. Instead of making tough decisions about closing schools due to steep enrollment declines, districts like Robbinsdale or Columbia Heights choose to aggressively market toward students eligible to participate in the Choice Is Yours and raise attendance and revenue. Without these students, each participating district, except for St. Anthony, would be facing even steeper declines in enrollment.

The Limitations of the Choice Is Yours Program

While the Choice Is Yours Program's interdistrict choice model is a promising approach and has been proved beneficial to the students involved, its limited geographic scope has been counterproductive. The program has so far been limited to eight school districts, six of which are located in stressed suburbs that have been struggling with social and fiscal strains.[215] Moreover, many of the program participants have been heavily concentrated in a few suburban school districts—Robbinsdale, Richfield, and Hopkins—that have already been experiencing residential demographic shifts and rapid segregation.

These factors put extreme pressures on many of the schools in participating inner suburbs and expose them to the risks of racial segregation and concentrated poverty. In less than five years, many schools in participating inner suburban districts experienced rapidly increasing segregation and concentrated poverty.

At the beginning of the Choice Is Yours Program in 2001, only three of the schools in participating suburban school districts were racially segregated (i.e., had minority student shares exceeding 40 percent). The number of racially segregated schools among participating suburban school districts jumped to twenty-one within just five years.

Similarly, concentrated poverty in schools spread rapidly among participating suburban districts. In 2001, only five of the schools in participating suburban school districts suffered from concentrated poverty (defined as more than 40 percent of students who are eligible for free or reduced-price lunch). Within merely five years, the number of these schools rose to nineteen. Overall, free/reduced-cost lunch percentages in the receiving schools increased 44 percent, from 16 percent in 2001 to 24 percent in 2006.

When participating students face growing segregation and concentrated poverty —exactly the same ills that plague urban schools—in the suburban schools, their performance and the gains associated with the program have begun to suffer. The latest evaluation of the Choice Is Yours Program provides evidence of deterioration in the academic performance of program participants.[216] Given the limited scope of the program, growing concentrated poverty and racial segregation among participating schools has begun to undermine the performance of participating students.

Expand the Geographical Scope of the Choice Is Yours Program to Ensure Its Success

The premise behind the Choice Is Yours is sound. As Figures 3.17 and 3.18 show, the program's academic benefits are realized as long as the program continues to integrate students by income. However, as the latest evaluations of the program demonstrate, moving students from high-poverty city schools to high-poverty suburban schools does not improve test scores. Two changes to the program can help reverse the detrimental effects of increasing racial and economic segregation.

The program should limit the number of program participants any individual school could enroll by instituting poverty caps on individual schools. This would prevent future concentrations of poverty in individual schools. The program should also ensure a wider distribution of program participants across districts by encouraging Choice Is Yours participation in more affluent suburban districts. This would help prevent overenrollment of participants in socially and economically transitioning suburbs.

However, participating suburban districts could not be fully relieved from the dual pressure of growing racial segregation and concentrating student poverty, unless the geographical scope of the program is expanded. In fact, to implement the program's original goal of integrating disadvantaged students into opportunity-rich, well-performing schools, the Choice Is Yours Program should be significantly expanded to encompass many more school districts.

Increasing the number of participating suburban school districts could help distribute poverty enrollments over a larger set of schools and school districts, and ensure that all participating schools remain economically and racially integrated. The program's continuing future success depends on avoiding concentrations of poverty and racial segregation in participating schools and school districts.

As the case of the Choice Is Yours demonstrates, when implemented on the inappropriate scale, school integration cannot be stable. Only large-scale integration plans can overcome the problem of resegregation that makes small-scale integration programs ineffective. By creating large-scale collaboration among school districts and by asking every school to educate a small share of the region's less fortunate children, regional plans prevent future concentrations of poverty and eliminate the need for families to flee increasing poverty enrollments.

CREATE REGIONAL SCHOOL INTEGRATION DISTRICTS

The idea of creating an institutional framework for collaboration among school districts is not new in the Twin Cities region. The region already has three integration districts, which cover Minneapolis, St. Paul and surrounding suburban districts of primarily first-ring suburbs (see Map 3.24).[217] These integration districts represent a good beginning for the type of school district cooperation that is necessary to integrate schools in the region. However, these districts are not geographically large enough and they lack the incentive and power to implement metrowide integration.

One way of achieving regionwide collaboration among school districts is to create "superdistricts." Map 3.25 shows the results of a simulation of one possible

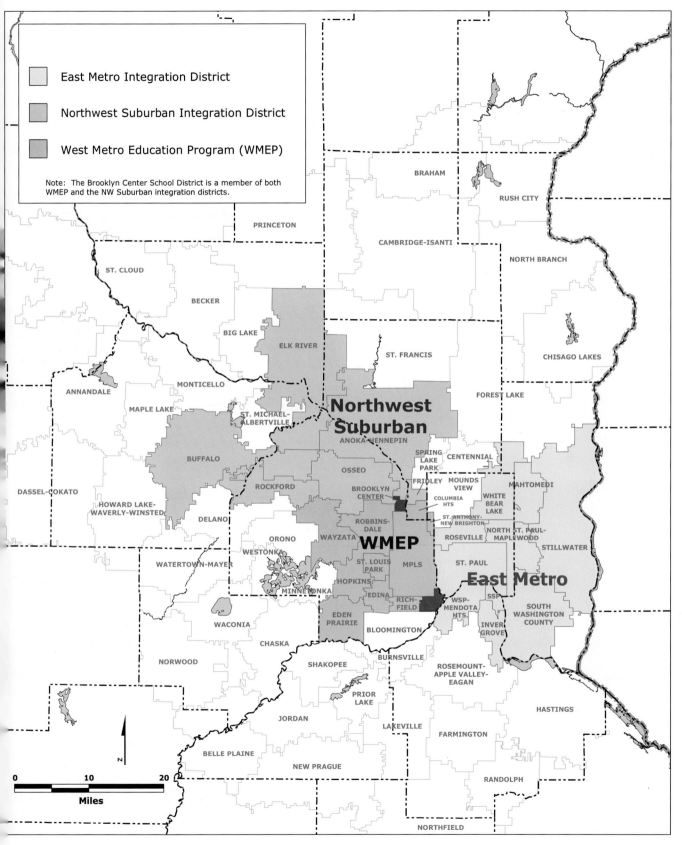

Northwest
Suburban

WMEP

East Metro

BRAHAM

RUSH CITY

PRINCETON

CAMBRIDGE-ISANTI

NORTH BRANCH

ST. CLOUD

BECKER

NORTH BRANCH

BIG LAKE

CHISAGO LAKES

ELK RIVER

ST. FRANCIS

ANNANDALE

MAPLE LAKE

FOREST LAKE

ST. MICHAEL-
ALBERTVILLE

ANOKA-HENNEPIN

BUFFALO

OSSEO

SPRING
LAKE
PARK

CENTENNIAL

DASSEL-COKATO

ROCKFORD

BROOKLYN
CENTER

FRIDLEY

MOUNDS
VIEW

MAHTOMEDI

COLUMBIA
HTS.

WHITE
BEAR
LAKE

HOWARD LAKE-
WAVERLY-WINSTED

DELANO

ST. ANTHONY-
NEW BRIGHTON

ROBBINS-
DALE

WAYZATA

ORONO

ROSEVILLE

NORTH ST. PAUL-
MAPLEWOOD

WESTONKA

ST. LOUIS
PARK

MPLS

ST. PAUL

STILLWATER

WATERTOWN-MAYER

MINNETONKA

HOPKINS

EDINA

RICH-
FIELD

WSP-
MENDOTA
HTS.

SSP

WACONIA

EDEN
PRAIRIE

BLOOMINGTON

INVER
GROVE

SOUTH
WASHINGTON
COUNTY

CHASKA

NORWOOD

SHAKOPEE

BURNSVILLE

ROSEMOUNT-
APPLE VALLEY-
EAGAN

HASTINGS

PRIOR
LAKE

JORDAN

LAKEVILLE

FARMINGTON

BELLE PLAINE

NEW PRAGUE

RANDOLPH

NORTHFIELD

MONTICELLO

0   10   20

Miles

N

MAP 3.24. Integration districts in Minneapolis–St. Paul region. *Sources:* Northwest Suburban Integration District; East Metro
Integration District; West Metro Education Program.

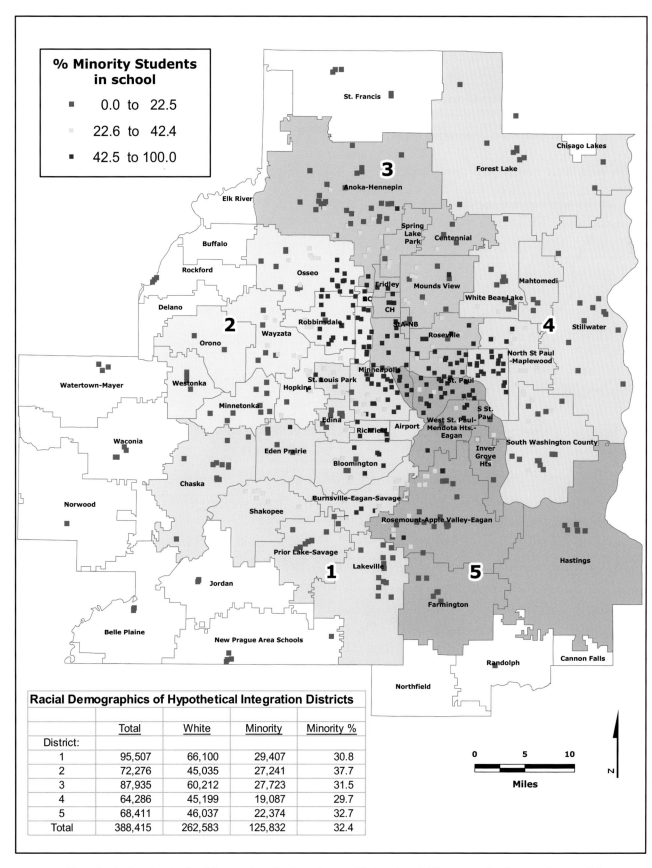

% Minority Students in school

- 0.0 to 22.5
- 22.6 to 42.4
- 42.5 to 100.0

Racial Demographics of Hypothetical Integration Districts				
District:	Total	White	Minority	Minority %
1	95,507	66,100	29,407	30.8
2	72,276	45,035	27,241	37.7
3	87,935	60,212	27,723	31.5
4	64,286	45,199	19,087	29.7
5	68,411	46,037	22,374	32.7
Total	388,415	262,583	125,832	32.4

0   5   10

Miles

MAP 3.25. Hypothetical regional school integration districts. *Source:* University of Minnesota, Institute on Race and Poverty; Minnesota Department of Education.

alignment of districts, where the Twin Cities metropolitan area is divided into five metro "superdistricts."

The boundaries of these superdistricts are drawn to maximize diversity within each district. Each district is designed as a contiguous zone spanning a similarly sized section of the metropolitan area. These superdistricts could be used to provide the necessary forum for planning across districts and schools. The superdistricts are not meant to replace existing school districts. They are simply meant to provide a larger integration geography within which individual school districts would be required to cooperate.

For instance, school districts in the superdistricts could be required to cooperate to maintain racial balance across the superdistrict. Schools within the superdistrict might be required to maintain a minority and low-income population share that is within 10 percentage points of the superdistrict's overall share. For example, if 35 percent of the students in the school district are students of color, schools within the district will be required to maintain a student of color population ranging between 25 and 45 percent. Research shows that if all the schools in the metro area achieve this level of integration, schools and neighborhoods are much less likely to resegregate.

The exact combination of sticks and carrots needed to push the superdistricts toward desegregation goals is debatable and could be subject to experimentation. The primary point of the simulation is to show that it is possible, given the existing distribution of students across the region, to define cooperative districts with balanced racial mixes.

4

Transportation and Employment

ACCESS TO GROWING JOB CENTERS

Thomas F. Luce Jr., Myron Orfield, Eric Myott, and Jill Mazullo

As in many U.S. metropolitan areas, there has been a steady movement of people and jobs into the suburbs in the Twin Cities. Rapid employment growth expanding deeper into the suburbs is decentralizing and dispersing jobs in a way that threatens to undermine efforts to control urban sprawl, implement transit, and provide equal access to opportunities to people in all parts of the region. These trends have been especially detrimental to low-income persons and people of color who are often concentrated in distressed inner-city neighborhoods and suburbs.

Although sprawl has not been as dramatic in the Twin Cities as in many comparable metropolitan areas, development in the region has been unbalanced, with growth in a few suburban areas outstripping the core and the rest of the suburbs. These places have attracted much of the wealth of the region—much of the high-end housing, transportation infrastructure, and many of the new high-paying employers.

An important outcome of this process is a mismatch between where job growth is occurring and where low-income households and people of color reside.[1] This maintains or exacerbates historic patterns of unequal opportunity. U.S. metropolitan areas with higher levels of employment decentralization exhibit greater spatial mismatch between the relative location of jobs and black residents, for instance.[2]

Job decentralization and dispersal in the Twin Cities at least partly reflect changes in regional policy. Early in its history, Metropolitan Council planning objectives encouraged job clustering as a way to use infrastructure most efficiently, route transit effectively, and encourage growth in the core of the region. However, this emphasis has nearly disappeared from more recent regional plans for the Twin Cities.

This chapter highlights job trends in the Twin Cities and contrasts them with two other metropolitan regions that have grown rapidly but have used differing approaches to regional planning and transportation policy—Atlanta, Georgia, and Portland, Oregon. Portland, like the Twin Cities, is known for its regional approach to land use and transportation planning. Unlike the Twin Cities, it is also known for its emphasis on transit and for close coordination of transportation and land use planning. Atlanta, on the other hand, is a region where urban growth is largely unconstrained—land use planning is highly localized—and where transportation planning has emphasized highway development and the automobile.

Strategies to promote job clustering work best when there is a commitment to guide growth within an urban boundary. The Twin Cities' Metropolitan Council's efforts to curb urban sprawl have been a necessary but not sufficient way to promote job clustering and transit in the region. Portland, Oregon, in contrast, has stronger urban growth containment policies and stronger links between development planning and transit.[3] This has led to less suburban sprawl and greater job clustering in the region. The result in Portland is a compact urban form more conducive to transit than in the Twin Cities.

Job clustering can also help close the mismatch between jobs, housing, and low-income workers who rely on transit. To do so, clustering policies need to synchronize with transportation and affordable housing policies. In Atlanta, for instance, there is a large spatial mismatch between where jobs are clustering and where affordable housing is located. This trend makes job clustering less beneficial to Atlanta's low-income, minority residents, many of whom reside on the opposite side of the region from fast-growing employment centers.

Traffic congestion worsens workers' access to employment and can magnify mismatches between jobs and housing as well. In the Twin Cities, increased traffic congestion in fast-growing suburbs has made it more difficult for low-income workers in the core of the region to access suburban jobs by means of reverse commuting. In Atlanta, on the other hand, congestion in the core of the region impedes movement to opportunity-rich parts of the region in the north from opportunity-poor parts of the region in the south.

Various strategies can encourage job centralization and clustering in a way that promotes transit and helps close jobs and housing mismatches. Stronger enforcement of regional policies that control urban sprawl lends itself to greater job centralization and clustering. Smart growth and transit-oriented development near clustered employment can help close the jobs–housing mismatch, especially when there are policies that help ensure fair and affordable housing throughout a region. Finally, such policies are supportive of a wider and more intensive regional transit system, which can help provide alternatives to commuting on congested roads.

JOB CLUSTERING AND EMPLOYMENT CENTERS

The cooperation of local governments and the containment of urban growth near already developed areas result in less decentralization and dispersal of jobs. Under these conditions jobs are more likely to cluster near transportation corridors and near the core of the region. Interlocal competition associated with highly fragmented local systems, on the other hand, encourages urban sprawl and can lead to very uneven growth (of housing and jobs).

Clustering is important for several reasons. Job clustering allows for more efficient use of infrastructure such as highways, major roads, and even sewer and waterlines.[4] Public services can be delivered at lower costs and services like day care can be provided in or near office buildings, enabling working parents to maintain reasonable commute times. Clustering is also necessary for agglomeration effects to occur, such as when complementary businesses locate near each other for ease of transactions.

Job and housing density is also a necessary precondition for the viability of transit. Transit enhances access for lower-income workers who lack automobiles. Clustering can also make smart growth designs for "walkable" neighborhoods near job sites more viable, reducing the vehicle miles traveled to work and the associated emissions that contribute to global warming.

Analysis of jobs data for the Twin Cities shows forty employment centers. (See sidebar, "Methods for Defining Employment Centers.") The job centers are scattered across the region but are more likely to be in the western and southwestern parts of the region (Map 4.1). The higher job concentrations in the west and southwest are not surprising. These parts of the region are home to disproportionate shares of the region's highest-income households and high-value homes.

Table 4.1 shows the full list of employment centers in the Twin Cities, jobs in 1990 and 2000, and growth from 1990 to 2000. The centers are quite diverse. They range in size from 140,930 to 2,305 jobs in 2000, show dramatically different growth rates, and range in density from 2,016 to 60,857 jobs per square mile.

Table 4.2 summarizes the job and growth data by employment center locations. There are two central business districts (CBDs), eight other central city, ten inner suburb, thirteen middle suburb, and seven outer suburb job centers. The data show several important patterns. Only a little more than half of total regional jobs are in the job centers, and this share is falling. This means that everyday availability of an automobile is becoming more and more important for accessing work, further disadvantaging lower-income workers who rely on public transportation.

There is also a very clear geographic pattern in job growth rates during the 1990s. Growth was much higher in the outer parts of the region than in the core—

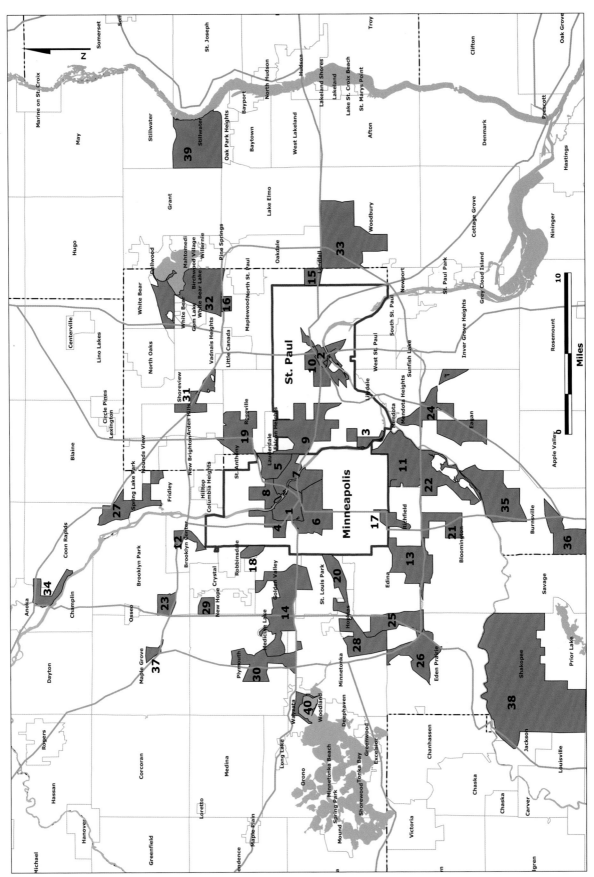

MAP 4.1. Employment centers in Minneapolis–St. Paul region. See Table 4.1 for job center information. *Source:* U.S. Census Bureau Transportation Planning Package, 1990 and 2000.

TABLE 4.1   Employment center jobs and job growth

Map number	Employment center	Total jobs 1990	Total jobs 2000	Percentage growth 1990–2000
1	Minneapolis CBD	128,395	140,930	10
13	Edina	43,963	53,490	22
9	St. Paul—Midway	43,163	48,245	12
10	St. Paul Center	40,402	45,150	12
14	Golden Valley—I-394	40,913	43,710	7
7	Minneapolis—University of Minnesota	48,276	42,645	-12
2	St. Paul CBD	40,278	38,140	-5
25	Eden Prairie—Highway 169	23,002	33,730	47
6	Minneapolis—Phillips / Whittier	33,361	29,305	-12
19	Roseville	23,080	26,580	15
24	Eagan	19,466	25,715	32
30	Plymouth—I-494	19,088	25,255	32
11	Airport/Fort Snelling	12,769	24,415	91
22	Bloomington—MOA	30,870	21,080	-32
27	Fridley / Coon Rapids	14,524	21,005	45
5	Minneapolis—Northeast	14,301	19,900	39
21	Bloomington—I-35W	17,407	19,765	14
20	St. Louis Park	13,604	17,905	32
26	Eden Prairie	11,335	14,715	30
28	Minnetonka/Hopkins	10,947	14,000	28
38	Shakopee	7,089	12,965	83
31	Shoreview/Arden Hills	9,196	11,475	25
39	Stillwater—Highway 36	8,082	10,910	35
32	White Bear	9,689	10,650	10
36	Burnsville Center	7,280	9,940	37
34	Anoka	9,516	8,995	-5
15	Maplewood—3M	9,674	8,855	-8
23	Brooklyn Park	4,831	8,755	81
12	Brooklyn Center	8,756	8,660	-1
8	Minneapolis–St. Anthony	7,726	8,475	10
4	Minneapolis—North	6,886	7,200	5
3	St. Paul—Highland	3,294	5,140	56
29	New Hope	4,430	4,325	-2
16	Maplewood—I-694	2,693	3,875	44
18	Robbinsdale	3,918	3,815	-3
33	Woodbury	1,315	3,805	189
17	Richfield—Crosstown	4,252	3,260	-23
40	Wayzata	2,609	3,175	22
37	Maple Grove	283	2,815	895
35	Burnsville—Highway 13	2,560	2,305	-10
	Total	743,223	845,075	14

Source: Census Transportation Planning Package, 1990 and 2000.

TABLE 4.2 Job growth by employment center type

Employment center	Number	Total jobs 2000	Percentage of regional jobs	Total jobs 1990	Percentage of regional jobs	Percentage growth 1990–2000
Central business districts	2	179,070	11	168,673	13	6
Other central city	8	206,060	13	197,409	15	4
Inner suburb	10	194,565	12	163,622	12	19
Middle suburb	13	214,275	13	176,100	13	22
Outer suburb	7	51,105	3	37,419	3	37
Total—employment centers	40	845,075	52	743,223	55	14
Nonclustered employment		783,405	48	596,045	45	31
Total—metropolitan area		1,628,480	100	1,339,268	100	22

Source: U.S. Census Transportation Planning Package, 1990 and 2000.

outer suburb employment centers grew more than five times faster than the CBDs and more than three times faster than other central city job centers. As a result the share of total Twin Cities' jobs that was in employment centers in the central cities fell from 29 percent to 25 percent. This clearly implies decreasing opportunities for groups disproportionately located in the core such as lower-income households and people of color.

COMPARISONS ACROSS METROPOLITAN AREAS

Portland and Atlanta show significantly different job and job growth patterns than the Twin Cities—differences that in many ways reflect the differing regional policies in the three areas. Jobs are much less centralized in Atlanta than in the Twin Cities and Portland. In a comparison of the thirty-two largest metropolitan areas, Portland, with its relatively strictly enforced growth boundary, shows the least job sprawl. The Twin Cities, where the Metropolitan Council uses a less strict "urban services area," shows the ninth-least amount of sprawl. Atlanta, on the other hand, ranks near the bottom, as the sixth most sprawling metropolitan area.[5]

The job center data reflect these patterns. The shares of regional jobs in the central cities were significantly higher in Portland and the Twin Cities than in Atlanta —29 percent in Portland's central city job centers and 24 percent in the Twin Cities compared to 17 percent in Atlanta (Table 4.3). Atlanta also shows three to four times as many jobs (measured by share of total regional jobs) in outer suburban centers as the other two metropolitan areas.

The job growth comparisons are markedly different. Middle and outer suburban

TABLE 4.3   Jobs and job growth by employment center type

	Percentage of regional jobs			Percentage change in jobs 1990–2000		
	Atlanta	Portland	Twin Cities	Atlanta	Portland	Twin Cities
Employment center						
Central business district	6	9	11	4	15	6
Other central city	11	20	13	13	33	4
Inner suburb	15	10	12	10	28	19
Middle suburb	6	9	13	72	60	22
Outer suburb	12	4	3	111	117	37
Total—employment centers	50	52	52	31	36	14
Nonclustered employment	50	48	48	57	34	31
Total—metropolitan area	100	100	100	43	35	22

Source: U.S. Census Transportation Planning Package, 1990 and 2000.

job centers are growing fastest in all three metropolitan areas, but Portland shows much stronger growth in the core of the region than the other two metros. Portland is also the only one of the three where clustered jobs are growing more rapidly than nonclustered jobs. The Twin Cities and Atlanta both show strong decentralization and deconcentration of jobs: outer job centers are growing much more rapidly than inner centers, and nonclustered employment is growing more rapidly than clustered jobs. Both trends make it more difficult to serve job centers with transit.

The regions also show different spatial patterns of growth. In Atlanta, employment centers are clustered in the northern part of the region and are growing much more rapidly there than in the south (Map 4.2). This means that living in Atlanta's outer suburbs is not in itself favorable. In Atlanta it is even more difficult for people living in the outer southern suburbs than for those in the core to connect to high-growth employment centers in the north.

Job clustering and growth rates are more uniform across the Portland region, as illustrated in Map 4.3. None of the centers in the central city lost jobs and suburban centers follow the interstate system closely, making it easier to route transit to employment centers throughout the region.

The patterns in the Twin Cities fall between Atlanta and Portland. As in Atlanta, many central city employment centers lost jobs and there is a favored quarter in the suburbs—the southwest suburban centers showed the strongest growth (Map 4.4). However, suburban employment centers are not as strongly clustered in one part of the region as in Atlanta.

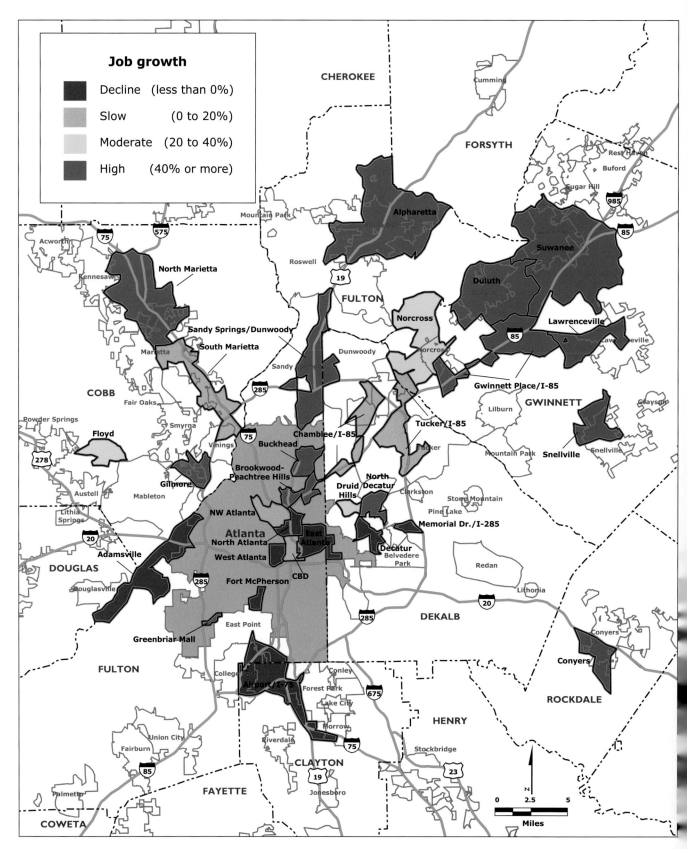

MAP 4.2. Employment centers by job growth in Atlanta region. *Source:* U.S. Census Bureau Transportation Planning Package, 1990 and 2000.

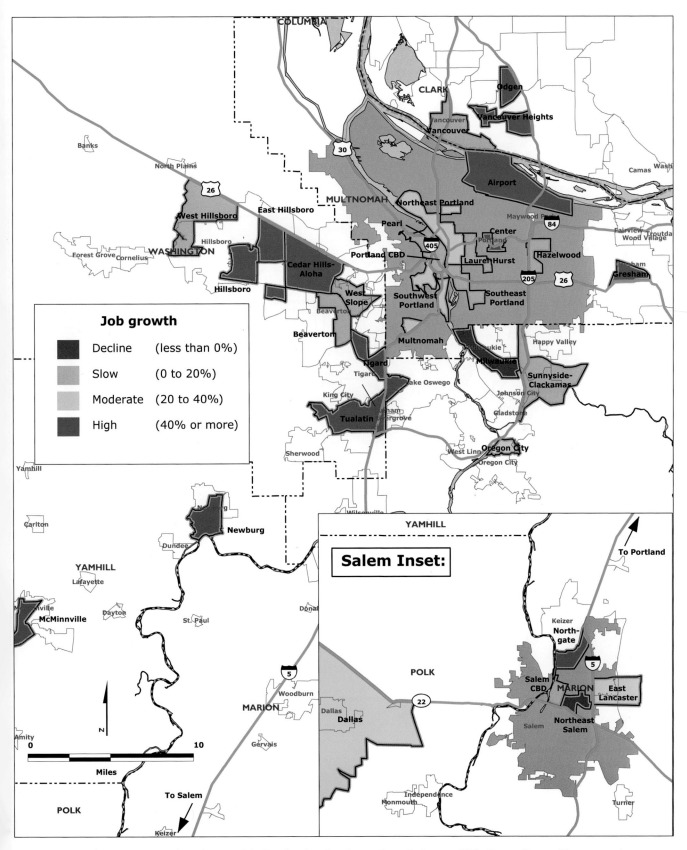

MAP 4.3. Employment centers by job growth in Portland region (central area). *Source:* U.S. Census Bureau Transportation Planning Package, 1990 and 2000.

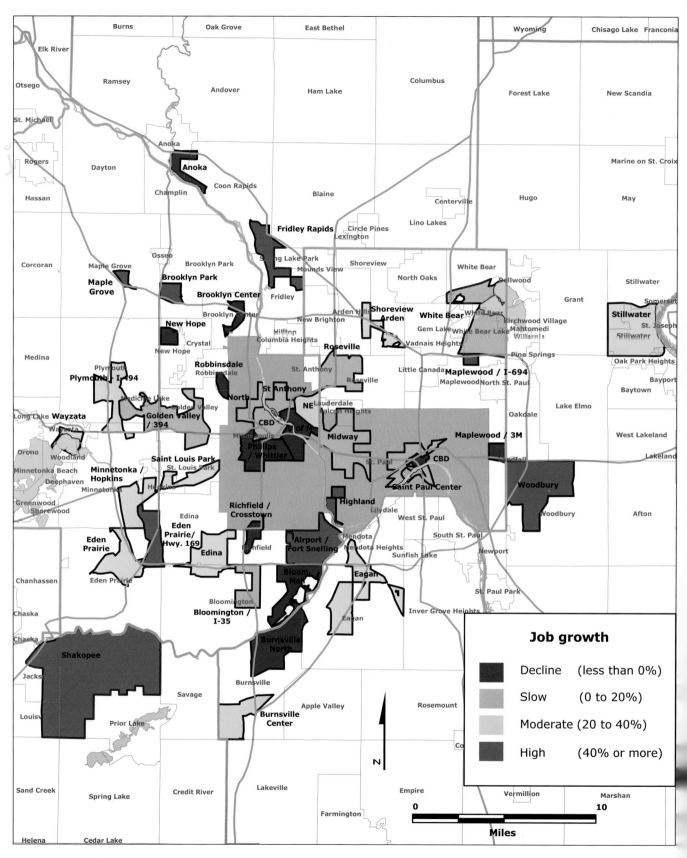

MAP 4.4. Employment centers by job growth in Minneapolis–St. Paul region. *Source:* U.S. Census Bureau Transportation Planning Package, 1990 and 2000.

METHODS FOR DEFINING EMPLOYMENT CENTERS

The analysis first documents the region's employment centers—where they are and how they grew during the 1990s. Census Transportation Planning Package (CTPP) data compiled by Traffic Analysis Zones (TAZs) in 1990 and 2000 were used both to find small- and large-scale job clusters and to show the racial breakdowns of the workers commuting to each center. Employment centers were defined as contiguous TAZs with greater than average numbers of jobs per square mile and total employment exceeding 1,800 jobs. Large job agglomerations like those in the centers of metropolitan areas were divided into multiple employment centers based on job densities in different parts of the larger clusters.

The employment centers were divided into five categories based on location to facilitate the analysis of access to jobs: (1) central business districts (CBDs) were the highest-density portions of the job clusters in the cores of central cities; (2) other central city job centers are those in the remainder of the central cities; (3) inner suburban job centers are those in suburbs that border one of the central cities; (4) middle suburban job centers are the job clusters in suburbs bordering inner suburbs but not a central city; and (5) outer suburban centers are the rest—the outermost job centers in the region. All remaining jobs were classified as nonclustered.

The CTPP also provides the regionwide journey-to-work matrix compiled at the TAZ level. The matrix shows how many residents from each TAZ work in every other TAZ in the region, along with the median travel time for each pair of TAZs. Geographic Information System techniques were used to derive the area around each job center accessible within twenty, thirty, and forty minutes. These "commuter sheds" were then overlaid on other demographic and housing data to compile the characteristics of workers and housing located within each commuter shed.

RACIAL DISTRIBUTION OF WORKERS IN THE EMPLOYMENT CENTERS

The decentralization and dispersal of jobs affect different groups of workers differently. Racial minorities, who often live in distressed neighborhoods near the core of the region, do not benefit as much from job growth opportunities near the edge of a region as suburban whites. Racial minorities are more likely than whites to work in the central cities, where job centers are growing slowly or declining. The combination of sprawl, segregation, decentralization, and dispersal undermines regional employment opportunities for people of color.

Table 4.4 shows the racial breakdown of workers by employment center types in Atlanta, Portland, and the Twin Cities. The table indicates that in 2000 most racial minority groups disproportionately worked in job centers in the central cities or inner-ring suburbs.

African Americans have the highest percentages of workers in central city employment centers. In Portland, nearly half (47 percent) of black workers had jobs in central city employment centers, followed by 40 percent in the Twin Cities and 23 percent in Atlanta.

Racial minorities were also less likely to work in unclustered jobs than whites. With the exception of Hispanics in Portland, every racial minority group was more likely to work in clustered employment centers than whites—a pattern that worked to their disadvantage in the Twin Cities and Atlanta, where unclustered jobs grew more rapidly than clustered.

TABLE 4.4 **Job growth and racial breakdowns by employment center type**

| | Percentage of regional total | | | |
| | Non-Hispanic | | | |
	White	Black	Other	Hispanic
Atlanta				
Central city	15	23	16	13
Inner suburb	15	17	16	14
Middle/outer suburb	19	14	23	23
Unclustered	52	46	45	50
Portland				
Central city	28	47	32	20
Inner suburb	10	7	9	8
Middle/outer suburb	13	9	16	14
Unclustered	49	38	43	59
Twin Cities				
Central city	22	40	32	30
Inner suburb	12	12	13	12
Middle/outer suburb	16	13	17	15
Unclustered	49	35	38	43

Source: U.S. Census Transportation Planning Package, 1990 and 2000.

Largely as a result of these spatial patterns, workers of color are more likely to work in declining and slow-growing employment centers than whites in all three metropolitan areas (Table 4.5). This pattern is strongest of all in the Twin Cities, where nearly half of black workers were employed in declining or slow-growth job centers in 2000. The lone exception was, again, Hispanics in Portland.

Why is this pattern so pronounced? A key determinant is residential location. If housing markets are segregated by race and/or income, then systematic geographic variations in job growth rates may generate corresponding variations in access to jobs. Maps 4.5 through 4.7 show the percentage of the population that is non-Asian minority in Atlanta, Portland, and the Twin Cities.[6]

The residential location of racial minorities in conjunction with regional job clustering and growth variations helps explain the racial differences across employment center types. In Atlanta, racial minorities (especially blacks) often reside in the southern portion of the metropolitan region, areas where most employment centers are either declining or growing very slowly. Conversely, moderate and high-growth centers are located on the opposite side of the region, where mostly whites live. As a result, blacks are less likely than whites to work in fast-growing job centers.

TABLE 4.5   **Job growth and racial breakdowns by employment center growth**

| | Percentage of regional total | | | |
| | Non-Hispanic | | | |
	White	Black	Other	Hispanic
Atlanta				
Declining/slow growth (< 20%)	20	31	24	22
Moderate/high growth (> 20%)	28	22	31	28
Unclustered	52	46	45	50
Portland				
Declining/slow growth (< 20%)	26	32	28	19
Moderate/high growth (> 20%)	25	30	33	22
Unclustered	49	38	39	59
Twin Cities				
Declining/slow growth (< 20%)	31	48	40	38
Moderate/high growth (> 20%)	20	17	22	19
Unclustered	49	35	38	43

Source: U.S. Census Transportation Planning Package, 1990 and 2000.

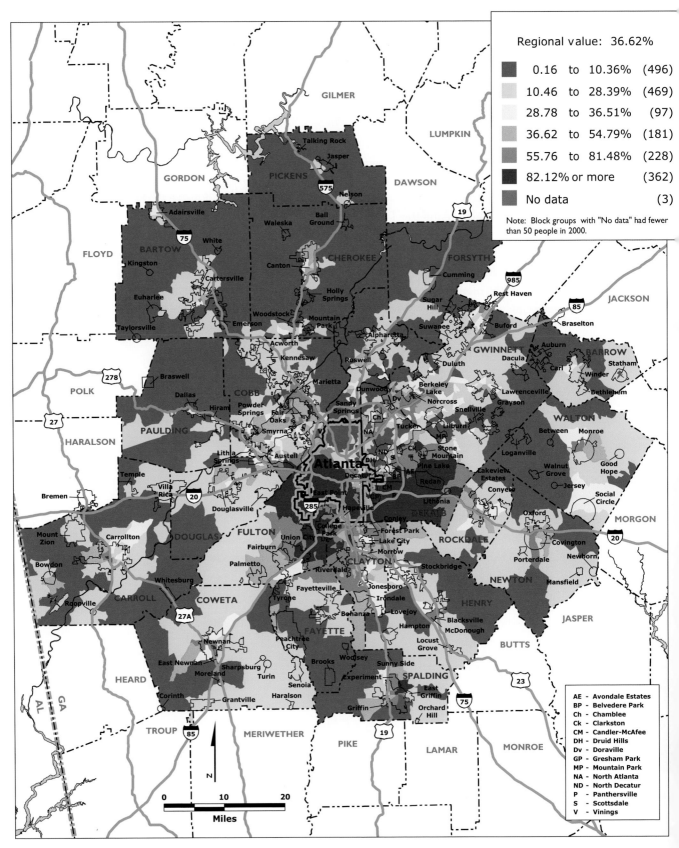

Regional value: 36.62%

	0.16 to 10.36%	(496)
	10.46 to 28.39%	(469)
	28.78 to 36.51%	(97)
	36.62 to 54.79%	(181)
	55.76 to 81.48%	(228)
	82.12% or more	(362)
	No data	(3)

Note: Block groups with "No data" had fewer than 50 people in 2000.

AE - Avondale Estates
BP - Belvedere Park
Ch - Chamblee
Ck - Clarkston
CM - Candler-McAfee
DH - Druid Hills
Dv - Doraville
GP - Gresham Park
MP - Mountain Park
NA - North Atlanta
ND - North Decatur
P - Panthersville
S - Scottsdale
V - Vinings

MAP 4.5. Percentage of non-Asian minority population by census block group, Atlanta region, 2000. *Source:* U.S. Census Bureau.

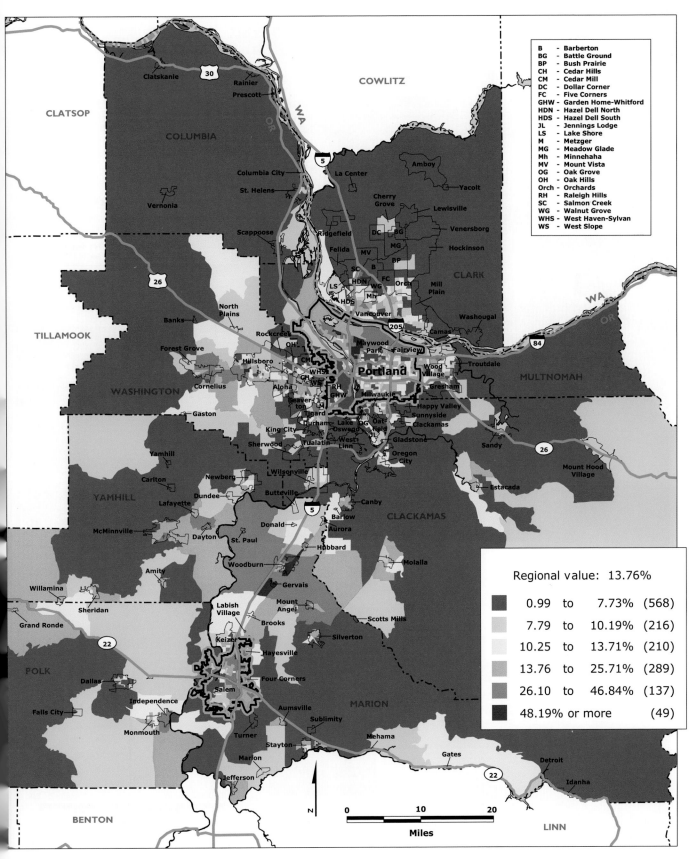

MAP 4.6. Percentage of non-Asian minority population by census block group, Portland region, 2000. *Source:* U.S. Census Bureau.

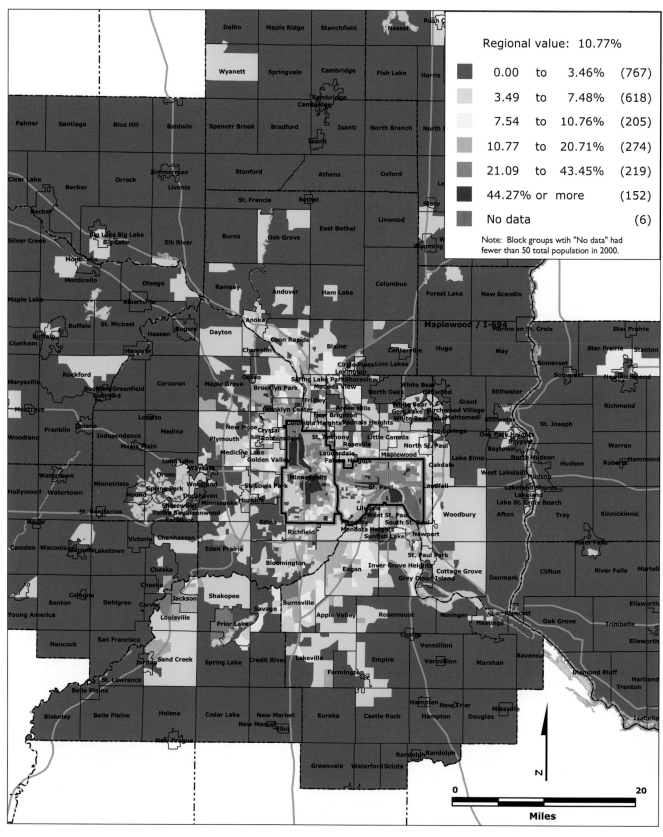

Regional value: 10.77%

	0.00	to	3.46%	(767)
	3.49	to	7.48%	(618)
	7.54	to	10.76%	(205)
	10.77	to	20.71%	(274)
	21.09	to	43.45%	(219)
	44.27%	or	more	(152)
	No data			(6)

Note: Block groups wtih "No data" had
fewer than 50 total population in 2000.

N

0   20

Miles

MAP 4.7. Percentage of non-Asian minority population by census block group, Minneapolis–St. Paul region, 2000.
Source: U.S. Census Bureau

In Portland, communities of color are often near employment centers that are more evenly distributed across the region. The fact that blacks work disproportionately in Portland's central city hurts them less, since central city job centers have fared better in Portland than in the other two metros. The result is a greater balance of employment opportunities for the various racial and ethnic groups in Portland's region.

In the Twin Cities, there are higher percentages of racial minorities in inner-city neighborhoods or in suburbs northwest of Minneapolis. Most employment centers in these areas are either declining or growing slowly. As a result, racial minorities are more likely to work in declining/slow growth centers than whites in the Twin Cities.

POPULATION DENSITIES AND PUBLIC TRANSPORTATION

In addition to minimizing job sprawl, local government cooperation and regional policies to contain urban growth also encourage housing and population densities that are more conducive for public transportation. When housing units are spaced far apart it is more difficult to generate adequate demand for transit.

Atlanta, Portland, and the Twin Cities have different regional policies that result in different urban densities and transit usage. Table 4.6 shows population densities in the urbanized portions of the regions broken down by central cities and suburbs.

TABLE 4.6 **2000 population density of urbanized area: Atlanta, Portland, and Twin Cities metropolitan areas**

	Population per square mile
Atlanta	
Central city	3,162
Suburbs	1,685
Total	1,784
Portland	
Central city	3,697
Suburbs	3,097
Total	3,296
Twin Cities	
Central city	6,220
Suburbs	2,186
Total	2,671

Source: U.S. Census Bureau.

Atlanta's lack of a regional policy to constrain growth helps make it the least dense of the three metropolitan areas. Portland's use of a strictly enforced urban growth boundary results in a higher overall population density and the densest suburbs of the three. The Twin Cities' use of an urban service boundary has helped to concentrate population in its core—its central cities are the densest of the three—but the lack of serious regulation outside the service area results in lower densities overall in the suburbs.

Higher population densities make transit more feasible. Table 4.7 shows this clearly. The proportion of workers who travel to work by transit varies directly with the densities in Table 4.6. Portland, the densest of the three regions, shows the greatest overall transit usage—10 percent compared to eight and six percent in the Twin Cities and Atlanta. Similarly, the Twin Cities show both the highest densities and the highest transit usage in the central cities—18 percent compared to 16 and 12 percent in the other two metros. All three metros show relatively little transit usage in the suburbs, but, again, the pattern matches the density comparison.

PUBLIC TRANSPORTATION AND RACE

The negative effects of job sprawl on people of color relate directly to their greater dependence on public transportation. In each of the regions racial minorities were more reliant on public transportation to get to work than whites. Table 4.8 shows the means of transportation workers used to get to jobs in the three regions broken down by race. Minorities, especially black workers, have the highest rates of transit usage, as well as walking or biking to work.

In Atlanta, blacks were four times more likely than whites to get to work without a car, the greatest disparity of the three regions. Still, 87 percent of blacks travel by automobile to their jobs, compared to 75 percent of blacks in the Twin Cities and 74 percent in Portland. The greater extent of African American suburbanization, higher black household income, and job sprawl in Atlanta help explain the greater automobile use for black workers in Atlanta than Portland or the Twin Cities.[7]

Portland had the greatest proportion of workers who did not use an automobile to get to work—25 percent of blacks, 17 percent of Hispanics and other nonwhites, and 14 percent of whites. Twin Cities workers were less reliant on automobiles than workers in Atlanta, but more so than people in Portland. In the Twin Cities, 25 percent of blacks did not use an automobile to get to work, followed by 21 percent of Hispanics, 17 percent of other nonwhites, and 11 percent of whites.

These comparisons reinforce the importance to low-income workers of regional efforts to slow sprawl and develop effective transit systems. The combination of greater dependence on transit for nonwhite workers, transit systems that are largely limited to core areas, and slower growth rates (or decline) in central cities

TABLE 4.7 Means of transportation to work, 2000:
Atlanta, Portland, and Twin Cities metropolitan areas (in %)

Atlanta

	Car, van, or truck	Public transportation, bike/walk	Work at home
Central business district	83	17	0
Central city	88	11	1
Unclustered central city	86	10	4
Total central city	86	12	2
Inner suburb	93	6	1
Middle suburb	96	3	1
Outer suburb	96	2	2
Unclustered suburb	90	4	6
Total suburb	92	4	4
Employment centers	92	7	1
Unclustered	90	5	6
Total	91	6	3

Portland

	Car, van, or truck	Public transportation, bike/walk	Work at home
Central business district	65	34	0
Central city	87	12	1
Unclustered central city	83	10	7
Total central city	81	16	3
Inner suburb	93	6	1
Middle suburb	91	6	2
Outer suburb	90	7	2
Unclustered suburb	86	6	8
Total suburb	88	6	6
Employment centers	85	13	1
Unclustered	85	7	8
Total	85	10	5

Twin Cities

	Car, van, or truck	Public transportation, bike/walk	Work at home
Central business district	73	27	0
Central city	85	14	1
Unclustered central city	82	10	8
Total central city	80	18	2
Inner suburb	95	4	1
Middle suburb	96	3	1
Outer suburb	96	3	2
Unclustered suburb	90	4	7
Total suburb	92	3	4
Employment centers	89	11	1
Unclustered	88	4	7
Total	89	8	4

Source: U.S. Census Transportation Planning Packages.

TABLE 4.8   Means of transportation to work by race and ethnicity, 2000: Atlanta, Portland, and Twin Cities metropolitan areas (in %)

Atlanta

	Car, van, or truck	Public transportation, bike/walk	Work at home
Black	87	12	2
Hispanic	86	13	2
Other	89	9	2
White	93	3	4
Total	91	6	3

Portland

	Car, van, or truck	Public transportation, bike/walk	Work at home
Black	74	22	3
Hispanic	83	15	2
Other	83	14	3
White	86	9	5
Total	85	10	5

Twin Cities

	Car, van, or truck	Public transportation, bike/walk	Work at home
Black	75	23	2
Hispanic	80	19	2
Other	82	15	2
White	89	7	4
Total	88	8	4

Source: U.S. Census Transportation Planning Package.

clearly limits opportunities for workers of color. Extending effective transit to fast-growing suburban areas is one way to reduce this disadvantage. A necessary condition to achieve this is high job densities in the suburbs—something that is achievable only if job clustering is strongly encouraged.

COMMUTING PATTERNS AND CONGESTION

Traffic congestion constricts worker access to employment and exacerbates existing mismatches between jobs and housing. In the Twin Cities, traffic congestion is worsening in the suburbs. Outer suburban employment centers start by having light levels of traffic and quickly become congested as development intensifies near the centers. This increased suburban congestion has made it even more difficult for low-income people of color in the core of the region to access the fastest-growing employment centers in middle and outer suburbs.

To illustrate changing commuting conditions in the Twin Cities, time contours around employment centers were mapped to show the time it takes to travel to the employment centers. Data for travel time to work were used to derive the areas around each employment center, representing twenty-, thirty-, and forty-minute commutes.[8] The time contours, or commuter sheds, can then be overlaid on demographic or housing data to analyze the characteristics of the commuter sheds. The size of commuter sheds is also of interest—a decline in the size of commuter sheds between 1990 and 2000 is indicative of increased traffic congestion.[9]

Four examples in Maps 4.8 through 4.15 illustrate changes in commuter sheds in the Twin Cities between 1990 and 2000. The commuter sheds are for the Minneapolis central business district job center, the Midway center (an "other central city" job center), Eden Prairie (a large, fast-growing, middle suburban center), and Shakopee (a very fast growing outer suburban employment center).

The Minneapolis CBD, the region's largest employment center, grew slowly during the 1990s. The commuter sheds are relatively circular, reflecting the fact that the job center can be reached by interstate highways from all four compass points. The twenty-minute commuter shed is relatively small—less than ten miles in diameter—because the roads in the immediate vicinity are the most heavily congested in the region. The twenty- to thirty-minute commuter shed extends more than twice as far from the job center, while the thirty- to forty-minute zone extends nearly thirty miles in all directions.

The three times contracted by 24, 26, and 22 percent, respectively, between 1990 and 2000. This reflects increases in traffic congestion during the decade. Another important change is in the shapes of the commuter sheds, especially for the two inner contours. Each of these became elongated along their east–west axis. This reflects two factors: the opening of I-394, which extends westward from Minneapolis CBD to the high-income suburbs to the west, and greater-than-average increases in congestion on I-35W, the major access from the north and south.

St. Paul's Midway employment center had an even more dramatic decrease in its twenty-minute commuting zone than did the Minneapolis central business district. The twenty-minute commuter shed declined by 51 percent between 1990 and 2000, making most of St. Paul and its southern suburbs inaccessible within twenty minutes. The thirty-minute and forty-minute zones also decreased, 22 and 23 percent, respectively, similar to the Minneapolis CBD.

Eden Prairie is a fast-growing, middle suburb southwest of Minneapolis. The employment center reflects these characteristics. It was the eighth-largest center

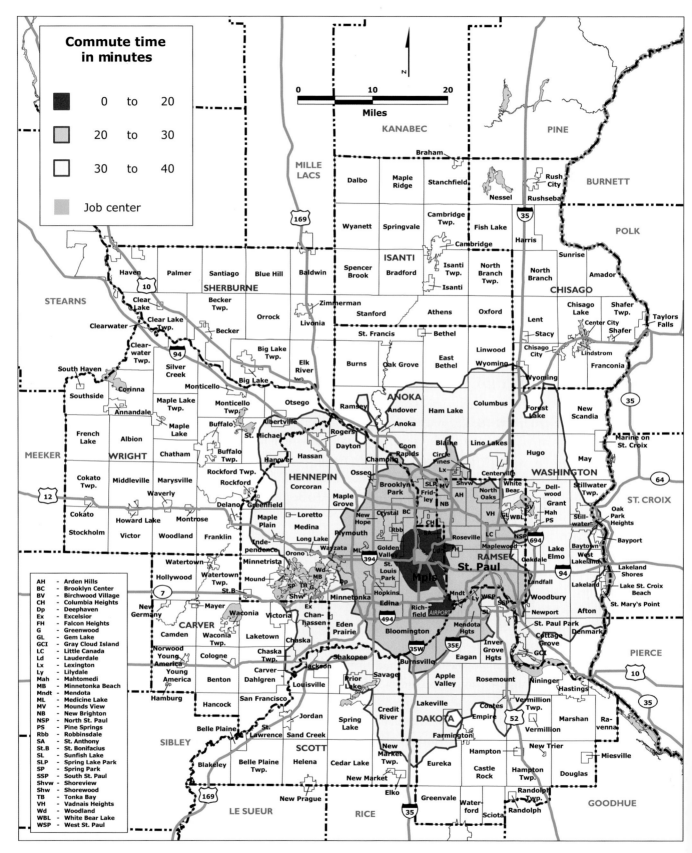

MAP 4.8. Commuter shed for Minneapolis central business district employment center, 1990. *Source:* U.S. Census Transportation Planning Package.

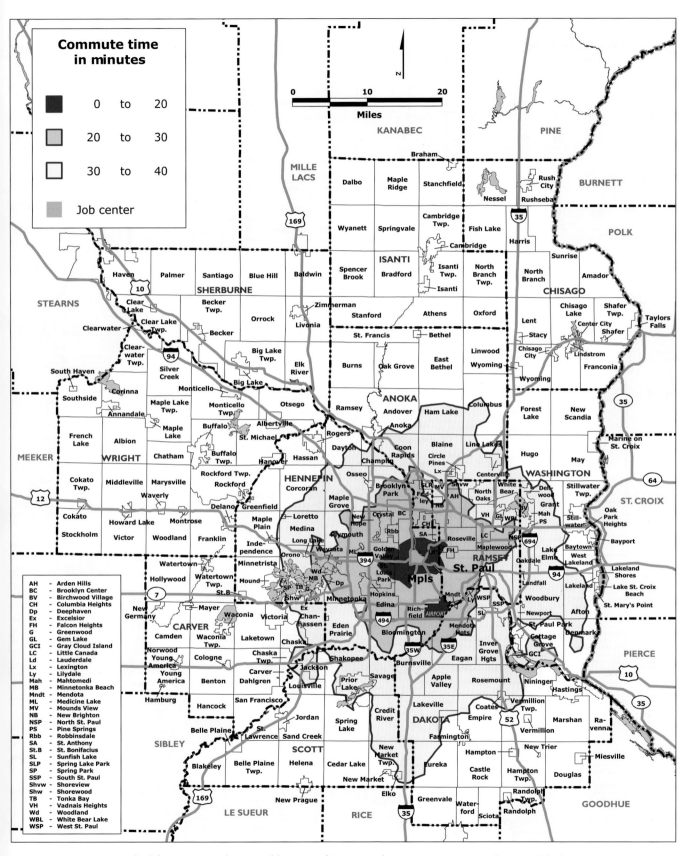

MAP 4.9. Commuter shed for Minneapolis central business district employment center, 2000. *Source:* U.S. Census Transportation Planning Package.

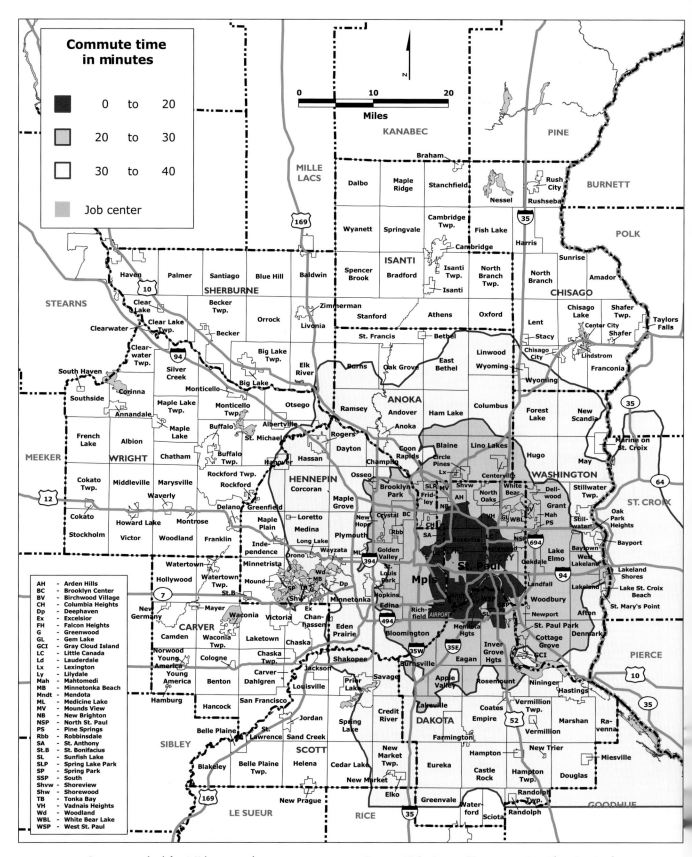

MAP 4.10. Commuter shed for Midway employment center, 1990. *Source:* U.S. Census Transportation Planning Package.

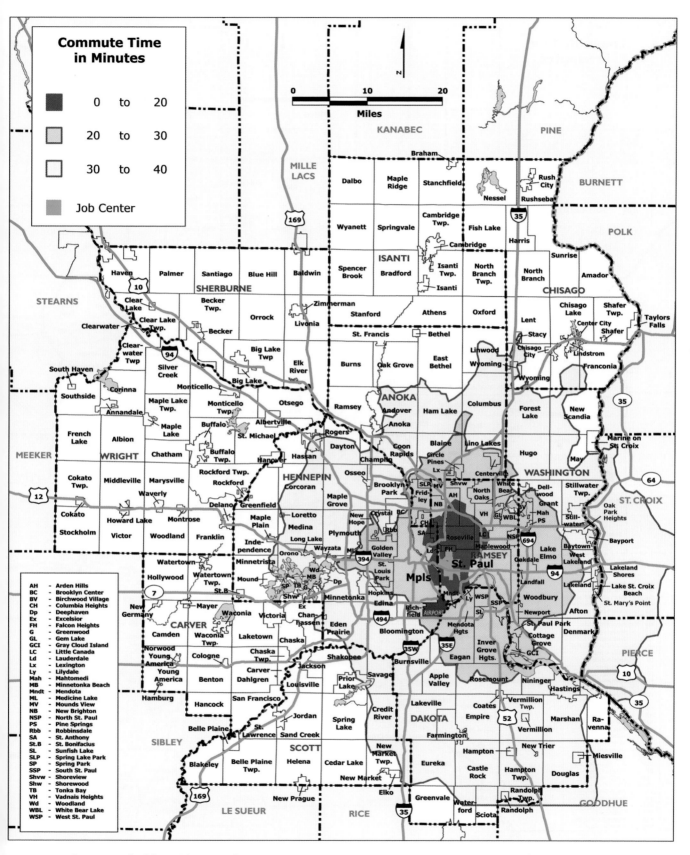

MAP 4.11. Commuter shed for Midway employment center, 2000. *Source:* U.S. Census Transportation Planning Package.

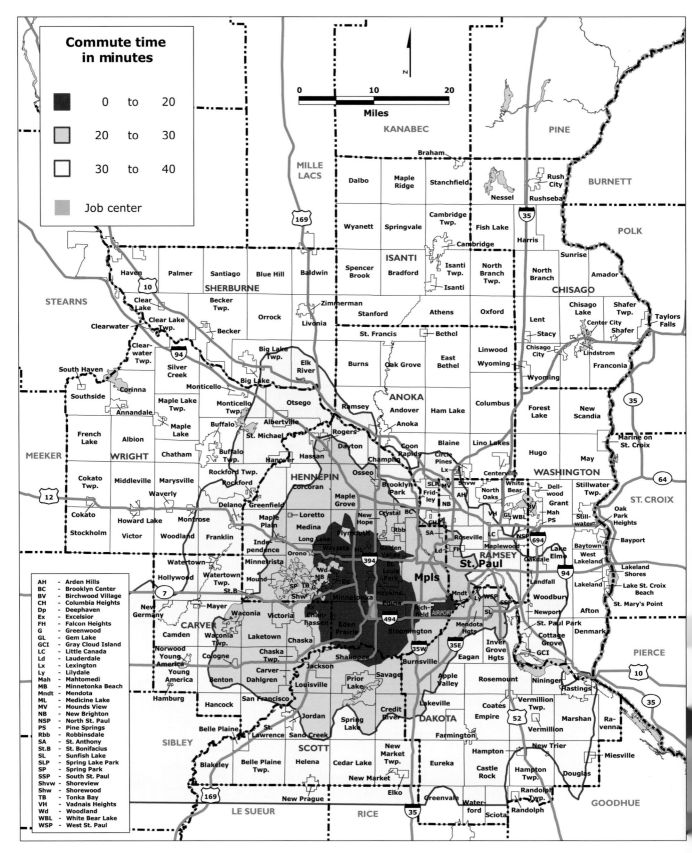

MAP 4.12. Commuter shed for Eden Prairie/169 employment center, 1990. *Source:* U.S. Census Transportation Planning Package.

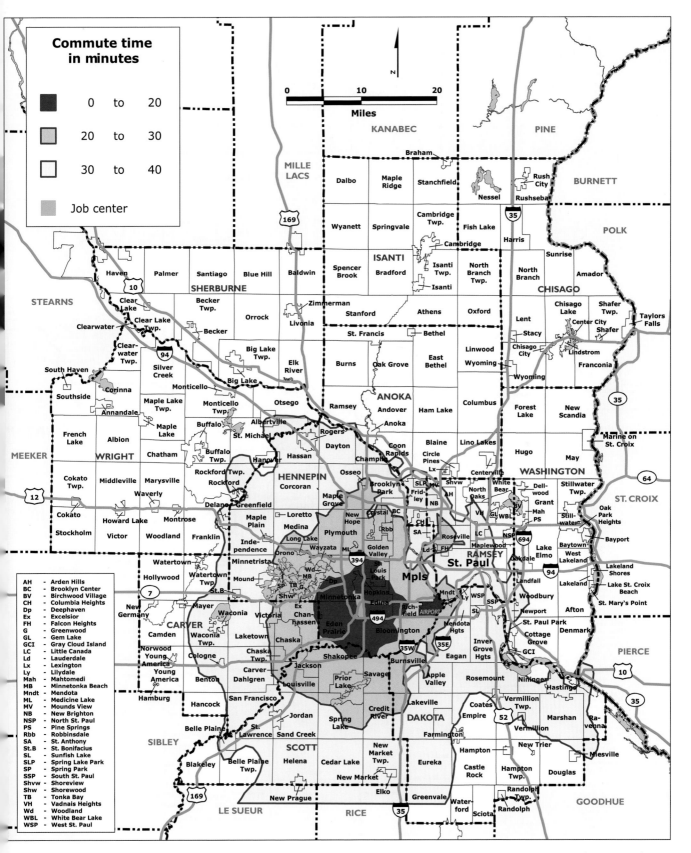

MAP 4.13. Commuter shed for Eden Prairie/169 employment center, 2000. *Source:* U.S. Census Transportation Planning Package.

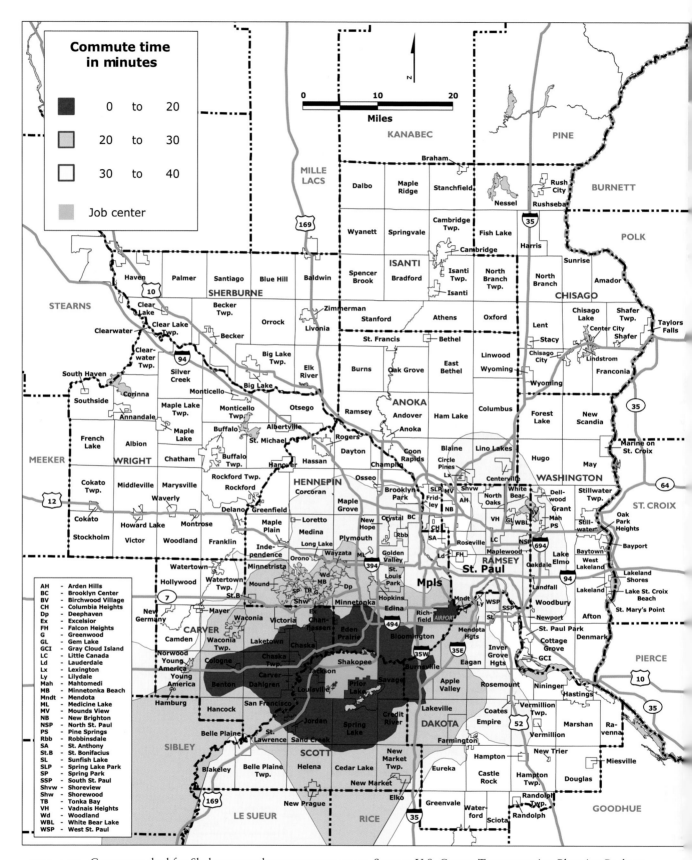

MAP 4.14. Commuter shed for Shakopee employment center, 1990. *Source:* U.S. Census Transportation Planning Package.

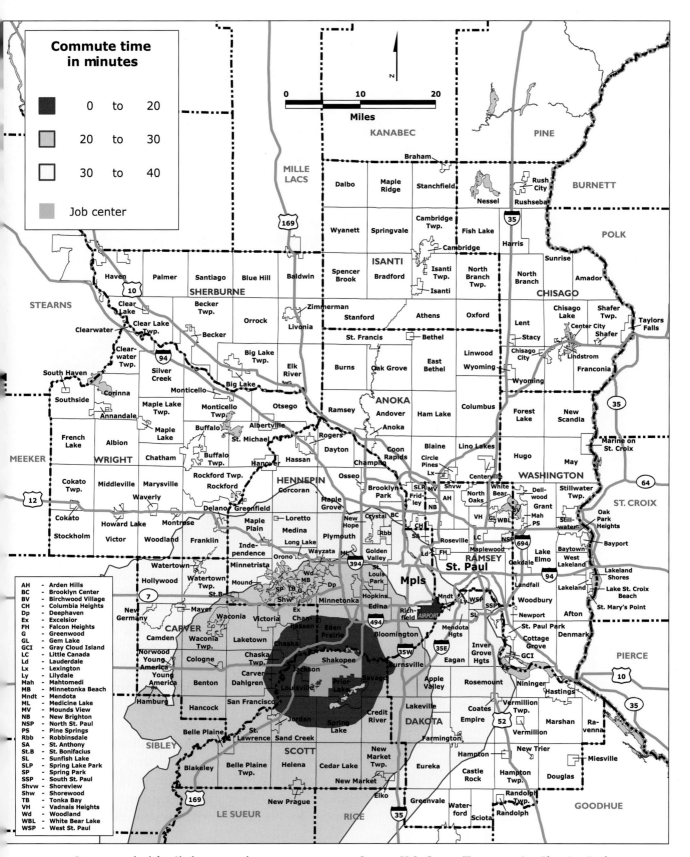

Commute time in minutes

Commute time in minutes

- 0 to 20
- 20 to 30
- 30 to 40
- Job center

AH – Arden Hills
BC – Brooklyn Center
BV – Birchwood Village
CH – Columbia Heights
Dp – Deephaven
Ex – Excelsior
FH – Falcon Heights
G – Greenwood
GL – Gem Lake
GCI – Gray Cloud Island
LC – Little Canada
Ld – Lauderdale
Lx – Lexington
Ly – Lilydale
Mah – Mahtomedi
MB – Minnetonka Beach
Mndt – Mendota
ML – Medicine Lake
MV – Mounds View
NB – New Brighton
NSP – North St. Paul
PS – Pine Springs
Rbb – Robbinsdale
SA – St. Anthony
St.B – St. Bonifacius
SL – Sunfish Lake
SLP – Spring Lake Park
SP – Spring Park
SSP – South St. Paul
Shvw – Shoreview
Shw – Shorewood
TB – Tonka Bay
VH – Vadnais Heights
Wd – Woodland
WBL – White Bear Lake
WSP – West St. Paul

MAP 4.15. Commuter shed for Shakopee employment center, 2000. *Source:* U.S. Census Transportation Planning Package.

in 2000 and had a job growth rate of 47 percent during the 1990s. Eden Prairie's commuter sheds are significantly larger than those for the Minneapolis CBD, reflecting lower overall congestion levels in the suburbs. However, traffic congestion increased much more rapidly in Eden Prairie in the 1990s—the area of the twenty- and thirty-minute commuter sheds decreased by about 40 percent, much faster than for the Minneapolis CBD.

Shakopee is a rapidly growing outer suburb near the periphery of development in the region. Its commuter sheds were the largest of the four job centers, reflecting lower absolute levels of congestion in the outer suburbs. However, the twenty-minute commuter shed shrank the most of the four centers—by 48 percent between 1990 and 2000. On the other hand, the thirty-minute commuter shed grew 23 percent. This indicates that traffic congestion worsened dramatically very close to the job center, but eased a bit farther away.

The overall patterns seen in these four examples are also evident in analysis of commuter sheds for all 40 job centers. Commuter sheds are smaller in the core, where absolute congestion levels are highest, but they are contracting more rapidly the farther the centers are from the core (where growth rates were greatest). The size of the thirty-minute commuter sheds varies from about 500 square miles for CBDs to about 850 square miles on average for outer suburban job centers (Table 4.10). However, the thirty-minute commuter sheds contracted more rapidly the farther from the core—by 23 percent for the CBDs compared to 36 percent for outer suburban centers.

COMMUTER SHED ANALYSIS: DEMOGRAPHICS

There are stark differences in housing and population characteristics in the commuter sheds serving different types of job centers. These differences correspond to their relative location in the Twin Cities region. For instance, the more distant from the core an employment center is, the greater are job growth rates and the lower are affordability rates for housing in the commuter sheds.

Table 4.9 shows that the data for the four sample job centers and differences across the centers are striking.[10] First, the racial compositions of the populations with greatest access to the job centers—the twenty-minute commuter sheds—are dramatically different. The population in the twenty-minute commuter sheds for the two central city job centers was very diverse in 2000 by Twin Cities' standards. Just 61 percent of the population was white in the Minneapolis CBD commuter shed, with 79 percent white in St. Paul's Midway. In contrast, the suburban twenty-minute commuter sheds of Eden Prairie and Shakopee were 90 percent white.

The income and poverty data show similarly dramatic patterns. Mean household income was lowest in the areas closest to the central city employment centers and increased with distance from it. Eden Prairie and Shakopee show the opposite

TABLE 4.9 Selected commuter shed characteristics in four Twin Cities employment centers

	Minneapolis Central business district	St. Paul Midway	Eden Prairie	Shakopee
Employment center type	CBD	Central city	Middle	Outer
Jobs in 2000	140,930	48,245	33,730	12,965
Job growth, 1990–2000	10%	12%	47%	83%
0 to 30-minute commuter shed area (square miles), 2000	349	544	481	790
Change in commuter shed size				
0 to 20-minute commuter shed	-24%	-51%	-42%	-48%
20 to 30-minute commuter shed	-26%	-22%	-40%	23%
30 to 40-minute commuter shed	-22%	-23%	-18%	-2%
Race of residents, 2000				
0 to 20-minute commuter shed				
White	61%	79%	90%	90%
Black	18%	7%	3%	1%
Other	21%	14%	7%	8%
20 to 30-minute commuter shed				
White	78%	76%	79%	91%
Black	8%	9%	9%	2%
Other	14%	15%	12%	7%
Mean household income, 2000				
0 to 20-minute commuter shed	$48,849	$57,840	$83,821	$87,727
20 to 30-minute commuter shed	$64,084	$61,246	$70,045	$80,325
30 to 40-minute commuter shed	$76,710	$77,011	$61,276	$63,682
Poverty rate, 2000				
0 to 20-minute commuter shed	22%	10%	4%	3%
20 to 30-minute commuter shed	8%	10%	8%	4%
30 to 40-minute commuter shed	4%	4%	9%	10%
Percentage of housing affordable to a household at 50% or less of the regional median income, 2000				
0 to 20-minute commuter shed	55%	38%	13%	11%
20 to 30-minute commuter shed	30%	35%	27%	15%
30 to 40-minute commuter shed	18%	15%	32%	33%

Sources: U.S. Census Transportation Planning Package; U.S. Census Bureau

trend with decreases in income at greater distances from the centers. Similarly, the poverty rate declines with distance from the Minneapolis CBD, while poverty climbs with distance from Eden Prairie and Shakopee.

The income and poverty patterns reflect the affordability of the housing stock in each of the commuter sheds. Within twenty minutes, 55 percent of the housing in the Minneapolis CBD was affordable to a household with 50 percent or more of the regional median income in 1999.[11] In St. Paul's Midway, 38 percent of housing was affordable. These percentages declined with distance from the job centers.

In contrast, just 13 percent of housing within twenty minutes to the Eden Prairie center was affordable, and the affordability rate increased with distance from the job center. Shakopee showed even lower affordability rates than Eden Prairie within its twenty- and thirty-minute commuter sheds.

COMPARATIVE ANALYSIS OF COMMUTER SHEDS IN ATLANTA, PORTLAND, AND THE TWIN CITIES

The location of regional jobs and affordable housing in a region has an impact on how accessible jobs are to workers. Traffic congestion also affects job accessibility for workers. To look at these issues commuter sheds were calculated for all of the employment centers in each of the three metropolitan areas.[12] The commuter sheds were then overlaid on demographic and housing data to repeat the analysis from the prior section for Atlanta and Portland.

Absolute congestion levels varied dramatically across the metros. Table 4.10 shows data for the thirty-minute commuter shed to illustrate this. Portland had the smallest commuter sheds by far—less than one-third the size of Atlanta's on average and one-sixth of the Twin Cities. (This ranking was true regardless of the type of employment center.) This reflects higher population densities in Portland, but also, more important, higher absolute congestion levels.

In each of the regions, commuter sheds tended to be larger in suburban areas, indicative of less-congested roads. For instance, Atlanta's CBD commuter shed had an area of 110.9 square miles, about a fourth the size of middle and outer suburb commuter sheds.

Of greater interest are the changes in commuter shed areas. Commuter sheds shrank in all regions, with Atlanta's shrinking the most, implying that traffic congestion grew most rapidly there. Atlanta's 2000 commuter sheds were 56 percent smaller in areas than in 1990. Traffic congestion increased less sharply in Portland and the Twin Cities, as their commuter sheds each decreased by about 42 and 34 percent, respectively.

The three regions also had different congestion trends within their areas. In Atlanta, traffic congestion worsened more in the core of the region than in the suburbs. The size of the thirty-minute commuter shed of the Atlanta CBD declined

TABLE 4.10 Commuter shed areas and percentage change by employment center type

Employment center type	Average 30-minute commuter shed area (square miles)			Percentage change: 30-minute commuter shed area, 1990–2000		
	Atlanta	Portland	Twin Cities	Atlanta	Portland	Twin Cities
Central business districts	110.9	34.0	490.1	-67.7	-54.6	-22.6
Other central city centers	248.7	64.7	570.5	-63.6	-35.8	-24.7
Inner suburb	229.6	138.0	699.6	-59.3	-39.6	-31.4
Middle suburb	397.1	114.5	663.9	-52.3	-25.1	-38.4
Outer suburb	388.6	117.8	848.8	-48.3	-51.3	-36.3
Total—employment centers	306.6	91.4	672.7	-55.7	-42.1	-33.6

Source: U.S. Census Transportation Planning Package, 1990 and 2000.

about 68 percent, compared to the outer suburban centers, which declined about 48 percent. Given that job growth was more rapid in suburban job centers, this implies that infrastructure improvements in the suburbs must have been more extensive than in the core.

In Portland, congestion worsened more in the central city and outer suburban employment centers. Portland CBD and outer suburban center's commuter sheds decreased by more than 50 percent, while the inner and middle suburbs decreased by less. Except for the CBD, this pattern reflects growth rates, implying that infrastructure investments were relatively balanced.

In the Twin Cities, congestion levels tended to worsen the farther an employment center was from the core of the region. While the CBDs had commuter sheds that decreased in size by about 23 percent, middle and outer suburban centers decreased by 38 and 36 percent, respectively. This pattern correlates well with job growth rates, which implies that, similar to Portland, infrastructure investments were relatively balanced.

Another way to measure accessibility of the job centers is to calculate the number or percentage of workers within a reasonable commute of the job centers. This measure controls for the fact that population densities (as well as congestion) vary significantly across the metros. Table 4.11 shows the average percentage of all workers within a thirty-minute commute of each type of job center in each of the metros. Atlanta shows the least accessible employment centers of the three regions. On average, just 15 percent of the population of Atlanta can access a given employment center, followed by 36 percent in Portland and 46 percent in the Twin Cities.

The fact that Portland's employment centers are more accessible for the region's population than Atlanta's are for its population is telling. Portland's centralization

TABLE 4.11 Percentage of regional population within 30 minutes of employment centers averaged by employment center type, 2000

	Atlanta	Portland	Twin Cities
Central business districts	10	34	43
Other central city	12	42	52
Inner suburb	14	35	52
Middle suburb	21	35	44
Outer suburb	15	25	34
Total—employment centers	15	36	46

Sources: U.S. Census Transportation Planning Package; U.S. Census Bureau.

of jobs and housing more than offset its high congestion levels (indicated by its very small commuter sheds). On the other hand, Atlanta's larger commuter sheds do little to offset the negative effects that job decentralization and urban sprawl have on accessibility for the region's population. The Twin Cities had the largest commuter sheds of any of the regions. On average, almost half of the Twin Cities' population (46 percent) can access a given employment center within thirty minutes.

In all three regions the central business district and the outer suburban employment centers tended to be the least accessible—almost certainly reflecting high congestion near CBDs and long distances in the periphery. In Atlanta, the central city was the least accessible for the region's population, while in the Twin Cities and Portland the outer suburban centers were the least accessible.

Accessibility also varies significantly by race. Tables 4.12 through 4.14 show the average percentages of regional populations within thirty-minute commutes from employment centers by race and location. In Atlanta, blacks and Hispanics had greater access than whites overall to each type of job center (Table 4.12). There was one exception: Atlanta's fastest-growing outer suburban centers were the least accessible to blacks—only half as accessible to blacks as whites. The fact that blacks overwhelmingly live in the southern part of the region and the outer suburban centers were located in the north explains this disparity. Compared to the other metropolitan areas, access rates were low for all races, but whites especially live farther from their jobs in Atlanta.

In Portland, Hispanics and whites showed similar access rates to job centers while blacks had greater rates, except for the outer suburban centers (Table 4.13). Less access to outer suburban centers is less detrimental in Portland because Portland's outer suburban centers have only a small share of the region's jobs and there was relatively strong job growth in the core of the region.

TABLE 4.12 Percentage of regional population within 30 minutes of employment centers by race and employment center type, 2000: Atlanta

	White	Black	Hispanic
Central business districts	10	11	11
Other central city	11	15	16
Inner suburb	13	14	20
Middle suburb	19	23	26
Outer suburb	16	8	24
Total—employment centers	14	15	21

Sources: U.S. Census Transportation Planning Package; U.S. Census Bureau.

In the Twin Cities blacks and Hispanics had greater accessibility rates than whites, regardless of location (Table 4.14).

The consistently greater access rates for workers of color are striking. They show that there are real advantages to central locations. In each of the three regions, people of color are much more likely to live in the core of the region. This often represents a clear disadvantage, given social and fiscal conditions in most regional cores. However, central location often bestows a real advantage when measuring access because all quadrants of the region are equally accessible and because transportation systems tend to focus on core areas. However, as jobs continue to decentralize, and if traffic congestion worsens in suburbs, the advantages of central locations diminish.

Another accessibility issue relates to affordable housing (Table 4.15). Afford-

TABLE 4.13 Percentage of regional population within 30 minutes of employment centers by race and employment center type, 2000: Portland

	White	Black	Hispanic
Central business districts	33	70	28
Other central city	41	74	32
Inner suburb	35	59	26
Middle suburb	35	46	31
Outer suburb	25	18	28
Total—employment centers	35	56	30

Sources: U.S. Census Transportation Planning Package; U.S. Census Bureau.

TABLE 4.14 Percentage of regional population within 30 minutes of employment centers by race and employment center type, 2000: Twin Cities

	White	Black	Hispanic
Central business districts	38	75	64
Other central city	48	82	74
Inner suburb	47	77	63
Middle suburb	40	57	56
Outer suburb	34	45	43
Total—employment centers	45	72	64

Sources: U.S. Census Transportation Planning Package; U.S. Census Bureau.

ability rates within thirty-minute commuter sheds decline with distance from the core in each of the three metropolitan areas. The gradient is sharpest in Atlanta, where only 8 percent of housing within thirty minutes of outer suburban job centers is affordable to households at 50 percent of the regional median income.

TRANSPORTATION STRATEGIES IN ATLANTA, PORTLAND, AND THE TWIN CITIES

Each of the three regions has emphasized different ways of addressing transportation issues and traffic congestion. In the past, Atlanta and the Twin Cities have relied on freeway development to accommodate growth, although this pattern has changed markedly in more recent years. Portland, in contrast, has consistently em-

TABLE 4.15 Percentage of housing affordable at 50 percent of regional median income in 0–30 minute commuter sheds by employment center type, 2000

	Atlanta	Portland	Twin Cities
Central business districts	25	19	35
Other central city centers	25	18	32
Inner suburb	19	17	30
Middle suburb	18	15	30
Outer suburb	8	13	27
All employment centers	18	17	30

Sources: U.S. Census Transportation Planning Package; U.S. Census Bureau.

phasized public transportation and containment of growth within an urban growth boundary.

Per capita freeway lane mileage decreased in all three regions during the 1980s and 1990s, with Atlanta showing sharp decreases beginning in the mid-1990s (Figure 4.1).[13] In 2005, the Twin Cities surpassed Atlanta in having more freeway lane miles per one thousand peak travelers, and the region actually saw a slight increase in per capita freeway lane miles between 2004 and 2005, counter to prevailing regional trends of decreasing per capita miles.

Building new roadways rarely, if ever, eases traffic congestion. When a new roadway is built, new development and changes in travel behavior increase demand for the new lane miles, making it impossible to alleviate traffic congestion with road building alone.[14] In the Twin Cities alone, estimates show that it cost $1.5 billion in 1998 for the maintenance and construction of streets and highways, a figure that is expected to jump to $2.2 billion in 2020.[15]

To ease urban travel, transportation planners also try to make the highway system more efficient by utilizing traffic management strategies, including ramp metering, monitoring freeways, and service patrols that tow inoperable vehicles from the roadways.[16] The Twin Cities more consistently incorporated these types of traffic management strategies, compared to Atlanta or Portland (Figure 4.2).

The Twin Cities outpaced the other regions with metering and monitoring most of its freeways while Atlanta hardly metered freeways at all. Atlanta only metered 2 percent of its freeway miles, compared to 86 percent of freeways in the Twin Cities. The Twin Cities also more often monitored its freeways with cameras to inform the public of crash incidents and to analyze congestion patterns. The Twin Cities monitored 80 percent of its freeway system, compared to 68 percent in Portland and only 55 percent in Atlanta.

Atlanta did incorporate one main feature to alleviate traffic congestion by hav-

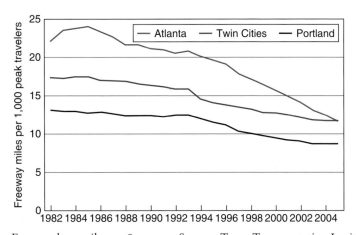

FIGURE 4.1. Freeway lane-miles, 1982–2005. *Source:* Texas Transportation Institute.

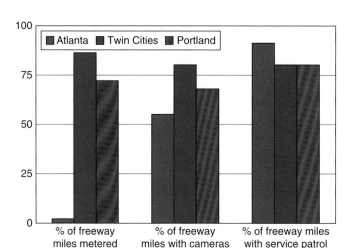

FIGURE 4.2. Traffic management statistics, 2005. *Source:* Texas Transportation Institute.

ing 91 percent of its freeways miles covered by service patrols that tow inoperable vehicles from the roadways. Portland and the Twin Cities also had high rates of service patrols on freeway miles, each with 80 percent coverage.

Using various traffic management strategies helps alleviate traffic congestion. Public transportation, however, plays an even larger role. According to the Texas Transportation Institute, in 2005, 510 million hours of traffic delays and $9.6 billion were saved by the use of public transportation systems in the eighty-five largest U.S. urban areas, almost twice the amount saved from combined operational improvements in traffic management strategies.[17]

When considering the amount of revenues generated by transit agencies, Portland's system is the most extensive and the Twin Cities' the least extensive. According to the U.S. Federal Transit Administration, in 2004 Portland generated $178 of public transportation revenue per person in the region, compared to $104 in Atlanta and only $83 in the Twin Cities.[18]

The generated revenue of the regions reflected the supply and use of the regional transit systems. In 2003 Atlanta operated 867 vehicles that traveled a total of 51 million miles annually while the Twin Cities operated 744 vehicles that covered 22 million miles and Portland operated 615 vehicles that covered 36 million miles.[19] However, when controlling for population, regional transit usage was greatest in Portland, followed by Atlanta and the Twin Cities.

In 2005, Portland's rate of passenger trips per person was twice that of the Twin Cities (Figure 4.3).[20] Portland's public transportation system also significantly outperformed Atlanta's. There were 64.4 unlinked passenger trips per person in Portland, compared to 36 in Atlanta and 32.1 in the Twin Cities.

Overall, commuters save time and fuel costs associated with traffic congestion

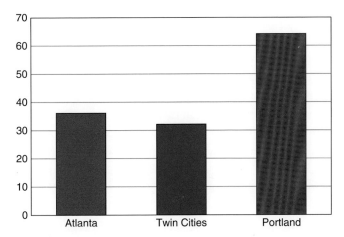

FIGURE 4.3. Unlinked public transportation passenger trips per person in 2005. *Source:* Texas Transportation Institute.

by having a transit system; and in the three regions, the greater use of the transit system reflected costs savings for peak time commuters.[21] The Texas Transportation Institute estimates that the existence of public transportation saved peak hour users an average of $140 in Portland, $112 in Atlanta, and $69 in the Twin Cities in costs associated with being stuck in traffic in 2005.[22]

Another major difference between the regions is the longer presence of light-rail in Atlanta and Portland. Until June 2004, the Twin Cities had no transit rail system and often had strong suburbanite resistance to light-rail development. Successful rail transit transports more passengers per vehicle, while reducing costs of fuel and wages, compared to bus transportation. In Atlanta and Portland, the operating expense per passenger mile and passenger trip are often half as much for trains as for buses.[23]

In more recent years, many Twin Cities suburbanites have reversed their resistance to light-rail. Leaders in suburban southwest Minneapolis now want to accelerate implementation of a light-rail route into job-rich sections of Minnetonka and Eden Prairie.[24] In the northwest Minneapolis suburbs, partnering communities wanted to ditch their original busway proposal in order to better consider a rail option for the area.[25]

Given that the Twin Cities may be moving more toward public transportation as a means to mitigate traffic congestion, it is important to consider the success of Portland. Portland's public transit success relates to the compactness and density of its urban area—a result of its strictly enforced urban growth boundary. Public transportation, especially rail, relies on supportive land use patterns, and the urban sprawl found in the Twin Cities and Atlanta works against the success of public transportation in those regions.

HIGHWAY INVESTMENT IN ATLANTA AND THE TWIN CITIES

In Portland, policy makers have placed greater emphasis on public transportation and containing urban sprawl, while Atlanta and the Twin Cities have tended to allow greater urban sprawl that is more conducive to the automobile. Regional highway policy and investments can, in the short term, ease the movement of transportation within metropolitan areas. Atlanta has focused on building more roads outward that connect to fast-growing middle and outer suburban areas, while the Twin Cities places greater emphasis on traffic management strategies and targets funding closer to the core of the region.

Highway funding can help direct growth and development in a region. Intraregional variations in spending can be very revealing of regional priorities and help to explain variations in congestion and growth.

The city of Atlanta and many of its inner-ring suburbs had low per capita highway spending (Map 4.16).[26] The greatest per capita highway spending in Atlanta occurred in the northwest suburbs, a part of the region with the fastest-growing employment centers. Higher per capita spending was also evident in suburbs to the north and west of Atlanta, but not in the south—the suburbs with the highest minority populations.

Overall the Twin Cities had greater per capita highway funding than Atlanta—$44,000 per one hundred persons for highways, compared to about $30,000 in Atlanta. This corresponds to Atlanta's sharp decline in per capita highway spending during the 1990s and recent increases in spending in the Twin Cities.

The Twin Cities also tended to put a greater proportion of their highway financing toward the core of the region. The central cities of Minneapolis and St. Paul had highway spending of $32,500 per one hundred residents compared to just $9,245 in the city of Atlanta. There were also a number of inner-ring suburbs in the Twin Cities that had high per capita spending (Map 4.17). In outer suburbs, Atlanta clearly outpaced the Twin Cities, with spending of $43,245 per one hundred residents compared to $22,912.

These trends indicate that the Twin Cities metro focuses more on maintaining the existing highway system, while Atlanta focuses funding toward areas that are expanding and urbanizing. These patterns are consistent with congestion trends. Figures 4.4 and 4.5 illustrate the changing levels of traffic congestion and the volume of highway spending broken down by a range of locations in the regions.[27]

In Atlanta there were decreases in highway spending the closer one gets to the core of the region, corresponding to increases in traffic congestion. In the city of Atlanta there was less than $10,000 per one hundred residents in highway spending, and there was a 65 percent increase in traffic congestion. In Atlanta's outer suburban areas, there was over $40,000 per capita spending and about a 50 percent increase in congestion.

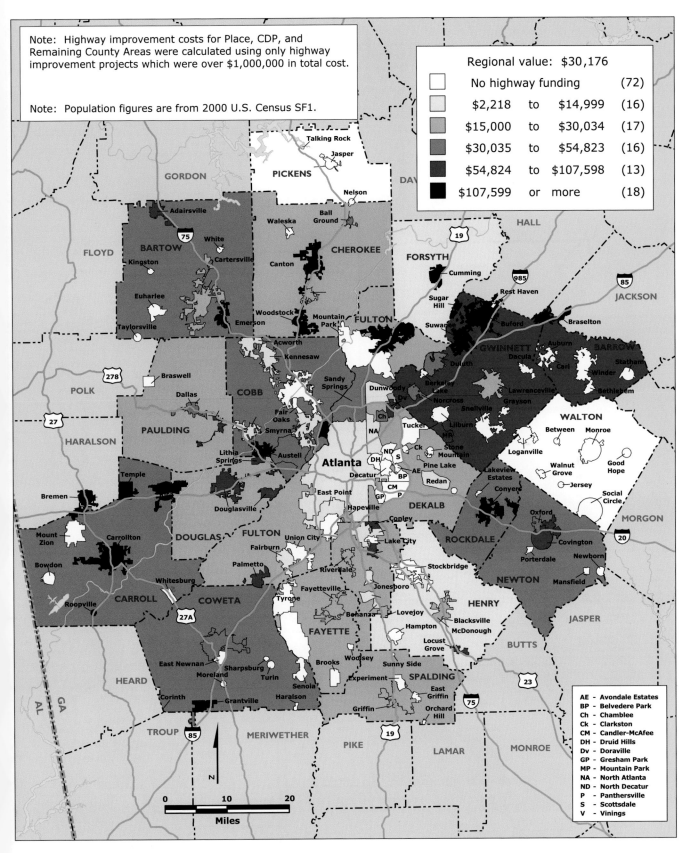

Note: Highway improvement costs for Place, CDP, and Remaining County Areas were calculated using only highway improvement projects which were over $1,000,000 in total cost.

Note: Population figures are from 2000 U.S. Census SF1.

Regional value: $30,176

	No highway funding		(72)
	$2,218	to	$14,999	(16)
	$15,000	to	$30,034	(17)
	$30,035	to	$54,823	(16)
	$54,824	to	$107,598	(13)
	$107,599	or	more	(18)

AE - Avondale Estates
BP - Belvedere Park
Ch - Chamblee
Ck - Clarkston
CM - Candler-McAfee
DH - Druid Hills
Dv - Doraville
GP - Gresham Park
MP - Mountain Park
NA - North Atlanta
ND - North Decatur
P - Panthersville
S - Scottsdale
V - Vinings

MAP 4.16. Highway improvement costs per hundred persons by place, census-designated place (CDP), and remaining county area, Atlanta region, 1992–2002. *Sources:* Georgia Department of Transportation; U.S. Census Bureau.

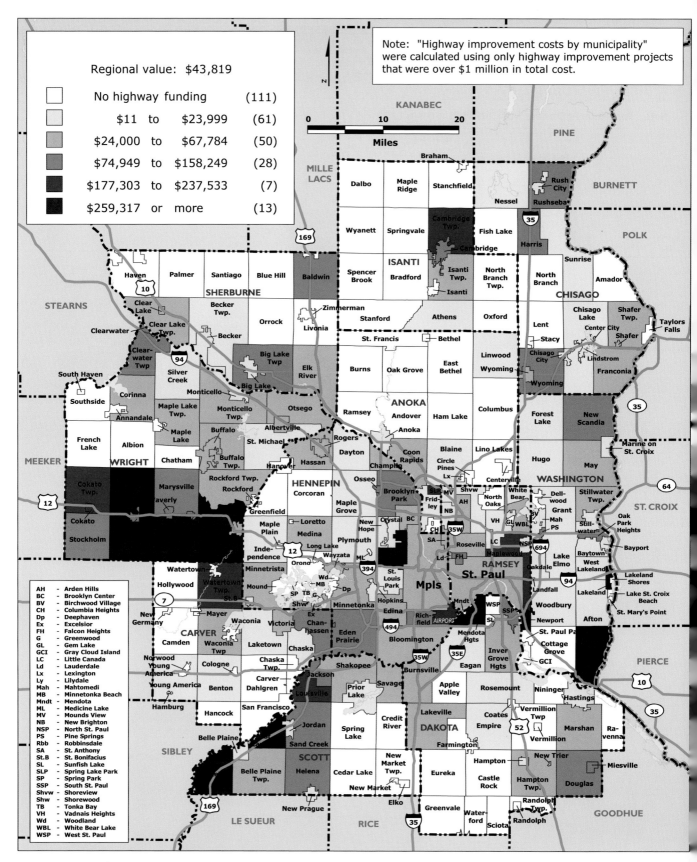

MAP 4.17. Highway improvement costs per 100 persons by municipality, Minneapolis–St. Paul region, 1992–2002.
Sources: Minnesota Department of Transportation; U.S. Census Bureau.

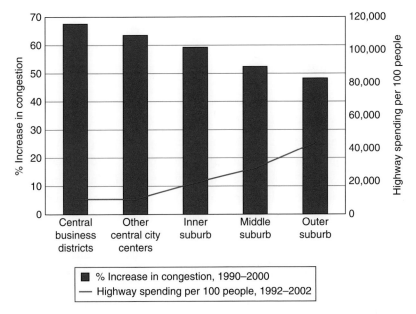

FIGURE 4.4. Increased traffic congestion and highway spending in Atlanta. *Sources:* U.S. Census Transportation Planning Package, 2000; Georgia Department of Transportation, 1992 and 2002.

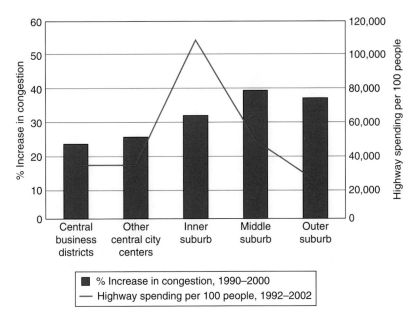

FIGURE 4.5. Increased traffic congestion and highway spending in Twin Cities. *Sources:* U.S. Census Transportation Planning Package, 2000; Minnesota Department of Transportation.

In the Twin Cities, inner-ring suburban highway spending, the highest in the region, corresponds with smaller increases in traffic congestion in the central city and inner-ring suburban job centers. Outer suburban job centers where spending was lowest had the greatest increases in traffic congestion.

CONCLUSIONS AND POLICY IMPLICATIONS

The ongoing decentralization of economic activity is an important issue in each of the three metropolitan areas included in the analysis. Middle and outer suburban job centers were the growth stars in all three metros. Increasing dispersal of jobs out of job clusters was also important in two of the three. In the Twin Cities, nonclustered jobs grew by 17 percentage points more than jobs in the employment centers during the 1990s. In Atlanta, the gap was 26 percentage points. Only in Portland did job center growth match that for nonclustered employment. If these trends continue, the viability of transit will continue to decline, especially in Atlanta and the Twin Cities.

The distributions of jobs and workers disadvantage workers of color, especially black workers. Minority workers are employed disproportionately in slower-growing job centers. Racial differences are greatest in the Twin Cities, where workers of color are concentrated in slow-growing core areas. Accessibility is the key. Black workers especially are much less likely to live within easy commuting distance of the fastest-growing job centers in middle and outer suburbs.

In Atlanta, racial segregation and affordable housing are concentrated in the southern part of the region, while the northern section of Atlanta saw the greatest clustering and growth of jobs. Portland again looked best of the three metros. Job growth, affordable housing, and racial groups are more uniformly spread across the region, creating conditions that make it easier for all groups to access employment.

Not surprisingly, outer areas are less congested in absolute terms in all three regions. However, changes in congestion patterns varied markedly. Congestion increased in all three metros, but the intraregional patterns were dramatically different. In the Twin Cities, highway funding patterns and slower growth near the core resulted in greater increases in congestion in outer parts of the region than in the core. In Atlanta, lagging transportation funding in the core led to greater congestion increases there than in outer areas, despite the fact that the core grew more slowly. One important outcome of this pattern is that it impedes commuting from slower-growing southern areas, where most workers of color live, to faster-growing northern job centers. The trends in Portland are more varied. Overall, congestion increased less there than in Atlanta but more than in the Twin Cities, and intraregional trends showed no clear pattern.

Portland clearly outperforms the other metros in transit usage. This reflects the fact that a primary transportation strategy in Portland is to guide growth into a compact urban area along transit corridors. As a result, job clusters grew more rapidly than nonclustered jobs in the 1990s, and Portland outperformed the Twin Cities and Atlanta by large margins in generating public transportation trips.

One very important policy implication of the findings is that, if current patterns continue, the potential for transit in the Twin Cities will decline. This will exacerbate the inequality in opportunity documented by this work. If jobs continue to migrate to low-density job centers at the fringe of the region and to nonclustered settings, job opportunities available to workers who rely on transit—lower-income workers who are disproportionately people of color—will decline. The Portland results show that this is not inevitable. Portland's use of a stricter growth boundary combined with coordination of transit and land use planning resulted in greater clustering of jobs during the 1990s, reinforcing the advantages of transit.

A variety of smart growth policies is available to slow or reverse the decentralization and dispersal of jobs that is happening in the Twin Cities. Incentives to encourage higher-density job development in the suburbs and a mix of housing, retail, and services around newly emerging job centers are one path. New town centers are gaining in popularity in developing suburbs in Minnesota. If new town centers become centers of gravity for future employment clusters in the planning stages, transit becomes more feasible. Planners should seek opportunities to cluster new development with an eye toward the job and housing densities required to support transit.

The findings also show that highway investment strategies matter. In Atlanta, where highway spending was clearly focused on the periphery, congestion increased most in the core, where growth was slowest. In the Twin Cities, more balanced spending led to congestion changes that reflected growth.

Growing public support for light-rail in the Twin Cities is a positive sign for transportation polices to promote transit. However, it is important to coordinate transit and transportation planning with land use planning. If local and regional planning do not have a strong focus on clustering jobs in transportation corridors, then greater transit spending may be futile. The Portland example is a good model of this concept: more compact urban development has resulted in more job clustering, making transit more viable.

This work also highlights the continuing problem of serious shortfalls in affordable housing in many suburban areas, especially near fast-growing job centers. Like most metropolitan areas, the Twin Cities have a long way to go in this regard. The existence of a regional planning agency with powers in this area is a big step, but the Metropolitan Council must develop and maintain a strong commitment to use its power to review local comprehensive plans to encourage or require more affordable housing in suburban areas with strong job growth.

The lack of racial diversity in the outer suburban job centers—areas where some affordable housing is already available—may also reflect steering or other discrimination in the housing market. Local and regional planners should be advocates for more aggressive testing studies to determine the presence of any racial steering by realtors and discrimination in the mortgage industry. As the Twin Cities have a more diverse workforce in the future, business leaders should be more aware of impediments that people of color face to access fast-growing job sectors and locations, including discrimination in housing and employment, and public education outcomes. In Chicago, Business and Professional People for the Public Interest, a collaboration of business, nonprofit, and governmental groups, is an example of an advocacy group that has taken a regional approach to these issues with some good results.

Finally, place-oriented strategies designed to enhance growth in current slow-growth areas in the core should play a role. One way to enhance access to growing job centers for disadvantaged workers and workers of color is to increase growth in centers in the core. A place in decline defines a worker's future opportunities, limits networks, and lessens the potential for higher earnings in the future. Stronger regional policies to direct more growth toward fully developed core areas instead of in green fields at the fringe can reduce the need for mobility strategies that help people get to scattered-site jobs.

5

The Environment and Growth

Thomas F. Luce Jr. and Sharon Pfeifer

During the past two decades, growth in the metropolitan region has rapidly expanded outward from the central cities and older suburbs into the rural areas of the region. As a direct result, many of the region's diverse natural habitats have been severely fragmented, if not completely converted to urban uses.

The public actors most often associated in the public's mind with natural resources conservation activities include several federal agencies, state government agencies in all fifty states, and thousands of special districts and counties. However, the role of local governments, with their powers to regulate land use, is often underestimated. Municipal governments often have the first and last word on whether specific parcels of land can or will be developed.

In many cases, local governments are not particularly well suited to regulate or protect sensitive natural areas. The full benefits of conserving natural resources are rarely concentrated in a single community. But, at the same time, the costs of conservation may be highly localized. In this situation, local governments do not face the proper incentives to conserve sensitive natural resources. If the benefits of protection are undervalued (because many of the benefits accrue to other areas), while the costs are not (because they are fully borne locally), then local governments can be expected to do too little to protect sensitive natural areas.

This happens not because residents or public officials value the resources any less than others or behave irrationally. Natural assets clearly have value at the local level. There have been more than thirty separate conservation finance measures in the eleven-county region since 1990. Recent successful initiatives in Wayzata, Woodbury, Minnetonka, and Dakota County to raise local taxes to preserve open space illustrate this point.[1] However, local residents often receive only a small portion of the benefits of protection, biasing decisions away from conservation when made solely at the local level.

Local governments also face a variety of incentives that push them to favor development over natural resource conservation. Local tax policy and land use regula-

223

tions are closely related. Local taxes must finance municipal services such as police and fire protection and public schools. The amount of revenue a local government can generate on its own depends largely on the value and types of land within its boundaries. If the property tax is the primary local tax, as it is in Minnesota, then local governments have a direct incentive to develop land use plans that maximize the value of property. Protected natural resources rarely meet this standard, at least in the short run.

The purpose of this chapter is to combine information about the metropolitan area's natural resource assets with a variety of demographic and fiscal data to assess how expected growth in the region is likely to affect the region's remaining land and water habitats. Specifically, the intent is to identify areas where natural resources might be most at risk from projected growth and development in order to assess the potential trade-offs between regional growth and natural resource conservation.

There are a variety of potential reasons to be concerned about these trade-offs. Sensitive natural areas create value in many ways. Historically, natural resources have been an important source of growth in the region's economy. Although today's economy relies much less on raw materials for growth, resource-related natural amenities make significant contributions to the area's quality of life. Lakes, rivers, streams, wooded areas, and the wildlife they support are magnets for residential development. Undeveloped areas also fill many other important, and often free, functions, including water and air purification, flood and stormwater control, wildlife habitat, and outdoor recreation.

The way in which development occurs—a factor controlled by local rules and regulations in most cases—also has implications for larger, worldwide concerns like global warming. Transportation is a major contributor to greenhouse gases. It accounts for a third of carbon dioxide emissions in the United States, a number that is growing. Compact development can reduce driving by reducing the number and length of trips made in cars. Mixed-use development puts housing in proximity to other destinations; grid street designs can reduce congestion on arterial roads; pedestrian-friendly streets can make it easier to walk or bicycle; and higher-density development can support transit usage.[2] One recent study shows that average vehicle miles traveled per person is nearly 25 percent lower in the ten most compact metropolitan areas than in the ten most sprawling areas.[3]

The region contains a variety of different types of communities, with very different sorts of pressures on sensitive natural areas. Data availability also limits analysis in some policy dimensions. As a result, two "regions" are used in this chapter to analyze the issues: (1) the eleven-county Twin Cities metropolitan area, and (2) the seven-county core of the metropolitan area.

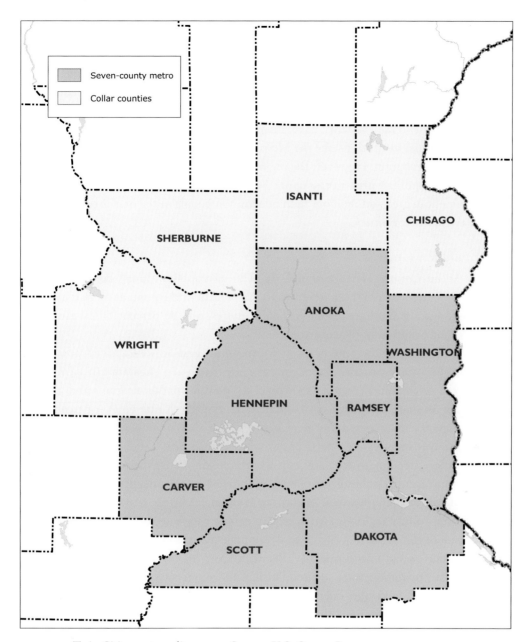

MAP 5.1. Twin Cities metropolitan area. *Source:* U.S. Census Bureau.

GROWTH PATTERNS IN THE ELEVEN-COUNTY
METROPOLITAN AREA

The eleven-county study area is home to 3.2 million people, nearly two-thirds of the state's population, and contains the state's primary growth engine: the Twin Cities metropolitan area economy. The eleven-county metropolitan area is projected to grow significantly by 2030, with the seven core metropolitan counties continuing to receive the majority of the state's new residents and jobs.[4]

Like most metropolitan areas in the United States, the Twin Cities metro has seen significant decentralization of population and jobs during recent decades. This pattern has not been as pronounced as in many large metropolitan areas owing, at least in part, to the existence of relatively strong (compared to other metropolitan areas) regional institutions like the Metropolitan Council and the Twin Cities Fiscal Disparities Program. However, the region has been growing more rapidly than any other metropolitan area in the upper Midwest, and current projections show the metropolitan area adding more than one million people in the first three decades of the twenty-first century.

Population Growth

The Seven-County Metropolitan Core. The metropolitan area's core is the most densely settled area in the state. In 1990, 94 percent of the population in the eleven-county metropolitan area lived in these counties, and 85 percent of the growth in the 1990s occurred in the core area.

While both of the core cities of Minneapolis and St. Paul gained population overall between 1990 and 2000, the two cities grew at a substantially slower rate than the seven-county region as a whole: 3.9 percent for Minneapolis and 5.4 percent for St. Paul, compared with a seven-county growth rate of 15.4 percent. The core region's inner-ring suburbs also saw either very modest growth or decline. Growth was strongest in outer-ring suburban communities, such as Woodbury and Lakeville, extending to the outer edges of the seven-county metro.

More recent population estimates show strong, continuing growth at the perimeter of the seven-county area. According to estimates by the Metropolitan Council, the seven-county region grew by 30,045 people between 2003 and 2004, and almost all of this growth occurred in developing suburbs (25,241 new residents) and rural areas (4,747 new residents).[5] Between 2000 and 2004, the ten cities adding the most population were all middle-ring and outer suburbs—Shakopee, Maple Grove, Blaine, Lakeville, Eden Prairie, Prior Lake, Plymouth, Farmington, Chaska, and Woodbury. These ten cities alone added a total of 54,303 new residents over the four-year time period.

The Collar Counties. All the metropolitan collar counties—Chisago, Isanti, Sherburne, and Wright—grew quickly during the 1990s. Although not as densely settled as the seven-county metropolitan core, these counties continue to grow rapidly. In 1990, the collar counties were home to just 6 percent of the population in the eleven-county metropolitan area, and in the 1990s they captured 15 percent of the region's growth. Most of Sherburne County, for instance, grew by more than 3 percent per year during the ten-year period.

Urbanization

While the spatial pattern of population growth is an important way to track growth, it does not capture all of what is important in growth patterns. Remote sensing from satellite imagery and aerial photography provide a means for visualizing the direct effect of growth and development on the landscape. The maps in chapter 1 show one major aspect of land use change—urbanization—in the seven-county core region over the period 1986 to 2002.[6] Urbanization in this report is defined as land in the following uses: residential, commercial, industrial, transportation, or communications. Based on satellite imagery analyzed by the Department of Forest Resources at the University of Minnesota, the map shows how growth in population and employment consumed previously undeveloped land during the sixteen-year period.[7]

Rapid urbanization occurred in areas immediately adjacent to previously urbanized areas (in inner and middle suburbs), as well as in locations along major roads and highways. The data show a pattern seen in most American metropolitan areas: as the region has grown, it has become less dense, consuming (or urbanizing) land at a rate greater than population has grown.

This is true even in the most densely settled parts of the region. Between 1986 and 2002, the amount of urbanized land in the seven-county metropolitan core grew from 450,000 to 625,000 acres, or by 38 percent. During the same period, population grew by just 29 percent: the growth rate in urbanized land was 53 percent greater than the population growth rate (Figure 5.1).

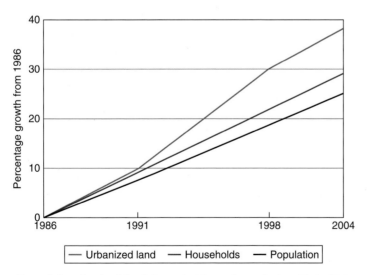

FIGURE 5.1. Growth in urbanized land, households, and population, Twin Cities seven-county metropolitan area, 1986–2002. *Sources:* Remote Sensing and Geospatial Analysis Laboratory, University of Minnesota; U.S. Census Bureau.

Growth during this time was also more "scattershot" than in previous years. For instance, in 1986, 79 percent of the urbanized land in the seven-county area was located within the Met Council's metropolitan urban service area (MUSA). However, only 50 percent of newly urbanized land during the subsequent sixteen years was inside the MUSA. The urbanized land map for 2002 (Map 1.6) shows a much more scattershot pattern of development than the 1986 map (Map 1.5).

Current population projections show the seven-county region growing by 33 percent between 2000 and 2030. If this growth urbanizes land at the same rate as in the recent past, then the amount of urbanized land in the seven-county region will grow by another 50 percent during that period, consuming hundreds of thousands of acres of previously undeveloped land.

Projected Future Growth

Population projections for the region show that future growth patterns are expected to look much like growth patterns of the recent past. More than 900,000 new residents are expected within the seven-county metropolitan core alone. Map 5.2 (which is the same as Map 1.11) shows projected population growth between 2000 and 2030 in relation to the metropolitan urban services area (MUSA), which defines the urbanized core of the region.[8] The current MUSA line forms a rough circle around the core of the region, passing through Andover, Blaine, and Lino Lakes in the north; Woodbury and Lake Elmo in the east; Lakeville and Savage in the south; and around the western end of Lake Minnetonka and through Plymouth and Maple Grove in the west. Sixty-three municipalities lie completely within the current MUSA and another thirty-eight are partly inside it.[9] Eighty-nine communities lie beyond the MUSA in the seven-county area.

Map 5.2 shows that the greatest projected growth rates are in the second- and third-ring suburbs just beyond the MUSA. This clearly implies that a large share of future growth will most likely consume currently undeveloped land. And, as Maps 1.12 and 1.13 show, current growth estimates almost certainly understate the share of future growth that will actually occur in these areas. Those maps strongly imply that the actual rate of urbanization that is likely to occur in this part of the region is even greater than Map 5.2 suggests.

In general, if the rate of land consumed continues to outstrip the rate of population growth, as it has in the past, the growth projections shown in Map 5.2 are almost certain to result in the loss of sensitive natural areas, valuable agricultural land, and other types of open spaces. To document these threats, the next section examines the locations of sensitive natural areas in the region and the variation in water sources available to meet demands from growth.

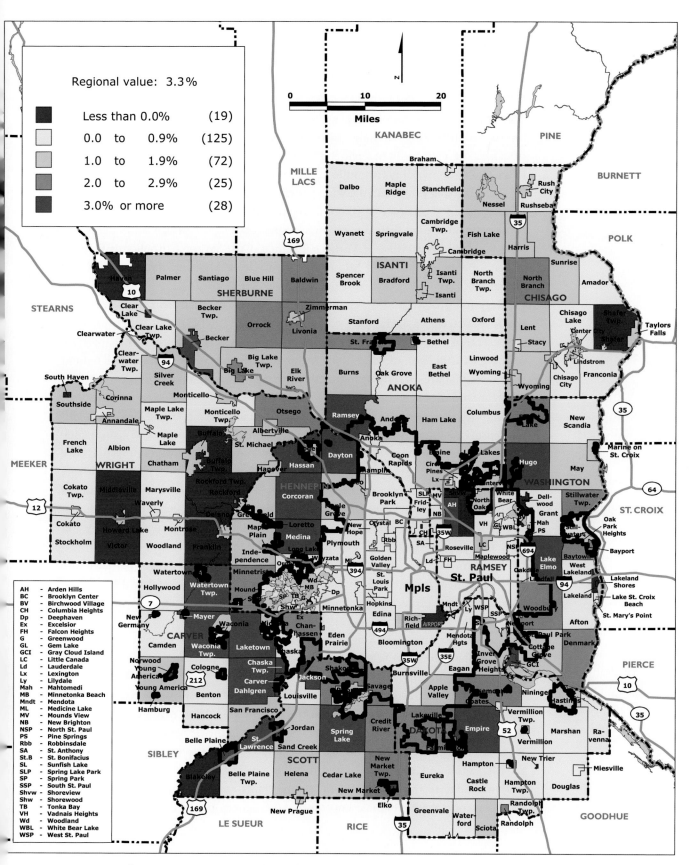

MAP 5.2. Percentage change per year in projected population by municipality, 2000–2030. *Source:* Minnesota Department of Administration, State Demographic Center.

SENSITIVE NATURAL AREAS

The Twin Cities metropolitan area lies at the nexus of coniferous and deciduous forests and grasslands, and abounds with wetlands, rivers, streams, and lakes. Bifurcating the metropolitan region from northwest to southeast is the Mississippi River and its outwash plains, hills, and moraines left from the last glaciation. The region's glaciated past created a wide variety of different landforms throughout the region and an abundance of different plant and animal communities. The eleven counties include nine different ecological subsections: the Anoka Sand Plain, Big Woods, Hardwood Hills, Mille Lacs Uplands, Oak Savanna, Rochester Plateau, St. Paul–Baldwin Plains and Moraines, the St. Croix Moraine, and the Blufflands (Map 5.3).

Regional growth and development since European settlement have converted nearly 60 percent of the region's 3.2 million acres to other types of land uses. With the exception of the two natural resource clusters discussed later in this chapter, remaining natural habitats exist in the regional landscape as smaller, isolated habitat fragments that are directly or indirectly affected by a wide variety of incompatible, adjacent land uses.

Map 5.4 provides a landscape perspective on the spatial relationships of remaining sensitive habitats in the eleven-county region. Three separate GIS (geographic information systems) layers, derived from a total of eighteen different existing data sets, make up this map. Because some of the data sets are "old" relative to the rate of development during the 1990s in the region, Map 5.4 undoubtedly overestimates the presence of remaining sensitive natural areas. The map is, however, a useful visual tool and provides limited planning guidance in where to focus land and water conservation efforts as growth occurs.

Habitats with the highest sensitivity to growth and development pressures are those identified through the Minnesota County Biological Survey and a DNR ecological modeling project that defined regionally significant ecological areas (RSEA). These highly sensitive habitats are shown in dark blue on the map and constitute a third of the region's remaining sensitive natural areas. These high-quality habitat areas are the remnants of the region's biologically diverse heritage and deserve protection for their many, free ecological services.

The data underlying Map 5.4 show that there are nearly 500,000 acres of unprotected sensitive areas remaining in the densely populated seven-county metropolitan region and nearly a million acres remaining in the eleven-county region. The RSEA assessment completed by the Minnesota DNR in 2003, in partnership with the Metropolitan Council, indicated that there were 280,000 acres of high-quality wetland and terrestrial habitats in the seven-county area, shown in Map 5.5. Of this total, 120,000 acres remained unprotected (i.e., not in public ownership).[10]

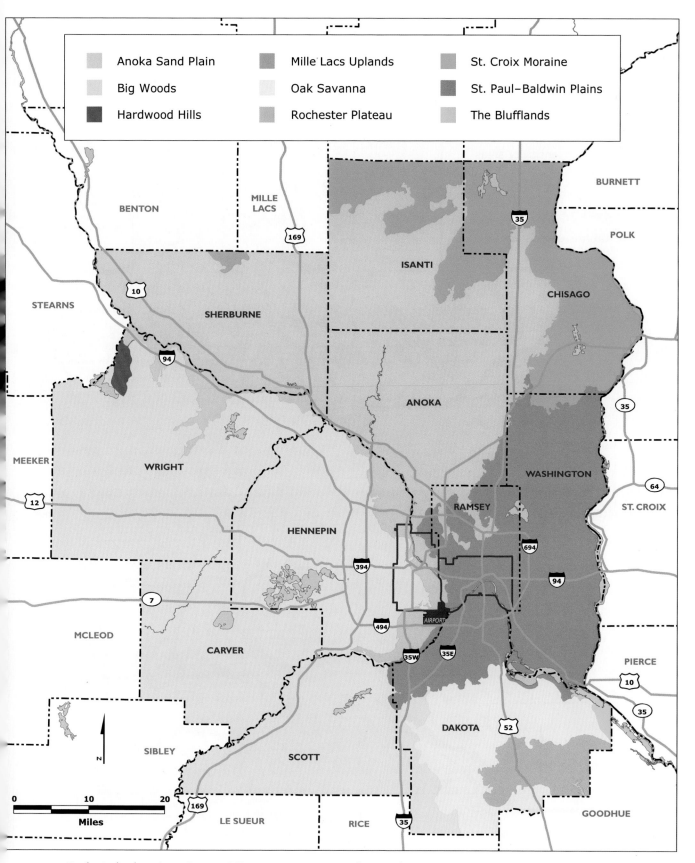

Anoka Sand Plain   Mille Lacs Uplands   St. Croix Moraine

Big Woods   Oak Savanna   St. Paul–Baldwin Plains

Hardwood Hills   Rochester Plateau   The Blufflands

MAP 5.3. Ecological subsections. *Source:* Minnesota Department of Natural Resources.

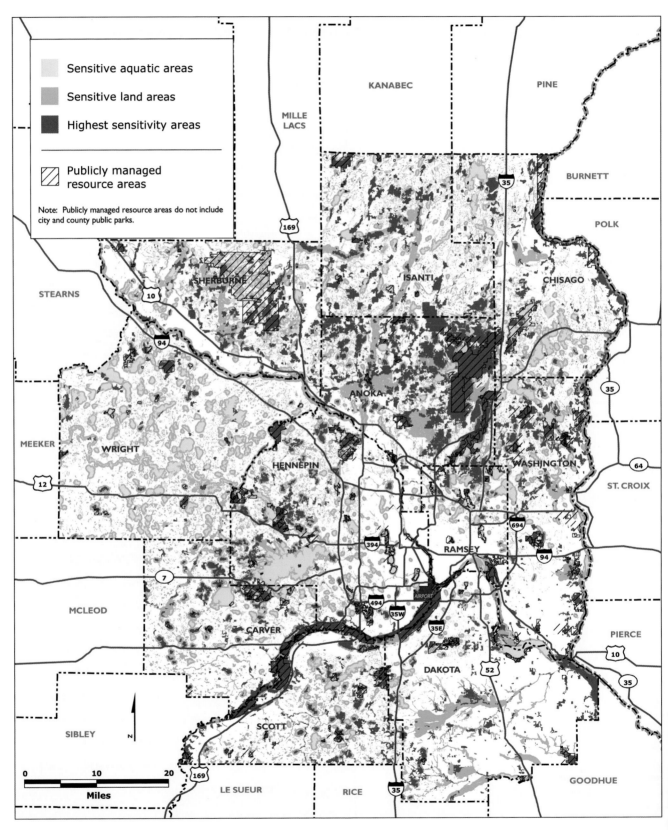

MAP 5.4. Sensitive natural areas. *Sources:* Minnesota Department of Natural Resources; Ameregis, Inc.

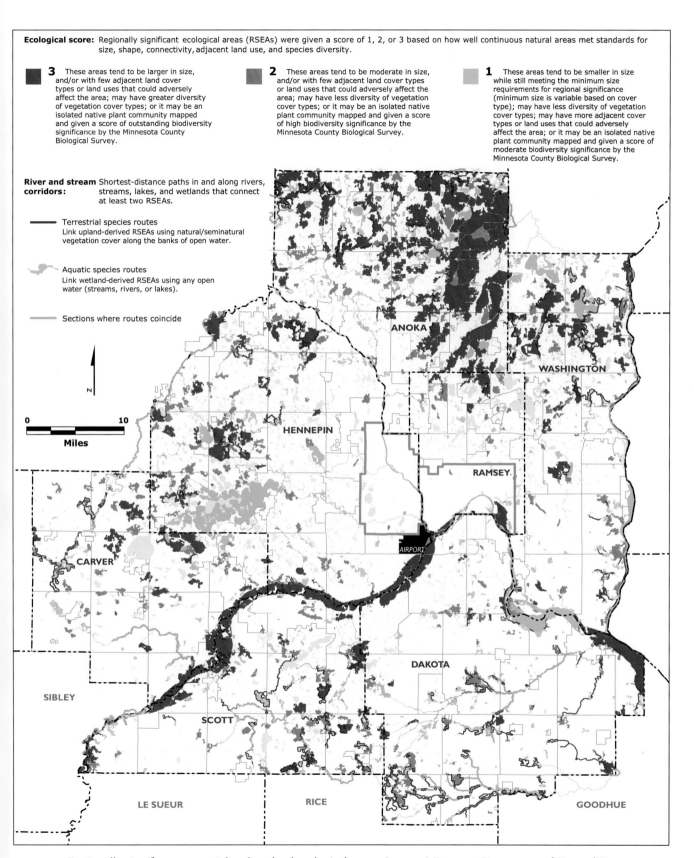

Ecological score: Regionally significant ecological areas (RSEAs) were given a score of 1, 2, or 3 based on how well continuous natural areas met standards for size, shape, connectivity, adjacent land use, and species diversity.

3 These areas tend to be larger in size, and/or with few adjacent land cover types or land uses that could adversely affect the area; may have greater diversity of vegetation cover types; or it may be an isolated native plant community mapped and given a score of outstanding biodiversity significance by the Minnesota County Biological Survey.

2 These areas tend to be moderate in size, and/or with few adjacent land cover types or land uses that could adversely affect the area; may have less diversity of vegetation cover types; or it may be an isolated native plant community mapped and given a score of high biodiversity significance by the Minnesota County Biological Survey.

1 These areas tend to be smaller in size while still meeting the minimum size requirements for regional significance (minimum size is variable based on cover type); may have less diversity of vegetation cover types; may have more adjacent cover types or land uses that could adversely affect the area; or it may be an isolated native plant community mapped and given a score of moderate biodiversity significance by the Minnesota County Biological Survey.

River and stream corridors: Shortest-distance paths in and along rivers, streams, lakes, and wetlands that connect at least two RSEAs.

Terrestrial species routes
Link upland-derived RSEAs using natural/seminatural vegetation cover along the banks of open water.

Aquatic species routes
Link wetland-derived RSEAs using any open water (streams, rivers, or lakes).

Sections where routes coincide

0   10
Miles

N

ANOKA

WASHINGTON

HENNEPIN

RAMSEY

CARVER

AIRPORT

DAKOTA

SIBLEY

SCOTT

LE SUEUR

RICE

GOODHUE

MAP 5.5. Regionally significant terrestrial and wetland ecological areas. *Source:* Minnesota Department of Natural Resources.

While areas sensitive to growth and development are scattered throughout the metropolitan area, there are two habitat clusters (dark blue) in the eleven-county region that are especially susceptible to development pressures. The most obvious clustering of highly sensitive habitat is located in the Anoka Sand Plain ecological subsection. It extends from the Mississippi River in central Sherburne County east and south into Anoka County, eastern Hennepin County, southern Isanti County, southwestern Chisago County, and northern Washington County. This entire area is part of a three-thousand-square-mile fine sand glacial outwash plain character-ized by shallow lakes, wetland depressions, rare dune habitats, oak savanna, and dry prairie. Within this cluster are multiple large protected areas: the 31,000-acre Sherburne National Wildlife Refuge, the surrounding Sand Dunes State Forest, the Uncas Dunes Scientific and Natural Area, and the 23,000-acre Carlos Avery Wild-life Management Area located in Anoka and Chisago counties. Despite the fact that much of the sand plain is not easily developed because of the abundance of wet-lands, growth is occurring rapidly in this area. In Anoka County alone, urbanized area increased 81 percent from 1986 (53,000 acres) to 2002 (96,000 acres). Signifi-cant population growth is projected for all of Sherburne County and areas adjacent to Interstate 35E that transects north–south through the Anoka Sand Plain.

The second, less obvious cluster of sensitive natural area is located in the vi-cinity of the 14,000-acre Lake Minnetonka and includes portions of Hennepin, Carver, and Scott counties. As the ninth-largest lake in the state (excluding the bor-der lakes), Lake Minnetonka was once the location of summer cottages for wealthy Minnesotans. Today, ringed by year-round, high-end residential homes, the lake's watershed is largely urbanized. Significant population growth is expected in nearby municipalities such as Minnetrista and Laketown Township, in part due to the natural amenities provided by the area's many smaller lakes, wetlands, and wooded areas. More development implies more fragmentation and conversion of existing sensitive natural areas that have made this portion of the region so attractive.

Map 5.6 displays this clustering of sensitive habitats more dramatically than Map 5.4. To create Map 5.6, the percentage of sensitive natural area was calculated as a percentage of total acreage for each minor civil division (see sidebar). The high-est percentages of remaining sensitive natural areas, not surprisingly, are primarily located at the fringe of the seven-county core region and just beyond in the adjacent collar counties. Many townships show 50–75 percent (red) of their total area in scattered, sensitive habitats.

Although growth pressures on high-quality natural habitats are of greatest con-cern, it is important *not* to dismiss those portions of the region where sensitive nat-ural areas are of lower ecological quality, smaller size, and more highly fragmented. These lower-quality habitats that make up 28 percent of the eleven-county region still provide many important ecological, social, and economic benefits.

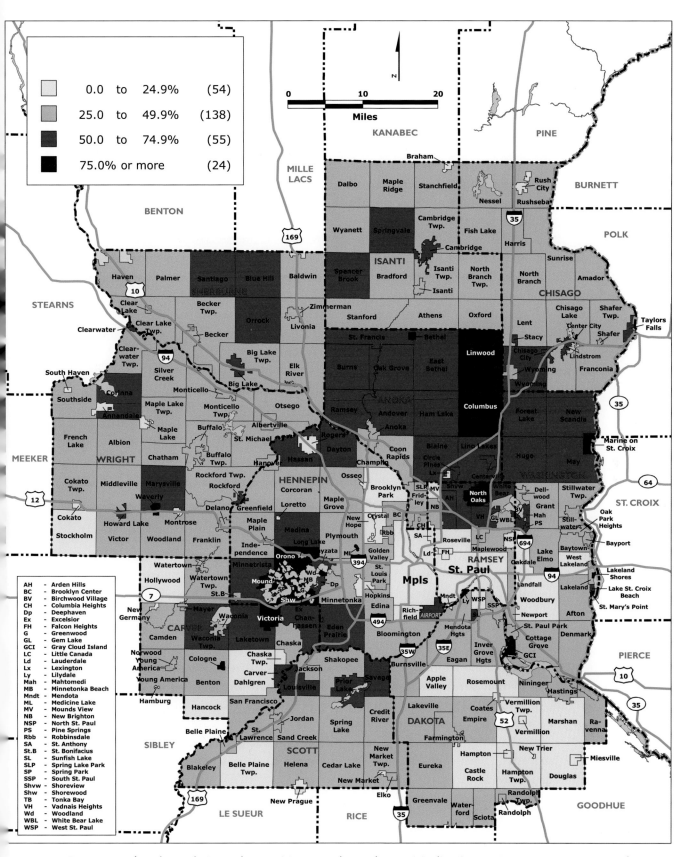

MAP 5.6. Percentage of total area designated as sensitive natural areas by municipality. *Source:* Minnesota Department of Natural Resources.

CREATION OF THE SENSITIVE NATURAL AREAS

Map 5.4, a GIS map created by the DNR's Central Region staff, combines nineteen different, existing data layers of varying ages. While some data sets are relatively current, others (like the National Wetland Inventory) date back to 1979–88. As a result, this map represents a "still shot in time" and the best approximation of remaining regional natural resources in 2005. Undoubtedly, this map overestimates the remaining sensitive natural areas in the region because land cover changes occur rapidly on a daily basis throughout much of the DNR's Central Region. Conversely, the map underestimates land in public protection, since county and city parks and privately owned lands such as corporate and academic land holdings are not included in the Publicly Managed Resource Lands overlay.

An essential step in the overall analysis was the creation of a regionwide sensitive natural areas (SNA) map. Initially, three separate natural resource layers were developed using different databases: highest sensitivity areas, sensitive aquatic areas, and sensitive land areas. These three layers were then combined to create the final SNA map. Although natural resources are not constrained by jurisdictional boundaries, municipal boundaries were overlaid on the resource map for purposes of analysis by minor civil division (MCD). By aggregating the three categories of sensitive natural areas and calculating percentages by MCD (Map 5.6), remaining sensitive natural areas could be compared directly with demographic, fiscal, and economic data used in analysis. The data sets used in the creation of the three separate natural resource layers included:

- Highest sensitivity areas
  Minnesota County Biological Survey (MCBS) Native Plant Communities (varies, 1986–present; excludes MCBS surveys for some counties)
  MCBS sites of biodiversity significance (varies, 1980–present)
  Regionally significant ecological areas (2000)
  Forest core patches (1991–93)
- Sensitive aquatic areas
  Shallow lakes (2004)
  Natural environment lakes (2004)
  Scientific and natural area (SNA) lakes (2004)
  Outstanding resource value water (ORVW) streams (2004)
  Trout streams (2002)
  Calcareous fens (2004)
  Public water basins (2004)
  Wetlands (1979–88; from the National Wetlands Inventory, Cowardin classes 4 through 8)
- Sensitive land areas
  Shoreland management zone—natural environment lakes (2004)
  Shoreland management zone—shallow lakes (2004)
  Trout stream protection zone (2004)
  Calcareous fen protection zone (2004)
  SNA lake protection zone (2004)
  Shoreland management zone—all other public water lakes (2004)
  Steep slopes (1997)
  Wetlands (1979–88; from the National Wetlands Inventory, Cowardin classes 1 through 3)

As a final caveat, this regional mapping of natural resources is not of sufficient resolution to detect remaining natural resources at the local level. Ground truthing is required to verify the presence and distribution of resources at these scales.

Relative to other growing metropolitan areas, the Twin Cities metropolitan region retains a fair percentage of important natural habitats. As this chapter illustrates, however, future growth and low-density development definitely threaten the continued existence of these sensitive, natural, undeveloped areas.

VARYING REGIONAL SOURCES OF GROUNDWATER

This region has relatively large supplies of groundwater for residential, commercial, and industrial uses. About 1.83 million residents in the metropolitan area obtain their water from bedrock aquifers that underlie much of the Twin Cities metropolitan area. These groundwater sources include the Prairie Du Chien–Jordan, Franconia–Ironton–Galesville, and Mt. Simon–Hinckley aquifers. Treated drinking water for an additional 870,000 people comes from the Mississippi River. In the seven-county core region and in the inner portions of the adjacent "collar" counties (Wright, Sherburne, Isanti, Chisago), both bedrock aquifers and the Mississippi River supply significant amounts of water. Although there have been reported incidences of interference with surface water features, such as fens and wetlands, in the core area of the region, the DNR's Waters Division believes that, if managed carefully, these combined ground- and surface water sources can supply enough water to meet future growth and development in the southern portion of the region (purple, tan, and blue areas of Map 5.7).

The water supply situation is least secure in the northern half of the region. As can be seen in the insert of Map 5.7, the water-bearing bedrock aquifers gradually disappear in the vicinity of the northern collar counties, and groundwater sources are restricted to unconsolidated sand and gravel deposits that can be at or near the land surface. These water-bearing deposits vary in thickness and in some areas can be virtually nonexistent. They are also spatially scattered and the locations of the buried sources are poorly known. Although these water sources are primarily used for low-volume domestic supplies and seasonal irrigation, it is uncertain whether these surficial and buried aquifers will be able to sustain increased withdrawals to meet the expected demand of 100,000 new residents in this portion of the region. Moreover, these shallow sand and gravel aquifers allow rapid infiltration of surface water, making these aquifers highly susceptible to contamination. In the future, the Mississippi River may prove to be the more reliable source of water supply for future development, although river water dependence will bear costs associated with water treatment and piping to location.

As growth occurs in the region, it will be important to balance the needs of sensitive natural areas with the water needs for homes, businesses, energy, and agriculture. To conserve the region's remaining sensitive aquatic natural resources, water managers will need to take into account the impacts of groundwater withdrawal

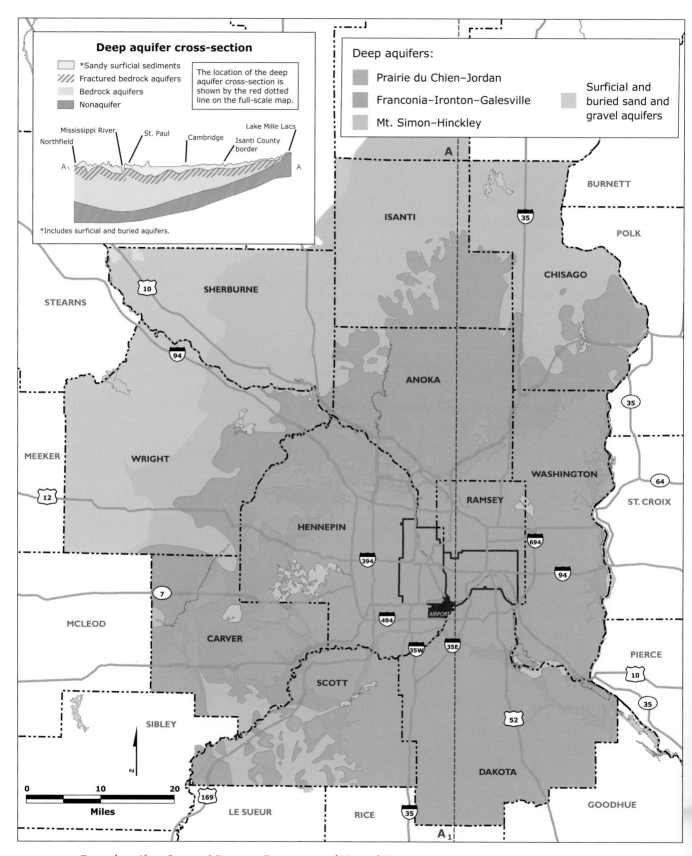

Deep aquifer cross-section

- *Sandy surficial sediments
- Fractured bedrock aquifers
- Bedrock aquifers
- Nonaquifer

The location of the deep aquifer cross-section is shown by the red dotted line on the full-scale map.

Northfield
Mississippi River
St. Paul
Cambridge
Lake Mille Lacs
Isanti County border

A₁
A

*Includes surficial and buried aquifers.

Deep aquifers:

- Prairie du Chien–Jordan
- Franconia–Ironton–Galesville
- Mt. Simon–Hinckley

Surficial and buried sand and gravel aquifers

BURNETT

POLK

ISANTI

CHISAGO

STEARNS

SHERBURNE

ANOKA

WRIGHT

MEEKER

WASHINGTON

RAMSEY

ST. CROIX

HENNEPIN

AIRPORT

MCLEOD

CARVER

SCOTT

PIERCE

SIBLEY

DAKOTA

LE SUEUR

RICE

GOODHUE

0   10   20
Miles

MAP 5.7. Ground aquifers. *Source:* Minnesota Department of Natural Resources.

on surface waters, such as groundwater-fed lakes, trout streams, springs, fens, and the black ash seepage swamp. Even if groundwater does not directly feed a lake, wetland, or river, groundwater depletion can result in a lowered water table that negatively affects sensitive aquatic plant communities adapted to specific hydrologic conditions.

POLLUTION OF THE REGION'S LAKES AND STREAMS

Map 5.8 shows how past development has affected water quality in the Twin Cities. It shows the lakes and streams in the region that are classified as "impaired" by the Environmental Protection Agency. A large share of the region's waters are impaired—27 percent of stream/river miles and 37 percent of lake area.

An important implication of the impaired designation is that it brings the body of water in question and its tributaries under the purview of the Clean Water Act regulations. In particular, the impaired designation greatly limits the ability of local authorities to build wastewater treatment facilities. The body of water in Minnesota that is most important in this context is Lake Pepin, which is downstream of virtually all the lakes and streams shown on Map 5.8. More than 80 percent of the population of Minnesota resides within Lake Pepin's watershed. This means that virtually all growth in the Twin Cities metropolitan area will fall under the regulations of the Clean Water Act for the foreseeable future.

A recent case illustrates the potential problems. On August 9, 2005, the Minnesota Court of Appeals reversed a decision of the Minnesota Pollution Control Agency that is likely to affect development in much of Minnesota for the near future. The case emerged from the plans of the cities of Annandale and Maple Lake for construction of a new wastewater treatment plant in late 2002. Both of the cities are located about forty-five miles to the northwest of Minneapolis–St. Paul. The area is experiencing dramatic growth as the population of the Twin Cities continues to spread out and grow, and the cities claimed they needed the new wastewater capacity to accommodate continued development.

The proposed plant would have discharged 3,600 pounds of phosphorus into the North Fork of the Crow River each year, 2,200 pounds more than the existing wastewater treatment facility discharges. This is where the cities ran into problems. The North Fork feeds into the Mississippi River, which flows into Lake Pepin. Both the North Fork and Lake Pepin are designated as "impaired waterways" according to the Federal Clean Water Act. Since the waterways are impaired, the Clean Water Act specifies that no additional pollutants can be added until a "total maximum daily load" (TMDL) is established for the waterway, and then the TMDL cannot be exceeded. Since there has not been a determination of the TMDL for the North Fork (anticipated 2012) and Lake Pepin (anticipated 2009), the court said that a

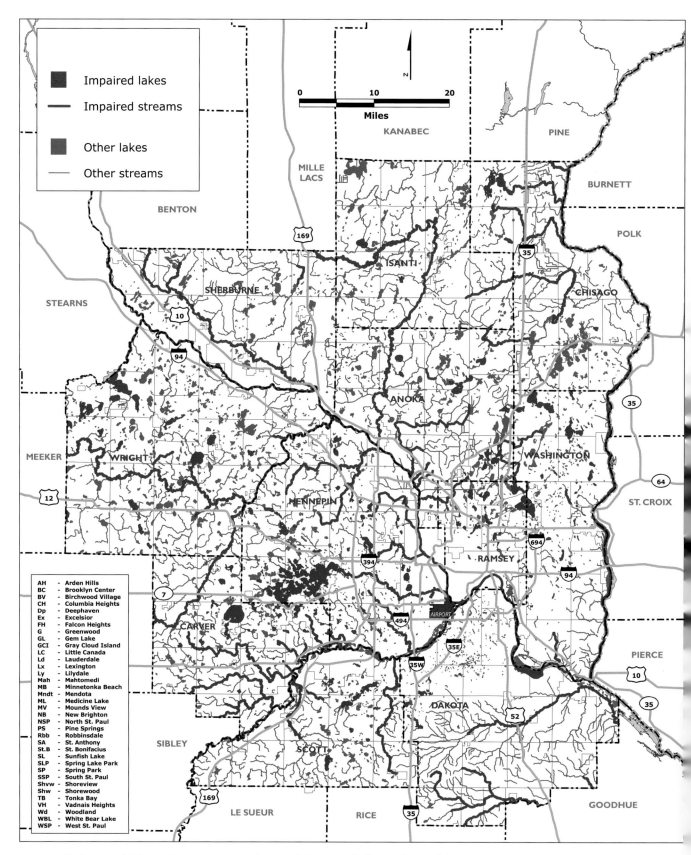

MAP 5.8. Impaired lakes and streams, 2006. *Source:* Minnesota Pollution Control Agency.

permit could be issued only if it did not cause increased impairment of the waterway. The Annandale permit would constitute an increased level of phosphorus and was deemed illegal under the Clean Water Act.

The cities had admitted that there was an increase in phosphorus, but argued that this was allowable because the new plant would be offset by the reduction of 53,500 pounds of phosphorus that the Litchfield Plant had been discharging into the North Fork. The court looked at the statutory history and found that an offset system had been considered five years before but was rejected as unworkable. The court therefore found that the Minnesota Pollution Control Agency had erred as a matter of law when it issued the permit for the new wastewater treatment plant.

This case was heard by the Minnesota Supreme Court in 2006, and the Appeals Court decision was overturned in 2008, allowing construction of the treatment plant. However, the controversy shows how much more carefully local and regional authorities must now treat these issues.

SENSITIVE NATURAL AREAS, LOCAL PLANNING, AND GROWTH

Local planning and economic development priorities often conflict with regional environmental needs. This conflict is a direct result of the incentives faced by local authorities when making decisions about whether and how to develop land. Because the property tax is the primary source of current revenues for local governments in Minnesota, development decisions directly influence the ability of local areas to raise revenues needed to finance public services.

If, as one would expect, the benefits of conservation are spread widely while the costs are largely borne locally—oftentimes in the form of foregone tax base—then localities face the wrong incentives. The likely result is overdevelopment of environmentally sensitive areas.

Different types of development often imply different obligations on the expenditure side of local budgets as well. Commercial–industrial development may enhance the tax base without increasing the demand for school services, for instance. In the end, it is the balance of costs (expenditure needs caused by the development) and benefits (the revenues generated) that local officials care about. Since protected resources rarely generate revenues directly, they often fare poorly in local fiscal decision making.

Sensitive Natural Areas and Local Fiscal Capacities

One very important characteristic to consider when comparing local government capacity is the ability to raise revenues locally. In Minnesota, the primary local tax instrument is the property tax. State law sets the rate structure for different types of property—the rate per dollar of assessed value is greater for commercial–industrial property than for owner-occupied residential property, for instance. A particular locality's mix of property types then determines how productive its tax base is (in terms of revenue generated per dollar of property values). This is the locality's "tax capacity." Local governments then determine their overall tax rate by varying the percentage of tax capacity that they assess.

Tax capacity per household—the revenue that the property tax would generate if the locality taxed its capacity at 100 percent—is therefore the proper measure of local ability to raise tax revenue. Map 5.9 (which is the same as Map 1.14) shows this measure in 2004 for each municipality in the region.

The maps show a great amount of diversity in the capacity of local governments to absorb the potential costs of growth and natural resource conservation. Tax capacities per household in 2004 varied from as low as $214 per household in the city of Osakis in Todd County to as high as $12,866 in the city of Becker in Sherburne County. The distribution increases relatively smoothly between these extremes, and 90 percent of municipalities fall in the range between $865 per household and $4,109 per household.

Municipalities in the core and at the fringes of the metropolitan area share lower than average tax capacities for the most part, while second- and third-ring suburbs are largely above average. The highest capacities are in the cities located in the southwest and western suburbs and along the St. Croix River valley.

The most distinctive pattern in the parts of the region that are growing the most is that tax capacities in the southern suburbs are consistently greater than those in the north. Unfortunately, this is also one of the most distinctive patterns in the map showing the distribution of sensitive natural areas. Most of the municipalities with the highest shares of sensitive natural areas are in the northern half of the region (Map 5.10). Thus the part of the region with the lowest capacities to finance conservation efforts is also the part of the region with the largest amounts of unprotected sensitive natural areas.

In sum, there is a great deal of variation in the ability of municipalities to finance public services from local taxes. If primary responsibility for conserving sensitive natural areas were left to local governments—through local planning and zoning decisions—the results would be a patchwork quilt of conservation efforts. An analogy would be each community independently planning and paying for its streets and highways with no knowledge of the timing, type, or location of roads being developed in adjacent communities or regionally. The resulting regional transportation system would be inefficient and ineffective.

Sensitive Natural Areas and Growth

The final step in the analysis is to examine the relationships among projected growth patterns, the community classification, and the sensitive natural areas mapping in order to explore questions such as:

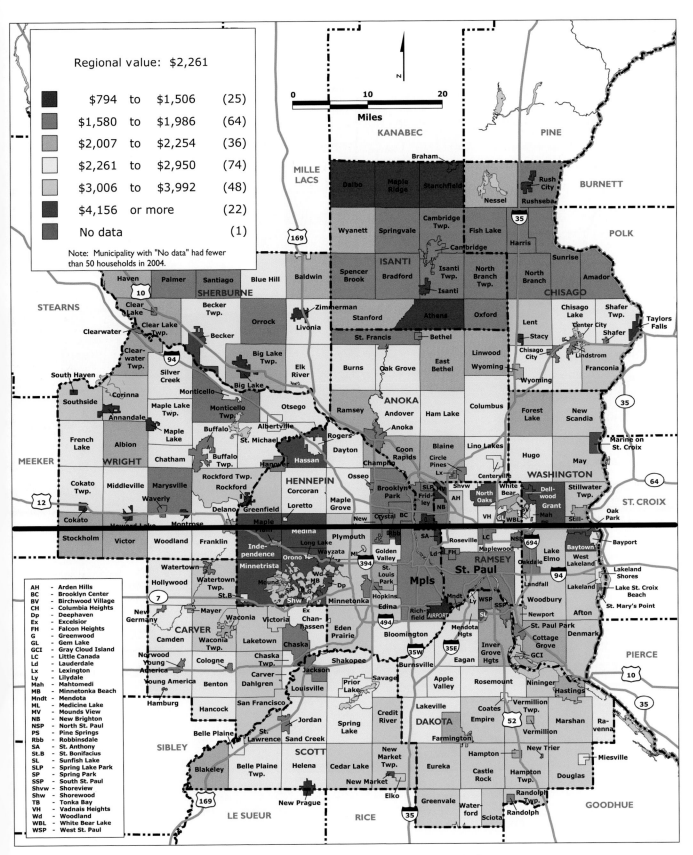

AH - Arden Hills
BC - Brooklyn Center
BV - Birchwood Village
CH - Columbia Heights
Dp - Deephaven
Ex - Excelsior
FH - Falcon Heights
G - Greenwood
GL - Gem Lake
GCI - Gray Cloud Island
LC - Little Canada
Ld - Lauderdale
Lx - Lexington
Ly - Lilydale
Mah - Mahtomedi
MB - Minnetonka Beach
Mndt - Mendota
ML - Medicine Lake
MV - Mounds View
NB - New Brighton
NSP - North St. Paul
PS - Pine Springs
Rbb - Robbinsdale
SA - St. Anthony
St.B - St. Bonifacius
SL - Sunfish Lake
SLP - Spring Lake Park
SP - Spring Park
SSP - South St. Paul
Shvw - Shoreview
Shw - Shorewood
TB - Tonka Bay
VH - Vadnais Heights
Wd - Woodland
WBL - White Bear Lake
WSP - West St. Paul

MAP 5.9. Tax capacity per household by municipality, 2004. *Source:* Minnesota State Auditor.

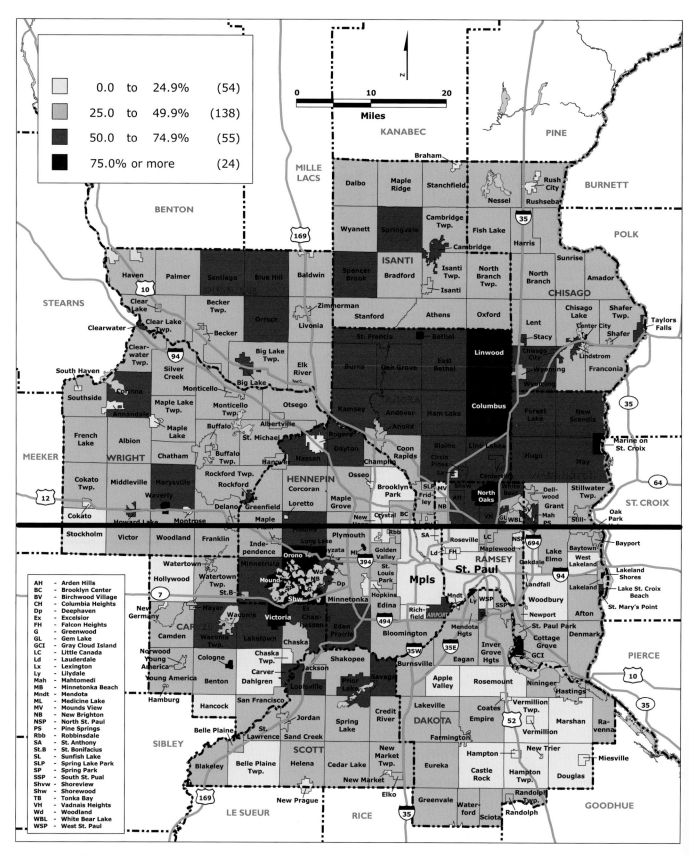

MAP 5.10. Percentage of total area designated as sensitive natural areas by municipality. *Source:* Minnesota Department of Natural Resources.

- What types of communities are projected to grow more or less quickly than the region as a whole? Do these communities contain sensitive natural areas?
- If new growth proceeds in the future at densities like the recent past, will there be enough available land—land that is not sensitive, protected, or already urbanized—in fast-growth communities to accommodate future growth while also conserving sensitive natural areas for their many benefits?

Much of the region's future growth is expected to occur in the seven-county core area. Nearly 900,000 new residents are expected in the core region with another 100,000 expected in the four adjacent collar counties. Figure 5.2 shows which types of communities in the seven core counties are expected to show the most increase in households between 2003 and 2030. The greatest expected growth rates are found in communities classified as developing job centers and bedroom developing. Although these two groups represented just 33 percent of households in the seven counties in 2003, they are projected to receive *67 percent* of growth in the coming decades. In short, much of the region's future growth is expected in relatively low-density middle-class communities at the fringe of the metropolitan area.

Figure 5.3 shows how the seven-county region's sensitive natural areas that are not already developed or protected are distributed across the six classes of communities. The affluent residential category shows the highest percentage of total

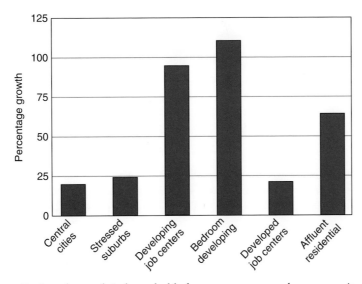

FIGURE 5.2. Projected growth in households from 2003 to 2030, by community type, seven-county core metro area. *Source:* Minnesota Department of Administration, State Demographic Center.

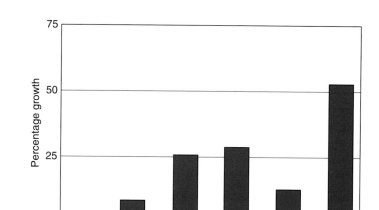

FIGURE 5.3. Percentage of total area that is nonurban, unprotected, and sensitive, by community type, seven-county core metro area. *Source:* Minnesota Department of Natural Resources.

land classified as nonurban, unprotected, and sensitive (53 percent), while the bedroom developing and developing job center categories are second and third (29 and 27 percent, respectively). However, because the latter two classes represent so much more total land area, bedroom developing and developing job centers contain fully 85 percent of the seven-county region's nonurban, unprotected, and sensitive areas.

In sum, two of the five community types—developing job centers and bedroom developing—are expected to receive 67 percent of the seven-county area's future growth, and they contain 85 percent of the area's nonurban, unprotected, and sensitive natural areas.

Growth produces tax base, but it also creates demand for infrastructure, schools, and public services. Given that they possess just average fiscal resources, developing job centers and bedroom developing communities are unlikely to be able to protect these sensitive resources alone. The costs of accommodating the bulk of the region's future growth will make it very difficult to also expend scarce local fiscal resources on natural resources conservation.

Trade-offs that jeopardize important, sensitive natural resource areas can be ameliorated based on how communities grow. This is illustrated by looking at how much currently undeveloped land will be needed if future growth occurs at densities like those of the past.

Table 5.1 compares the amount of currently available land that will be needed to

TABLE 5.1 Distribution of households and developable land by community type

Community type	Households 2003	New households 2003–2030	Developable land (acres) 2000	2010	2020	2030
Central cities	267,520	52,480	1,425	-4,474	-8,332	-11,273
Stressed suburbs	254,899	62,361	9,249	-3,146	-14,032	-23,446
Developing job centers	250,359	236,431	104,356	29,501	-50,740	-106,238
Bedroom developing	57,427	63,280	488,752	464,387	403,104	363,422
Developed job centers	208,883	43,997	35,949	23,558	15,384	4,747
Affluent residential	9,110	5,820	7,812	5,402	1,403	-1,721

Sources: U.S. Census Bureau; Ameregis, Inc.

accommodate new households in each of the community types if each new household consumes as much land as current households.[11] "Available" is defined as nonurban, unprotected, nonsensitive land. The results show that, although the seven-county area as a whole has enough land to accommodate projected growth, there are shortfalls in available land for four of the six community classes. The most glaring shortfall is in those communities classified as developing job centers—the classification expected to receive the most growth. If growth in these communities occurs at current densities, it would consume 106,000 more acres than is currently available, an area equivalent to the total areas of Minneapolis, St. Paul, and Bloomington combined (97,800 acres).

Developing job centers contain about 118,000 acres of unprotected, nonurban, sensitive land. This means that, if these communities grow in the same manner they have grown in the past, one of two things must happen. Either new growth will consume most or all of the remaining sensitive natural areas, or new growth will be pushed farther out into the fringes of the region. Developing job centers form a nearly complete ring around the region's core (see Map 1.17). If they cannot accommodate all the growth they are expected to receive, the likeliest place for it to go is outward into the fringes of the seven-county region and the collar counties. It will be difficult for growth to be pushed inward, since the communities inside the ring of developing job centers—central cities, stressed suburbs, and developed job centers—already are expected to grow at rates that will consume all, or nearly all, available land there. Each of these community types shows either a shortfall or very small surplus of available land for development when sensitive natural areas are removed from development consideration.

Very recent growth patterns—from 2000 to 2006—suggest that the land crunch in these developing suburbs will come sooner rather than later. The 2000–2030

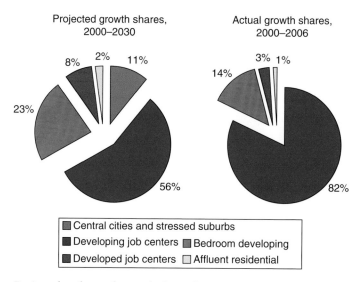

FIGURE 5.4. Projected and actual growth shares by community classification in the Twin Cities metropolitan area. *Sources:* Minnesota Department of Natural Resources; Ameregis, Inc.

growth projections described earlier estimated that roughly half the growth in that period would fall in developing job centers. However, Figure 5.4 (which is the same as Figure 1.11) shows that in the first half of this decade these municipalities actually absorbed *82 percent* of the region's growth.

On the other hand, infill or new development in the core of the region, in central cities and stressed suburbs, did not even offset population declines elsewhere in these places. As a result, they absorbed none of the region's growth during this period, when they had been projected to capture 11 percent. Similarly, developed job centers, projected to capture 8 percent of growth, actually absorbed only 3 percent.

The actual growth patterns suggest that projections were very ambitious about growth in the already-developed portions of the region. Actual patterns show that the overwhelming majority of growth is occurring on previously undeveloped tracts. This means that the simulations shown in Tables 5.1 and 5.2 almost certainly understate the threats to the region's remaining sensitive natural areas.

Another way to view the potential trade-offs facing the region is to look at the growth projections in the context of the Metropolitan Council's metropolitan urban services area (MUSA). The MUSA is perhaps the most important tool the council uses to guide development in the region. It defines the area within which the council provides important regional infrastructure like wastewater conveyance and treatment. The primary objective of the MUSA is to ensure orderly, contiguous development as the region moves outward.

TABLE 5.2   Distribution by development patterns

Municipalities	Households 2003	New households 2003–2030	Developable land (acres)			
			2000	2010	2020	2030
Within current MUSA	559,320	110,490	10,969	-6,343	-18,381	-32,549
Developable land depleted 2000–2010	195,924	148,266	23,618	-27,890	-77,143	-110,753
Developable land depleted 2010–2020	155,605	104,795	46,572	18,580	-24,973	-53,025
Developable land depleted 2020–2030	46,767	50,110	58,332	43,104	7,295	-12,746
Developable land still available in 2030	90,582	50,708	508,110	487,776	459,989	434,564

Sources: U.S. Census Bureau; Ameregis, Inc.

The MUSA, as it now stands, is boxed in along much of its length by municipalities with very high percentages of their land in sensitive natural areas (Map 5.11). In fact, nearly the entire MUSA from its northeastern corner in Washington County running north, west, south, and eventually east to its southernmost link in Scott County, is bordered by municipalities with 50–75 percent of land in sensitive natural areas. Only the southeastern and eastern parts of the MUSA lie in and next to areas below 50 percent. The direct proximity of the region's two largest clusters of sensitive natural areas—the Anoka Sand Plain and the Lake Minnetonka area—means that large amounts of sensitive areas are likely to be in the direct path of development. Simulations confirm this projection.

If the MUSA boundary were expanded to include all the area in the municipalities currently split by the MUSA, this would add about 280,000 acres of new area inside the MUSA. If each new household projected for this part of the region by 2030 consumes land at rates like those of the recent past, then there will be a shortfall of more than 115,000 acres of available land inside the expanded MUSA to accommodate future growth. This is true even though the 280,000-acre increase assumed for the purposes of this assessment is substantially more than the Metropolitan Council currently plans to accommodate future growth.[12]

The shortfall of 115,000 acres represents about 65 percent of the nonurban, unprotected, sensitive land in these communities. This reinforces the conclusions from the calculations based on the community classification: if the region grows the way it has in the past, future growth either will have to occur beyond the areas targeted for development by the Metropolitan Council (primarily within the current MUSA and in areas immediately adjacent to it) or it will consume much of the region's remaining unprotected, sensitive natural areas.

Another way to view the growth pressures is simply to simulate when individual communities will run out of developable land—nonsensitive, nonurbanized

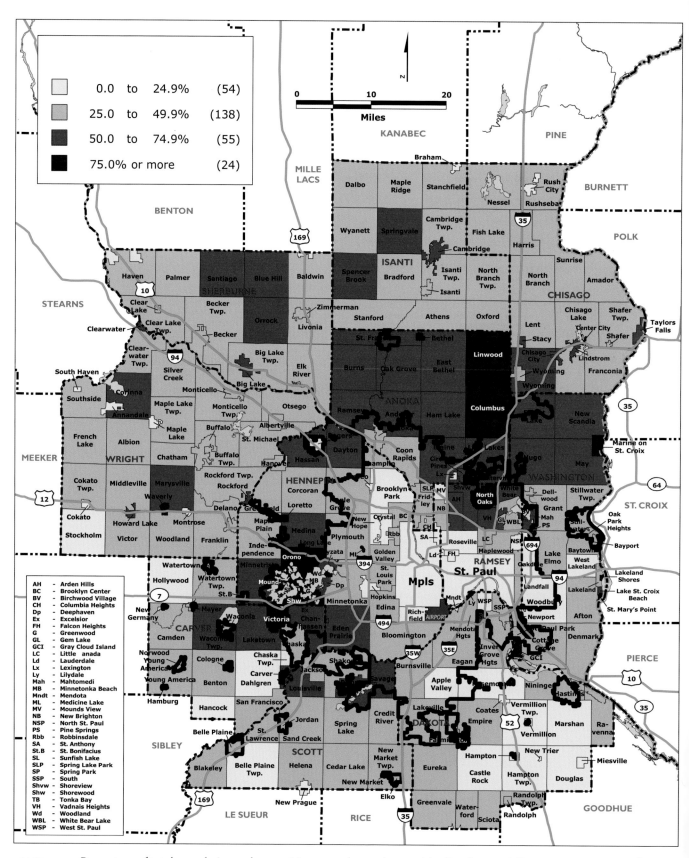

MAP 5.11. Percentage of total area designated as sensitive natural areas by municipality. *Source:* Minnesota Department of Natural Resources.

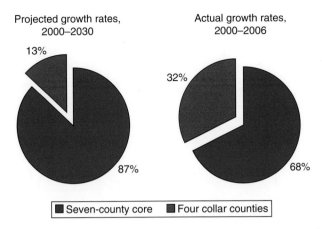

FIGURE 5.5. Projected and actual growth shares in the seven-county core region and the collar counties. *Sources:* U.S. Census Bureau; Minnesota Department of Administration, State Demographic Center.

land—if they grow at projected rates. Map 5.12 and Table 5.2 show these results. The simulation assumes that future growth in a given community will occur at a density equal to existing development (current households per acre of currently urbanized land). The results are that one-fourth of the municipalities on or outside the MUSA (36 of 139) will have consumed all of their remaining developable land by 2010 and another one-fifth (28) will have done so by 2030. If these 64 municipalities absorb all of the new households projected for them at current densities, their land shortfalls would total 176,000 acres, an area larger than Minneapolis, St. Paul, Bloomington, Plymouth, Eden Prairie, and Woodbury combined. The total shortfall is very nearly the same amount of sensitive lands in these municipalities, namely, 156,000 acres. This means that if they do in fact grow at projected rates, they will very likely develop most or all of their sensitive natural areas.

Actual recent growth patterns show the same disturbing trend with respect to the geography of growth as they did with respect to the community classifications. The forecasts used in the simulations shown in Table 5.2 projected that roughly 13 percent of growth during the thirty-year period would occur in the four collar counties. In reality, 32 percent of growth between 2000 and 2006 occurred in these counties (Figure 5.5).

CONCLUSIONS AND POLICY RECOMMENDATIONS

The overriding conclusion from each of the simulations is that we must find new ways to grow if we want to both conserve the region's remaining sensitive natural areas and avoid inefficient expansion into the far reaches of the metropolitan area.

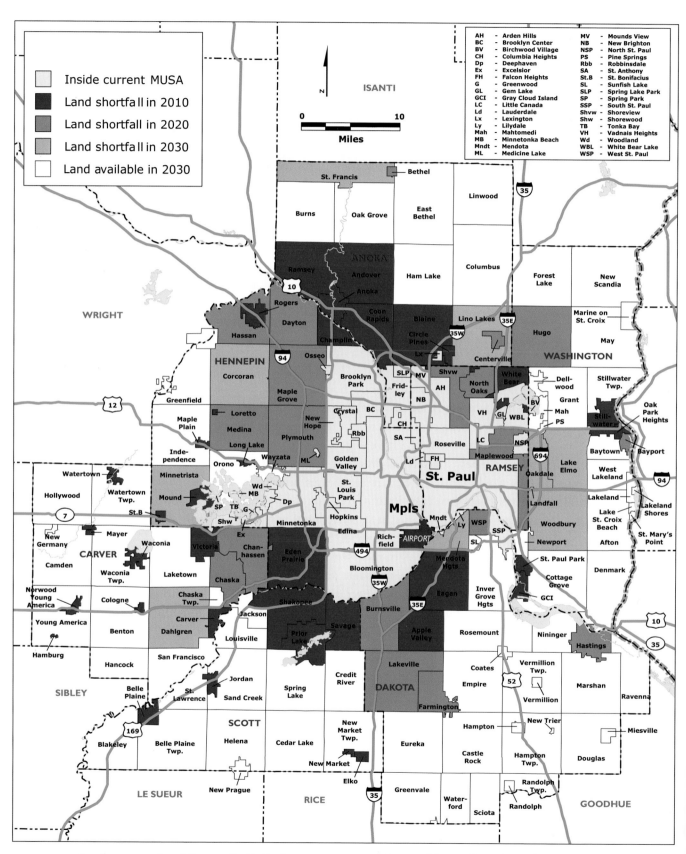

MAP 5.12. Land consumption, Minneapolis–St. Paul seven-county area. *Source:* Metropolitan Council.

To do this while accommodating the amount of growth that is currently projected to 2030, new development on currently undeveloped land must occur at greater densities than in the past, and "infill" development on already developed land must represent much greater portions of growth than in the recent past. Further, even if new development occurs in ways that consume less land than in the past, it still must be directed to nonsensitive areas as much as possible. Natural resource planning must play a significant role in local and regional development and land use planning.

Policy Recommendations—State Government

Regional growth projections put much of the region's growth in coming years at the fringes of the Metropolitan Council's seven-county domain and in the four collar counties. Growth is also expected in parts of the state just beyond the collar counties—especially north along the Highway 169 corridor to Lake Mille Lacs.[13] Much of this area also contains disproportionate shares of sensitive natural areas.

Without institutional reforms in the way the region regulates growth, much of this growth will "fall through the cracks" of the current planning system. Current institutions make it very difficult, if not impossible, to coordinate growth in the region's seven core counties—which are still the state's primary growth engine—with growth in the collar counties and beyond. Two policy options requiring state action could remedy this: expansion of the Metropolitan Council to include the four collar counties and reinstatement of the Minnesota Planning Agency.

The hows and whys of expanding the Metropolitan Council into the four collar counties are discussed extensively in chapters 2 and 6. The environmental issues raised in this chapter clearly strengthen the argument for doing this. Forty-two percent of the sensitive natural areas in the eleven-county region are in the four collar counties, and they are expected to grow nearly twice as quickly as the seven-county core in coming decades. The need to coordinate planning in the two parts of the region will only intensify as more and more growth crosses into the collar counties.

A simple thought experiment using the current growth projections illustrates how important this coordination could be to the municipalities and residents of the collar counties. The original projections for the eleven-county region estimated that the metro would grow by 1.1 million residents between 2000 and 2030. Eighty-seven percent of this growth, representing 970,000 people and a growth rate of 37 percent, was forecast for the seven-county core with the remaining 140,000, a 65 percent growth rate, projected for the four collar counties. If the core seven counties grow by just a bit less—by 30 percent instead of 37 percent, for instance—the distribution between core and collar counties would be dramatically different. This modest seven-point difference would mean that the core seven counties would grow by 793,000 instead of 970,000. The resulting spillover of growth into the collar counties would more than double projected growth there—from 140,000 to 316,000. Figure 5.5 shows that exactly this type of imbalance is already occurring.

The clear implication is that what happens in the seven-county core can have profound effects on the collar counties. Expanding the Metropolitan Council to eleven counties is the surest way to reserve seats at the table for the collar counties when the core counties plan their futures.

Regional growth is also spilling over into areas beyond the four collar counties. Since these areas are not yet fully integrated into the regional economy, the case for including them in the Metropolitan Council is much weaker. Nonetheless, these areas are profoundly affected by the way the metropolitan area is growing. Managing the interface between the metro and adjoining areas (in all four directions) is a job for the state. However, the state agency best suited to the task—the Minnesota Planning Agency—was disbanded in 2002.

A state planning agency could also help other state agencies coordinate better on key regulatory and permit issues facing local governments. Land use, water quality and supply, and habitat conservation are all interrelated and need to be addressed in a more comprehensive fashion rather than piecemeal by separate agencies and by different divisions within agencies. Improved interagency coordination, in combination with some clear guidance on state-level priorities and expectations on how to address key resource development issues, could only help decision makers of rapidly growing communities, who face a myriad of development decisions and trade-offs on a daily basis.

While many argue that land use planning is a local issue, and requires no higher-level governmental involvement, there is a very real need for "big picture" land use planning guidance, technical assistance, and financial incentives to help create more effectively functioning systems throughout the state, no matter what type of infrastructure system is considered—transportation, communication, or green space. Reinstatement of the state planning agency to address these issues should be a high priority.

The Minnesota Department of Natural Resources (DNR) could also do more to help alleviate growth pressures on natural habitats by developing a comprehensive statewide green infrastructure map and plan, dealing with desired linkages among its many public holdings.[14] It is essential that other levels of government know which habitats are of greatest importance for future conservation as well as those that serve as vital links between existing or desired publicly held lands. The DNR's Central Region, which includes the entire major growth corridor of the state, has taken several major steps in this direction. It has identified its regionally significant habitats based on ecological modeling, as well as assessed those sensitive natural areas most threatened by future population growth. The Central Region has a "green infrastructure" map derived from scientific data as well as local expertise and input. This template forms the basis for the Metro Conservation Corridor funding partnership made up of nongovernmental organizations and the DNR. Other parts of the state also have developed larger-scale conservation frameworks to help guide conservation and (re)development. The Red River Greenway in west-central Minnesota is an example.

Policy Recommendations—Regional and Local Government

At the regional level, the eleven-county region collectively has a negative green space balance that is growing larger every year. In other words, the conservation of green space (e.g., sensitive natural areas) is not keeping pace with urbanization. This is true even though the Twin Cities region is one of only two in the nation that has a true regional multipurpose government with land use planning authority. The Metropolitan Council's *Regional Development Framework* (2004) provides guidance to almost two hundred communities in the seven-county core region and provides the basis for review of local comprehensive plans for compliance with four regional "system" plans: wastewater services, transportation, airports, and parks and open space. However, although the framework includes the goal to "work with local and regional partners to reclaim, conserve, protect, and enhance the region's vital resources,"[15] there is no council "system" that embraces the full range of environmental concerns—green space, sensitive natural areas, or other important environmental issues. Since inconsistency with a regional "system" plan is necessary for the Met Council to require changes in a local plan, the council's role in environmental issues is limited. It can encourage, but not require, local governments to incorporate natural resource considerations into local comprehensive plans. There have been suggestions over the years that the council broaden its definition of its "Parks and Open Space" system to include natural resource conservation. A stronger alternative would be to adopt a fifth regional "system" that targets conservation of natural habitats and sensitive natural areas, requiring integration of these issues into local comprehensive plans.

The regional plan that immediately preceded the 2004 *Framework,* the 2002 *Blueprint 2030,* modified the council's metropolitan urban services area in a way that is potentially important for environmental concerns. The MUSA defines the area within which the council provides regional services. Until 2002, municipalities that were astride the MUSA were cut into two contiguous parts—one inside the MUSA and one outside. The *Blueprint* changed this practice, designating municipalities astride the MUSA as "MUSA Cities." These cities, while assigned a limit on the amount of land to be provided regional services, were given more flexibility on which areas within their boundaries would be within the MUSA. In particular, they are now allowed to designate noncontiguous additions to the MUSA, provided they stay within their overall MUSA acreage limits.

This increased local flexibility creates the potential for more effective environmental policies at the local level. If the land just beyond the current MUSA is environmentally sensitive, cities now have the option to skip over it to nonsensitive areas. Similarly, a more flexible MUSA may permit municipalities to develop new areas currently outside the MUSA in exchange for refraining from developing sensitive areas currently within the MUSA.

It is important, however, that flexibility inside the MUSA be coupled with increased vigilance by the council *outside* the MUSA. Moderate-density development now (such as single-family housing on two- to four-acre lots) in areas just beyond the MUSA makes it very difficult or impossible to accommodate future development in ways that conserve land. Currently, the council is much more likely to exercise its service or regulatory powers inside the MUSA than it is to use its regulatory powers outside the MUSA. The priority outside the MUSA should be to enforce very low *maximum* densities so that when the land is added to the MUSA, it can be developed at high enough densities. (Land developed at one housing unit per two acres is much more difficult to develop more intensely later than land that is currently developed at one housing unit per ten acres.) The analysis in chapter 2 shows that density requirements outside the MUSA have been relaxed, making it easier for municipalities to develop now at moderate densities that will make it very difficult to increase densities later.

Traditional local planning decisions are also very important. It is critical to have local policies and ordinances in place that direct development to less sensitive portions of communities and encourage (or require) design standards that minimize impacts to land, water, and air. This can involve a wide variety of policies, including denser, more compact, mixed-use development patterns; transit-, bike- and pedestrian-friendly development; and priority for infill development in already developed areas.

However, as noted earlier, fiscal incentives can discourage local areas from pursuing these kinds of policies. The seven-county core of the metropolitan area already has a unique institution, which, if expanded, could meet at least some of the equity concerns raised by regional or state limitations on the development of sensitive lands by municipalities. The region's Fiscal Disparities Program since 1971 has combined 40 percent of the increase in commercial–industrial tax base in each municipality in a regional pool. The pooled tax base is then redistributed to municipalities according to their population and total market value of property. The lower a place's market value per capita, the more tax base it receives from the pool. This means that municipalities that forego development of sensitive lands (and the market value increases associated with that development) are compensated to some extent for that decision. Tax base sharing effectively encourages sensible land use planning, especially when governance is as fragmented as it is in the Central Region.[16]

Coupling more regional or state control over local land use decisions with expansion of the Fiscal Disparities Program would reduce the potential costs of conserving sensitive natural areas in places rich in resources. For instance, the current Fiscal Disparities Program clearly helps the developing suburbs that are most likely to face difficult trade-offs between development and resource conservation in the coming years. Of the 102 municipalities in the seven-county core region in the developing job center and bedroom developing classifications, 88 (or 86 percent) currently receive more tax base from the pool than they contribute.

Similarly, expanding the Fiscal Disparities Program to include the next ring of counties likely to face these trade-offs—Chisago, Isanti, Sherburne, and Wright—would benefit the vast majority of places in those counties as well. If they had been part of the program from its inception, seventy-eight of the eighty-eight municipalities would now be receiving more tax base from the pool than they contributed, and a typical municipality would receive enough to increase its tax capacity by 11 percent. These places now contain 80 percent of the population in the collar counties.[17]

Finally, communities should be required to use comprehensive land cover data, where available, as the framework by which all development decisions are made. By using land cover information upfront, ecologically sensitive areas deserving of protection can be easily identified as part of the community's vision, and not be treated as an afterthought. In natural resource planning workshops offered around the eleven-county region in 2006–7 by the DNR and its partners, local government participants emphasized how important it was for each community to have a clearly stated vision that laid out the future desired areas for development and conservation to both community members and to developers.

6

An Overview of Policy Recommendations

Myron Orfield and Thomas F. Luce Jr.

Debates about governance and policy in metropolitan areas are highly contentious. A major reason for this is that metropolitan growth patterns have made the traditional distribution of governmental powers largely obsolete. American metropolitan areas have evolved from relatively simple city–suburb economies where most jobs were in the center of the region into extremely complex mosaics where jobs and housing are scattered across large areas governed (in most metros) by large numbers of local governments. Very few metropolitan residents now live, work, shop, and play in a single municipality. As a result, policy decisions in individual municipalities have consequences well beyond their borders with impacts on many people with no power to affect those decisions.

Resolving the resulting mismatches is no simple matter. Governments guard their powers closely, and proposals to increase the scale of existing entities (through consolidation or annexation) threaten existing prerogatives. Similarly, proposals to create alternative units that are properly scaled (regional governments) are criticized as "big government" or for adding to public sector complexity by "creating a new layer of government."

This chapter approaches the thorny policy questions raised in prior chapters in two steps. First, the analyses in preceding chapters are used to evaluate individual policy areas. The policy objectives proposed in prior chapters are restated and an appropriate division of powers among state, regional, county, and local authorities is recommended for each policy area. Second, the final section outlines a revised division of powers among the major public sector actors that reflects the discussion of policy areas.

POLICY AREAS

Land Use Planning

Land use planning is one of the most controversial policy areas in metropolitan areas. The authority to regulate housing and commercial–industrial development is one of the most jealously guarded powers held by municipal governments. At the same time, most American metropolitan areas are home to a large number of municipalities. The outcome in most areas is a patchwork quilt of land use planning carried out by many local authorities, each with its own, largely unfettered, planning powers. The resulting regulatory scheme is extremely complex. It also violates a central tenet of the correspondence principle by allocating decision making to areas much smaller than the scope of costs and benefits of their actions.

A region's land use planning system affects all of the policy areas covered in previous chapters and more. Local decisions about where to put development, how much of it to allow, and what types to pursue affect how much the region sprawls, social and racial diversity in regional housing markets and schools, the location of and access to job centers, and the region's ability to conserve sensitive natural resources. Obviously, planning policies alone cannot fully address all these needs, but the planning system should and can be designed to complement direct initiatives in each of these areas.

To meet needs in all these areas a planning system must promote development practices that:

- Cluster development on a regional scale. This conserves land at the fringes of the region, relieving pressures (in most metropolitan areas) on environmentally sensitive areas and farmland. It also concentrates demand for transportation infrastructure, takes advantage of economies of scale, and facilitates transit and other non-automobile modes of transportation.
- Require that new development on previously undeveloped land occur at reasonable densities on land adjacent to already developed land. This conserves land and resources while lowering the costs of providing regional services.
- Regulate land use outside the developed area to maintain densities low enough to allow higher-density infill when these lands are required for future growth. Moderate density development (such as one housing unit per two acres) in areas just beyond the developed core of the region can make it very difficult to increase densities later as the urbanized core expands.
- Leave control of issues with purely local consequences to local authorities. For instance, decisions regarding where to locate particular kinds of activity within municipal boundaries are usually best left to local areas.

In the Twin Cities, these general guidelines imply a set of policies, including:

- Refocus on growing within the limits of the MUSA. Recent trends include dramatic increases in the amount of scattered-site development outside the MUSA.
- Greater enforcement of density limits outside the MUSA. The Metropolitan Council currently takes its planning responsibilities outside the MUSA much less seriously than inside the MUSA.
- Serious review of local plans for consistency with regional objectives.
- A reinvigorated state planning system that manages how the metropolitan area (and other urbanized areas in the state) interact with nearby rural areas. This interface is more important now than ever, as the region's influence spreads beyond the official eleven-county metropolitan area.

Housing and Schools

Housing policy and schools are closely related. On the one hand, housing patterns determine the makeup of neighborhood schools. On the other, school characteristics are an important determinant of location decisions for many households. This two-way causation exacerbates vicious circles in housing markets that result in segregation and rapid transition in neighborhoods and schools. If poverty rates increase in a neighborhood's schools, nearby housing becomes less and less attractive to middle-income families. At some point, middle-class households will exclude the neighborhood from consideration. Even without active flight by middle-class families, normal turnover in the housing market will lower average incomes in nearby neighborhoods, which, in turn, increases poverty rates in schools, beginning the cycle again. This means that maintaining economic diversity in schools cannot be achieved independently of a housing strategy that emphasizes distributing affordable housing evenly across the region, rather than concentrating it in a few places.

As in most metropolitan areas, the problem in the Twin Cities is not simply one of maintaining diversity in schools and neighborhoods. Many neighborhoods and schools in the central cities and inner suburbs have already made the transition to concentrated poverty, and grossly disproportionate shares of the region's nonwhite population attend schools and live in these areas. More proactive policies are needed to overcome the tendency toward vicious circles in local housing markets and the incentives facing local officials in growing areas to limit housing development to housing that "pays its way."

All these factors imply that coordinated housing and school policies are needed to achieve integrated schools and neighborhoods. Affordable housing strategies must require that all parts of the region provide their fair share of affordable housing and current residents in neighborhoods of concentrated poverty must have schooling options beyond the all-poor, all-minority schools in their neighborhoods.

Necessary first steps include:

- Serious affordable housing goals, especially in growing areas. In addition to traditional criteria, like access to jobs, housing targets should be used to promote integration by income and race in neighborhoods and schools.
- Performance on these goals should be among the most important criteria used by the Met Council when reviewing local comprehensive plans, and plan approval should be linked to spending in other policy areas to give the review process teeth.
- Funding under existing affordable housing programs—the Low Income Housing Tax Credit and HUD's Section 8 programs—should be distributed based on overall population proportions, the distribution of school-age population, and integration goals, deemphasizing the current focus on the core of the region. The Metropolitan Council has a distinguished history of using its powers over federal funding to steer affordable housing funds toward the parts of the region where affordable housing is most needed. The council used federal policy 13(39) to do this very effectively during the 1970s and early 1980s. (See chapter 2, n. 81.) Compared to other parts of the country, the council has also done reasonably well steering LIHTC and HUD Section 8 funding toward suburban areas.[1] However, the simulations described in chapter 3 make it clear that more could be done. Indeed, existing funding streams could be used to significantly reduce segregation by race and income in the region's schools.
- Multidistrict school programs like the Choice Is Yours that promote integration by income and race should be expanded—in size and geographic scope—to increase options for students in highly segregated districts.
- Rules must reflect regional targets, rather than relying solely on comparisons to nearby areas. For instance, the current definition of "racially identified schools" compares school or district characteristics only to nearby schools or districts. This must be revised to reflect regionwide targets to avoid transitions that cascade from one school or district to the next.
- The incentives facing local officials in these policy areas make it very unlikely that local areas will pursue these goals on their own. The vicious circles associated with income and racial transition in neighborhoods and schools are well known and local officials are very wary of them. Increased oversight by regional and state authorities is needed to ensure that responsibilities are shared, so that individual schools and neighborhoods don't reach "tipping points."

Economic Development and Transportation

Economic development and transportation policy are also closely related. On the one hand, location decisions by businesses and residents are strongly affected by the existing (and planned) transportation system. People and firms want easy access to other parts of the region and the rest of the world. On the other hand, decisions about where to locate transportation infrastructure and what type of infrastructure to emphasize are influenced by where jobs and residents are currently located. For instance, congestion relief is unquestionably the dominant factor raised in public discussions of transportation issues in most metropolitan areas.

As with schools and housing, policy should recognize this two-way relationship. Economic development planning should reflect both the current transportation system and objectives about how we want the transportation system to work in the future. Transportation decisions should be conditioned both by current settlement and job patterns and by objectives about how we want future growth to occur.

The overall objectives of development and transportation policies follow directly from the planning, housing, and schools goals described earlier. Planning priorities mean that economic development policy should encourage growth in the already developed parts of the region and immediately adjacent areas to conserve land and infrastructure. Housing and school objectives imply that development policy should foster access to jobs across the income spectrum by promoting growth in areas with the greatest access by transit and the existing road system. Finally, there is widespread agreement that local public resources devoted to incentives for firms and high-income households to locate in one part of the region rather than another are inefficient from the point of view of the region as a whole. Reducing incentives for this wasteful competition is therefore another legitimate concern on the regional scale.

Taken together, these objectives imply regional economic development policies that emphasize:

- Clustered development to conserve land and infrastructure. The implied strategy is to focus development efforts along existing transportation corridors or at the intersection of current major highways.
- Infill and new development near the core of the region to enhance access to opportunity for the disadvantaged populations disproportionately residing there.
- Reduced incentives for interlocal competition for commercial and high-end residential development.

In the Twin Cities, the first two objectives correspond to long-standing goals of the Met Council. However, both urbanized land data (chapter 1) and job growth data (chapter 5) show that regional growth is happening more and more on scattered sites beyond the urbanized core and away from major transportation infrastructure. The council clearly could do more. One way would be to put greater emphasis on transportation improvements that complement these goals. These improvements would include:

- Expanded transit opportunities. Transit both relies on and promotes the desired kinds of development patterns. It promotes job and housing clustering by enhancing access to limited areas along and at the end points of transit corridors. However, it also relies on the existence of such clustering to be viable. In the context of the Twin Cities, where current development patterns are of the result of decades with very limited transit, transit planning needs more than ever to work in conjunction with development planning.
- More efficient use of the existing highway system—congestion relief.
  - Appropriate pricing of fuel and roads that makes users face the full cost of their transportation decisions not only would promote more efficient use of existing infrastructure but also would generate additional revenues for further needs.
  - Greater emphasis should be placed on transit and/or high-occupancy vehicle lanes along already developed transportation corridors.

The final objective—incentives to reduce interlocal competition—is one of the primary motivations for the Twin Cities' unique tax base sharing system, the Fiscal Disparities Program. This program reduces the incentives for interlocal competition by reducing the fiscal windfalls for municipalities that accompany many types of commercial–industrial development, as well as promotes regional cooperation by sharing the fiscal benefits among all participating communities. However, the program covers only the seven core counties of the region, leaving out the rapidly growing collar counties (Chisago, Isanti, Sherburne, and Wright). The program also excludes another portion of the tax base that can provide equally enticing fiscal windfalls—high-end residential development.

Environment

Much of the region's sensitive natural areas are threatened by growth. We must find new ways to accommodate our expanding economy—ways that consume less land and allow us to grow while also conserving the region's valuable natural assets. New development on undeveloped land must be at greater densities than in the past, and we must find ways to channel more growth to already developed areas. This approach will require actions at the state, regional, and local levels. However, because of the fiscal and development incentives they face, local governments are not particularly well suited to regulate or protect sensitive natural areas in many cases. This means that state and regional decision makers must take the lead. First steps should include:

- Providing state-level leadership and guidelines for growth in the metropolitan area and in the exurbs just beyond the region's official boundaries. Reconstituting the state planning agency would be a good first step.
- Creating state-level financial incentives to encourage conservation and help offset the local costs. The state's local government aid system provides one way to do this; new aid programs could also be beneficial.
- Integrating environmental issues into local plan reviews and elevating environment to a "system" in the Met Council review process. This would effectively integrate environmental issues into Met Council planning for transportation, economic development, and housing.
- Expanding the Met Council's planning powers and services into the four collar counties, which contain nearly half of the metropolitan area's sensitive natural areas.
- Combining this expansion with the extension of the Fiscal Disparities Tax Base Sharing into the four collar counties.
- Strategically applying Met Council infrastructure decisions—wastewater collection and treatment, transportation planning, and MUSA expansions— to support environmental goals.

GOVERNANCE

The preceding sections describe a wide variety of proposals across several policy areas. Many metropolitan area public sectors are too ill equipped to deal with these recommendations. The most glaring shortcoming in most cases is the lack of regionwide institutions with the needed powers. The Twin Cities is one of the few regions where this is not an issue—the Metropolitan Council has the statutory powers needed to fill this void. However, the council operates in a highly fragmented local public sector in which a large number of local authorities resist regional approaches to many of the problems described in the preceding chapters. As a result, the council's actions often fall short of its powers.

This section addresses the question of what sort of governance structure could best address all of the issues raised by the proposals outlined above. Put another way, the question is what distribution of responsibilities to the various levels of government provides the best way to meet these objectives at the lowest possible cost while remaining responsive to voters.

Regional Government

Chapter 2 describes the Metropolitan Council's powers and how they have expanded since 1972. This discussion found several areas where its powers need to be expanded and a few others where the council should use its current powers more aggressively.

Boundaries. The council's current boundaries include only the seven core counties of the metropolitan area. In 1972 this area represented the full metropolitan economy. Since then, the four collar counties—Chisago, Isanti, Sherburne, and Wright—have become fully integrated into the region's housing and labor markets.[2] Housing and labor markets are the major engines that spread the costs and benefits of local actions across the metropolitan landscape, and effective regional policy making implies that the collar counties should be added to the council's territory.

Such an expansion would likely meet resistance in the collar counties. From their point of view, they would be taking on costs (in the form of potential limitations on how they could grow) without receiving commensurate benefits (which would be spread across the region over the long term). One way to reduce the opposition would be to couple expansion of the Metropolitan Council's planning powers with expansion of the Fiscal Disparities Program—the region's tax base sharing system. Such an expansion would clearly provide financial benefits in the collar counties. Map 6.1 shows the net distributions of tax base across the region if the collar counties were now in the program. Because of their relatively small amounts of commercial–industrial tax base (the source of contributions to the regional pool of tax base) and relatively low total tax base per capita (the primary determinant of distributions from the pool), the overwhelming majority of municipalities in the collar counties—seventy-seven out of eighty-eight, representing 80 percent of population—would receive financial benefits from the program. In many cases the benefits would be substantial.

Representation. Although the sixteen members who sit on the Metropolitan Council ostensibly represent specific districts, they are not currently elected by voters in those districts; they are instead appointed by the governor. Since 1994 the council has produced four separate long-term plans, each with significant differences from its predecessor. In large measure this reflects the fact that the council's makeup can change very dramatically from one gubernatorial election to the next. Indeed, since governors normally appoint members of their own party to the council, it could change from sixteen Republicans and no Democrats to sixteen Democrats and no Republicans and back again in just four years. In actuality, the council has shifted from 100 percent Republican during most of the 1990s (largely moderate Republicans appointed by Arne Carlson) to eight Democrats, four Independents, and four Republicans (during Jesse Ventura's single four-year term), to 100

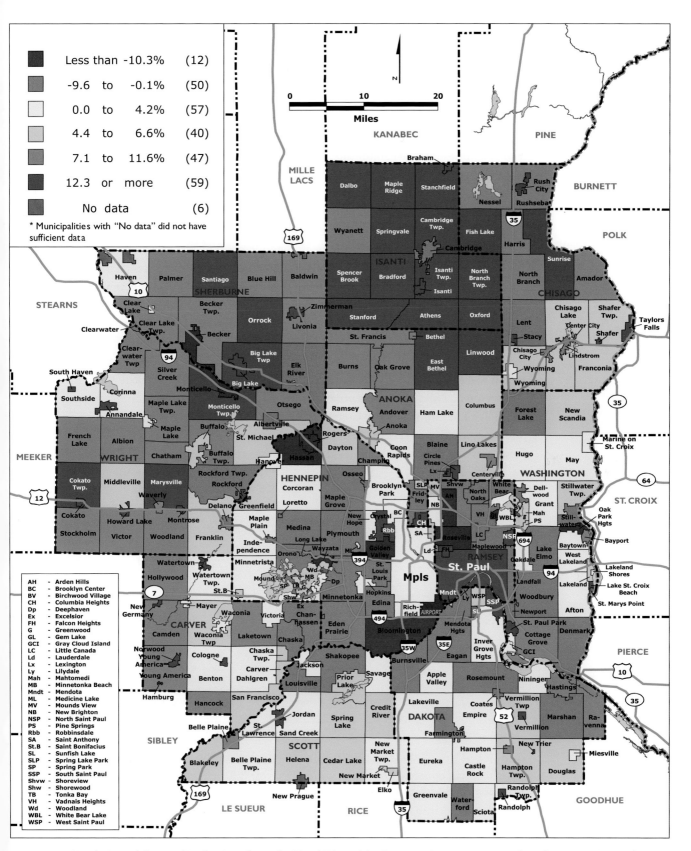

Legend:

Less than -10.3%	(12)
-9.6 to -0.1%	(50)
0.0 to 4.2%	(57)
4.4 to 6.6%	(40)
7.1 to 11.6%	(47)
12.3 or more	(59)
No data	(6)

* Municipalities with "No data" did not have sufficient data

MAP 6.1. Simulation of the net distributions from the Fiscal Disparities Program (as a percentage of total tax capacity) with the four collar counties included in the program, Twin Cities eleven-county metropolitan area, 2004. *Source:* House Research, Minnesota House of Representatives.

percent Republican (more conservative Republicans, for the most part, appointed by Tim Pawlenty) since 2002.

These dramatic partisan shifts lead to significant philosophical shifts, which make long-term planning more difficult and expensive. Most of the council's service responsibilities involve capital-intensive activities where current decisions can have very long-term consequences—transportation, transit, wastewater collection and treatment. If the planning philosophy underlying decisions in these areas frequently changes from one extreme to another, long-run planning will clearly suffer. Further, in a region that has been split fairly evenly along partisan lines during the past two decades, these shifts are fundamentally undemocratic.

If the council were elected, it would almost certainly have been much more stable during the 1990s and 2000s. Figure 6.1 shows the council's actual composition from 1992 to 2006 (red line) and its likely composition if it had been elected (blue line).[3] It is clear that control of the council would have been tightly contested during the entire period. Democrats would have controlled the council in five elections and Republicans would have won control in three.[4] More important, each part of the region would have had a voice representing its interests during the entire period.

Regional Land Use Planning and the Metropolitan Urban Services Area (MUSA). The Metropolitan Council has become less aggressive in the use of its planning powers in recent years. Two trends most clearly illustrate this statement. First, the way the council defines the MUSA has shifted from a clearly delineated

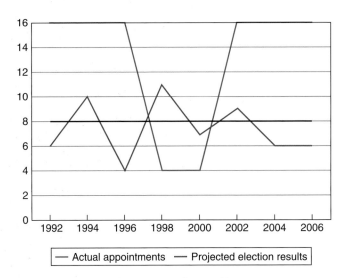

FIGURE 6.1. Metropolitan Council districts with Republican representatives, 1992–2006. A Republican is projected to hold a seat in a given year if Republicans won the majority of actual races in that district in that year. *Sources:* Minnesota Secretary of State; Metropolitan Council.

line to "MUSA Cities." In the past, the MUSA was a distinct line, beyond which metropolitan services (transportation, wastewater collection and treatment) were not provided. Jurisdictions split by the MUSA had to plan development in ways that did not force the council to provide (more costly) services to leapfrog development that was noncontiguous with already developed areas. In recent years the council has changed the way the MUSA is defined to allow municipalities that are split by the MUSA to receive metropolitan services in new developments on noncontiguous tracts within the jurisdiction as long as those municipalities stay within an overall limit for urbanized land. Not only is this more expensive for regional taxpayers, but it also makes it much more difficult for the council to limit the total amount of land added to the MUSA in the future. Providing infrastructure to noncontiguous developments is inherently more expensive, and if a municipality wishes to develop the land between the current, continuous MUSA and noncontiguous development added to the MUSA under the new guidelines, it would be very difficult for the council to refuse services to the new development. In effect, individual municipalities can increase the total amount of their land receiving metropolitan services by staging development in strategic ways, weakening the council's ability to regulate the total amount (and location) of urbanized land in the region.

The second trend that shows the council's weakening resolve is the actual pattern of urbanization that is occurring in the region. In 1986, just 22 percent of urbanized land in the Metropolitan Council's seven counties was outside the MUSA as it was then defined. During the next sixteen years, however, 47 percent of newly urbanized land occurred outside the MUSA as it was defined in 2002. During this time, the council was clearly exercising less control over development patterns outside the MUSA and the spread of urbanized land in the region became much more "scattershot." (See Maps 1.5–1.7.)

Both of these patterns illustrate how the council has become less and less aggressive about exercising its powers. This trend must be reversed if the planning objectives outlined earlier in this chapter are to be met.

Schools

School districts are major actors in local public sectors. In the Twin Cities, as in most parts of the country, school districts spend substantially more than municipalities or counties. Conditions in local schools can have dramatic effects on local housing markets, affecting home values and the kinds of households moving into and out of neighborhoods. Local schools also, and perhaps most important, contribute mightily to the long-run opportunities available to children and families.

Chapters 2, 3, and 4 highlighted a pattern of segregation by race and income in Twin Cities metropolitan area schools. Remedies proposed there and earlier in this chapter emphasized expanding the choices available to children in neighborhoods with segregated or poorly performing schools. However, since several of the region's largest districts have districtwide poverty and minority shares well in excess of 50 percent, expanded choice *within* existing school district boundaries is clearly not enough. At the other extreme, regionwide remedies in a region as large as the Twin Cities face the inevitable problems created by long distances. An intermediate remedy clearly is needed.

The Twin Cities region has the basic framework in place for just such a remedy. Multidistrict consortia that combine all or parts of central city and inner suburban districts (with high poverty and minority shares) with growing suburban areas already exist. The West Metro Education Partnership (WMEP), the Northwest Suburban Integration District (Northwest Suburban), and the East Metro Integration District (East Metro) provide excellent starting points for further efforts to stabilize schools and neighborhoods. However, although the consortia each have a superintendent and are recognized as "local governments" under state law, their powers to act are very limited.

It is not only local or regional organizations that must play an expanded role in this area. The state government is a very important actor, financing and regulating local districts. The areas in which increased state vigilance is most needed are (1) policing local boundary decisions and (2) defining where local actions or school characteristics create schools that are segregated enough to warrant state or regional oversight.

Cities and Townships

Regardless of how aggressively a region pursues a regional governance strategy, cities and townships will still fill important functions: building and maintaining local infrastructure such as streets and sewers; providing local police and fire protection; and regulating new development. Ideally, municipalities should be large enough to provide these services at efficient scales. In sparsely settled areas, this idea may be impractical and in these areas county governments often provide local services. However, very small municipalities are not uncommon even in relatively densely settled or developing areas. For instance, in 2005 roughly half of the cities and townships in the eleven-county Twin Cities metropolitan area (129 out of 270) had fewer than 2,500 residents. Even in the mostly developed seven core counties, there were 78 such places—more than 40 percent of cities and townships. There were another 53 municipalities with between 2,500 and 5,000 residents—33 in the seven core counties and 20 in the collar counties.

There are no hard and fast estimates of the optimal size for local governments, but it is difficult to defend a system in a large metropolitan area where two-thirds (182 of 270) of the cities and townships have fewer than 5,000 residents. The extreme degree of fragmentation clearly implies that policies should be designed to encourage localities to take advantage of any opportunities to reduce fragmentation through consolidation or annexation. In the Twin Cities, the most likely opportunities for this involve cases where cities border on townships. The State's Office of Administrative Hearings handles a steady stream of annexation cases, but they are disproportionately outside the metropolitan area and rarely involve large tracts of land. For instance, in September 2007 there were 144 pending boundary change cases, and just 28 of them were in the Twin Cities metropolitan area. (This represents 20 percent of cases, while the metro houses 60 percent of the state's population.) Of these 28 cases, only 4 involved annexations of more than one hundred acres of land.

7

The Politics of Regional Policy

Myron Orfield, Thomas F. Luce Jr.,
Geneva Finn, and Baris Gumus-Dawes

THE SURPRISINGLY STABLE GEOGRAPHY OF A SWING REGION

The Twin Cities metropolitan area has a reputation as a swing region, electing Republican and Independent governors, Democratic presidents, and hosting both Democratic and Republican majorities in the Minnesota House of Representatives and Minnesota Senate over the past fifteen years. The election of former pro wrestler Jesse Ventura exposed the fickleness of the Minnesota voter—and left both the Minnesota Republican and Democratic-Farm-Labor (DFL) parties scrambling to win over wayward suburban voters. Despite these political swings, votes in the Twin Cities metropolitan region remained relatively evenly split from 1992 to 2006. Democrats secured slightly more than half of the votes in the region in most of election years, barring some minor fluctuations, depending on voter turnout and the presence of third-party candidates (Figure 7.1).[1]

Voters' party preferences differed systematically within the region, and these geographic differences did not change over time; the region becomes more Republican the farther away one moves from the region's urban core. The central cities are Democratic strongholds, while inner suburbs remained more Democratic than both middle and outer suburbs. The outer suburbs had the highest percentages of Republican voters among all types of suburbs (Figure 7.2).

While the party preferences of various suburb types remained relatively constant, the geographical distribution of votes in the region changed, reflecting demographic changes in the Twin Cities region. As the region suburbanized, population in the outer suburbs grew at a much faster rate than the rest of the region. The outer suburbs provide a growing share of the votes in the region, while the share of votes coming from central cities and inner cities has declined (Figure 7.3).

These trends changed the geography of politics in the Twin Cities—despite a regional political divide that remained relatively evenly split across time. Central cities and inner suburbs became more Democratic; middle suburbs became more

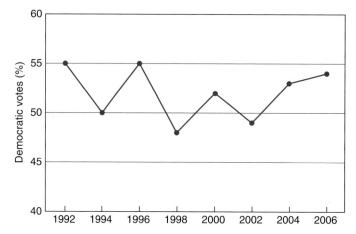

FIGURE 7.1. Democratic votes as a percentage of Democratic and Republican votes in the Twin Cities metropolitan area, 1992–2006. *Source:* Minnesota Secretary of State.

tightly contested and some shifted party affiliation; and outer suburbs became increasingly and more strongly Republican. Most of the municipalities that became Republican between 1992 and 2006 were fast-growing places. Most municipalities that grew faster than the regional average were Republican (Figure 7.4).[2]

Changes in the geography of party preferences affected the distribution of legislators in both chambers of the state legislature. Democratic house members and senators maintained their stronghold in the central cities while solidifying their position in the inner suburbs. Democrats made gains in middle suburban house

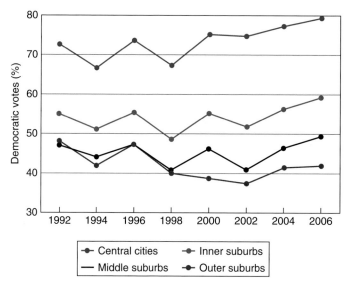

FIGURE 7.2. Democratic votes as a percentage of Democratic and Republican votes by Twin Cities locations, 1992–2006. *Source:* Minnesota Secretary of State.

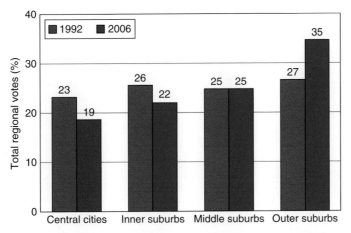

FIGURE 7.3. Distribution of total votes by Twin Cities locations, 1992 and 2006. *Source:* Minnesota Secretary of State.

and senate districts; however, middle suburban districts still remain highly contested—both parties win middle suburbs by narrow margins. Republicans have had a growing domination of the outer suburban state senate districts (Map 7.1).

None of these patterns is particularly surprising. However, if voters' preferences are analyzed by the community typology described in chapter 1, rather than simply by geography, clearer patterns emerge (Map 7.2). While the inner cities and stressed suburbs are solid Democratic strongholds and the outer suburbs are Republican, developing and developed job centers have swinging, volatile voters—whose votes will go to the party most willing to represent their best interests.

The rest of this chapter examines the political interest of the Twin Cities region's communities and the importance of these communities to political strategists

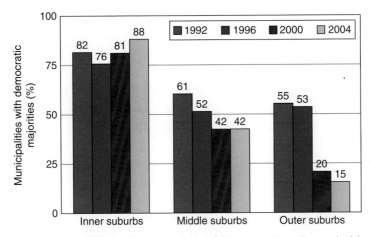

FIGURE 7.4. Percentage of Twin Cities suburbs with Democratic voting majorities by location, 1992–2004. *Source:* Minnesota Secretary of State.

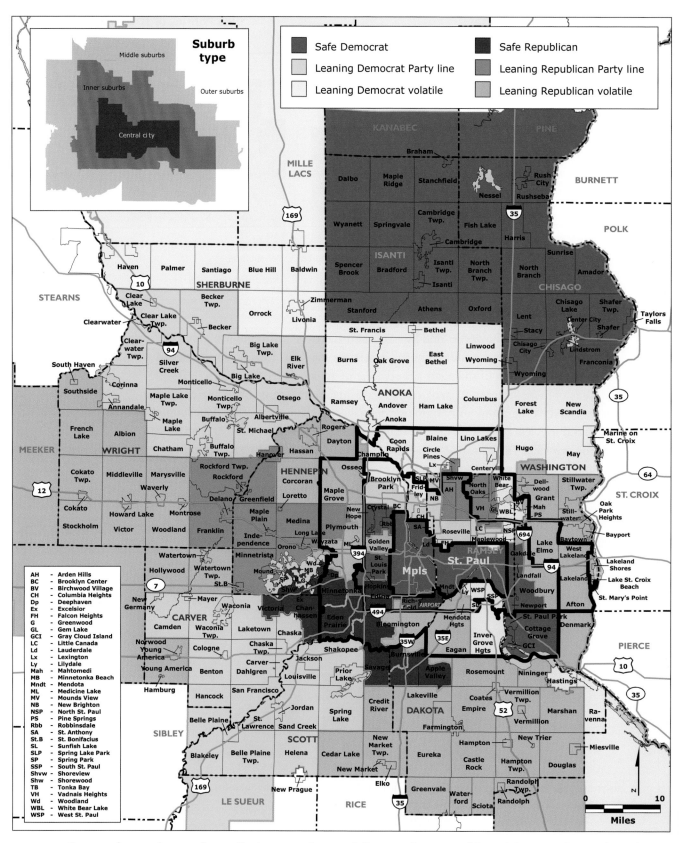

MAP 7.1. Party preferences by state Senate district, 1992. *Sources:* Minnesota Secretary of State; Minnesota Geographic Information Services.

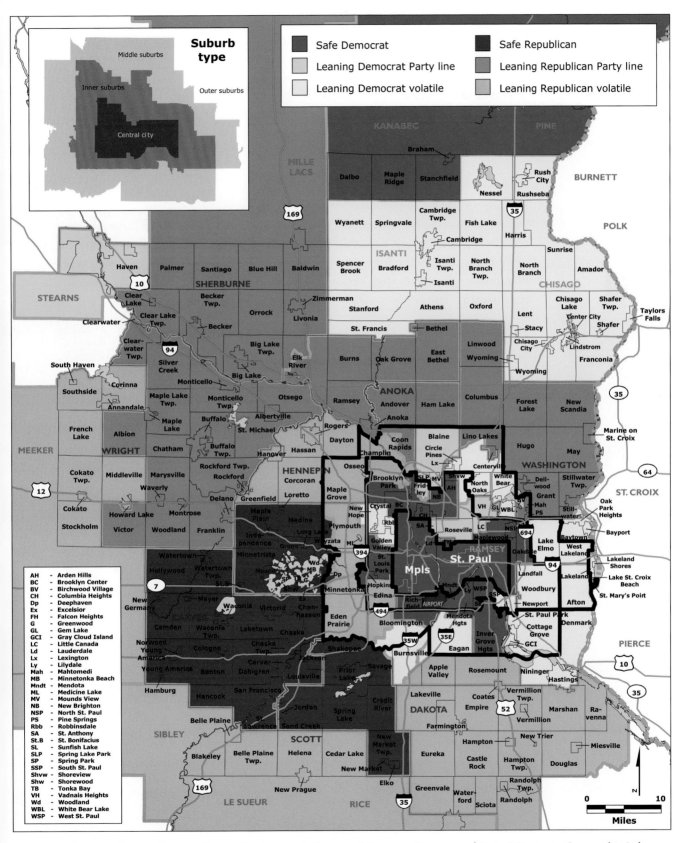

MAP 7.2. Party preferences by state Senate district, 2006. *Sources:* Minnesota Secretary of State; Minnesota Geographic Information Services.

seeking to build a winning coalition for a regional agenda. It then shows how regionalism can meet the needs of all types of Twin Cities communities, with special attention to the needs of political battleground communities. The final sections then describe how a political party that embraces a regional agenda can build solid majority control over state politics.

THE COMMUNITIES

Developing and developed job centers provide about 48 percent of the region's votes, something that did not change much between 2000 and 2006. While these job centers are key to forming a successful coalition for a regionalist agenda, communities of all types can benefit from regional reforms. Understanding the ways each type of community benefits from regional reforms is essential for making the case for regionalism (Figure 7.5).

Democratic Strongholds: Central Cities and Stressed Suburbs

Both central cities and more than 70 percent of stressed suburbs voted Democratic in 2000 and 2006 (Figure 7.6).[3]

Swing Communities: Developed Job Centers

Developed job centers, overall, switched allegiance during the period.[4] This change in party preferences is noteworthy. In 2000 nearly two-thirds of these job centers

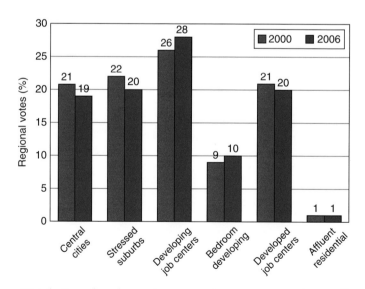

FIGURE 7.5. Distribution of total votes by community type, 2000 and 2006. *Sources:* Minnesota Secretary of State; Ameregis, Inc.

were Republican. Merely six years later, more than half showed Democratic majorities. This rather dramatic shift in party alignment was reflected in the composition of the votes cast in developed job centers.

Republican Strongholds: Developing Job Centers, Bedroom Developing, and Affluent Residential Places

Affluent residential places voted Republican consistently in this period.[5] Less than one-tenth of these communities voted Democratic in both years. The party preferences of bedroom developing places did not change much either from 2000 to 2006. Democrats carried only about one in five of these places in 2000 and 2006. Developing job centers looked very similar, with Democrats carrying only 22 percent of these places in 2006.

VOLATILITY: IDENTIFYING REPUBLICANS WHO VOTE FOR DEMOCRATS

Volatile districts are places where voters are not strongly tied to a single party— places where Republicans are willing to split their ballot and vote for selected Democrats and where Democrats are similarly willing to vote for selected Republicans. Volatility is a statistical measure to identify and locate the voters most open to persuasion. The measure used for the analysis shows how much party shares vary from race to race in a single election. (See the sidebar for a complete description of

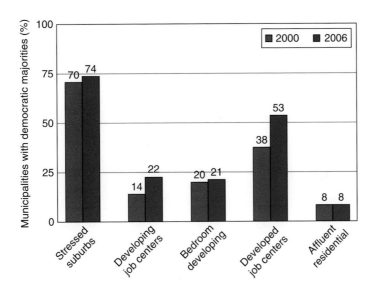

FIGURE 7.6. Party preferences of Twin Cities suburban communities by community type. *Sources:* Minnesota Secretary of State; Ameregis, Inc.

the methods.) If the Democratic or Republican share varies a great deal from race to race, this implies that individual voters are not voting for the same party in all races. Voters split their ticket because they either are not aligned with a specific party or are undecided on public policy issues. These volatile voters are likely to be more open to education and persuasion. This means that volatile districts are often important battlegrounds, especially in statewide elections. All parties have a strong interest in addressing the concerns of these places, and effectively addressing the needs of volatile communities is key to a winning regionalist agenda.

Overall, the Twin Cities region became politically less volatile from 1992 to 2006, despite some fluctuations in average voter volatility along the way (Figure 7.7). This decline in average voter volatility implies that *the region's voters are increasingly polarized in their political party preferences*. In other words, a declining share of the region's voters are "ticket splitters" who vote for different parties in a single election either because they are not aligned with a specific party or because they are undecided on public policy issues.

However, volatile voters still exist in substantial numbers in the region. Middle and outer suburbs were more politically volatile than the central cities and inner suburbs during the 1990s and early 2000s (Figure 7.8; Map 7.3). Developing and developed job centers have consistently cast the majority of volatile votes in the Twin Cities region, highlighting the political importance of these areas. Together, these places cast nearly two-thirds of the volatile votes in the Twin Cities metropolitan area in both years.[6] Developing job centers are especially important because they provide a growing share of the region's volatile votes. By 2006, nearly 40 percent of the volatile votes in the region came from developing job centers (Figure 7.9).

The most highly contested areas are likely to be places that are both closely contested—neither Democrats nor Republicans win with large majorities—and

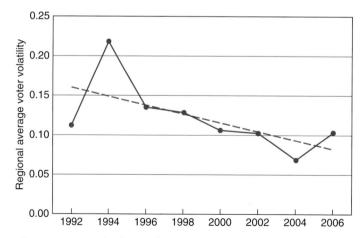

FIGURE 7.7. Average voter volatility in the Twin Cities metropolitan area, 1992–2006. *Source:* Minnesota Secretary of State.

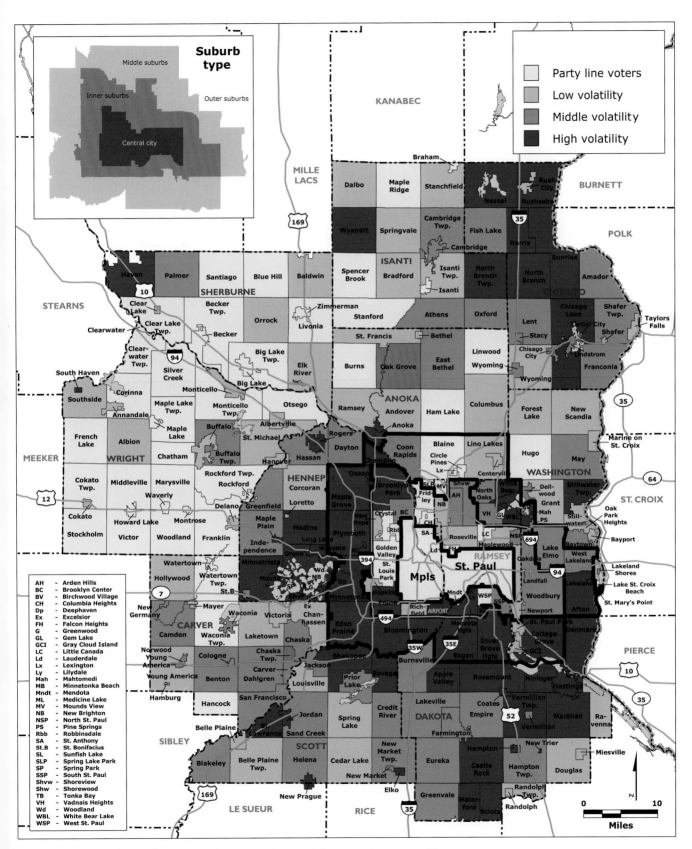

Party line voters

Low volatility

Middle volatility

High volatility

AH   - Arden Hills
BC   - Brooklyn Center
BV   - Birchwood Village
CH   - Columbia Heights
Dp   - Deephaven
Ex   - Excelsior
FH   - Falcon Heights
G   - Greenwood
GL   - Gem Lake
GCI - Gray Cloud Island
LC   - Little Canada
Ld   - Lauderdale
Lx   - Lexington
Ly   - Lilydale
Mah - Mahtomedi
MB   - Minnetonka Beach
Mndt - Mendota
ML   - Medicine Lake
MV   - Mounds View
NB   - New Brighton
NSP - North St. Paul
PS   - Pine Springs
Rbb - Robbinsdale
SA   - St. Anthony
St.B - St. Bonifacius
SL   - Sunfish Lake
SLP - Spring Lake Park
SP   - Spring Park
SSP - South St. Paul
Shvw - Shoreview
Shw - Shorewood
TB   - Tonka Bay
VH   - Vadnais Heights
Wd   - Woodland
WBL - White Bear Lake
WSP - West St. Paul

MAP 7.3. Voter volatility by municipality, 2006. *Source:* Minnesota Secretary of State.

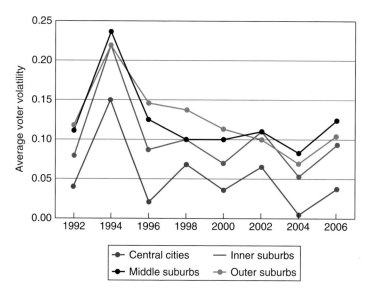

FIGURE 7.8. Average voter volatility by suburban community type, 1992–2006. *Source:* Minnesota Secretary of State.

volatile—many voters are willing to split their tickets. Analysis of these types of places—leaning volatile places—shows that developing and developed job centers are important political battlegrounds. The share of leaning volatile votes cast in developing and developed job centers increased from 64 percent in 2000 to 67 percent in 2006. In 2006, developing job centers alone cast 37 percent of the leaning volatile votes in the region, up from 22 percent in 2000 (Figure 7.10).

MAKING THE CASE FOR REGIONALISM

In Minnesota, the metropolitan region is home to a significant part of the state's population; major political parties cannot maintain legislative majorities unless they control the developing or developed job centers or both. Once these communities realize their strategic role in regional politics and the detrimental consequences for their communities of social and economic segregation, intense intraregional competition for tax base, sprawling development, and congestion, the party that addresses these crucial regional issues will exert great political power.

Racial and economic segregation destabilizes communities and undermines their economic vitality by triggering a process of disinvestment in these communities. This process of disinvestment not only negatively impacts the housing values in these communities but also drives out the businesses providing jobs and tax base. In addition, racial segregation and concentration of poverty impose a number of social costs on communities, inflating the expenditure side of their fiscal ledgers. Communities are put in a double bind, as racial segregation and concentrated pov-

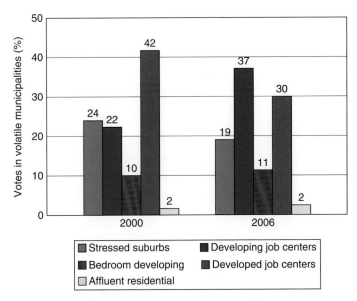

FIGURE 7.9. Distribution of votes in volatile places by community type, 2000 and 2006. *Sources:* Minnesota Secretary of State; Ameregis, Inc.

erty sap their fiscal capacities while their financial obligations accelerate because of growing social costs.

Racial and economic segregation impacts various types of communities in the region. Many neighborhoods in the central cities have already been hard hit by the disinvestment caused by segregation. Even impressive local efforts to revitalize these neighborhoods have limited success without the implementation of regional

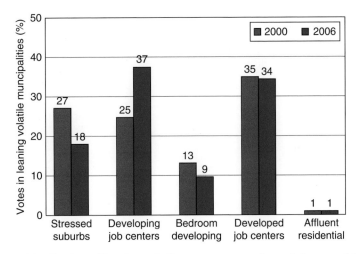

FIGURE 7.10. Distribution of leaning volatile votes, 2000 and 2006. *Sources:* Minnesota Secretary of State; Ameregis, Inc.

POLITICAL VOLATILITY

The voter volatility measure is an indicator of the extent to which voters in a particular precinct, municipality, or other geographic area split their tickets between Democrats and Republicans. It is computed by calculating how much the share of votes going to Democrats and Republicans varies from race to race in a specific place in a single election year. Specifically, it is the coefficient of variation in the share of votes going to Democrats (in places where Democrats receive more votes than Republicans) or Republicans (in places where Republicans receive more votes than Democrats). Or mathematically:

Voter volatility in a municipality = SD_{dem} ÷ $Mean_{dem}$ (in municipalities where Democrats receive more votes than Republicans) or SD_{rep} ÷ $Mean_{rep}$ (in municipalities where Republicans receive more votes than Democrats)

Where: SD_{dem} (or SD_{rep}) is the standard deviation of the percentages of votes going to Democrats (or Republicans) across all the races in a single year; and $Mean_{dem}$ (or $Mean_{rep}$) is the simple mean of the percentages of votes going to Democrats (or Republicans) across all races in a single year.

A low coefficient of variation indicates a municipality where the percentage of votes received by one or the other party is roughly the same across all races and a high value is one where the percentage varies a great deal across races.

The volatility categories are determined by the quartile volatility values across municipalities in the relevant year. "Party line" municipalities are those where the volatility measure is between zero and the 25th percentile; "low volatility" refers to those between the 25th and 50th percentiles; "middle volatility" designates those between the 50th and 75th percentiles; and "high volatility" municipalities are those above the 75th percentile.

The party preference categories are determined with a combination of the average share of votes received by a particular party and the volatility measure. "Safe" municipalities are places where the average vote for either party exceeds 60 percent. "Leaning" municipalities are the places where the average percentage is between 50 and 60 percent. "Party line" places are those where the volatility measure is less than the 50th percentile, and "volatile" municipalities are those above the 50th percentile. Safe municipalities are not subdivided into party line and volatile categories because voter volatility in these places is less likely to result in party shifts from election to election. On the other hand, in tightly contested municipalities, a tendency for voters to split tickets is more likely to result in different parties winning in different years.

All party shares are calculated as a percentage of the sum of votes for Democratic and Republican candidates. The classification system ignores votes for other parties.

policies that can reverse the social and economic segregation trends in the Twin Cities metropolitan area. For instance, a regional housing policy, which distributes affordable housing fairly across different types of communities in the region, would be a crucial component of reducing racial segregation and decentralizing poverty in the region.

Racial and economic segregation is no longer confined to central cities; segregation is now a regional concern, threatening the vitality of different types of suburban communities. Schools, which are powerful indicators of a community's health, are already experiencing social and economic changes that signal growing segregation in stressed suburbs. However, stressed suburbs are not alone in experiencing these disturbing segregation patterns. These patterns are emerging even in developed job centers that are close to stressed suburbs. These suburban communities face the risk of decline unless they can preempt spreading racial and economic segregation before it undermines the vitality of their communities.

The region's increasing racial diversity does not have to result in growing racial and economic segregation and disinvestment in various types of communities. Regional policies can help prevent the harms of unstable integration and resegregation. In fact, in metropolitan regions where such policies are in effect, stably integrated communities continue to thrive and generate opportunities for their residents. Only through an effective combination of pro-integrative school and housing policies, can central cities, stressed suburbs, and developed job centers defend themselves against the growing problem of racial and economic segregation and ensure the vitality of their communities.

A regional land use policy can revitalize central cities and stabilize stressed suburbs and developed job centers. A strictly enforced and well-defined urban growth boundary can geographically redirect development away from newer developments in the suburbs and infill development in the already developed parts of the region. A policy of recycling places prioritizes fixing and improving places in the already developed parts of the region before enabling new developments in the fringes of the region. Similar recycling policies have proved successful in revitalizing central cities and stabilizing stressed suburbs in Maryland.

By encouraging stronger land use planning at the periphery of the region, a well-implemented regional land use policy can strengthen developed job centers. By discouraging new development outside the regional growth boundary, planning can curtail the sprawling of jobs and households and enhance the competitiveness of developed job centers in the regional economy.

Regional land use planning can also prevent central cities, stressed suburbs, and developed job centers from subsidizing the costs of poorly planned new development and its remediation. By implementing infrastructure concurrency requirements, a regional land use plan can postpone new development until adequate infrastructure is in place and force newer suburbs to bear the full costs of development. This plan can also reduce the infrastructure costs for all types of communities by making the provision of infrastructure more efficient. Planning that more holistically takes into account the infrastructural needs of the region avoids costly duplications and rules out myopic investments that undermine the long-term effectiveness of a regional infrastructure network.

A *regional transportation policy,* which prioritizes transit, could also help revitalize communities in the already developed parts of the region. Transit investments can help central cities and developed job centers to reduce the infrastructural costs associated with their high job and household densities. Transit-oriented growth can also boost housing values and tax capacity in central cities and stressed suburbs without contributing to further congestion, and thus enhance the vitality of these communities as job centers. A transit-oriented regional transportation policy ensures the continuing vitality of developed job centers by containing job sprawl.

Central Cities

Social and economic segregation hurts central cities more than any other type of community in the region by turning them into sites of urban blight. A *regional affordable housing policy,* which distributes affordable housing fairly across all types of communities in the region, could reduce urban blight by decentralizing poverty and reducing racial segregation. By addressing the true causes of urban blight, a regional affordable housing policy can increase the ability of central cities to raise revenues from local resources and reduce the costs associated with concentration of poverty and racial segregation.

Central cities can also benefit from *regional land use planning* that boosts their tax capacities. Regional land use planning, more specifically the strict enforcement of a well-defined urban growth boundary, redirects development away from newer developments in the suburbs to infill development in the central cities.

A *regional transportation policy,* which prioritizes transit, can also help central cities. Transit investments in central cities can significantly reduce the costs associated with their high job and household densities. Transit-oriented growth can also boost housing values and tax capacity in central cities without contributing to congestion. As a result, a regional transportation policy can maintain and enhance the vitality of central cities as job centers.

Stressed Suburbs

A *regional tax equity policy,* which promotes regional tax base sharing to reduce excessive competition among municipalities, benefits stressed suburbs more than any other type of suburb. By providing additional resources to stressed suburbs, this policy helps stressed suburbs simultaneously reduce tax rates and provide crucial services necessary to stay competitive within the metropolitan economy.

Stressed suburbs need to be especially vigilant regarding factors that threaten to import racial and economic segregation from central cities to suburban areas. Racial segregation and concentration of poverty destabilize communities and undermine their economic vitality by weakening their fiscal strength and by imposing costly services on them. The stressed suburbs are already witnessing early signs of trouble in their schools.

Schools are a powerful indicator of a community's health and a predictor of the future. Middle-class families choose to live in the least poor school district they can afford. When a place's schools begin to become poorer, in more cases than not, middle-class families leave the community. This triggers a process of disinvestment that not only affects the housing market but also the businesses providing jobs in that community. Slow household growth rates usually herald the beginnings of such disinvestment. Between 1993 and 2003, stressed suburbs had the lowest average household growth rate among all suburbs—roughly a third of the regional average rate of 18 percent.

While the average poverty rate in stressed suburbs is still slightly below the regional average, growing school poverty in these suburbs signals growing social and economic stress for these communities. Of the six nonwhite segregated suburban schools with high concentrations of poverty in the Twin Cities region, five of them were located in the stressed suburbs in 2002. If unchecked, growing racial and economic segregation in suburban schools could destabilize these suburbs by triggering residential segregation.

A regional housing policy can help stressed suburbs protect themselves from the destabilizing effects of racial segregation and concentration of poverty. This policy can take the pressure off stressed suburbs and prevent racial segregation and concentration of poverty in these communities by distributing affordable housing fairly across all types of communities in the region. After all, stressed suburbs already provide more than their fair share of affordable housing. Home to 23 percent of the region's households, these suburbs provide 26 percent of the region's affordable housing.[7]

Moreover, among all suburban communities, stressed suburbs have the highest share of affordable housing stock (28 percent)—more than twice the corresponding share in the remaining suburbs. The stressed suburbs need to collaborate to make sure that newer suburbs bear their fair share of affordable housing. Only a coalition of stressed suburbs can ensure that stressed suburbs do not exclusively bear the tax capacity burden of having disproportionately high shares of affordable housing. Stressed suburbs are natural allies of the central cities, which also provide a disproportionately high portion of the region's affordable housing stock.

Regional land use planning can be another powerful stabilizing tool for stressed suburbs. A well-implemented regional land use plan can discourage new development until adequate infrastructure is in place. It could achieve this by requiring newer suburbs to bear the full costs of development through infrastructure concurrency requirements. Requiring new development to bear the full costs of development prevents stressed suburbs from subsidizing the costs of poorly planned new development and its remediation.

A regional plan that prioritizes the rehabilitation of existing infrastructure over the construction of new infrastructure in sprawling suburbs can also channel regional resources into stressed suburbs. Regional resources above and beyond the individual capacities of stressed suburbs could help restore the streets, sewer systems, parks, and schools that need additional maintenance and upgrades and assist in financing expensive brownfield developments. By making crucial infrastructural reinvestments possible, a regional plan could redirect regional growth back into stressed suburbs and help them revitalize their communities.

Developing Job Centers

With higher than average children-to-household ratios, developing job centers face very high school costs per household. Since schools are the most expensive local public service provided in the United States, school districts in developing job centers tend to have very low spending per pupil figures. As communities with modest fiscal capacities, developing job centers struggle with the costs of educating their students. Schools in these communities tend to be overcrowded because these communities usually lack the resources to build new facilities to meet the educational needs of a rapidly growing student body.

A *regional tax equity policy*, which promotes regional tax base sharing, can offer lower taxes and better services to developing job centers. Developing job centers have relatively low tax capacity relative to the rest of the region, so they would benefit from tax base sharing.[8]

Lacking the tax capacities required for meeting the costs of rapid growth, developing job centers seek additional development far more aggressively than developed job centers. Facing pressures to attract development at any price, these centers tend to neglect long-term infrastructural planning for schools, roads, and sewers. In the absence of central planning, developing job centers frequently face escalating costs as they are forced to remedy the problems associated with neglected infrastructure.

For instance, developing job centers allow rapid household growth along small country roads that have limited capacity to handle growing traffic. This quickly generates traffic bottlenecks and specific sites of congestion in these communities. Remedying this problem, in turn, imposes additional costs on these cash-strapped communities because widening these roads by moving strip malls and houses back from the right of way costs a lot more than planning and constructing roads that could accommodate future growth in the first place.

Similarly, because of their limited tax capacities, developing job centers tend to build septic systems rather than the more expensive sewerage infrastructure. These systems invariably fail and endanger public health by polluting the groundwater. Remedying these problems by eventually building sewerage in these places is once again far more expensive than initially developing these communities with the proper infrastructure. Building interceptors and trunk lines through developed areas involves very costly activities such as digging up existing public infrastructure and private lawns as well as bypassing lakes and stands of trees.

Developing job centers can benefit from *regional planning,* which helps them obtain infrastructure in more orderly and cost-effective ways. Long-range road and interceptor planning at the regional scale can help developing job centers share their infrastructural costs. Regional authorities can lower the financial costs of building infrastructure in these centers by pooling regional resources and by creating regional funds and bonding authorities that create access to capital at more favorable terms.

Under pressure to attract development at any price, developing job centers also risk loss of open space and natural amenities that make suburban living such an attraction for many residents. As the growth projections summarized in chapter 6 show, developing job centers are the places where a significant portion of new growth in the region is likely to happen. Very recent growth patterns confirm that if developing job centers continue to grow at current densities, they will be encountering developable land shortages much sooner than any other community type in the region.

As a result, many of these places will face hard choices between accepting development and conserving sensitive natural areas. Accommodating the costs of this new growth will make it harder for these places to spend their scarce fiscal resources on conservation efforts. Policies designed to absorb the costs of conservation at the regional level can provide additional resources to developing job centers, preventing them from sacrificing valuable natural amenities to excessive and unplanned growth.

Developed Job Centers

Despite developed job centers' relatively limited costs and high tax capacities, some centers have been undergoing the same social and economic changes as stressed suburbs. Developed job centers such as Bloomington, Roseville, and Eden Prairie are already showing signs of growing racial and economic segregation. Unless these trends are stopped, segregation could eventually destabilize these communities and undermine their economic vitality. Developed job centers have an important stake in fighting racial segregation and concentration of poverty along with central cities and stressed suburbs.

Racial and economic segregation is a regional problem that cannot be effectively addressed without regionwide measures. A *regional housing policy,* which prioritizes a fair distribution of affordable housing across the region, can address segregation. Developed job centers undergoing social and economic transition could preserve the stability and vitality of their communities by making sure that *all* communities, including other developed job centers, provide their fair share of affordable housing.

A more even regional distribution of affordable housing can also help reduce traffic congestion, especially in places with high concentrations of jobs. As a group, developed job centers have a limited supply of affordable housing, despite having the highest concentration of jobs in the region. This combination makes congestion a pressing problem for these communities. Streamlining regional housing and transportation policies can ease congestion on a regional level.

A *regional transportation policy,* which prioritizes transit, can reduce congestion in developed job centers, since most of these communities have reached job agglomeration thresholds needed to support transit. A transit-oriented transportation policy can also help contain job sprawl, ensuring the continuing vitality of developed job centers in the face of competition from developing job centers.

Regional land use planning can supplement regional housing and transportation policies, preserving the stability and vitality of developed job centers. Developed job centers can benefit immensely from stronger land use planning at the periphery of the region. By prioritizing growth at the already developed parts of the region, regional land use policies can effectively curtail the sprawling of jobs and households and boost the standing of developed job centers among their competitors.

Bedroom Developing Places

Most households move to bedroom developing communities to live a suburban lifestyle in a natural or farmlike setting. Sprawl hurts bedroom developing places by threatening the open spaces that are valuable to their residents. Bedroom developing communities frequently resort to local growth moratoriums in order to protect their open space and sensitive areas. Growth moratoriums by individual communities are at best ineffective in stopping sprawl, and at worst likely to export the sprawl problem to the next town by encouraging leapfrog development.

These communities can benefit immensely from *regional land use planning,* which can effectively curtail sprawl at the fringes of the region by encouraging higher densities in the region's core. In the long run, the creation of a regional growth boundary as part of a strictly enforced regional land use plan is more effective than unilateral action by individual communities in protecting open space and containing sprawl.

Affluent Residential Places

Since high land prices make it costly to preserve open spaces in these communities, sprawl becomes a pressing issue for the residents of the affluent residential places.

As a result, these communities could benefit from *regional land use planning,* which can effectively curtail sprawl and help preserve open space at a regional level.

WINNING COALITIONS FOR REGIONALISM

An analysis of voter patterns shows that Minnesota is a more polarized place than it used to be. Even more, the share of voters for either party has not changed very much over the past fifteen years. These facts tend to lead to fatalism, political parties giving up on the prospect of developing winning coalitions. An analysis of community types and voter volatility, however, leads to a much different conclusion: the Twin Cities region has plenty of communities of volatile voters, and voter volatility is increasing in the fast-growing developing job centers. What's more is that these voters are leaning volatile voters, the voters who are the most likely to change their votes in response to a party platform that addresses their core interests and the needs of their communities.

Regionalism does just that. In the 1990s, a coalition for regionalism emerged within the Minnesota DFL. Inner-suburban and city legislatures worked together to pass the Livable Communities Act, a strong piece of affordable housing legislation that was supported by cities throughout the region. In addition, the legislature consolidated regional agencies into the Met Council, passed a bill to elect the Met Council (this was vetoed by the governor), gave the Met Council superseding planning authority, and pushed through a transit line. These bills addressed the needs of the region's swing communities of the 1990s, the inner suburbs, which were just starting to experience core city types of stresses.

Today, the case for regionalism is stronger than ever. Suburbs are poorer than they used to be, and most school districts are struggling to keeps schools open in the face of mounting costs and declining budgets. Even Eden Prairie, a Twin Cities developed job center that used to have little or no interest in regionalist issues, is struggling with urban issues, like school funding and increasing diversity and segregation. There is hope for regionalism in these patterns and success for political parties that address the common concerns of struggling suburban and city communities.

APPENDIX A

Neighborhood and School Typology

The twelve neighborhood types used in the analysis are based on four racial-ethnic groups in the population—white, black, Hispanic, and other (sum of Asian Pacific Islanders and American Indians). Eight of the neighborhood types are considered *segregated* and four are considered *integrated*. Two characteristics differentiate segregated neighborhoods from integrated neighborhoods: the presence or not of significant numbers of residents of more than one racial/ethnic group and the presence or not of a significant share of white residents. Thus, the segregated group includes neighborhoods where the share of blacks, Hispanics, or others exceeds 50 percent as well as neighborhoods with varying combinations of black, Hispanic, and other residents, where the relative share of white residents in the neighborhoods does not exceed 30 percent. Although these racially mixed neighborhoods could be regarded as integrated because they include a mix of races, they are treated as segregated in this work because they are dominated by racial/ethnic groups that have traditionally faced discrimination of various kinds. The same typology was created for schools.

SEGREGATED TYPES

1. Predominantly white: Less than or equal to 10 percent black *and* less than or equal to 10 percent Hispanic *and* less than or equal to 10 percent other.

2. Predominantly black: Greater than 50 percent black *and* less than or equal to 10 percent Hispanic *and* less than or equal to 10 percent other.

3. Predominantly Hispanic: Greater than 50 percent Hispanic *and* less than or equal to 10 percent black *and* less than or equal to 10 percent other.

4. Predominantly other: Greater than 50 percent other *and* less than or equal to 10 percent black *and* less than 10 percent Hispanic.

5. Black and Hispanic: Less than 30 percent white *and* greater than 10 percent black *and* greater than 10 percent Hispanic *and* less than or equal to 10 percent other.

6. Black and other: Less than 30 percent white *and* greater than 10 percent black *and* greater than 10 percent other *and* less than or equal to 10 percent Hispanic.

7. Hispanic and other: Less than 30 percent white *and* greater than 10 percent Hispanic *and* greater than 10 percent other *and* less than or equal to 10 percent black.

8. Multiethnic segregated: Less than 30 percent white and greater than 10 percent black *and* greater than 10 percent Hispanic *and* greater than 10 percent other.

INTEGRATED TYPES

9. White and black: Greater than 10 percent and less than or equal to 50 percent black *and* less than or equal to 10 percent Hispanic *and* less than or equal to 10 percent other.

10. White and Hispanic: Greater than 10 percent and less than or equal to 50 percent Hispanic *and* less than or equal to 10 percent black *and* less than or equal to 10 percent other.

11. White and other: Greater than 10 percent and less than or equal to 50 percent other *and* less than or equal to 10 percent black *and* less than or equal to 10 percent Hispanic.

12. Multiethnic integrated: Greater than or equal to 30 percent white *and* at least two of the three nonwhite groups greater than 10 percent.

Supplemental Data for Neighborhoods
and Schools in the Twin Cities, Portland, and
the Twenty-five Largest Metropolitan Areas

TABLE B.1 Percentage distribution of population across neighborhood types by race–ethnicity in the 25 largest metropolitan areas, 1980–2000

Neighborhood type	White			Black			Hispanic			Other			Total		
	1980	1990	2000	1980	1990	2000	1980	1990	2000	1980	1990	2000	1980	1990	2000
Total population share	75	69	62	13	13	14	9	12	17	3	5	7	100	100	100
Segregated															
Predominantly white	76	67	55	7	7	6	22	14	9	39	26	17	60	50	37
Predominantly black	1	1	1	57	47	39	3	2	1	3	2	1	9	7	6
Predominantly Hispanic	1	1	2	0	1	1	29	29	32	3	2	3	3	4	6
Predominantly other	0	0	0	0	0	0	0	0	0	2	2	3	0	0	0
Black/Hispanic	1	1	1	14	17	20	20	20	20	3	2	3	4	5	7
Black/other	0	0	0	0	1	1	0	0	0	1	1	1	0	0	0
Hispanic/other	0	0	1	0	0	1	3	8	9	4	9	12	0	2	3
Multiethnic, segregated	0	0	0	1	2	4	1	3	4	2	5	6	0	1	2
Segregated	79	70	60	79	75	72	78	75	75	55	48	46	76	69	62
Segregated Setting	76	67	55	72	68	66	56	61	67	16	22	29	72	64	57
Integrated															
White/black	6	7	6	12	11	9	3	2	2	5	4	3	7	7	6
White/Hispanic	10	11	13	2	3	3	0	0	0	13	10	8	10	11	12
White/other	1	4	8	0	1	2	1	2	2	7	12	16	1	4	6
Multiethnic, integrated	4	8	12	7	10	14	18	20	21	20	26	27	6	10	15
Integrated	21	30	40	21	25	28	22	25	25	45	52	54	24	31	38
Integrated setting	24	33	45	28	32	34	44	39	33	84	78	71	28	36	43

TABLE B.2 Percentage distribution of population across neighborhood types by race–ethnicity in the Twin Cities, 1980–2000

Neighborhood type	White			Black			Hispanic			Other			Total Population		
	1980	1990	2000	1980	1990	2000	1980	1990	2000	1980	1990	2000	1980	1990	2000
Total population share	95	92	85	2	3	6	1	1	3	2	4	5	100	100	100
Segregated															
Predominantly white	96	93	87	38	35	32	86	73	49	73	57	49	94	89	80
Predominantly black	0	0	0	24	10	1	2	0	0	1	1	0	1	0	0
Predominantly Hispanic	0	0	0	0	0	0	0	0	0	0	0	0	0	0	0
Predominantly other	0	0	0	0	0	0	0	0	0	0	0	0	0	0	0
Black/Hispanic	0	0	0	0	0	2	0	0	2	0	0	0	0	0	0
Black/other	0	0	0	2	9	14	0	1	3	1	6	8	0	1	2
Hispanic/other	0	0	0	0	0	0	0	0	0	0	0	0	0	0	0
Multiethnic, segregated	0	0	0	0	0	6	0	0	8	0	0	5	0	0	1
Segregated	96	93	87	64	53	54	88	74	61	75	64	62	95	90	83
Segregated setting	96	93	87	26	19	23	2	2	12	2	7	13	91	86	76
Integrated															
White/black	2	3	4	27	22	15	5	7	8	6	7	6	3	4	5
White/Hispanic	0	0	1	0	0	1	0	0	0	1	0	1	1	0	1
White/other	1	1	3	3	2	3	4	4	4	11	9	8	1	2	3
Multiethnic, integrated	0	2	5	6	22	26	3	14	27	7	20	23	1	4	8
Integrated	4	7	13	36	47	46	12	26	39	25	36	38	5	10	17
Integrated setting	4	7	13	74	81	77	98	98	88	98	93	87	9	14	24

TABLE B.3 Percentage distribution of population across neighborhood types by race–ethnicity in Portland, 1980–2000

Neighborhood type	White			Black			Hispanic			Other			Total Population		
	1980	1990	2000	1980	1990	2000	1980	1990	2000	1980	1990	2000	1980	1990	2000
Total population share	92	90	82	2	2	3	2	4	9	3	4	6	100	100	100
Segregated															
Predominantly white	95	88	65	35	36	32	94	89	59	87	78	45	93	86	60
Predominantly black	0	0	0	21	24	0	1	2	0	1	1	0	1	1	0
Predominantly Hispanic	0	0	0	0	0	0	0	0	8	0	0	0	0	0	1
Predominantly other	0	0	0	0	0	0	0	0	0	0	0	0	0	0	0
Black/Hispanic	0	0	0	0	0	3	0	0	0	0	0	0	0	0	0
Black/other	0	0	0	6	0	0	0	0	0	1	0	0	0	0	0
Hispanic/other	0	0	0	0	0	0	0	0	0	0	0	0	0	0	0
Multiethnic, segregated	0	0	0	0	0	0	0	0	0	0	0	0	0	0	0
Segregated	95	88	65	63	61	35	95	91	67	89	79	45	94	86	61
Segregated setting	95	88	65	28	25	3	1	2	8	3	1	0	89	80	54
Integrated															
White/black	2	2	2	34	32	19	4	4	3	5	4	2	3	3	2
White/Hispanic	2	5	17	0	2	12	0	0	0	1	4	15	2	6	19
White/other	1	4	12	1	4	12	0	4	16	4	13	30	1	4	13
Multiethnic, integrated	0	0	4	2	2	23	0	1	15	1	1	9	0	0	5
Integrated	5	12	35	37	39	65	5	9	33	11	21	55	6	14	39
Integrated setting	5	12	35	72	75	97	99	98	92	97	99	100	11	20	46

TABLE B.4   **Racial change in integrated tracts, Twin Cities, 1980–2000**

		Segregated in 2000 (%)							
Tract status in 1980	Number of tracts	Predominantly white	Predominantly black	Predominantly Hispanic	Predominantly other	Black and Hispanic	Black and other	Hispanic and other	Multiethnic segregated
White/black	23	4	0	0	0	9	22	0	17
White/Hispanic	3	0	0	0	0	0	0	0	33
White/other	10	0	0	0	0	0	0	0	70
Multiethnic integrated	7	0	0	0	0	0	29	0	29
Total	43	2	0	0	0	5	16	0	33

	Integrated in 2000 (%)					
Tract status in 1980	White and black	White and Hispanic	White and other	Multiethnic integrated	Segregated	Integrated
White/black	22	0	0	26	52	48
White/Hispanic	0	33	0	33	33	67
White/other	20	0	10	0	70	30
Multiethnic integrated	14	0	0	29	57	43
Total	19	2	2	21	56	44

TABLE B.5 Racial change in segregated tracts, Twin Cities, 1980–2000

Tract status in 1980	Number of tracts	Segregated in 2000 (%)							
		Predominantly white	Predominantly black	Predominantly Hispanic	Predominantly other	Black and Hispanic	Black and other	Hispanic and other	Multiethnic segregated
Predominantly white	677	81	0	0	0	0	1	0	0
Predominantly black	7	0	14	0	0	14	57	0	14
Predominantly Hispanic	0								
Predominantly other	0								
Black/Hispanic	0								
Black/other	1	0	0	0	0	0	100	0	0
Hispanic/other	0								
Multiethnic segregated	7	0	0	0	0	0	29	0	29
Total	692	80	0	0	0	0	2	0	0

Tract status in 1980	Integrated in 2000 (%)					
	White and black	White and Hispanic	White and other	Multiethnic integrated	Segregated	Integrated
Predominantly white	5	2	3	8	82	18
Predominantly black	0	0	0	0	100	0
Predominantly Hispanic						
Predominantly other						
Black/Hispanic						
Black/other	0	0	0	0	100	0
Hispanic/other						
Multiethnic segregated	14	0	0	29	57	43
Total	5	2	3	7	83	17

TABLE B.6 **Racial change in integrated tracts, 25 largest metropolitan areas, 1980–2000**

Tract status in 1980	Number of tracts	Predominantly white	Predominantly black	Predominantly Hispanic	Predominantly other	Black and Hispanic	Black and other	Hispanic and other	Multiethnic segregated
					Segregated in 2000 (%)				
White/black	1,943	7	22	0	0	6	1	0	2
White/Hispanic	3,026	3	0	23	0	5	0	6	3
White/other	318	3	0	1	6	0	0	2	4
Multiethnic integrated	1,638	2	2	5	2	20	1	17	11
Total	6,925	4	7	11	1	9	1	7	5

Tract status in 1980	White and black	White and Hispanic	White and other	Multiethnic integrated	Segregated	Integrated
			Integrated in 2000 (%)			
White/black	33	2	1	26	38	62
White/Hispanic	0	32	1	26	40	60
White/other	1	1	47	34	17	83
Multiethnic integrated	1	3	2	34	60	40
Total	10	16	3	28	43	57

TABLE B.7 Racial change in segregated tracts, 25 largest metropolitan areas, 1980–2000

Tract status in 1980	Number of tracts	Segregated in 2000 (%)							
		Predominantly white	Predominantly black	Predominantly Hispanic	Predominantly other	Black and Hispanic	Black and other	Hispanic and other	Multiethnic segregated
Predominantly white	17,355	59	1	1	0	1	0	0	0
Predominantly black	2,323	0	79	0	0	16	1	0	1
Predominantly Hispanic	776	0	0	79	0	5	0	10	1
Predominantly other	29	3	3	0	66	0	10	17	0
Black/Hispanic	991	0	4	6	0	79	0	1	6
Black/other	27	0	7	0	4	19	22	0	33
Hispanic/other	114	0	0	9	0	1	0	86	0
Multiethnic segregated	1,638	0	0	5	1	12	0	21	58
Total	23,253	48	10	4	0	6	0	1	1

Tract status in 1980	Integrated in 2000 (%)					
	White and black	White and Hispanic	White and other	Multiethnic integrated	Segregated	Integrated
Predominantly white	6	12	9	11	62	38
Predominantly black	1	0	0	2	97	3
Predominantly Hispanic	0	3	0	2	95	5
Predominantly other	0	0	0	0	100	0
Black/Hispanic	0	0	0	3	96	4
Black/other	0	0	0	15	85	15
Hispanic/other	0	0	0	4	96	4
Multiethnic segregated	0	0	0	3	97	3
Total	5	10	7	9	69	31

TABLE B.8 Racial change in integrated tracts, Portland, 1980–2000

| | | Segregated in 2000 (%) | | | | | | | |
Tract status in 1980	Number of tracts	Predominantly white	Predominantly black	Predominantly Hispanic	Predominantly other	Black and Hispanic	Black and other	Hispanic and other	Multiethnic segregated
White/black	11	0	0	0	0	0	0	0	0
White/Hispanic	8	13	0	13	0	0	0	0	0
White/other	5	40	0	0	0	0	0	0	0
Multiethnic integrated	3	0	33	0	0	0	0	0	0
Total	27	11	4	4	0	0	0	0	0

| | Integrated in 2000 (%) | | | | | |
Tract status in 1980	White and black	White and Hispanic	White and other	Multiethnic integrated	Segregated	Integrated
White/black	55	0	0	45	0	100
White/Hispanic	0	75	0	0	25	75
White/other	0	0	60	0	40	60
Multiethnic integrated	67	0	0	0	33	67
Total	30	22	11	19	19	81

TABLE B.9 Racial change in segregated tracts, Portland, 1980–2000

Tract status in 1980	Number of tracts	Segregated in 2000 (%)							
		Predominantly white	Predominantly black	Predominantly Hispanic	Predominantly other	Black and Hispanic	Black and other	Hispanic and other	Multiethnic segregated
Predominantly white	440	64	0	0	0	0	0	0	0
Predominantly black	4	0	0	0	0	25	0	0	0
Predominantly Hispanic	0								
Predominantly other	0								
Black/Hispanic	1	0	0	0	0	0	0	0	0
Black/other	1	0	0	0	0	0	0	0	0
Hispanic/Other	0								
Multiethnic segregated	3	0	33	0	0	0	0	0	0
Total	449	63	0	0	0	0	0	0	0

Tract status in 1980	Integrated in 2000 (%)					
	White and black	White and Hispanic	White and other	Multiethnic integrated	Segregated	Integrated
Predominantly white	2	17	13	4	65	35
Predominantly black	25	0	0	50	25	75
Predominantly Hispanic						
Predominantly other						
Black/Hispanic	0	0	0	100	0	100
Black/other	0	0	0	100	0	100
Hispanic/Other						
Multiethnic segregated	67	0	0	0	33	67
Total	2	16	13	5	64	36

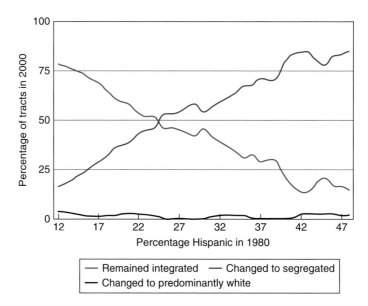

FIGURE B.1. Housing segregation: Status in 2000 of 3,026 tracts that were white–Hispanic integrated in 1980 in the twenty-five largest U.S. metropolitan areas. Conclusion: When the Hispanic population share was 24 percent or greater in 1980, the tract was more likely to resegregate during the next twenty years than it was to remain integrated.

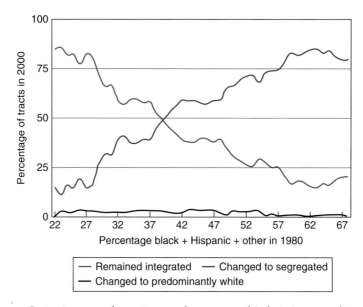

FIGURE B.2. Status in 2000 of 3,026 tracts that were multiethnic integrated in 1980 in the twenty-five largest U.S. metropolitan areas. Conclusion: When the black plus Hispanic plus other population share was 38 percent or greater in 1980, the tract was more likely to resegregate during the next twenty years than it was to remain integrated.

TABLE B.10 **Percentage distribution of elementary students by race and school type in the 25 largest metropolitan areas**

	1992						2002					
	Total	White	Black	Hispanic	Other	Free lunch eligible	Total	White	Black	Hispanic	Other	Free lunch eligible
% of total students	100	56	19	19	6	25	100	47	19	27	7	31
Predominantly white	34	56	4	4	16	10	25	48	3	3	11	7
Predominantly black	9	1	44	1	1	14	9	1	41	1	1	17
Predominantly Hispanic	8	2	1	32	3	18	12	3	2	39	5	23
Predominantly other	0	0	0	0	2	0	0	0	0	0	4	0
White/black integrated	8	10	11	1	4	6	5	8	7	1	3	4
White/Hispanic integrated	9	11	2	11	6	9	9	14	2	9	6	6
White/other integrated	4	5	1	1	13	1	5	7	1	1	13	1
Black/Hispanic	9	1	21	23	3	17	13	2	26	24	5	21
Black/other	0	0	1	0	2	1	0	0	1	0	2	1
Hispanic/other	3	1	1	7	12	5	3	1	1	7	15	4
Multiethnic integrated	13	12	12	15	27	14	14	15	12	12	24	11
Multiethnic segregated	2	1	4	4	10	5	4	1	5	5	12	5
Segregated	66	62	75	72	51	70	66	56	79	78	54	78
Integrated	34	38	25	28	49	30	34	44	21	22	46	22
Segregated setting	60	56	71	67	35	60	60	48	76	75	44	71
Integrated setting	40	44	29	33	65	40	40	52	24	25	56	29

TABLE B.11   Percentage distribution of elementary students by race and school type in the Twin Cities metropolitan area

	1992						2002					
	Total	White	Black	Hispanic	Other	Free lunch eligible	Total	White	Black	Hispanic	Other	Free lunch eligible
% of total students	100	85	7	1	7	18	100	73	12	5	9	21
Predominantly white	78	87	18	47	32	41	60	76	13	23	24	22
Predominantly black	1	0	8	1	1	3	1	0	5	0	0	2
Predominantly Hispanic	0	0	0	0	0	0	0	0	0	3	0	1
Predominantly other	0	0	0	0	0	0	1	0	0	1	5	2
White/black integrated	5	4	18	6	6	9	8	8	10	7	6	8
White/Hispanic integrated	0	0	0	1	0	0	2	2	1	8	1	2
White/other integrated	2	1	2	3	10	5	2	3	1	2	4	2
Black/Hispanic	0	0	0	0	0	0	2	0	6	12	1	5
Black/other	1	0	6	1	5	4	7	1	27	5	22	22
Hispanic/other	0	0	0	0	0	0	0	0	0	0	0	0
Multiethnic integrated	13	8	49	39	47	38	13	9	25	21	22	20
Multiethnic segregated	0	0	0	0	0	0	5	1	12	19	15	15
Segregated	80	87	31	50	37	47	75	78	63	63	67	69
Integrated	20	13	69	50	63	53	25	22	37	37	33	31
Segregated setting	75	87	14	3	5	6	68	76	50	39	43	47
Integrated setting	25	13	86	97	95	94	32	24	50	61	57	53

TABLE B.12   **Racial change in integrated schools, Twin Cities, 1992–2002**

School status in 1992	Number of schools				Segregated in 2002 (%)				
		Predominantly white	Predominantly black	Predominantly Hispanic	Predominantly other	Black and Hispanic	Black and other	Hispanic and other	Multiethnic segregated
White/black	20	0	0	0	0	10	35	0	5
White/Hispanic	0								
White/other	8	13	0	0	13	0	25	0	13
Multiethnic integrated	51	0	0	0	0	4	24	0	29
Total	79	1	0	0	1	5	27	0	22

School status in 1992	Integrated in 2002 (%)					
	White and black	White and Hispanic	White and other	Multiethnic integrated	Segregated	Integrated
White/black	5	10	0	35	50	50
White/Hispanic						
White/other	0	0	0	38	63	38
Multiethnic integrated	4	0	0	39	57	43
Total	4	3	0	38	56	44

TABLE B.13 Racial change in segregated schools, Twin Cities, 1992–2002

School status in 1992	Number of schools	Predominantly white	Predominantly black	Predominantly Hispanic	Predominantly other	Black and Hispanic	Black and other	Hispanic and other	Multiethnic segregated
					Segregated in 2002 (%)				
Predominantly white	273	76	0	0	0	0	0	0	0
Predominantly black	5	0	0	0	0	0	80	0	0
Predominantly Hispanic	0								
Predominantly other	0								
Black/Hispanic	0								
Black/other	3	0	0	0	0	0	33	0	67
Hispanic/other	0								
Multiethnic segregated	0								
Total	281	74	0	0	0	0	2	0	1

School status in 1992	White and black	White and Hispanic	White and other	Multiethnic integrated	Segregated	Integrated
		Integrated in 2002 (%)				
Predominantly white	11	2	3	8	76	24
Predominantly black	0	0	0	20	80	20
Predominantly Hispanic						
Predominantly other						
Black/Hispanic						
Black/other	0	0	0	0	100	0
Hispanic/other						
Multiethnic segregated						
Total	11	2	3	8	76	24

TABLE B.14   **Racial change in integrated schools, 25 largest metropolitan areas, 1992–2002**

School status in 1992	Number of schools	Segregated in 2002 (%)							
		Predominantly white	Predominantly black	Predominantly Hispanic	Predominantly other	Black and Hispanic	Black and other	Hispanic and other	Multiethnic segregated
White/black	1,535	6	13	0	0	5	1	0	1
White/Hispanic	1,467	2	0	27	0	3	0	1	1
White/other	776	9	0	0	4	0	0	1	1
Multiethnic integrated	2,242	0	0	6	0	21	1	8	12
Total	6,020	3	3	9	1	10	1	3	5

School status in 1992	Integrated in 2002 (%)					
	White and black	White and Hispanic	White and other	Multiethnic integrated	Segregated	Integrated
White/black	41	2	1	30	27	73
White/Hispanic	0	48	0	19	33	67
White/other	1	2	51	31	15	85
Multiethnic integrated	1	4	2	45	49	51
Total	11	14	7	33	35	65

TABLE B.15   Racial change in segregated schools, 25 largest metropolitan areas, 1992–2002

School status in 1992	Number of schools	Segregated in 2002 (%)							
		Predominantly white	Predominantly black	Predominantly Hispanic	Predominantly other	Black and Hispanic	Black and other	Hispanic and other	Multiethnic segregated
Predominantly white	6,542	71	0	0	0	0	0	0	0
Predominantly black	1,568	0	85	0	0	12	1	0	0
Predominantly Hispanic	943	0	0	94	0	3	0	2	0
Predominantly other	30	0	0	0	70	0	3	17	7
Black/Hispanic	1,237	0	3	12	0	81	0	0	2
Black/other	78	0	15	0	9	18	23	0	32
Hispanic/other	344	0	0	23	1	1	0	71	3
Multiethnic segregated	347	0	0	4	0	17	1	13	63
Total	11,089	42	12	10	0	12	0	3	3

School status in 1992	Integrated in 2002 (%)					
	White and black	White and Hispanic	White and other	Multiethnic integrated	Segregated	Integrated
Predominantly white	5	12	5	6	71	29
Predominantly black	1	0	0	1	98	2
Predominantly Hispanic	0	1	0	1	99	1
Predominantly other	0	0	3	0	97	3
Black/Hispanic	0	0	0	1	99	1
Black/other	0	0	0	3	97	3
Hispanic/other	0	0	0	1	99	1
Multiethnic segregated	0	0	0	1	99	1
Total	3	7	3	4	82	18

TABLE B.16   **Racial change in integrated schools, Portland, 1992–2002**

		Segregated in 2002 (%)							
School status in 1992	Number of schools	Predominantly white	Predominantly black	Predominantly Hispanic	Predominantly other	Black and Hispanic	Black and other	Hispanic and other	Multiethnic segregated
White/black	8	13	0	0	0	0	0	0	13
White/Hispanic	22	0	0	45	0	0	0	0	0
White/other	29	17	0	0	0	0	0	0	0
Multiethnic integrated	8	0	0	13	0	0	0	0	50
Total	67	9	0	16	0	0	0	0	7

	Integrated in 2002 (%)					
School status in 1992	White and black	White and Hispanic	White and other	Multiethnic integrated	Segregated	Integrated
White/black	38	0	0	38	25	75
White/Hispanic	0	55	0	0	45	55
White/other	0	10	31	41	17	83
Multiethnic integrated	0	0	0	38	63	38
Total	4	22	13	27	33	67

ACKNOWLEDGMENTS

This book grew out of several projects of the Institute on Race and Poverty (IRP) at the University of Minnesota Law School and Ameregis, Inc. IRP is a research institute that investigates how policies and practices disproportionately affect people of color and the disadvantaged. Its work focuses on the geography of social and economic change in metropolitan areas and on the intersection of trends in these areas with access to opportunities for people of color and the poor. Ameregis is a research and demographic consulting firm that has combined traditional social science analysis with geographic information system (GIS) methods to analyze land use, public finance, regional governance, and election outcomes in more than forty metropolitan areas across the country during the past fifteen years.

Many talented people associated with these organizations were also contributors to *Region*. Coauthors Baris Gumus-Dawes, Geneva Finn, Eric Myott, Jill Mazullo, and Nick Wallace are excellent colleagues involved with both organizations and the book. Dawn Hoover, the administrative backbone of IRP, offers irreplaceable support to everyone in the organization and excellent research and editing skills to the Institute's projects. Bill Lanoux contributed mapping and other GIS work. Aaron Timbo of Ameregis has provided years of exemplary programming, GIS, and administrative work. Jeff Rosenberg, Jessica Burke, and Joanna Vossen accomplished excellent research and development work with Ameregis projects associated with the book, and Scott Crane and Ann Olsen made important contributions to IRP's research.

In addition to coauthor Sharon Pfeiffer, many people provided expertise, data, or comments for the joint project of Ameregis and the Minnesota Department of Natural Resources that was the basis for chapter 5. They include Josh Williams of Ameregis; Jim Berg and Jan Falteisek of the Minnesota Department of Natural Resources; Ann Beckman, Rick Gelbman, and Todd Graham of the Metropolitan Council; Jean Coleman of CR Planning; Jim Erkel of the Minnesota Center for Environmental Advocacy; Mark Lindquist of the Minnesota Project; and Marvin Bauer and Brian Loeffelholz of the University of Minnesota Department of Forestry.

We thank the regional researchers and public officials who in October 2008 participated in a two-day conference devoted to the primary themes of *Region*. These include Doug Anderson (mayor of Dayton, Minnesota); Peter Bell (chairman, Metropolitan Council); Jan Callison (mayor of Minnetonka); Thomas M. Crosby (mayor of Medina; Faegre & Benson LLP); Debbie Goettel (mayor of Richfield); Bill Green (superintendent, Minneapolis Public Schools); Ben Kanninen (Community Action Council); Judith Martin (Department of Geography and the Urban Studies

Program, University of Minnesota); Tonja Orr (assistant commissioner, Minnesota Housing and Finance Agency); Guy Peterson (community development director, Metropolitan Council); Sharon Pfeiffer (director of community relations, Minnesota Department of Natural Resources); R. T. Rybak (mayor of Minneapolis); John W. Shardlow (Bonestroo, Inc.); and Carl Wahlstrom (superintendent, East Metro Integration District). The conference was cohosted by IRP, the Association of Metropolitan Municipalities, and the Association of Metropolitan School Districts. Several organizations gave financial support, including the University of Minnesota Metropolitan Consortium, the Center for Urban and Regional Affairs, the University of Minnesota's Office of Public Engagement, and the Spring Hill Center, Minneapolis Foundation.

A great many national and regional researchers deserve thanks for reading or commenting on early drafts of *Region,* including John Adams, David Barron, Richard Briffault, Robert Burchell, Ingrid Gould Ellen, Robert Fishman, Richard Frase, Gerald Frug, Ed Goetz, Brad Karkkainen, Bruce Katz, Alexandra Klass, Judith Martin, Paloma Pavel, John Powell, Rip Rapson, Kevin Reitz, Laurie Reynolds, David Rusk, Tom Scott, Lisa Servon, Deb Swackhamer, Tim Thompson, and Michael Tonry.

Production and promotion of *Region* was facilitated by the University of Minnesota Press and its staff, including Todd Orjala (senior editor), Andrea Rondoni (editorial assistant), Daniel Ochsner (production and design manager), Maggie Sattler (marketing coordinator), and Heather Skinner (publicist).

We are very grateful for the generous support of the foundations that have sustained IRP and Ameregis over the years with general and project support, including some of the most prestigious in the nation: the McKnight Foundation, the Ford Foundation, the Bush Foundation, the Minneapolis Foundation, the Northwest Area Foundation, the Open Society Institute and Soros Foundations Network, the Otto Bremer Foundation, the Kresge Foundation, the Annie E. Casey Foundation, and the Rockefeller Foundation. The University of Minnesota Law School also contributed much-appreciated assistance, including space, support services, and funding.

Finally, we wish to thank our families. Tom sends his gratitude to Karen and Jesse for all of their support over the years, and Myron would like to thank Jeanne, Sam, and Will for their love, support, patience, and good questions.

Myron Orfield
Thomas F. Luce Jr.

NOTES

Metropolitan Council reports are available from the council (http://www.metrocouncil.org).

I. LOCAL GOVERNANCE, FINANCE, AND GROWTH TRENDS

1. Paul Jargowsky, *Poverty and Place: Ghettos, Barrios, and the American City* (New York: Russell Sage Foundation, 1997); Douglas S. Massey and Nancy A. Denton, *American Apartheid: Segregation and the Making of the Underclass* (Cambridge, Mass.: Harvard University Press, 1993); David Rusk, *Cities without Suburbs* (Baltimore: The Johns Hopkins University Press, 1994), 27–31; Myron Orfield, "Racial Integration and Community Revitalization: Applying the Fair Housing Act to the Low Income Housing Tax Credit," *Vanderbilt Law Review* 58 (2005), 1747.

2. Among the best-known works engaging with new regionalism are Gerald Frug, *City Making: Building Communities without Building Walls* (Princeton, N.J.: Princeton University Press, 1999); Anthony Downs, *New Visions for Metropolitan America* (Washington, D.C.: Brookings Institution, 1994); Richard Briffault, "Our Localism" (parts 1 and 2), *Columbia Law Review* 90 (1990); Laurie Reynolds, "Intergovernmental Cooperation: Metropolitan Equity and the New Regionalism," *Washington Law Review* 78 (2003), 93; Richard Thompson Ford, "The Boundaries of Race: Political Geographies in Legal Analysis," *Harvard Law Review* 107 (1994), 1841; Sheryll D. Cashin, "Localism, Self-Interest, and the Tyranny of the Favored Quarter: Addressing the Barriers to New Regionalism," *Georgetown Law Journal* 88 (2000), 1985.

3. This is the Twin Cities' rank with each of the two most commonly used fragmentation indexes—the number of local governments per ten thousand residents or the Herfindahl index (a measure that controls for size differences across individual governments within a metropolitan area).

4. See Ronald Fisher, *State and Local Public Finance* (Boston: South-Western College Publishing, 2006), 129–30, for a full description of the correspondence principle. Another common name used by some authors for the principle is "fiscal equivalence."

5. The state allows for two types of cities, including statutory cities with controls and powers set by the state and home rule charter cities that have duties and powers established by their charters. Cities are further divided into fours classes by size. The powers of townships are also determined by state law. Some townships are granted additional powers if they have a thousand or more people living in them. Townships often become incorporated cities when they become more populated or may be annexed by neighboring cities. There are ninety-seven townships in the Twin Cities eleven-county area, mostly near the periphery of the eleven-county metropolitan area (see Figure 1.1).

6. Minnesota Statutes sec. 382.01; Minnesota Statutes sec. 375A.10.

7. Minnesota House of Representatives, House Research (last visited November 2, 2006), http://www.house.mn/hrd/issinfo/cntyoptn.htm.

8. Public Law 87-866, October 23, 1962, 76 Stat. 1147, 23 U.S.C. 307 note.

9. National Association of Regional Councils, "Metropolitan Planning Organizations," http://narc.org/activities/transportation/metropolitan.html (last visited October 23, 2006).

10. The Transportation Advisory Board (TAB) was created by the state legislature in 1974.

11. Metropolitan Council, "Transportation Advisory Board," http://www.metrocouncil.org/services/tab.htm (last visited October 23, 2006).

12. Map 1.1 shows property taxes as a percentage of total tax capacity. Total tax capacity is the amount of revenue that would be generated if tax rates exactly equaled the state-set rates for different kinds of property (residential vs. commercial–industrial, for instance).

13. *2007 Minnesota Tax Incidence Study: An Analysis of Minnesota's Household and Business Taxes* (St. Paul: Minnesota Department of Revenue, Tax Research Division, 2007), Table 2.3, 29. A taxpayer at the tenth percentile is one whose income is greater than 10 percent of all taxpayers and less than 90 percent of taxpayers. At the ninetieth percentile, the taxpayer's income is greater than 90 percent of taxpayers and less than 10 percent.

14. Ibid., Table 2.3, 29.

15. Ibid., Table 1.4, 13.

16. Myron Orfield, *American Metropolitics: The New Suburban Reality* (Washington, D.C.: Brookings Institution, 2002).

17. Consistent urbanization data were not available over the full time period for the eleven-county region.

18. See Fei Yuan, Kali E. Sawaya, Brian C. Loeffelholz, and Marvin E. Bauer, "Land Cover Classification and Change Analysis of the Twin Cities (Minnesota) Metropolitan Area by Multitemporal Landsat Remote Sensing," *Remote Sensing of Environment* 98 (2005): 317–28, for a complete description of the methods used to classify land uses.

19. The relationship also exists using alternative measures of fragmentation that account for the size distribution of local governments. The sprawl ratio in Figure 1.7 shows the relationship between population growth and the increase in land settled at "urban densities" between 1970 and 2000. Both parts of the ratio are measured by simple ratio of the 2000 value to the 1970 value. This method avoids negative values and reduces scale biases resulting from very low population growth rates. "Urban density" was defined as census tracts with more than one housing unit per four acres, a value consistent with the census definition for urbanized land at the fringes of metropolitan areas. The census definition for urbanized land could not be used because it changed in 2000 and values for prior census years are not available.

20. The line in Figure 1.7 shows a log-linear relationship. The simple correlation between the sprawl measure and the log of the fragmentation measure is .53, a value significant at the 99 percent confidence level. The relationship remains significant when controlling for metro population, population growth, natural barriers to growth, and the existence of a strong regional planning organization.

21. The line in Figure 1.8 shows a log-linear relationship. The simple correlation between the logs of job growth and the fragmentation measure is –.42, a value significant at the 99 percent confidence level.

22. The commuter sheds were generated from Census Transportation Planning Package journey to work data shown by traffic analysis zones (TAZs). TAZs are usually slightly smaller than census tracts. The commuter sheds were derived by finding the circumference of TAZs around the job center with the relevant median travel time and smoothing the contour using inverse distance weighting (IDW) interpolation. IDW estimates values for areas by averaging from surrounding values of point samples, giving greater weight to nearby points. The commuter shed boundaries were interpolated from TAZ commuting times, using the TAZ centroids as the point samples. IDW was used with the Geostatistical Analyst extension to ESRI's ArcMap.

23. Minnesota Department of Administration, Office of the State Demographer; "Projected Population to 2030 for Cities and Townships Outside the Twin Cities Area"; http://server.admin .state.mn.us/resource.html?Id=7376.

24. See "Voters Being Asked to Raise Taxes for Parks," *Minneapolis Star Tribune*, November 2, 2005, B1.

25. The line in Figure 1.10 shows a log-linear relationship. The simple correlation between the sprawl measure and the log of the fragmentation measure is .35, a value significant at the 98 percent confidence level. The relationship remains significant when controlling for metro population, population growth, natural barriers to growth, and the existence of a strong regional planning organization.

26. For a more extensive discussion of tax base sharing, see Thomas Luce, "Regional Tax

Base Sharing: The Twin Cities Experience," in *Local Government Tax and Land Use Policies in the United States: Understanding the Links,* ed. Helen Ladd, 234–54 (Cambridge, Mass.: Lincoln Institute of Land Policy, 1998).

27. For examples, see the studies available at http://www.ameregis.com.

2. GOVERNING THE TWIN CITIES

1. Arthur Naftalin, *Making One Community Out of Many: Perspectives on the Metropolitan Council of the Twin Cities Area* (St. Paul: The Council, 1986), 11.

2. 42 U.S.C. 3334 (1966).

3. Circular A-95, which was later replaced by President Ronald Reagan's Executive Order 12372. 47 FR 30959, 3 CFR, 1982, Comp., 197.

4. Naftalin, *Making One Community Out of Many,* 19.

5. Senator Wiger stated, "People should have power in electing representatives that have a direct impact on taxation." Jennifer Bjorhus, "Letting the People Pick the Planners; Bill Calls for Met Council Elections, Four-Year Terms," *St. Paul Pioneer Press,* January 27, 2007.

6. Myron Orfield, *American Metropolitics: The New Suburban Reality* (Washington, D.C.: Brookings Institution, 2002), 176–77.

7. Mike Kaszuba and Steve Brandt, "Schreiber's Activities Questioned; Some See Conflict in 2 Projects," *Minneapolis Star Tribune,* December 6, 1994

8. Metropolitan Council, *Metropolitan Council 2006 Proposed Budget—Budget Summary and Financial Resources,* 3–1, 3–10, http://www.metrocouncil.org/about/2006Budget/Budget Summary.pdf (last visited October 23, 2006); Metropolitan Council, *Metropolitan Council 2007 Preliminary Unified Budget—Environmental Services Division,* http://www.metrocouncil.org/about/2007Budget/MCES.pdf (last visited October 23, 2006).

9. Naftalin, *Making One Community Out of Many,* 23.

10. Minnesota Statutes sec. 473.175 (1992).

11. Metropolitan Council, "History of the Metropolitan Council," http://www.metrocouncil.org/about/about.htm (last visited July 16, 2006).

12. Minnesota Statutes sec. 473.851–473.872.

13. In 1991 the U.S. Intermodal Surface Transportation Efficiency Act (ISTEA) directed MPOs to expand regional transportation planning to consider related issues, such as traffic congestion, transportation alternatives to the automobile, and Clean Air Act amendments.

14. Thomas Sanchez, *An Inherent Bias? Geographic and Racial-Ethnic Patterns of Metropolitan Planning Organization Boards* (Washington, D.C.: Brookings Institution, 2006).

15. Under federal statute, MPOs must be composed of elected officials, but former Minnesota congressman Martin Sabo helped pass special legislation that made the all-appointed Met Council acceptable—if combined with the newly created TAB.

16. Metropolitan Council, *Blueprint 1994* (1995), 9.

17. "Previously, the regional growth strategy focused on how much development occurred in growing communities at the regions urbanizing edge. *Blueprint 2030* pays more attention to how development occurs—such as the mix of land uses, the number of housing units per acre, and the potential for transit and local street connections." Metropolitan Council, *Blueprint 2030* (2002), 4.

18. Metropolitan Council, *Local Planning Handbook* (September 2005); *Framework 2030* (2004), 1–6, 31.

19. Elizabeth Deakins and Christopher Porter, *Transportation Impacts of Smart Growth and Comprehensive Planning Initiatives* (Cambridge, Mass.: Cambridge Systematics, 2004), D-6.

20. Brian W. Ohm, "Growth Management in Minnesota: The Metropolitan Land Planning Act," *Hamline Law Review* 16 (1993), 359, 381.

21. Edward Goetz, "Fair Share or Status Quo? The Twin Cities Livable Communities Act," *Journal of Planning Education and Research* 40 (2000): 37–51.

22. Minnesota Statutes sec. 473.25 (1995).

23. Orfield, *Metropolitics*, 149–52.

24. Goetz, "Fair Share or Status Quo?" 37.

25. *Village of Euclid v. Ambler Realty Co.* 272 U.S. 365 (1926).

26. 685 N.W. 2d 1 (Minn., Aug. 5, 2004).

27. 685 N.W. 2d at 5 quoting Minnesota Statutes sec. 473.175, subd. 1 (emphasis added). This language regained prominence after the repeal of Minnesota Statutes sec. 473.858 subd. 1 (1994), also known as the "Merriam Amendment." The Merriam Amendment provided that local plans took priority over a conflicting comprehensive plan.

28. *Alliance for Metropolitan Stability v. Met Council* 671 N.W. 2d 905 (Minn. Ct. App. 2003).

29. Metropolitan Council, *Metropolitan Development Guide* (1975), 21–27.

30. Metropolitan Council, *Metropolitan Development and Investment Framework* (1988), 11–13; *Blueprint 1994* (1995), 59–60.

31. Metropolitan Council, *Blueprint 2030* (2002), 43.

32. Regional Strategies Working Group, *Designing a Better Regional Blueprint* (Minneapolis: McKnight Foundation, 2002), 16–17.

33. Calculations made for urbanized land inside and outside the MUSA are from the 2000 MUSA GIS file from the Metropolitan Council's Comprehensive Plan Composite (http://www.datafinder.org/metadata/comp_plan_composite.htm); 2002 land cover satellite data used to calculate urbanized areas in and outside the MUSA come from the Remote Sensing and Geospatial Analysis Laboratory at the University of Minnesota.

34. Metropolitan Council, *Local Planning Handbook* (March 2006), 2–3; *Framework 2030* (2004), 19, B-5.

35. Metropolitan Council, *Local Planning Handbook* (March 2006), 2–3; *Framework 2030* (2004), 21, B-5.

36. Metropolitan Council, *Framework 2030* (2004), 9; *Local Planning Handbook* (March 2006), 2–3.

37. Metropolitan Council, *Framework 2030* (2004), 9, B-5; *Local Planning Handbook* (March 2006), 2–3.

38. Metropolitan Council, *Framework 2030* (2004), 10; *Local Planning Handbook* (March 2006), 2–3; Regional Strategies Working Group, *Designing a Better Regional Blueprint*, 9–10.

39. Metropolitan Council, *Framework 2030* (2004), 9–10, 28; *Local Planning Handbook* (March 2006), 2–3.

40. Metropolitan Council, *Framework 2030* (2004), 9, 10, 28–29; *Local Planning Handbook* (March 2006), 2–3.

41. Metropolitan Council, *Framework 2030* (2004), B-1.

42. Ibid., B-1, B–5.

43. Ibid., 25–28. Areas that have rural densities as low as one unit to ten acres include diversified rural areas.

44. Ibid., 10.

45. Richard S. Bolan, "Is the Twin Cities 'Permanent Rural' Area Truly Permanent? A Case Study on the Rural–Urban Edge," *CURA Reporter*, September 2000, 24.

46. David Peterson, "Suburban Sprawl: Is There Another Way?" *Minneapolis Star Tribune*, April 30, 2008.

47. Regional Strategies Working Group, *Designing a Better Regional Blueprint*, 9–10.

48. Metropolitan Council, *2030 Water Resources Management Policy Plan* (2005), 32–34.

49. Eric M. Hanson, "City Wrestles with Growth, Rural Identity," *Minneapolis Star Tribune*, February 9, 2008.

50. Collar County Study Committee, *Balancing Minnesota's Growth: Capturing Benefits, Reducing Costs, and What's at Stake* (St. Paul: 1000 Friends of Minnesota, 2006).

51. Minnesota House Research, H.F. No. 313 as introduced—81st Legislative Session (1999–2000).

52. Metropolitan Council, *Metropolitan Development and Investment Framework* (1988), 21–22.

53. Metropolitan Council, *Blueprint 1994* (1995), 60–61.

54. Metropolitan Council, *Blueprint 2030* (2002), 8–10.

55. Ibid., Appendix C.

56. Compare *Blueprint 2030*, 44–45 and 48–49, to *Framework 2030*, chapter 3.

57. See transportation policy objectives highlighted in Metropolitan Council, *Framework 2030* (2004), 10–11.

58. Metropolitan Council, *2030 Water Resources Management Policy Plan*, 17–20 (2005).

59. Metropolitan Council, *Wastewater Services Fact Sheet* (2006), 3, http://www.metro council.org/about/facts/WastewaterServicesFacts.pdf.

60. Metropolitan Council Environmental Systems, *Survey of 2006 Municipal Residential Wastewater Rate* (2006), 3.

61. Metropolitan Council, *2030 Water Resources Management Policy Plan*, 3.

62. Metropolitan Council, *Water Resource Management: Part 1, Wastewater Treatment and Handling Policy Plan* (1988), 17.

63. Metropolitan Council, *2030 Water Resources Management Policy Plan*, 30.

64. Thomas Luce, Barbara Lukermann, and Herbert Mohring, *Regional Sewer System Rate Structure Survey* (Minneapolis: University of Minnesota, Hubert H. Humphrey Institute of Public Affairs, 1992), 50–52.

65. Metropolitan Council, *2004 Stream Monitoring and Assessment Report* (2004), 10. http://www.metrocouncil.org/planning/environment/StreamWQ2004.pdf.

66. Metropolitan Council, *2005 Census of Twin Cities' Lake Water Quality* (2005). http://www.metrocouncil.org/planning/environment/TCWaterClarity2005.pdf.

67. Minnesota Statues sec. 473.1565 (2006).

68. Minnesota Statutes sec. 473.859 (2008) requires communities with a water supply entity to provide water plans as a part of their local comprehensive plans. Minnesota Statutes sec. 103G.291 (2008) requires that water suppliers serving over a thousand people prepare conservation and emergency water plans that can be approved by the Minnesota Department of Natural Resources. Metropolitan Council, *Water Supply Planning in the Twin Cities Metropolitan Area* (2007), 27, 40.

69. Watersheds are geographic units that capture the directional flow of surface water; all flows travel toward one side of the watershed. In the Twin Cities, local governments called watershed management organizations create local watershed plans that address water quality protection, flood management, drainage system management, and other issues associated with the flow and runoff of water. Metropolitan Council, *2030 Water Resources Management Policy Plan* (2005), 2.

70. Metropolitan Council, *Water Supply Planning in the Twin Cities Metropolitan Area*, 29–30.

71. The 1988 Met Council already exerted influence with the Minnesota Department of Transportation, the ultimate transportation public authority in the state, because the council approved controlled-access highway construction and set highway improvement guidelines. Metropolitan Council, *Metropolitan Development and Investment Framework* (1988), 34. The primary goal of the council in the 1980s was the maintenance and reconstruction of regional facilities in poor working condition, especially highway infrastructure and other urban services near business centers. Ibid., 11.

72. Metropolitan Council, *2007–2010 Transportation Improvement Project for the Twin Cities* (2006), 1.

73. Metropolitan Council, *2030 Transportation Policy Plan* (2004), 1.

74. Ibid., 4.

75. Tragically, the I-35W bridge collapse shows there is a much greater need to fund older transportation infrastructure in Minnesota and elsewhere in the United States. Highway expansion not only entails the costs of building roads and bridges but also involves large costs for maintaining a safe transportation network for commuters.

76. Metropolitan Council, *2030 Transportation Policy Plan,* 65–67.

77. A housing study of twenty-five fast-growing Twin Cities suburbs found that only twenty out of every one hundred acres of land set aside in 1980 for higher housing density had dense housing in 2000, and only five acres had low- to moderate-income housing. Edward Goetz, Karen Chapple, and Barbara Lukermann, "The Minnesota Land Use Planning Act and the Promotion of Low- and Moderate-Income Housing in Suburbia," *Law and Inequality: A Journal of Theory and Practice* 22 (2004): 31–72, esp. 63–64.

78. Frequent service routes are those that run every fifteen minutes between 6 a.m. and 7 p.m. on weekdays and from 9 a.m. to 6 p.m. on Saturdays. Calculations for the length of the Twin Cities transit routes are from Bus Route and Hi-Frequency Transit Service data provided by the Met Council: http://www.datafinder.org/catalog/index.asp.

79. Regional Strategies Working Group, *Designing a Better Regional Blueprint,* 12; Deakins and Porter, *Transportation Impacts of Smart Growth and Comprehensive Planning Initiatives,* D-9.

80. Metropolitan Council, *1979 Subsidized Housing Activity in the Twin Cities Metropolitan Area* (1980), 1 (on file with author) (hereinafter Metropolitan Council, *1979 Subsidized Housing*).

81. A major component of the council's success was use of its intergovernmental authority from federal policy 13(39) to encourage prioritization of federal housing funds according to how well a community had provided low- and moderate-income housing in the past. See, e.g., Metropolitan Council, *1979 Subsidized Housing,* 33 (describing Section 8, the federal government's program for "assisting lower-income families to secure decent, safe and sanitary housing").

82. See Metropolitan Council, *1979 Subsidized Housing,* 6 (noting an increase of 2,721 units from 1,878 to 4,599, which represented an 8 percent jump in the share of subsidized housing units located in the suburbs).

83. Ibid., 14.

84. Ibid.

85. Ibid., Table 1, 14.

86. Metropolitan Council, *Report to the Minnesota Legislature on Affordable and Lifecycle Housing in the Twin Cities* (2005), 2.

87. Metropolitan Council, *Guidelines for Priority Funding for Housing Performance* (2003), 3.

88. Minneapolis/St. Paul Housing Finance Board, *2008 Low Income Housing Tax Credit Procedural Manual* (2008), 1–5.

89. Data were calculated from information provided by the Minnesota Housing Finance Agency. LIHTC data are derived from representational 53 percent survey of LIHTC housing sites. About 60–80 percent of central city subsidized units have African American households living in them.

90. Though federal law does not require suballocations of LIHTC, in Minnesota suballocatees of LIHTC are cities and suburban counties that applied for the special status within a forty-five-day window in June 1987, a date set by the state legislature.

91. BBC Research and Consulting, *The Next Decade of Housing in Minnesota* (2003), sec. 3, p. 6; "Understanding Affordable Housing Planning Requirements" (June 8, 2007) http://www.tchousingpolicy.org/understanding/index.php?strWebAction=article_detail&intArticleID=182.

92. BBC Research and Consulting, *The Next Decade of Housing in Minnesota,* sec. 3, p. 1.

93. Housing affordability calculations made by author were derived from U.S. Census data on income, housing values, and rent. Percentages of affordable housing in central cities reflect totals for the seven-county metropolitan area.

94. Metropolitan Council, *Summary Report: Determining the Affordable Housing Need in the Twin Cities 2011–2020* (2006).

95. In the Twin Cities, there is one local government for about every 9,000 persons. In Portland, one local government typically represents about 27,000 persons.

96. The line in Figure 2.3 shows a log-linear relationship. The simple correlation between the sprawl measure and the log of the fragmentation measure is .53, a value significant at the 99 percent confidence level.

97. In the Twin Cities, urbanized land grew approximately 130 percent more quickly than population growth from 1970 to 2000. In Portland, urban land growth was actually slower than population growth—urban land grew 90 percent as quickly as the population.

98. While the Metropolitan Council had an annual budget of about $650 million, and a bonded debt that exceeded $1 billion in 2005, the 2007–8 budget of Portland's Metro includes just above $328 million in expenditures and bonded debt of approximately $185 million in 2007.

99. The Metropolitan Council operates both a housing authority and the major transit agency in the Twin Cities, reflecting its larger budget compared to Portland's Metro.

100. In the past, the Met Council actively advocated for transit and wastewater powers, while Portland's Metro has judiciously expanded its powers. For instance, while the Met Council conflicted over planning authority with the Metropolitan Transit Commission in the early 1970s, Portland's Metro has failed to absorb the region's transit operator (called Tri-Met) even though it has maintained the authority to do so since 1979.

101. Robert Liberty, "Planned Growth: The Oregon Model," *Natural Resources and Environment,* Summer 1998. Metropolitan Council, *Framework 2030,* 25–26.

102. Or. Rev. Stat. ch. 197 (also known as Senate Bill 100); H. Jeffrey Leonard, *Managing Oregon's Growth: The Politics of Development Planning* (Washington, D.C.: The Conservation Foundation, 1983).

103. Carl Abbott, "The Portland Region: Where City and Suburbs Talk to Each Other—and Often Agree," *Housing Policy Debate* 8:1 (1997), 28.

104. Liberty, "Planned Growth"; Metropolitan Council, *Framework 2030,* 25–26.

105. Portland's UGB is often thought of as a fixed containment boundary; however, in 2002 Metro added over 18,000 acres to the UGB after determining its existing urbanized area could not contain growth. Metro, *2002–2022 Urban Growth Report: A Residential Land Need Analysis,* http://www.metro-region.org/library_docs/land_use/ugr-land.pdf (last visited May 30, 2007). Metro, "2002 urban growth boundary decision," http://www.metroregion.org/article .cfm?ArticleID=266 (last visited May 30, 2007).

106. Oregon Administrative Rule 660-007-0035.

107. Metropolitan Council, *Framework 2030,* B5.

108. Metropolitan Service District, *Regional Transportation Plan for the Portland Metropolitan Area,* Ordinance No. 82-135 (Portland: Metropolitan Service District, 1982); Metropolitan Service District, *Regional Transportation Plan: 1989 Update,* Ordinance No. 89-282 (Portland: Metropolitan Service District, 1989).

109. Metro, *2000 Regional Transportation Plan* (Portland: Metro, 2000).

110. Metro Code sec. 3.07.170(A).

111. In Portland, a series of political and legal actions culminated in the passage of Measure 37. This law makes it difficult for regional planning to contain growth to within Oregon UGBs, by requiring property owner compensation for the loss or having waivers for the land use regulation, if the land use regulation demonstrates a reduction in the value of a property. Within the

Portland region, Measure 37 requests have spanned 148,880 acres, a potential urban expansion of 58 percent. Measure 37 has the potential to undermine the effect of Portland's UGB. In the Twin Cities, the outcomes of legal challenges are more positive. The *Lake Elmo* decision has given the Met Council greater leverage in determining when elements of a local plan constitute an impact or departure from regional systems plans by means of the Minnesota Land Planning Act. Furthermore the decision affirms the densities the council establishes in its systems plans for within and outside the MUSA. Given the court's decision, the council clearly has power to maintain low rural densities and establish higher urban densities and can revise local plans not in conformance.

112. Regional Strategies Working Group, *Designing a Better Regional Blueprint*, 15.

113. State of Minnesota, Office of the Legislative Auditor, *Program Evaluation Report: Affordable Housing* (2001), 80–81. LCA includes brownfield redevelopment and smart growth goals that receive greater funding to support LCA's goal to create affordable housing opportunities. The Livable Communities Demonstration Account was a small dedicated fund from which the Met Council could provide grants to cities to achieve Livable Communities Act goals.

114. See Metro, *2004 Performance Measures Report*, http://www.oregonmetro.gov/files/planning/full_2004_perf_meas_report_.pdf.

3. NEIGHBORHOOD AND SCHOOL SEGREGATION

1. See, e.g., John Lukehart, Tom Luce, and Jason Reece, *The Segregation of Opportunities: The Structure of Advantage and Disadvantage in the Chicago Region* (Chicago: Leadership Council for Metropolitan Open Communities, 2005).

2. According to Mary J. Fischer, while the share of residential sorting based on race and ethnicity was 81 percent in 1970, this number dropped to 65 percent in 2000. In other words, while two-thirds of residential segregation could be explained by race/ethnicity in 2000, only a third could be explained by income segregation. See Mary J. Fischer, "The Relative Importance of Income and Race in Determining Residential Outcomes in U. S. Urban Areas, 1970–2000," *Urban Affairs Review* 38, no. 5 (May 2003): 669–96, 684.

3. While over 18 percent of poor blacks and nearly 14 percent of poor Hispanics lived in high-poverty communities, less than 6 percent of poor whites resided in such communities in 2000. Paul Jargowsky, *Stunning Progress, Hidden Problems: The Dramatic Decline of Concentrated Poverty in the 1990s* (Washington, D.C.: Brookings Institution, 2003), 10.

4. John Logan, Deirdre Oakley, and Jacob Stowell, *Segregation in Neighborhoods and Schools: Impacts on Minority Children in the Boston Region* (Albany: State University of New York, Lewis Mumford Center for Comparative Urban and Regional Research, 2003), 16. Moreover, the neighborhood gap for blacks and Hispanics increased during the 1990s. See John R. Logan, *Separate and Unequal: The Neighborhood Gap for Blacks and Hispanics in Metropolitan America* (Albany: State University of New York, Lewis Mumford Center for Comparative Urban and Regional Research, 2002).

5. Studies document the close link between racial composition and poverty rates in schools. See, for instance, Gary Orfield and Chungmei Lee, *Brown at 50: King's Dream or Plessy's Nightmare* (Cambridge, Mass.: The Civil Rights Project at Harvard University, 2004); Gary Orfield and Chungmei Lee, *Why Segregation Matters: Poverty and Educational Inequality* (Cambridge, Mass.: The Civil Rights Project at Harvard University, 2005). In 2002–3, 88 percent of high-minority schools—defined as at least 90 percent minority—were high-poverty schools in which more than 50 percent of students received free or reduced-price lunches. In contrast, only 15 percent of low-minority schools—defined as less than 10 percent minority—were also high-poverty schools. See Orfield and Lee, *Brown at 50*.

6. Nonwhite segregated schools are defined either as schools in which the share of black,

Hispanic, or Asian students exceeds 50 percent or as schools with varying combinations of black, Hispanic, and Asian students, in which the relative share of white students in the schools does not exceed 30 percent. In predominantly white schools, the share of each nonwhite group is smaller than 10 percent. Any school that is neither nonwhite segregated nor predominantly white is considered integrated.

7. 2004 U.S. Department of Education report cited in note 11, p. 7, of Orfield and Lee, *Why Segregation Matters.*

8. Orfield and Lee, *Why Segregation Matters,* 29.

9. Ibid., 16.

10. Gary Orfield and Chungmei Lee, *Racial Transformation and the Changing Nature of Segregation* (Cambridge, Mass.: The Civil Rights Project at Harvard University, 2006), 30.

11. R. Balfanz and N. Legters, "Locating the Dropout Crisis: Which High Schools Produce the Nation's Dropouts," in *Dropouts in America: Confronting the Graduation Rate Crisis,* ed. Gary Orfield, 57–84 (Cambridge, Mass.: Harvard Education Press, 2004); C. Swanson, "Sketching a Portrait of Public High School Graduation: Who Graduates? Who Doesn't?" in *Dropouts in America,* 13–40.

12. Richard D. Kahlenberg, *All Together Now* (Washington, D.C.: Brookings Institution Press, 2001), 28–29.

13. Ibid., 31.

14. Ibid.

15. Roslyn Arlin Mickelson, "Segregation and the SAT," *Ohio State Law Journal* 67 (2006): 157–99; Roslyn Arlin Mickelson, "The Academic Consequences of Desegregation and Segregation: Evidence from the Charlotte-Mecklenburg Schools," *North Carolina Law Review* 81 (2003): 1513–62; Kathryn Borman et al., "Accountability in a Postdesegregation Era: The Continuing Significance of Racial Segregation in Florida's Schools," *American Educational Research Journal* 41, no. 3 (2004): 605–31; Geoffrey D. Borman and N. Maritza Dowling, "Schools and Inequality: A Multilevel Analysis of Coleman's Equality of Educational Opportunity Data" (paper presented at the annual meeting of the American Educational Research Association, San Francisco, 2006).

16. R. L. Crain and J. Strauss, *School Desegregation and Black Occupational Attainments: Results from a Long-Term Experiment* (Baltimore: Center for Social Organization of Schools, 1985), report no. 359; Goodwin Liu and William Taylor, "School Choice to Achieve Desegregation," *Fordham Law Review* 74 (2005), 791; Jomills H. Braddock and James M. McPartland, "How Minorities Continue to Be Excluded from Equal Employment Opportunities: Research on Labor Market and Institutional Barriers," *Journal of Social Issues* 43, no. 1 (1987): 5–39; Janet Ward Schofield, "Maximizing the Benefits of Student Diversity: Lessons from School Desegregation Research," in *Diversity Challenged: Evidence on the Impact of Affirmative Action,* ed. Gary Orfield and Michal Kurlaender, 99–109 (Cambridge, Mass.: Harvard Education Press, 2001), 99.

17. Orley Ashenfelter, William J. Collins, and Albert Yoon, "Evaluating the Role of *Brown vs. Board of Education* in School Equalization, Desegregation, and the Income of African Americans," *American Law and Economics Review* 8, no. 2 (2006): 213–48; Michael A. Boozer et al., "Race and School Quality Since Brown v. Board of Education," *Brookings Papers on Economic Activity. Microeconomics,* 1992, 269–338.

18. Maureen Hallinan and Richard Williams, "Students' Characteristics and the Peer Influence Process," *Sociology of Education* 63 (April 1990): 122–32.

19. Jomills H. Braddock, Robert L. Crain, and James M. McPartland, "A Long-Term View of School Desegregation: Some Recent Studies of Graduates as Adults," *Phi Delta Kappan* 66, no. 4 (1984): 259–64.

20. Maureen Hallinan and Richard Williams, "The Stability of Students' Interracial Friendships," *American Sociological Review* 52 (1987): 653–64; Kahlenberg, *All Together Now.*

21. Thomas Pettigrew and Linda Tropp, "A Meta-Analytic Test of Intergroup Contact Theory," *Journal of Personality and Social Psychology* 90 (2006): 751–83; Melanie Killen and Clark McKown, "How Integrative Approaches to Intergroup Attitudes Advance the Field," *Journal of Applied Developmental Psychology* 26 (2005): 612–22; Jennifer Jellison Holme, Amy Stuart Wells, and Anita Tijerina Revilla, "Learning through Experience: What Graduates Gained by Attending Desegregated High Schools," *Equity and Excellence in Education* 38, no. 1 (2005): 14–24.

22. Michal Kurlaender and John T. Yun, "Fifty Years After Brown: New Evidence of the Impact of School Racial Composition on Student Outcomes," *International Journal of Educational Policy, Research and Practice* 6, no. 1 (2005): 51–78.

23. See Brookings Institution, *Mind the Gap: Reducing Disparities to Improve Regional Competitiveness in the Twin Cities* (2005), available at http://www.brookings.edu/metro/pubs/20051027_mindthegap.pdf (visited May 2006).

24. Ibid., 5.

25. Ibid.

26. Erica Frankenberg, "The Impact of School Segregation on Residential Housing Patterns," in *School Resegregation: Must the South Turn Back?*, ed. John Charles Boger and Gary Orfield, 164–84 (Chapel Hill: University of North Carolina Press, 2005).

27. Unpublished 1995 research by Robert Crain, Diana Pearce, et al., cited in Frankenberg, ibid., 180. See also Gary Orfield, "Metropolitan School Desegregation: Impacts on Metropolitan Society," in *In Pursuit of a Dream Deferred: Linking Housing and Education Policy,* ed. john powell, Gavin Kearney, and Vina Kay, 121–57 (New York: Peter Lang Publishing, 2001), 121, 135.

28. Myron Orfield and Thomas Luce, *Minority Suburbanization and Racial Change: Stable Integration, Neighborhood Transition, and the Need for Regional Approaches* (Minneapolis: University of Minnesota, Institute on Race and Poverty, 2005).

29. Orfield, "Metropolitan School Desegregation," 121, 125.

30. Frankenberg, "The Impact of School Segregation on Residential Housing Patterns," 165.

31. Diana Pearce, "Breaking Down the Barriers: New Evidence on Impact of Metropolitan School Desegregation on Housing Patterns" (1980). Pearce's 1980 research for the National Institute of Education showed that "in areas without metropolitan desegregation plans, housing advertisements were replete with racial signals." "Such racial signals were absent, however, in the metropolitan areas with area-wide desegregation." See Orfield, "Metropolitan School Desegregation," 121, 135.

32. Andrew Haughwout and Robert Inman, *How Should Suburbs Help Their Central Cities?* Federal Reserve Bank of New York Staff Report no. 186 (May 2004), available at http://www.newyorkfed.org/research/staff_reports/sr186.pdf (accessed February 2008); Robin Leichenko, "Growth and Change in U.S. Cities and Suburbs," *Growth and Change* 32 (2001): 326–54.

33. Haughwout and Inman, *How Should Suburbs Help Their Central Cities?;* Leichenko, "Growth and Change in U.S. Cities and Suburbs"; Richard Voith, "Do Suburbs Need Cities?" *Journal of Regional Science* 38, no. 3 (1998): 445–64.

34. Leichenko, "Growth and Change in U.S. Cities and Suburbs."

35. Voith, "Do Suburbs Need Cities?" Similar results from more refined research came from advanced modeling using employment data rather than income. For twenty-eight Spanish metro regions across thirty-five years, results showed that a 1 percent increase in economic activity in large central cities (populations over 300,000) resulted in a 2 percent increase in suburbs; for smaller central cities, the result was a 1 percent increase for the suburbs. Albert Solé Ollé and Elisabet Viladecans Marsal, "Central Cities as Engines of Metropolitan Area Growth," *Journal of Regional Science* 44, no. 2 (2004): 321–50. See also Leichenko, "Growth and Change in U.S. Cities and Suburbs."

36. Neighborhoods were originally categorized into twelve types based on their racial/ethnic

composition. Appendix A includes a detailed description of these categories. These twelve types were then aggregated into nonwhite segregated, predominantly white, and integrated categories. Nonwhite segregated neighborhoods are defined either as neighborhood where the share of blacks, Hispanics, or Asian residents exceeds 50 percent or as neighborhoods with varying combinations of black, Hispanic, and Asian residents, where the relative share of white residents in the neighborhoods does not exceed 30 percent. In predominantly white neighborhoods, the share of each nonwhite group is smaller than 10 percent. Any neighborhood that is neither nonwhite segregated nor predominantly white is considered integrated.

37. The analysis, however, shows that despite being more integrated, whites mostly mix with Asians and Hispanics, and not with blacks.

38. See Table B.1 in Appendix B for details of the data underlying Figure 3.5.

39. See Table B.2 in Appendix B for details of the data underlying Figure 3.6.

40. See Table B.3 in Appendix B for details of the data underlying Figure 3.7.

41. See Tables B.4, B.6, and B.8 in Appendix B.

42. See Tables B.5, B.7, and B.9 in Appendix B.

43. See Figures B.1 and B.2 in Appendix B.

44. See Table B.10 in Appendix B for details of the data underlying Figure 3.9.

45. See Table B.11 in Appendix B for details of the data underlying Figure 3.10.

46. See Tables B.12, B.14, and B.16 in Appendix B.

47. See Table B.13 in Appendix B.

48. The turnover points for schools were greater than the turnover points for neighborhoods simply because racial transition was examined over one decade compared to two decades for neighborhoods. When compared over the same decade, the turnover points for schools and neighborhoods were almost identical.

49. George Galster and Erin Godfrey, "By Words and Deeds: Racial Steering by Real Estate Agents in the U.S. in 2000," *Journal of the American Planning Association* 71, no. 3 (Summer 2005): 251–68.

50. National Fair Housing Alliance, *Unequal Opportunity—Perpetuating Housing Discrimination in America: 2006 Fair Trends Housing Report* (Washington, D.C.: National Fair Housing Alliance, 2006), 12.

51. Diana M. Pearce, "Gatekeepers and Homeseekers: Institutional Patterns in Racial Steering," *Social Problems* 26, no. 3 (February 1979): 325–42.

52. Research suggests that minorities often find themselves trapped in poor neighborhoods, not because of their inability to move out, but because of their inability to stay out of poor neighborhoods. See Lincoln Quillian, "How Long Are Exposures to Poor Neighborhoods? The Long-Term Dynamics of Entry and Exit from Poor Neighborhoods," *Population Research and Policy Review* 22 (2003): 221–49. As soon as minority households leave poor neighborhoods for better neighborhoods, a process of resegregation in neighborhoods and schools destabilizes these neighborhoods and undermines their efforts to escape poor neighborhoods.

53. Camille Zubrinsky Charles, "The Dynamics of Racial Residential Segregation," *Annual Review of Sociology* 29 (2003): 167–207, 185.

54. Ibid., 186.

55. Ibid., 185.

56. Camille Zubrinsky Charles, "Can We Live Together? Racial Preferences and Neighborhood Outcomes," in *The Geography of Opportunity: Race and Housing Choice in Metropolitan America*, ed. Xavier de Souza Briggs, 45–80 (Washington, D.C.: Brookings Institution Press, 2005), 72.

57. Mary Pattillo, "Black Middle Class Neighborhoods," *Annual Review of Sociology* 31 (2005): 305–29, 321.

58. Lincoln Quillian, "Why Is Black-White Residential Segregation So Persistent? Evidence on Three Theories from Migration Data," *Social Science Research* 31 (2002): 197–229.

59. Keith R. Ihlanfeldt and Benjamin Scafidi, "Whites' Neighborhood Racial Preferences and Neighborhood Racial Composition in the United States: Evidence from the Multi-City Study of Inequality," *Housing Studies* 19, no. 3 (2004): 325–59.

60. For examples of these studies, see Charles, "The Dynamics of Racial Residential Segregation," 182.

61. Charles, "Can We Live Together?"

62. Ibid., 73.

63. Ibid., 62.

64. See, e.g., John Iceland and Rima Wilkes, "Does Socioeconomic Status Matter? Race, Class, and Residential Segregation," *Social Problems* 53, no. 2 (2006): 248–73; John Iceland, Cicely Sharpe, and Erika Steinmetz, "Class Differences in African American Residential Patterns in US Metropolitan Areas: 1990–2000," *Social Science Research* 34 (2005): 252–66.

65. Iceland and Wilkes, "Does Socioeconomic Status Matter?"; Iceland et al., "Class Differences in African American Residential Patterns in US Metropolitan Areas."

66. In 1970, racial and ethnic sorting accounted for 81 percent of residential sorting. In contrast, it accounted for 65 percent of residential sorting in 2000. See Fischer, "The Relative Importance of Income and Race in Determining Residential Outcomes in U.S. Urban Areas," 684.

67. Margery Austin Turner and Stephen L. Ross, "How Racial Discrimination Affects the Search for Housing," in *The Geography of Opportunity* (see note 56), 81–100.

68. For black and Hispanic renters, denial of information about available houses and denial of opportunities to inspect units are the most common forms of discrimination. Black homebuyers may find information about available units but still encounter discrimination in inspecting those units. In addition, they are frequently steered away from white neighborhoods, and receive inferior assistance with regards to financing their home purchases as well as in other stages of the home purchasing process. Hispanic homebuyers, in contrast, encounter discrimination mostly in the form of geographic steering and receiving inferior assistance with regards to financing their home purchases. See Turner and Ross, ibid., 86–91.

69. "In the sales market, steering of African American homebuyers increased by 11 percentage points during the 1990s, and steering against Hispanic homebuyers showed no decline during the period." Stephen Ross and Margery Austin Turner, "Housing Discrimination in Metropolitan America: Explaining Changes between 1989 and 2000," *Social Problems* 52, no. 2 (2005): 152–80, 176. See also Margery Austin Turner et al., *Discrimination in Metropolitan Housing Markets: National Results from Phase I of HDS 2000* (Washington, D.C.: U.S. Department of Housing and Urban Development, 2002); Turner and Ross, "How Racial Discrimination Affects the Search for Housing."

70. Turner and Ross, "How Racial Discrimination Affects the Search for Housing," 94.

71. Jan Ondrich, Stephen Ross, and John Yinger, "Now You See It, Now You Don't: Why Do Real Estate Agents Withhold Available Houses from Black Customers?" *Review of Economics and Statistics* 85, no. 4 (November 2003): 854–73.

72. Turner et al., "Discrimination in Metropolitan Housing Markets."

73. National Fair Housing Alliance, *Unequal Opportunity,* 5.

74. Of 290 total visits, there were 51 instances in which black or Latino testers were offered no service or reduced service. Ibid., 9.

75. Ibid., 12.

76. Margery Austin Turner and Stephen Ross, "Housing Discrimination in Metropolitan America: Findings from the Latest National Paired Testing Study" (University of Connecticut, Department of Economics, working paper 2003–08). Available at http://www.econ.uconn.edu/working/2003-08R.pdf.

77. John Yinger, *Closed Doors, Opportunities Lost: The Continuing Costs of Housing Discrimination* (New York: Russell Sage Foundation, 1995).

78. Charles, "The Dynamics of Racial Residential Segregation," 176.

79. Guy Stuart, *Discriminating Risk: The U.S. Mortgage Lending Industry in the 20th Cen-*

tury (Ithaca, N.Y.: Cornell University Press, 2003); Stephen Ross and John Yinger, *The Color of Credit: Mortgage Discrimination, Research Methodology and Fair Lending Enforcement* (Cambridge, Mass.: MIT Press, 2003).

80. Ross and Yinger, *The Color of Credit;* William Apgar and Allegra Calder, "The Dual Mortgage Market: The Persistence of Discrimination in Mortgage Lending," in *The Geography of Opportunity* (see note 56), 101–23, 102. Melvin L. Oliver and Thomas M. Shapiro suggest that racial discrepancies in mortgage rejection rates emanate from the fact that "loan officers were far more likely to overlook flaws in the credit scores of white applicants or to arrange creative financing for them than they were in the case of black applicants." Melvin L. Oliver and Thomas M. Shapiro, *Black Wealth/White Wealth: A New Perspective on Racial Inequality* (New York: Routledge, 1995), 139.

81. Richard Williams, Reynold Nesiba, and Eileen Diaz McConnell, "The Changing Face of Inequality in Home Mortgage Lending," *Social Problems* 52, no. 2 (2005): 181–208; Apgar and Calder, "The Dual Mortgage Market."

82. Apgar and Calder, "The Dual Mortgage Market," 102.

83. Ibid., 111–15.

84. Margery Austin Turner et al., *All Other Things Being Equal: A Paired Testing Study of Mortgage Lending Institutions* (report prepared for the U.S. Department of Housing and Urban Development Office of Fair Housing and Equal Opportunity, April 2002).

85. These predatory lending practices range from equity stripping and charging excessively high interest rates and fees to disregarding the borrower's ability to pay. For a detailed study on predatory lending, see Kathleen C. Engel and Patricia A. McCoy, "A Tale of Three Markets: The Law and Economics of Predatory Lending," *Texas Law Review* 80, no. 6 (2002): 1257–1381.

86. For evidence on the concentration of foreclosures in minority neighborhoods, see U.S. Department of Housing and Urban Development and U.S. Department of Treasury, *Curbing Predatory Home Lending: A Joint Report* (2000), and Mark Duda and William Apgar, *Mortgage Foreclosure Trends in Los Angeles: Patterns and Policy Issues,* Los Angeles Neighborhood Housing Service (Washington, D.C.: Neighborhood Reinvestment Corporation, 2004).

87. Gregory D. Squires, ed., *Insurance Redlining: Disinvestment, Reinvestment, and the Evolving Role of Financial Institutions* (Washington, D.C.: Urban Institute Press, 1997).

88. Gregory D. Squires, "Racial Profiling, Insurance Style: Insurance Redlining and the Uneven Development of Metropolitan Areas," *Journal of Urban Affairs* 25, no. 4 (2003): 391–410.

89. Gregory D. Squires and Jan Chadwick, "Linguistic Profiling: A Continuing Tradition of Discrimination in the Home Insurance Industry," *Urban Affairs Review* 41, no. 3 (2006): 400–415. For a similar study that documents the prevalence of linguistic profiling in mortgage lending, see Douglas S. Massey and Nancy A. Denton, "The Social Ecology of Racial Discrimination," *City and Community* 3 (2004): 221–43.

90. Squires, "Racial Profiling, Insurance Style," 400. For a discussion of these guidelines and their adverse effects on communities of color, see D. J. Powers, "The Discriminatory Effects of Homeowners Insurance Underwriting Guidelines," in *Insurance Redlining* (see note 87), 119–40.

91. For a detailed discussion of these exceptions, see Philip D. Tegeler, "The Persistence of Segregation in Housing Programs," in *The Geography of Opportunity* (see note 56), 197–216, 199–200.

92. For a detailed discussion of how these housing programs contribute to racial segregation, see ibid.

93. For a detailed discussion of how these housing programs contribute to racial segregation, see ibid.

94. Florence Wagman Roisman, "Mandates Unsatisfied: The Low Income Housing Tax Credit Program and the Civil Rights Law," *University of Miami Law Review* 52 (1998): 1011–12; Khadduri and colleagues estimate that the number of LIHTC units is comparable to the number of public housing units. See Jill Khadduri, Larry Buron, and Ken Lam, "LIHTC and Mixed In-

come Housing: Enabling Families with Children to Live in Low-Poverty Neighborhoods?" (paper prepared for presentation at the annual meeting of the Association of Public Policy Analysis and Management, Atlanta, October 30, 2004), 1. Available at http://www.prrac.org/mobility/pdf/ Khadduri.pdf (accessed May 2, 2007).

95. Sandra Nolden et al., *Updating the Low Income Housing Tax Credit Database: Projects Placed in Service through 2001* (Cambridge, Mass.: Abt Associates Inc., 2003). Available at http://www.huduser.org/Datasets/lihtc/report9501.pdf; David A. Smith, *The Low-Income Housing Tax Credit Effectiveness and Efficiency* (Boston: Recapitalization Advisors, Inc., 2002), 3. This does not include the federal commitment for voucher-based housing programs.

96. Tax Reform Act of 1986, Pub. L. No. 99-514, sec. 252, 100 Stat. 2095, 2189–2208 (1986).

97. Tegeler, "The Persistence of Segregation in Housing Programs," 201.

98. Larry Buron et al., *Assessment of Economic and Social Characteristics of LIHTC Residents and Neighborhoods* (Cambridge, Mass.: Abt Associates Inc., 2000), 4:16–4:18; Nolden et al., *Updating the Low Income Housing Tax Credit Database;* Smith, *The Low-Income Housing Tax Credit Effectiveness and Efficiency,* 3.

99. Jill Khadduri et al., *Are States Using the Low Income Housing Tax Credit to Enable Families with Children to Live in Low Poverty and Racially Integrated Neighborhoods?* (Cambridge, Mass.: Abt Associates Inc., 2006).

100. Data provided by the U.S. Department of Housing and Urban Development.

101. Kevin M. Cremin, "The Transition to Section 8 Housing: Will the Elderly Be Left Behind?" *Yale Law and Policy Review* 18, no. 23 (2000): 405, 409; National Low Income Housing Coalition, *2004 Advocates Guide to Housing and Community Development Policy* (Washington, D.C.: National Low Income Housing Coalition, 2004), 96.

102. Cremin, "The Transition to Section 8 Housing," 409.

103. See U.S. Department of Housing and Urban Development, "Section 8 Rental Voucher Program" available at http://www.hud.gov/progdesc/voucher.cfm (accessed May 2, 2007). Recent limitations on the funding of Section 8 vouchers are effectively making these vouchers less portable. For a detailed discussion of these limitations, see Tegeler, "The Persistence of Segregation in Housing Programs," 198.

104. See chapter 4 for a more detailed discussion of the job–housing spatial mismatch and its implications for the region's residents of color.

105. See Independent School Board 196, meeting minutes, March 27, 2006. Available at http://isd196.granicus.com/viewpublisher.php?view_id=4; http://www.district196.org.

106. Minnesota Rules, sec. 3535 (2007).

107. See, for instance, Julie Wageman, "Racial Compliance Draws Board Impasse," *Osseo–Maple Grove Press,* June 24 1998, 32, for a discussion of the battle between Osseo parents and the school board on redrawing attendance boundaries and compliance with civil rights laws.

108. School Board Meeting Minutes, Osseo School District (November 15, 1994).

109. School Board Meeting Minutes, Osseo School District (February 21, 1994).

110. Osseo's 2001–2 integration plan does provide money, including transit money, to help students open-enroll across the district. See *2001–2 Intra-district Integration Budget Osseo Area Schools,* Report to Minnesota Department of Education, July 31, 2001.

111. School Board Meeting Minutes, Osseo School District (May 19, 1998). The effect of the new attendance boundaries on the racial composition of the schools was initially a parameter in the attendance boundary changes. In this school board meeting, members voted to remove the parameter.

112. School Board Meeting Minutes, Osseo School District (May 19, 1998); School Board Meeting Minutes, Osseo School District (June 2, 1999); Lauri Winters, "Osseo School Board Remains Deadlocked," *Brooklyn Park Sun Post,* June 17, 1998, 1A.

113. Julie Wageman, "Boundary Progress Made, Despite Tempers," *Osseo–Maple Grove Press,* September 9, 1998.

114. School Board Meeting Minutes, Osseo School District (February 2, 1999).

115. See Mike Kaszuba, "District Wrestles with Racial Imbalance," *Minneapolis Star Tribune,* October 11, 1998, B1 (quoting a Maple Grove parent: "Fine, spend the money to make those better schools, just don't bus from east to west").

116. Osseo's 2001–2 integration plan does provide money, including transit money, to help students open-enroll across the district. *2001–2 Intra-district Integration Budget Osseo Area Schools.*

117. Letter to Susan Hintz, superintendent of Osseo Area Schools, from Cindy Jackson, principal state program administrator, November 8, 2006.

118. Norman Draper, "Parents Speaking Up against Plans to Close Osseo Schools," *Minneapolis Star Tribune,* January 26, 2008.

119. Sue Scharebroich, "Hopkins Public Schools Are Serious about Restoring the District's Financial Stability," *Minneapolis Star Tribune,* December 20, 2006; Jason McGrew-King, "Enrollment Decline Means Less Revenue for Hopkins Schools," *Lakeshore Weekly News,* November 7, 2005.

120. Hopkins School Board, Meeting Minutes, November 16, 2007.

121. Hopkins School District Boundary Task Force, *Boundary Options for Board of Education Consideration,* February 2007.

122. Interview with Emily Wallace Jackson, Katherine Curren parent, March 2007.

123. Patricia Releford, "Hopkins New District Map Will Relocate the Fewest Students," *Minneapolis Star Tribune,* February 20, 2007.

124. Economist Charles Clotfelter found that in the most segregated metropolitan areas, between-district segregation in schools represented an astonishing 84 percent of all segregation in schools in 2000 compared to just 4 percent in 1970. He also found that between-district segregation was much more significant than segregation between public and private schools. See Charles T. Clotfelter, *After Brown: The Ruse and Retreat of School Desegregation* (Princeton, N.J.: Princeton University Press, 2004).

125. Gregory R. Weiher, *The Fractured Metropolis: Political Fragmentation and Metropolitan Segregation* (Albany, N.Y.: SUNY Press, 1991); A. I. Frank, "Geopolitical Fragmentation: A Force in Spatial Segregation in the US?" (paper presented at the Lincoln Institute of Land Policy International Seminar on Segregation in the City, July 26–28, 2001). http://66.223.94.76/pubs/PubDetail.aspx?pubid=601.

126. Rolf Pendall, "Local Land Use Regulation and the Chain of Exclusion," *Journal of the American Planning Association* 66, no. 2 (Spring 2000): 125–42.

127. Ibid.

128. J. M. Quigley, S. Raphael, and L. A. Rosenthal, "Local Land-Use Controls and Demographic Outcomes in a Booming Economy," *Urban Studies* 41, no. 2 (2004): 389–421; Pendall, "Local Land Use Regulation and the Chain of Exclusion."

129. *Swann v. Charlotte-Mecklenburg Bd. of Educ.,* 402 U.S. 1, 15 (1971).

130. There is no federal constitutional right to a public school education. *San Antonio Indep. Sch. Dist. v. Rodriguez,* 411 U.S. 1 (1973).

131. *Brown v. Board of Education,* 347 U.S. 483 (1954); 349 U.S. 294 (1955).

132. *Green v. County Sch. Bd.,* 391 U.S. 430 (1968).

133. *Keyes v. School District No. 1,* 413 U.S. 189 (1973)

134. *Milliken v. Bradley,* 418 U.S. 717 (1974).

135. *Missouri v. Jenkins,* 515 U.S. 70 (1995), 94.

136. Orfield, "Metropolitan School Desegregation," 121, 129. The aftermath of *Milliken* illustrates how intradistrict remedies tended to trigger white flight and destabilize neighborhoods. The best example of the failure of remedies after *Milliken* is the Detroit School District, which covers a small area of the Detroit metro region and was the subject of *Milliken*'s ruling. In 1973, Detroit's student enrollment was 70 percent nonwhite—amid a metro region that was only 19 percent nonwhite. These percentages are similar to those in the Twin Cities today. *Milliken* re-

quired that Detroit schools be "desegregated" only by rebalancing enrollments within the boundaries of Detroit's isolated, nonwhite district. In 1986, twelve years after *Milliken* was decided, the typical black student in Detroit attended a school with white enrollment under 12 percent. By the 1990s, Detroit was the nation's most segregated school district, and white enrollments had evaporated to 4 percent. Gary Orfield, *Schools More Separate: Consequences of a Decade of Resegregation,* The Civil Rights Project, Harvard University, July 2001, Table 6, p. 25, available at http://www.civilrightsproject.ucla.edu/research/deseg/Schools_More_Separate.pdf.

137. If a school board had complied in good faith with a federal desegregation decree, and "the vestiges of past discrimination had been eliminated to the extent practicable," then the desegregation order can be dissolved irrespective of segregation levels. *School Bd. of Oklahoma City v. Dowell,* 498 U.S. 237 (1991).

138. E.g., *Missouri v. Jenkins,* 515 U.S. 70, 87 (1995).

139. *Parents Involved in Community Schools v. Seattle School Dist. No. 1,* 127 S. Ct. 2738 (2007) (Kennedy, J., Concurring).

140. Justice Kennedy's concurrence in the Seattle Schools holding tells metropolitan areas that most integration plans are constitutional, and it gives guidance in implementing desegregation plans that do not violate the Fourteenth Amendment. Districts may explicitly attempt to achieve racial balance in schools through "strategic site selection of new schools, drawing attendance zones with general recognition of the demographics of neighborhoods, allocating resources for special programs, recruiting students and faculty in a targeted fashion and tracking enrollments, performance and other statistics by race." Ibid.

141. *Skeen v. Minnesota,* 505 N.W.2d 299, 313 (Minn. S. Ct. 1993). See William E. Thro, "An Essay: The School Finance Paradox: How the Constitutional Values of Decentralization and Judicial Restraint Inhibit the Achievement of Quality," *Education Law Reporter* 197 (June 30, 2005), 482.

142. The educational finance system was found to be constitutional. The *Skeen* holding, however, is limited to the issue of whether the existing differences in school funding, which the plaintiffs asserted did *not* result in an inadequate education, violated the Minnesota Constitution.

143. *Skeen v. Minnesota,* 505 N.W.2d at 312.

144. The *Skeen* court's holding is particularly important to plaintiffs challenging segregation because whether plaintiffs must prove *intentional* racial discrimination, in addition to proving racially unequal outcomes, depends on whether a fundamental right is involved. Even under federal constitutional law, when a fundamental right is affected, plaintiffs are not required to prove that the government intended to discriminate. In fact, proving governmental awareness and *inaction* in the face of racially disparate impacts on the fundamental right to vote is sufficient evidence to establish that the government violated the federal constitution. *Sheff v. O'Neill,* 238 Conn. 1, 678 A.2d at 1279, citing, e.g., *Reynolds v. Sims,* 377 U.S. 533, 561–63 (1964). For instance, there is no meaningful distinction between a court's requiring legislative action to "protect the fundamental right to vote" and requiring legislative action "to protect the fundamental right to a substantially equal educational opportunity." *Sheff v. O'Neill,* at 1280. Thus, there is no reason to require proof of discriminatory intent to prove violation of a state's fundamental right to educational opportunity.

145. *Sheff v. O'Neill,* 678 A.2d at 1267.

146. William E. Thro, "An Essay: The School Finance Paradox: How the Constitutional Values of Decentralization and Judicial Restraint Inhibit the Achievement of Quality," *Education Law Reporter* 197 (June 30, 2005), 482.

147. *Sheff v. O'Neill,* 678 A.2d at 1280. The court was interpreting the education clause, as well as Connecticut's unusual equal protection clause, which, like the constitutions of Hawaii and New Jersey, prohibit both discrimination and segregation. Ibid. at 1281–82, 1281 n. 29.

148. Keith R. Ihlanfeldt, "Exclusionary Land-Use Regulations within Suburban Commu-

nities: A Review of the Evidence and Policy Prescriptions," *Urban Studies* 41, no. 2 (February 2004), 272.

149. According to Goetz et al., the fair share program in the Twin Cities during this period was "one of the highest-performing regional programs in the entire nation." Edward G. Goetz, Karen Chapple, and Barbara Lukermann, "The Rise and Fall of Fair Share Housing: Lessons from the Twin Cities," in *The Geography of Opportunity* (see note 56), 247–65, 251. For evidence on the success of the program during the seventies, see Myron Orfield, "Land Use and Housing Policies to Reduce Concentrated Poverty and Racial Segregation," *Fordham Urban Law Journal* 33, no. 3 (March 2006): 919–22.

150. The Metropolitan Council was granted this authority by the Office of Management and Budget in its Circular A-95.

151. Orfield, "Land Use and Housing Policies to Reduce Concentrated Poverty and Racial Segregation," 920.

152. Ibid., 921.

153. Ibid.

154. Ibid., 922.

155. Goetz et al., "The Rise and Fall of Fair Share Housing," 251. The early eighties saw a reversal of the program's fortunes. The repeal of Circular A-95 by the Reagan administration eliminated the Metropolitan Council's authority to review local applications for federal grants. As a result, the council lost an important tool to leverage local compliance with its regional land use and housing plans. Similarly, the dramatic budget cuts experienced by HUD in the early eighties undermined the federal housing subsidies available to the council to implement its regional fair share housing policies. Changes in the leadership of the council as well as changes in the demographics of the region's population also contributed to the council's gradual retreat from its former regional fair share housing policies. For a detailed discussion of the decline of the program, see Goetz et al., ibid., 251–53.

156. For a detailed discussion of the jurisdictions with inclusionary housing programs, see Business and Professional People for the Public Interest, *Opening the Door to Inclusionary Housing,* 60–103, available at http://www.bpichicago.org/documents/OpeningtheDoor.pdf (accessed February 20, 2008).

157. Ibid., 4.

158. Unpublished Institute on Race and Poverty research. Data file available from the IRP upon request.

159. Myron Orfield, *Metropolitics: A Regional Agenda for Community and Stability* (Washington, D.C.: Brookings Institution Press, 1997), 28.

160. Isles Inc., *Milestones and Accomplishments,* available at http://www.isles.org/mileston.html (accessed February 15, 2008).

161. Isles Inc., *Isles Newsletter,* Spring 2003, 5, available at http://www.isles.org/spring2003.pdf (accessed February 18, 2008).

162. These agreements enable opportunity-rich suburbs to buy their way out of providing their fair share of affordable housing in the region and to burden central cities with the full responsibility of housing low-income persons.

163. See john powell, "Segregation and Educational Inadequacy in Public Schools," *Hamline Journal of Public Law and Policy* 17 (1996), 337, 360.

164. For this simulation, the region was defined as the seven core counties of the metropolitan area—Anoka, Carver, Dakota, Hennepin, Ramsey, Scott, and Washington. To simplify the analysis, the simulations deal only with segregation of black and white students. The numbers of students of other races and ethnicities, especially Hispanics, are on the rise. However, blacks are clearly the dominant racial minority in area schools. In addition, the simulations are meant to be illustrative, and adding a third or fourth group to the analysis complicates the discussion considerably.

165. Housing simulations for the Choice Is Yours Program adjust school racial enrollments according to whether (1) the racial populations of low-income housing were placed uniformly within existing housing units and (2) the housing units themselves were placed uniformly across the Twin Cities area. First, we determined how many more or fewer children would attend a school if the population of each low-income housing unit had the same proportional racial distribution within the units. The child populations of low-income housing units closest to elementary schools were used to adjust the schools' population. Second, we determined how many more or fewer children would attend a school if low-income housing were placed uniformly according to school populations. We used racial demographic data for 2002 elementary schools and 2004 low-income housing for the Twin Cities. For low-income housing, child population data are provided with LIHTC households and are estimated with project-based Section 8 households. Our estimate of children in Section 8 households is derived by multiplying the Twin Cities average number of children in a household for each racial group (derived from U.S. census data) by the racial population results. To place low-income housing units uniform to student populations we determined each school's population as a percentage of total schools and multiplied it by the total population of LIHTC and project-based Section 8 households by race. We assume that spatially uniform low-income populations are also racially uniform in their distributions.

166. Zip code level race data were used for the analysis of Section 8 vouchers.

167. A school is considered racially identifiable if its proportion of protected students exceeds by 20 percentage points the proportion of protected students in the district as a whole for those grades served by the school. Minnesota Revised Code, sec. 3535.0110, subd. 6 (West 2007).

168. A school district is considered racially isolated if its proportion of protected students exceeds that of a neighboring district by more than 20 percentage points. When a school district qualifies as a racially isolated one, both the racially isolated district and the adjoining districts become eligible for integration revenue. See State of Minnesota, Office of the Legislative Auditor, *School District Integration Revenue: Evaluation Report (St. Paul: Office of the Legislative Auditor, Program Evaluation Division, 2005)*, 7.

169. For the specific rates, see Table 1.3 in ibid., 9.

170. State of Minnesota, Office of the Legislative Auditor, *School District Integration Revenue.*

171. Ibid., 30.

172. Ibid., 32.

173. For latest efforts, see, for instance, *National Access Network Campaign for Fiscal Equity,* available at http://www.schoolfunding.info/states/state_by_state.php3 (accessed May 2, 2008).

174. Molly S. McUsic notes that socioeconomic integration would be more effective than expanded funding in increasing the educational attainment of low-income students of color. See Molly S. McUsic, "The Future of *Brown v. Board of Education:* Economic Integration of the Public Schools," *Harvard Law Review* 117, no. 5 (March 2004): 1334–77.

175. Ibid.

176. Minnesota Department of Education, *Minneapolis Public School District, Report to Tax Payers, Fiscal Year 2007,* available at http://education.state.mn.us/ReportCard2005/loadFinanceAction.do?SCHOOL_NUM=000&DISTRICT_NUM=0001&DISTRICT_TYPE=03 (accessed October 3, 2008).

177. Ibid.

178. Minnesota Department of Education, *Bethune Elementary School Report Card, 2007 Results,* available at http://education.state.mn.us/ReportCard2005/loadFinanceAction.do?SCHOOL_NUM=107&DISTRICT_NUM=0001&DISTRICT_TYPE=03 (accessed October 3, 2008).

179. Minnesota Department of Education, *Barton Open Elementary School Report Card, 2007 Results,* available at http://education.state.mn.us/ReportCard2005/loadFinanceAction.do?

SCHOOL_NUM=106&DISTRICT_NUM=0001&DISTRICT_TYPE=03 (accessed October 3, 2008).

180. Minnesota Department of Education, *Bethune Elementary School Report Card 2008,* available at http://education.state.mn.us/ReportCard/2008/RCF000103107.pdf (accessed October 3, 2008).

181. Minnesota Department of Education, *Barton Open Elementary School Report Card 2008,* available at http://education.state.mn.us/ReportCard/2008/RCF000103106.pdf (accessed October 3, 2008).

182. Kara Finnegan et al., *Evaluation of the Public Charter Schools Program: Final Report* (Washington, D.C.: U.S. Department of Education, 2004), ix, available at http://www.ed.gov/rschstat/eval/choice/pcsp-final/finalreport.pdf (accessed May 30, 2007).

183. Institute on Race and Poverty, *Failed Promises: Assessing Charter Schools in the Twin Cities* (Minneapolis: University of Minnesota, Institute on Race and Poverty, 2008), available at http://www.irpumn.org/uls/resources/projects/2_Charter_Report_Final.pdf.

184. State of Minnesota, Office of the Legislative Auditor, *Charter Schools: Evaluation Report* (St. Paul: Office of the Legislative Auditor, Program Evaluation Division, 2008), 9. Between the 2000–2001 and 2005–6 academic years, Minnesota's charter school enrollments mushroomed, increasing nearly 120 percent, while traditional public school enrollments fell 2.1 percent. See Martha McMurry, "Minnesota Education Trends, 2000 to 2005," *Minnesota State Demographic Center Population Notes,* September 2006, 3, available at http://www.demography.state.mn.us/documents/MinnesotaEducationTrends20002005.pdf (accessed 04/26/07).

185. State of Minnesota, Office of the Legislative Auditor, *Charter Schools: Evaluation Report,* 10.

186. Ibid. For a more detailed breakdown of the charter and district school students by region, see Table 1.3, ibid., 11.

187. Ibid., 6.

188. Ibid., 6–7.

189. Institute on Race and Poverty, *Failed Promises,* 12.

190. Ibid.

191. Ibid., 13.

192. See especially Chart 10 in ibid., 14.

193. Ibid.

194. See Bruno V. Manno, Gregg Vanourek, and Chester E. Finn Jr., "Charter Schools: Serving Disadvantaged Youth," *Education and Urban Society* 31, no. 4 (August 1999), especially 439–41.

195. For details of the regression results, see Table 1 in Institute on Race and Poverty, *Failed Promises,* 27.

196. Ibid., 41.

197. Ibid.

198. Wameng Moua, "Are Hmong Students Making the Grades?" *Twin Cities Daily Planet,* March 25, 2008.

199. Mary Turck, "Loving It and Leaving It: Phalen Lake Hopes to Reverse the Trend," *Twin Cities Daily Planet,* February 25, 2008.

200. For a detailed discussion of the history of this lawsuit and the ensuing settlement process, see Institute on Race and Poverty, *The Choice Is Ours: Expanding Educational Opportunity for All Twin Cities Children* (Minneapolis: University of Minnesota, Institute on Race and Poverty, 2006), 35–36.

201. Aspen Associates, *Minnesota Voluntary Public School Choice, 2005–2006: Evaluation Report* (Edina, Minn.: Aspen Associates, 2007), 1. In addition to these eight suburbs, another West Metro Education Program school district, Eden Prairie, started receiving students participating in the Choice Is Yours Program during the 2005–6 school year under the West Metro Education Program's comprehensive desegregation plan.

202. Ibid., i.

203. The eligibility income cutoffs for the federal free and reduced-cost lunch programs depend on the size of families. In general, families whose incomes are less than 135 percent of the federal poverty line qualify for free-lunch programs. Families with incomes less than 185 percent of the federal poverty line are eligible for the reduced-cost lunch program.

204. The Institute on Race and Poverty obtained information on the per school attendance of the Choice Is Yours participants in the 2005–6 school year from two different sources. Seven of the nine participating districts use the Wide Area Transportation System (WATS) cooperatively for transporting the students who participate in the Choice Is Yours Program. For these districts, IRP obtained from WATS the number of students transported to the schools that took part in the Choice Is Yours, as well as the Minneapolis zip codes from which they left. Two participating school districts—St. Anthony–New Brighton and Hopkins—now use their own transportation system. IRP contacted these districts directly to obtain the 2005–6 student enrollment numbers for each participating school. Map 3.23 was created using this data. The total number of students represented on the map is 1,858. In contrast, the total number of the Choice Is Yours students reported leaving Minneapolis for the 2005–6 school year is approximately 1,680. This 178-student difference is explained by the fact that some open enrollment students use WATS along with the Choice Is Yours participants. The number of students represented in the first seven districts may be an underestimate of the actual number, as some of the Choice Is Yours participants may take rides from their parents, drive, or even walk to school. The information for Hopkins and St. Anthony–New Brighton gives no indication of the number of students benefiting from the respective busing programs.

205. Aspen Associates, *Minnesota Voluntary Public School Choice, 2004–2005: Evaluation Report* (Edina, Minn.: Aspen Associates, 2006).

206. Institute on Race and Poverty communication with Marsha Gronseth, executive director, West Metro Education Program, September 14, 2005.

207. State of Minnesota, Office of the Legislative Auditor, *School District Integration Revenue: Evaluation Report,* Table 2.3.

208. Elisabeth A. Palmer, *The Choice Is Yours after Two Years: An Evaluation* (Edina, Minn.: Aspen Associates, 2003), 40.

209. Ibid., Table 2.16, 44.

210. Ibid., Table 3.2, 66.

211. Aspen Associates, *Minnesota Voluntary Public School Choice, 2005–2006,* 21.

212. Ibid.

213. Ibid., vi.

214. James E. Ryan, "Schools, Race, and Money," *Yale Law Journal* 109 (1999): 263–64.

215. Except for Wayzata and Edina, all the suburban school districts participating in the Choice Is Yours Program were located in suburbs categorized as stressed places according to the community classification outlined in Chapter 1. It is worth noting that relatively better-off school districts such as Edina, Wayzata, and Hopkins consistently underenrolled program participants in their school districts, rarely filling half of their allocated Choice Is Yours spaces in most years. See Institute on Race and Poverty, *The Choice Is Ours,* 42–43.

216. Aspen Associates, *Minnesota Voluntary Public School Choice, 2005–2006,* 34–39.

217. School districts participate in these integration districts for two reasons. Some school districts have to participate because the district is racially isolated (i.e., the district's share of students of color is 20 percent greater than that of the surrounding districts). Other school districts that are not racially isolated can also choose to participate in an integration district to receive integration revenue funding (Minn. Stat. 124D.896). Many metro area school districts are not part of integration districts. Instead, they cooperate in collaboration councils, which also allow the schools to receive integration aid. Currently, these collaboration councils generally provide social programming and teacher development, but do little to actually integrate the racially isolated districts. See, for instance, "Lakeville's Answers to Parents about Its Collaboration

with Burnsville," available at http://www.isd194.k12.mn.us/integration3.shtml (accessed May 1, 2008). Participation in the collaboration councils is voluntary, and districts can withdraw their students and their integration aid dollars. Ben Goessling, "North St. Paul-Maplewood-Oakdale Might Withdraw from the East Metro Integration District to Start Its Own Project in 2009," *Minneapolis Star Tribune,* January 15, 2008.

4. TRANSPORTATION AND EMPLOYMENT

1. john powell, "Race and Space: What Really Drives Metropolitan Growth," *Brookings Review* 16, no. 4 (1998): 20–22.

2. Michael A. Stoll, *Job Sprawl and the Spatial Mismatch between Blacks and Jobs,* Brookings Institution Survey Series (Washington, D.C.: Brookings Institution, 2005).

3. See Myron Orfield and Thomas Luce, "Governing American Metropolitan Areas: Spatial Policy and Regional Governance," in *Megacities and Megaregions: Frontiers in Spatial Planning,* ed. Cheryl Contant and Catherine Ross (Cambridge, Mass.: MIT Press, forthcoming), for a comparison of planning systems in Portland and the Twin Cities.

4. Peter Calthorpe and William Fulton, *The Regional City: Planning for the End of Sprawl* (Washington, D.C.: Island Press, 2001).

5. Edward L. Glaeser, *Job Sprawl: Employment Location in U.S. Metropolitan Areas* (Washington, D.C.: Brookings Institute, Center on Urban and Metropolitan Policy, 2001). Job sprawl is defined as percentage of jobs within ten miles of a metropolitan area's central business district.

6. We exclude Asians from the racial minority maps because Asians often have much greater levels of education, higher incomes, and wealth generation than other minority groups. There are also large differences between Asian subgroups. For instance, recent immigrants from Southeast Asia often have incomes and home ownership rates as low as African Americans and Hispanics. However, because there were great differences in the composition of the Asian population within and between regions and it is difficult to derive reliable data on Asian immigrant subgroups, we did not include them on our maps for the racial minority population.

7. Census data show that African American median household income was $39,073 in Atlanta, $31,119 in Portland, and $29,417 in the Twin Cities in 1999.

8. The method is similar to that used in Richard S. Bolan, Thomas F. Luce Jr., and Hin Kim Lam, "Changing Commutation Patterns in Twin Cities Metropolitan Area Job Centers: 1980–1990" (unpublished manuscript). However, because their focus was on the size and orientation of commuter sheds, Bolan et al. derived commuter sheds with standard deviational ellipses around the centers. Since access is the emphasis in this work, time contours were used. An added advantage of this procedure is that it does not force a specific shape on the commuter sheds, instead allowing the effects of transportation corridors and congestion to be fully reflected in the estimates.

9. Decreasing commuter sheds may also be attributable to road construction, added highway lines, and new road development.

10. Table 4.9 shows the results of overlaying commuter sheds on block group–level data from the 2000 Census of Population to derive the characteristics of the population and housing within the contours.

11. "Affordable" was defined as a rent or mortgage plus tax cost representing less than 50 percent of gross income.

12. In Portland, five employment centers in Salem, a city that is about forty miles from Portland, were excluded. With less population and traffic, Salem's commuter sheds are larger, but they capture a small percentage of the region's overall population because of the city's distance from Portland.

13. Data reported from Texas Transportation Institute, performance measure summary for Atlanta, Portland, and Minneapolis–St. Paul, in David Schrank and Tim Lomax, *The 2007*

Urban Mobility Report (College Station: Texas A&M University, Texas Transportation Institute, 2007).

14. Schrank and Lomax, *2007 Urban Mobility Report,* 50; Anthony Downs, *Stuck in Traffic: Coping with Peak-Hour Traffic Congestion* (Washington, D.C.: Brookings Institution, 1992).

15. David Anderson and Gerald McCullough, *The Full Cost of Transportation in the Twin Cities Region* (Minneapolis: University of Minnesota, Center for Transportation Studies, 2000), 82.

16. The Texas Transportation Institute mobility data indicate that cities reporting on operational treatments had a 5 percent decrease in congestion when freeway entrance ramps were metered and saw a 7 percent decrease in congestion when there were incident management operations in place (including the use of cameras and service patrols). David Schrank and Tim Lomax, *The 2005 Urban Mobility Report* (College Station: Texas A&M University, Texas Transportation Institute, 2005), 8–9.

17. Schrank and Lomax, *The 2007 Urban Mobility Report;* computed from averages for the eighty-five urban areas included in the analysis.

18. Statistics included are the major regional transit providers, including MARTA in Atlanta, Metro Transit in the Twin Cities, and Tri-Met in Portland.

19. The mileage reported is annual vehicle revenue miles, which are the total miles traveled by vehicles from when they pull out into service until they pull in from service.

20. Unlinked passenger trips include each time a passenger boards a vehicle, even when transferring from another transit route.

21. Consumption costs are calculated by the Texas Transportation Institute by the value of time delay, $13.45 per hour of personal travel, and $71.05 for trucks per hour, as well as fuel excessively consumed, which are estimated by using costs per gallon (state averages). Schrank and Lomax, *2005 Urban Mobility Report,* 14.

22. Schrank and Lomax, performance measure summary for Atlanta, Portland, and Minneapolis–St. Paul in the *2007 Urban Mobility Report,* average personal congestion cost savings calculated by author.

23. According to the Federal Transit Administration's 2004 National Transit Database, in Portland the operating expense per passenger mile was $0.76 for buses and $0.31 for light-rail; and operating expense of $1.81 per passenger trip for train and $2.78 per bus. In Atlanta the operating expense per passenger mile was $0.60 for buses and $0.27 for light-rail; and operating expense of $1.78 per passenger trip for train and $2.48 per bus.

24. Laurie Blake, "Suburbs Want Train Plan on Fast Track," *Minneapolis Star Tribune,* March 17, 2007.

25. Laurie Blake, "NW Suburbs Pull Plug on Proposed Minneapolis-Rogers Busway," *Minneapolis Star Tribune,* March 23, 2007.

26. Highway spending data used in the report only include larger projects that have more than $1 million of spending.

27. The congestion measure reflects decreases in the sizes of zero- to thirty-minute commute zones. For example, the 67 percent increase in traffic congestion in the Atlanta central business district reflects the 67 percent decrease in the size of its thirty-minute commuter shed.

5. THE ENVIRONMENT AND GROWTH

1. See "Voters Being Asked to Raise Taxes for Parks," *Minneapolis Star Tribune,* November 2, 2005, B1.

2. See Reid Ewing, Keith Bartholomew, Steve Winkelman, Jerry Walters, and Don Chen, *Growing Cooler: The Evidence on Urban Development and Climate Change* (Washington, D.C.: Urban Land Institute, 2007), for a much more complete analysis of these issues.

3. Reid Ewing, Rolf Pendall, and Don Chen, *Measuring Sprawl and Its Impact* (Washington, D.C.: Smart Growth America, 2002), 18.

4. This section summarizes the discussion of growth trends and important planning institutions in the region provided in chapter 1. See that chapter for maps, charts, and a more detailed discussion.

5. Metropolitan Council, news release, July 19, 2005.

6. Consistent urbanization data were not available over the full time period for the eleven-county region.

7. See Fei Yuan, Kali E. Sawaya, Brian C. Loeffelholz, and Marvin E. Bauer, "Land Cover Classification and Change Analysis of the Twin Cities (Minnesota) Metropolitan Area by Multi-temporal Landsat Remote Sensing," *Remote Sensing of Environment* 98 (2005): 317–28, for a complete description of the methods used to classify land uses.

8. Minnesota Department of Administration, Office of the State Demographer, *Projected Population to 2030 for Cities and Townships Outside the Twin Cities Area,* http://server.admin .state.mn.us/resource.html?Id=7376.

9. Municipalities with 97 percent or more of their land inside the MUSA were treated as completely within the MUSA for these calculations.

10. See http://www.dnr.state.mn.us/rsea/map.html.

11. Densities and land consumption were calculated separately for each municipality. Density was estimated as 2002 households divided by 2002 land classified as urbanized. Land consumption was estimated by this density times the number of projected new households for the municipality. Total land consumption for a community type is the sum of estimated land consumption for each of the municipalities in the group.

12. See *Growth Pressures on Sensitive Natural Areas in DNR's Central Region* (Minneapolis: Ameregis; St. Paul: Minnesota Department of Natural Resources, 2006), 41–43, for a description of the simulations. The Metropolitan Council currently plans to expand the MUSA by significantly less—by 121,637 acres in 2020, or about 21 percent of current area inside the MUSA. (This was calculated with GIS data from the Metropolitan Council at http://www.datafinder .org.) However, since the planned MUSA expansion does not follow municipality boundaries while the population projections do, it is not possible to match population changes and MUSA changes acre by acre.

13. For projected growth beyond the eleven-county metropolitan area, see *Growth Pressures on Sensitive Natural Areas in DNR's Central Region,* 4–5.

14. Sharon Pfeifer, *A Comparative Examination of Selected Regional Green Infrastructure Programs in the United States and Northern Europe* (final report to the Bush Foundation Leadership Fellowship, 2005).

15. Metropolitan Council, *Regional Development Framework,* 2004, 14.

16. See Robert W. Burchell, Anthony Downs, and Sahan Mukherji, *Sprawl Costs: Economic Impacts of Unchecked Development* (Washington, D.C.: Island Press, 2005), and Myron Orfield, *American Metropolitics: The New Suburban Reality* (Washington, D.C.: Brookings Institution, 2002).

17. The findings for the current program and the expansion to the collar counties were calculated from work performed by Steve Hinze of the Research Department of the Minnesota House of Representatives.

6. AN OVERVIEW OF POLICY RECOMMENDATIONS

1. Sandra Nolden et al., *Updating the Low Income Housing Tax Credit (LIHTC) Database: Projects Placed in Service through 2001* (Cambridge, Mass.: Abt Associates Inc., 2003). Available at http://www.huduser.org/Datasets/lihtc/report9501.pdf.

2. Two Wisconsin counties—Pierce and St. Croix—are also now part of the official metro-

politan area and, in principle, should be included in metropolitan planning. However, adding counties outside the state to the Metropolitan Council's domain raises special issues beyond the scope of this analysis.

3. The projected election outcomes use the results of actual elections in each year. They assume that a Democrat (Republican) would have won a district if the average number of votes for Democrats (Republicans) exceeded the average number of votes for Republicans (Democrats) in the district's precincts in that year. Current Metropolitan Council districts (which did not change during this period) were used in the simulations.

4. This assumes that the entire council was reelected every two years. If terms were staggered, the composition would have been smoother.

7. THE POLITICS OF REGIONAL POLICY

1. Voter turnout rates in presidential election years (1992, 1996, 2000, 2004) were consistently higher than the voter turnout rates in gubernatorial election years (1994, 1998, 2002, 2006). The minor fluctuations in Figure 7.1 can be explained by this systematic difference in voter turnout rates as Democrats tend to fare slightly better in high turnout years.

2. In order to understand the changing geography of party preferences over time, the following analysis focuses on changes in the party preferences of different types of suburbs. The analysis tracks these changes at four different points in time: 1992, 1996, 2000, 2004—all presidential election years. The purpose of focusing on these presidential election years is to control for fluctuations that might be a mere artifact of variations in turnout rates. In other words, by eliminating gubernatorial election years, when turnout rates are consistently lower compared to presidential election years, the analysis intends to capture long-term political trends more clearly because this focus on the presidential races also reduces the effect of third-party candidates on the results. Gubernatorial races usually have a viable third candidate. As a result, gubernatorial election years tend to be more volatile years.

3. See chapter 1 for a full description of the community types. Central cities are home to nearly a quarter of the region's households and experience significant social and fiscal stress. Central cities in the Twin Cities region face higher costs than any other type of community with the lowest average tax capacity per household in the region. The factors that increase their costs include the highest poverty rate in the region—more than twice the regional average—that increases needs for local services; high demand for services by nonresidents due to above average job concentrations; greater than average housing ages, which raise the costs of maintaining or upgrading infrastructure. Stressed suburbs accommodate almost a quarter of the metropolitan households and are beginning to experience the social and fiscal challenges the central cities face. Like the central cities, they deal with high cost factors with lower than average tax capacities—in fact, the lowest average tax capacity among suburbs. Old housing stock and the highest poverty rate among the suburbs are the main factors contributing to their high costs.

4. Developed job centers, home to nearly one-fifth of the region's households, are located mostly in second-ring suburbs across the south and west of the metropolitan region. As a group, they face limited cost factors with the second-highest tax capacity per household in the region. While the developed job centers have the highest job density in the region, population growth in these centers has lagged behind the regional average.

5. Developing job centers are home to one of every four households in the region. These fast-growing centers experience higher than average costs with tax capacities that are around the regional average. These centers have the highest growth rates for both households and jobs among all the community types. As a result, they tend to be stressed by costs associated with rapid growth, including crowded schools, congested roads, and rapidly growing infrastructure needs. Bedroom developing places, located mostly at the periphery of the metropolitan area, represent 8 percent of the households in the region. While these places experience rapid population growth, they have the lowest concentration of jobs in the region. Residential properties provide

a majority of the tax base in bedroom developing places, where tax capacity remains slightly above the regional average. Affluent residential places are home to merely 1 percent of the region's households. These communities have the highest average tax capacity per household in the region and the lowest poverty rate among all types of communities.

6. The analysis of party preferences and voter volatility in different types of communities only covers the period between 2000 and 2006. Unlike suburban types, which are relatively fixed over time, the social and fiscal data underlying the classification of community types change over time. For instance, a municipality that was classified in one community type can switch to another type in less than a decade. The data used in this chapter to classify communities in the Twin Cities region reflect the social and fiscal characteristics of these communities during the short period between 2000 and 2006. An analysis of these characteristics during the 1990s would require another classification based on the data sets for the 1990s.

7. Affordable housing stock is defined as the housing units affordable to residents with 50 percent of the regional median income.

8. Compare Maps 1.16 and 1.17 in chapter 1.

CONTRIBUTORS

GENEVA FINN is a research fellow at the Institute on Race and Poverty at the University of Minnesota.

BARIS GUMUS-DAWES is a research fellow at the Institute on Race and Poverty at the University of Minnesota.

WILLIAM LANOUX is a GIS specialist at the Institute on Race and Poverty at the University of Minnesota.

THOMAS F. LUCE JR. is research director at the Institute on Race and Poverty at the University of Minnesota.

JILL MAZULLO is director of communications at 1000 Friends of Minnesota and editor of *Planning Minnesota*, the monthly newsletter of the Minnesota chapter of the American Planning Association.

ERIC MYOTT is a research fellow at the Institute on Race and Poverty at the University of Minnesota.

MYRON ORFIELD is executive director at the Institute on Race and Poverty at the University of Minnesota. He is the author of *Metropolitics: A Regional Agenda for Community and Stability* and *American Metropolitics: The New Suburban Reality.*

SHARON PFEIFER is community assistance manager for the central region (twenty-three counties) of the Minnesota Department of Natural Resources.

NICK WALLACE is a research fellow at the Institute on Race and Poverty at the University of Minnesota.

INDEX

Affordable Housing Enhancement Demonstration (AHED), 74, 82

African Americans: automobile use, 192; community types, distribution, 91; and housing, integrated/segregated, 96–98, 100, 114–15; in housing, subsidized, 320n89; housing and socioeconomic status, 115; housing sales, steering of, 116, 326n69; job growth, 187; median household income, 335n6; and neighborhood types, 293–94, 324n36; population growth, xv; students, 93–94, 105–6, 163, 322n6; workers in employment centers, 186

agricultural areas: growth projections, 63, 64

AHED. *See* Affordable Housing Enhancement Demonstration

AHOP. *See* Area-wide Housing Opportunity Program

airports, special district for. *See* Metropolitan Airports Commission

Alliance for Metropolitan Stability, 149

Andover: new subdivisions and urbanization, 16; population growth, 2, 16, 228

Annandale: wastewater treatment, 239–40

Anoka County, 7; SNAs and urbanization, 234; wastewater treatment, 69–70

Anoka Sand Plain, 230, 234, 249

Apple Valley: population growth, 2, 16

Area-wide Housing Opportunity Program (AHOP), 145

Asians: community types, distribution, 91; housing and socioeconomic status, 115; housing/neighborhoods, integrated/segregated, 96–98, 100, 104, 114–15; and neighborhood types, 293, 324n36; population growth, xv, 293, 335n6; racial minority maps, exclusion from, 335n6; students, 93–94, 106, 164, 165, 322n6

Atlanta, Georgia: commuter sheds, 206–10; highways, investment in, 214–17; job growth, 180–84; MPOs, 56; transportation and employment, 175–76, 180–83, 186–89, 191–92, 206–14, 218

Barton Open Elementary School, 156

Becker: tax capacity per household, 36, 242

bedroom developing communities, xiv; classification, 45–46, 245–48, 257; growth trends, 47–49; opportunity in, 88; and regional land use planning, 290; as Republican stronghold, 279; and sprawl, 290

Bethune Elementary School, 156

Big Woods, 230

Blaine: new subdivisions and urbanization, 16; population growth, 2, 16, 226, 228

Bloomington: as developed job center, 289; growth predicted, 64; growth and land use, 247, 251; wastewater treatment, 69–70

Blueprint 2030, 60, 68, 255, 317n17. *See also Framework 2030*; regional performance plans

Blufflands, 230

Brooklyn Park: new subdivisions and urbanization, 16; population growth, 16; schools, segregated, 112, 136

Brown v. Board of Education, 141–42, 164

Burnsville: population growth, 2; schools, integrated, 334n217; wastewater treatment, 69–70

Bush (George W.) administration, 167

Business and Professional People for the Public Interest (Chicago), 220

Carlos Avery Wildlife Management Area, 234

Carlson, Arne (governor), 53, 58, 266

Carver County, 7; projected growth, 29; wastewater treatment, 71

CBDs. *See* central business districts

CDCs. *See* Community Development Corporations

Cedar Park Elementary School, 133–35

Census Transportation Planning Package (CTPP), 179–81, 185, 186–87, 193–94, 205, 207–10, 218, 316n22

Central Americans: population growth, xv

central business districts (CBDs), 177, 180, 185, 195, 204–8

Chanhassen: population growth, 2, 16

charter schools: performance metrics, 160–63; and public school segregation, 163–64; as segregated, 157–60

Chaska: population growth, 226

345

segregation: of charter schools, 157–60; and discontinuous attendance school zone boundaries, 133–36; dynamics of, 112; economic, and regional policy, 282–83, 286–87; and equality of opportunity, 88–93, 96–98, 104–7; and exclusionary zoning, 138–41, 144, 145; and fragmentation/decentralization, 2–3; legal remedies, 141–44; multiethnic neighborhoods, 103, 104; in neighborhoods, 85–91, 103, 104, 112–33, 138–41, 293–94, 324n36; persistence of, 114–33; racially isolated school, defined, 135; and real estate practices, 115–16; and regionalism, 95–96, 282–83, 285, 286–87; resegregation, 107–8, 111, 112–13; and residential preferences, 114–15; school district decisions, 133–38; in schools, xv, 85–88, 91–93, 112–13, 133–38, 141–44, 157–60, 269–70, 293–94, 322n6; and socioeconomic status, 115; solutions to, 87; in suburbs, 96
sensitive natural areas (SNAs): creation of, 236; and development, 224, 230–35; GIS layers, 230; and growth, 230–37, 241–51, 264; and local fiscal capacities, 241, 242; spatial analysis of, xi. See also environment
service areas: and costs/benefits, 4; local vs. broader, 4–5
Service Availability Charges (SACs), 71
Shakopee: commuter shed, 195, 204, 206; new subdivisions and urbanization, 16; population growth, 2, 16, 226; urbanization of rural areas, 64, 67
Shannon Park: schools, 133
Shapiro, Thomas M., 326n80
Sheff v. O'Neill, 143–44, 330n144, 330n147
Sherburne County: commuting patterns, 27, 29; and decentralization, 24, 26; and fiscal disparities tax base sharing, 264; growth, 67–68; as part of metropolitan area, 24, 26; population growth, 29, 32, 226; and regional governance, 266; rural to suburban transition, 24, 26; tax capacity per household, 36
Sherburne National Wildlife Refuge, 234
Skeen v. Minnesota, 143, 330n142, 330n144
SNAs. See sensitive natural areas
southwest counties: tax capacity per household, 36, 39
special taxing districts. See taxation
sports facilities: special district for. See Metropolitan Sports Facilities Commission

sprawl: and bedroom developing communities, 290; and fragmentation, 22–23, 51–52, 77–78, 316n25, 320n96; and job centers, 68
state taxes, 13
streams. See lakes and streams
subdivisions, new: and urbanization, 16
suburbs: affluent, xiv; population growth in, xiv, 2, 16; and regional policy, 286–88; school integration in, 111–12; and segregation, 96; stressed, xiv, 96, 278, 286–88; and traffic congestion, 2
Suits index: measure of regressivity/progressivity, 13–14

TAB. See Transportation Advisory Board
taxation: incentives, 35–36; local taxes, 13–14, 35–43; low-income housing tax credit program, 121–25; rate changes, 39; regressivity/progressivity measurement, 13; sales taxes, 13; tax base equality, 39; tax capacity, 36–39, 42, 315n12; taxing districts, 7–8, 9, 12. See also Fiscal Disparities Program
tax base sharing. See under Fiscal Disparities Program
Tax Reform Act of 1986, 121
TAZs. See Traffic Analysis Zones
TEA-21. See Transportation Equity Act for the 21st Century
telecommuting, 24
Texas Transportation Institute (TTI), 211–13
TLC. See Transit for Livable Communities
townships: governance of policy recommendations, 270–71; powers, 315n5
Traffic Analysis Zones (TAZs), 185, 316n22
traffic congestion, xvi, 2, 26–29, 29, 176, 194–204, 264
Transit for Livable Communities (TLC), 149
transportation: comparative strategies, 210–13; and counties, 74; and economic development, xvii, 263–64; and employment, xvi, 175–76; highway investment, 214–17; and housing density, 73; improvement, 26, 73; infrastructure support, 319n75; and land use, 73–74, 80, 81–82; light-rail systems, xv, 56, 73, 213, 219, 336n23; mass transit, xv, 68–69, 73–74, 177, 191–92; policy recommendations, xvii–xviii, 58, 73, 81–82, 218–20, 263–64; and population densities, 191–92; and race, 192–94;